REMEMBERING LASTS SO LONG

To David + Jennifer with warm wishes

Thomas A. Greenlaw

THOMAS A. GREENLAW

PAGE PUBLISHING, INC.
New York, NY

First originally published by Page Publishing, Inc. 2015

ISBN 978-1-63417-995-9 (pbk)
ISBN 978-1-63417-996-6 (digital)

Printed in the United States of America

DEDICATION

Two special people made this dream come true. For your love and belief in me and my story I gratefully dedicate this book to Royal Latuch, more than a friend forever & my sister, Patricia McSherry who helped start this journey.

CONTENTS

Part 2

Part 3

ACKNOWLEDGEMENT

A special thanks to my writers group family: my editor, Cindy Davis, Dee Currier who encouraged me to pursue this story, Jennifer, Susan, Darren, Al and so many more. Thanks to you all.

Ecstasy is so short but the remembering lasts so long.
—Walt Whitman

PROLOGUE

1995

The two-hundred-year-old Federal overlooking the Piscataqua River gave little clue to the confrontation I feared was imminent. The July sun beat down mercilessly as I piloted my ten-year-old Volvo into the driveway beside Dad's antique Mercedes. I was sweating, and not from the sun.

Last evening, after finally confiding my lifestyle to my parents, Dad went haywire, and I stormed out. For Mom's sake, at least, I hoped we could come to some kind of resolution.

Mom, red-eyed, met me at the kitchen door this morning, hugged me, and motioned toward his study. The only thing I could read in her demeanor was alarm.

"Lil," my father shouted, "is someone out there? Not Damon?"

Mom squeezed my hand tearfully and hurried up the stairs as I entered his study.

"Damon, what are you doing here?" my father demanded, rising. "I thought I made it clear, you are no longer welcome in this house." He stood behind his desk, facing me, eyes cold and unforgiving. "I'm sorry, but that's the way it has to be."

"And how does Mother feel about it?" I asked belligerently, slumping onto an antique side chair, the delicate legs protesting under my weight. A flash of sun pierced through a cranberry glass plate in the window. *Blood of the lamb* sprang to my mind from the crimson reflection on the wide pine floor, but I was hardly a Jesus figure.

"She concurs with me. Don't you see the position this puts me in? What about my business, and the neighbors, with you parading that man in and out of here, and God knows who else?"

Not an iota of understanding registered with him.

"But I'm still your son," I argued, my voice rising.

"Not since our conversation last evening. Your mother wept most of the night. Neither of us slept a wink." A blood vessel bulged on his temple. "No son of mine can be—"

I snatched up a delicate hand-painted vase off the table beside me. It had been in the family for generations. It almost trembled as I tossed it hand to hand.

"Put the vase down, Damon."

"Then say the fucking word, Dad. 'No son of mine can be...what?"

All civility abandoned me, replaced by a blind rage that had been twenty-three years in the building.

"Don't you dare use that foul word in my house." Spittle oozed from a corner of his mouth.

"I'm not asking you to say *faggot*, *fairy*, or even *queer*," I shouted, jumping up and overturning the chair. "Just say the three letter word, Dad, say it."

He stood with his mouth set, outrage distorting his face. I heaved the vase with all my strength, barely missing his right ear. It crashed into the wall behind him and exploded into a sea of kaleidoscopic fragments, plunging noisily to the floor.

He sprang from behind the desk and grabbed me by the arm, his hand like a vise.

"You little bastard, do you know how much that vase was worth?"

I hammered his arm and shoulder with my fist. He was flummoxed. I had never challenged him before. He released me and shoved me away. I caught my balance and staggered back toward him, rubbing the bruise on my arm.

"I'm a grown man now and no longer your little bastard. That vase means more to you than I ever did."

Although close to it, I was damned if I would shed any tears.

"I'm sorry I couldn't meet the high standards you set. Don't worry, your friends in New Castle will never know because they won't be seeing me again."

Fists jammed into my pockets, our faces not a foot apart.

"I never told you about Mike and me before because I knew it would end this way."

I snatched one of his favorite Cuban cigars out of a humidor on his desk, snapped it open, and flung it at him.

"This is what you and I have become now. I'm gay, goddamn it, g-a-y."

In that fleeting moment, truth sank in; I hate him. This room, this house, this world is suffocating me. I turned and strode toward the front door.

"Tell Mother I love her, if it still means anything."

The heavy oak door closed resoundingly behind me.

∽

The next few days passed in a blur. Sleep was sporadic, and my waking hours were spent struggling to convince myself I was okay. In a weak moment, I called home. Dad answered but hung up when he heard my voice. I banged the phone down and punched the wall with my fist. Life was suddenly purposeless. New Castle was now an anathema and held no future.

But my shattered ego was yet to collect another blow.

Mike and I shared an apartment after I got out of college. For the past month or so, he slunk in later and later each night, some nights not at all. Something was wrong between us, but I was too involved with my own feelings to pay enough heed.

Around ten the following evening, his key rattled in the lock. The door pushed open and then slammed. He stomped into the kitchen, red-faced, a little unsteady on his feet, avoiding my gaze.

"What?" I finally asked.

His underlip curled, and he spit out, "Damon, I'm seeing a woman, an old friend. We're getting married."

"Married? You son of a bitch." I struggled for hurtful words, but my mind was in disbelief. "And all this time I thought we were a couple."

He shrugged his shoulders and turned to leave. I grabbed for his arm, but he pasted me on the cheek. I sprawled backwards onto the table. Apples rolled in every direction after the wooden bowl struck the floor and split in half. I lay there, stunned, rubbing the bruise on my jaw.

"Grow up, Damon." Scorn twisted his mouth. "Can't you see we're from two different worlds? Have you been so stupid you didn't see this coming?" His speech was slurred, and I knew he'd been drinking. "What didja think was going on when we haven't seen much of each other lately?" He eyed me with scorn.

"All I know is, you cheating bastard, I wasn't out fucking someone else."

With a snap of the fingers, we were suddenly strangers. The derisive look on his face was so like my father's just two days ago. Filled with fury, I lunged at him. Mike was stronger and wrestled me to the floor. I was no match for him; he outweighed me by twenty-five pounds. He stood up, brushed his arms as though I had defiled him, turned on his heel, and strode out.

I scrambled back to my feet, momentarily feeling sorry for myself. Then it dawned on me—I'm free. I would escape this pretentious, impossible world where I had spent my entire life.

After a sleepless night, half-expecting yet dreading Mike's return, I fried some eggs, burned the toast, and brewed coffee. It repulsed me, and I threw the plate against the wall.

I yanked out drawers and dumped them, tossing records and receipts in all directions, like a ticker tape parade. Everything I wanted to save filled a duffel bag and a small suitcase. The rest lay scattered on the floor. I made up my mind no one would ever hurt me again.

My hand shook as I scribbled a note to Mike with my share of the month's rent. Crushing the bills in my hand, I flung them onto the table.

"Thank you for doing me a favor," I scrawled. "Go fuck yourself."

An hour later, after pacing up and down the street, one more unpleasant task faced me. I had to give notice at the bank where I worked. My self-esteem rose slightly with the reaction I received from the bank president. With great reluctance, he accepted my resignation, wished me well, and assured me of a job waiting if I was to return.

PART 1

CHAPTER

1

Half the seats on the Trailways bus were empty. It was midsummer, during a hot spell, shorts-and-sandals weather. The bus rolled into Boston and circled up to the South Station Terminal. I was last off the bus. The driver handed out my duffel bag and suitcase from the cargo space, and I trailed the other passengers changing to a Greyhound headed west. A dozen or so people got on and filled most of the remaining forward seats. I took the wider rear seat and spread out books and magazines to while away the time. We were about to depart when a loud rap sounded on the metal door, and a male voice shouted. The driver swung the door open, and another passenger, out of breath from running, climbed on. He rummaged through a zipper compartment on the side of his duffel bag and produced a ticket then worked his way up the narrow aisle, pitching from side to side with the movement of the bus. Our eyes locked for a second. With difficulty, I attempted to read once more, wary of making eye contact again.

He was probably on his way to meet his wife or girlfriend.

"Mind if I join you? It's pretty crowded up front." His husky voice had a pleasant cadence.

I looked up from my book. A delicious bulge hidden behind his zipper caught my attention a second too long. I sensed his gaze. My eyes rose hastily to spot a yellow silk shirt contrasting against his ruddy complexion and curly black hair. A tiny gold stud glistened in his left ear. His chiseled features and dark flashing eyes mesmerized me.

"Not at all," I replied tentatively, extending my hand. "Hi, I'm Damon." I tried to keep my voice steady in spite of my accelerated heartbeat.

"Nice to meet you, Damon. I'm Carlos."

His firm handshake sent a shiver up my arm. I was both charmed by, but wary of his instant charisma. I cleared a space on the seat. He shrugged the duffel bag off his shoulder and eased down beside me.

"Where ya headed?"

"California. I've been living in Boston the last eight years. Can't take the New England winters any longer. I was born in Miami."

He proceeded to unbutton his shirt straining against his buffed shoulders and muscular biceps.

"Hope you don't mind me making myself comfortable." His shirt was now open to the waist.

"Not at all." Heat stoked in my cheeks.

"Where are you headed?" he asked.

"Fort Worth. Going to stay with my sister for a while, trying to put my life back together after a difficult breakup."

"Yeah, girls can do that to you sometimes!"

I had a feeling he was fishing. I wasn't biting—yet.

"Same thing with you?" Turnaround is fair play.

"Nah, I've learned to stay away from women." A lopsided grin animated his handsome face.

"Smart move." Our eyes met again momentarily.

He stretched and yawned. A pair of sunglasses rested casually on his hair. My eyes wandered to his open shirt that revealed a muscular chest, probably a gym nut. A dusting of black fuzz thickened somewhat at the navel, and a tiny red rose was tattooed over his left nipple. A heady mixture of Irish Spring and testosterone filled my nostrils.

My stash of magazines slid, and I made a grab for them. A gay issue hit the floor. He grabbed it up before I could reach it, inspected the cover, and flipped a couple of pages. "Is this research or natural inclination?"

My face felt hot, and I tried to think of something clever to say.

"Some of both, I guess," I replied inanely, my heart beating in my ears.

He continued thumbing through the pages, each time stopping to inspect a colored spread with a naked male model in full arousal.

"Research or natural inclination?" I rebutted.

"Some of the former, more of the latter."

We turned to each other, my smile matched by his. I had the sensation those dark, liquid eyes could see right through my façade and into my soul. Had we met before? Hardly. I would have remembered.

As the afternoon wore on, we chatted and laughed about trivialities—nothing of substance—each waiting for the other to break the spell. I drew my left leg up under me while moving closer to him. Throwing caution to the wind, I slid my hand over and rested it on his thigh.

He leaned toward me, lifted my chin with his index finger, brushed my cheek with his lips, and then gently rotated my face. We kissed. The action so intimate, so tender, I responded by leaning toward him. His left arm encircled my shoulders, and his right palm rested on my waist. I half-wished it to be lower. I slid my arm around his back, and we embraced. Although I was aroused, the time was not right. I luxuriated in a nonsexual intimacy I had never experienced with Mike.

The bus exited into a Burger King around six thirty. The sky was dark with a gathering storm. Rain swept in, pelting us as we raced for the entrance. Most passengers had umbrellas or raincoats. We had neither and reveled in the refreshingly cool downpour. Carlos stepped into a puddle and lost a sandal. Water splashed onto us both, and we had a laughing jag. We ended up cupping our hands and throwing water at each other. Soaked to the skin, we ran back to the bus to change.

The bus was empty, so we were able to strip. We pawed through our duffel bags and pulled out dry clothes. Carlos straightened up and moved close. He towered above me as we embraced even though I'm just under six feet. Five frustrated minutes later we dashed back in line with the last of the passengers. While waiting for our order, Carlos put his hand on my shoulder, kind of guy-to-guy, and whispered in my ear, "Tonight, we're going to finish what we started in the bus."

My ears felt hot, and my pulse raced.

Three or four of us took our trays to a back table. Carlos sat opposite me. He slipped off a sandal and put his foot up onto my crotch. Thank God I didn't have to get up quick! I tried to eat and stay composed, but that's like watching the water rise before an approaching tsunami.

The other passengers drifted away, either ducking through the rain to board the bus or to have a last cup of joe. The bus driver sat in a booth chatting with one of the passengers. Carlos and I stood together by a plate glass window, each lost in thought, watching the rain. Our reflections in the glass were an apparition of two strangers unknown to me. Could this really be me, a small-town New Hampshire guy?

✐

On the road again, we traveled in a heavy rain. Lightning flashes lit the sky and the cabin with brief shocks of light. Most of the passengers were dozing or discussing the storm. The steady rumble of the huge tires on the pavement cast a hypnotic spell, like an ocean liner sloughing through the waves to an exotic land.

Carlos's whisper jolted me out of my reverie.

"Here's the idea. I'll go into the john. Give me a couple of minutes and come in."

"It's pretty small in there, what's up?"

"You are. Do as I say."

"What if somebody needs to take a crap?"

"Fuck 'em, they had a chance to dump back at Burger King."

The next few minutes dragged as my respiration increased. I checked my watch a dozen times. Rising from my seat and checking for anyone approaching, I tried the door. It was locked. I tapped gently and whispered his name. He released the latch, and I slid in. He was a naked Greek god.

My T-shirt yanked easily off while Carlos fumbled with my zipper. Our bodies pressed urgently together, our mouths melding. The scent of his body and the confinement of the space forcing us together were an overpowering aphrodisiac. My last anxiety was stemmed when I sensed he was using a condom. The next several minutes were a contest of athletic skill as we performed our active lovemaking in such close quarters. New Castle and Mike seemed forever ago.

A rap on the door brought us back to reality. I scrambled into my shorts. Carlos grabbed for his. I slid them up onto his legs. He chortled, and I shushed him. We prepared to face the person on the other side of the door.

"What in hell are two men doing in the restroom at the same time?" demanded a rather stuffy-looking middle-aged man as we slid out by him.

"I had to take a shit," Carlos said cockily.

The man snorted then eyed me, the corners of his mouth drawn down.

"I had an uncontrollable desire to wash my hands, if it's any of your freaking business," I retorted with a smile.

"Disgusting queers."

"Hey, buddy, just 'cause you ain't getting any doesn't mean we shouldn't." A devilish grin spread over Carlos's face, and he patted the man's butt.

The door slammed, the latch clicked sharply into place. Carlos was all for unzipping and exposing himself when the guy came back out. I prevailed upon him to behave. He finally pulled his shirt on, and we sat like giggling teenagers. Shortly, the old geezer reappeared. I pretended to snooze. God knows what Carlos was doing. I dared not look.

Carlos elbowed me after he passed by. "The old fart was probably playing with himself."

"Or cleaning up the floor."

Carlos smirked.

The passengers adjusted themselves the best they could, settling down for the night, doing whatever possible to ease the long ride. Carlos nodded off, his breath coming slow and easy. An occasional flash of lightning illuminated his handsome face. I wondered what he was really like and if this nascent attraction would turn into something more. I only knew his first name and that he was a great fuck.

∽

We pulled into Dallas around 5:00 a.m. a day and a half later. From a slight knoll, lights shone to infinity in every direction. I already missed the hills of New England but was determined to start a new life far from the heartbreak back east. Carlos stirred and yawned, running his fingers through his rumpled hair. He would soon be on his way, and I would be taking the bus to Fort Worth. How can you love someone you have known less than forty-eight hours? Yet I knew I did. And it was more than physical. Carlos, the extrovert and protector. And me? Certainly the introvert. Strangers on a bus. Shit, I didn't want it to end.

"I don't want to say good-bye, Damon." Was he reading my mind? "Come to California with me."

"No, stay here in Texas with me...for a few days at least." I couldn't believe I was saying it so urgently.

"What about your sister? She expects you to be here alone, doesn't she? Is she aware that you're..." He jiggled his outspread fingers.

"Yeah, she's the only one in the family who didn't give me a hard time when I came out." I didn't mention the ugly scene back at my folk's house in New Castle.

The Greyhound bus pulled into the terminal off Commerce Street.

"There must be plenty of motels in the area." I flipped open my travel guide and ran my finger down the motel listings. "Hey." I snapped my fingers. "Ilka doesn't need to know I'm here yet. Let's rent a room. We can spend two or three days here in Dallas then bus over to Fort Worth for a couple more." I tried to keep my voice light.

"Is that fair to your sister? Won't she wonder where you are?"

"I'll call and say I've stopped for some sightseeing," I said as we worked our way down the aisle, our arms full of magazines and overnight bags. I bumped a woman's elbow, and she gave me a dirty look.

"You don't think your sister will catch on?" A frown wrinkled his forehead.

"I suppose I could tell her I'm in town with my fuck buddy," I said in sotto voce.

Carlos's face clouded, and his smile faded.

"Damon, if that's all I am to you, maybe I should say good-bye now and move on."

At first I thought he was joking, but his expression remained serious. I was horrified he had taken my facetious remark as the truth. It was such a stupid statement, but how to make him believe it was only in jest?

"Point well taken. As good as the sex has been," I lowered my voice again and glanced around, "the rest of the time has meant so much more to me. I don't want you to go."

A broad smile broke over his face. "I knew what you meant, just wanted to tease you a little."

~

The streets in Dallas were the busiest I had ever seen. Highways spread like spider's legs in every direction. My knees felt a little weak as we descended the steep steps from the bus. A blast of hot air slammed onto us when we hit the pavement.

Taxis were parked helter-skelter around the terminal and snapped up fast. Carlos hailed one; we tossed our bags in and were off. I had scouted out a Howard Johnson on my map just a few blocks away at the corner of Elm and North Griffin.

I had plenty of traveler's checks and a credit card. My severance pay for vacation time from the bank alone was a good chunk of change. Not knowing Carlos's financial condition, I offered to pay for our room. He laughed and showed me a wad of bills. We finally agreed to go Dutch.

It was still only six in the morning, but neither of us felt like sleeping. Nobody was behind the desk in the lobby. We had to ring to be admitted. The clerk yawned as he informed us all the rooms were occupied, but there would be vacancies after eleven. We registered for a suite (my idea, Carlos loved it) and headed for the dining room.

The place was empty save for a lone man absorbed in a newspaper, holding a cup to his lips. We took a booth away from him and piled our luggage on one of the seats. A door from the kitchen swung open a few minutes later, and a rather handsome young black man approached with a pad and pencil. We ordered coffee. I went for scrambled eggs, toast, and jam. Carlos ordered poached eggs, dark toast, and juice. The waiter returned shortly with our coffee. I made up a face when Carlos drank his black.

"Have to watch my weight," he said, seeing my reaction. He reached for a complimentary flyer from a stack on the back of the table. "I need to find a gym." He thumped his stomach. The waiter reappeared and served us from the tray balanced on his hand.

"By the way"—I peered over the rim of my coffee cup—"we're having breakfast and sharing a room, and I don't even know your last name."

"I thought you'd never ask." A devilish smile spread over his face.

"Well?"

"Carlos Santos Bravara." He rolled his tongue pronouncing it, then bit off a piece of toast and chewed noisily as he eyed me for a reaction.

"Nice Irish name." I grinned and cocked an eye at him. "My last name is Duncan, Damon Edward Duncan, to be exact. Pretty dull compared with yours, huh?"

"Sounds Hispanic to me." He snickered. "Damon Edward Duncan, hmm." His face sobered. "I like it, sounds so established, middle-class American." He reached across the table, and we shook hands. "Nice to meet you, Damon Edward Duncan."

"Same here, Carlos Santos Bravara."

We finished breakfast, pushed our dishes aside, and spread out a map of Dallas. Another waiter, glancing our way, wandered in our direction and eased his tray down. He fiddled around piling our few dishes but seemed far more interested in cruising Carlos. Not unusual, I was sure. The dining room was still almost empty, so we engaged him in conversation, asking for advice. We would be in Dallas for three or four days and wanted to see the sights.

He nonchalantly slipped into the seat opposite us. "In the first place"—he slid his rump forward, feet sticking out, hands behind his head—"you need about three or four weeks to scratch the surface. What are ya interested in seeing?"

"Dealey Plaza, the zoo, farmers' market, some nightlife."

"A gym," Carlos cut in, "dancing."

He gave us the once-over. "Together?" A slight leer crossed his face.

"You have a problem with that?" Carlos challenged.

"As a matter of fact, no." His face colored a bit. "A friend and I know a neat place over on McKinney Avenue, dancing all night, a great bar, awesome cruising. We go there a lot." His gaze never left Carlos; I might as well not have been there. "You staying here at the hotel?"

"Yeah, we just got off the bus," Carlos replied.

I looked at him and snorted.

"Waiting for a room," he said, cuffing at me.

"My name's Jeff Pinter."

He proffered his hand. He was around twenty, I figured, blond with a narrow brown birthmark from his left jaw down toward his neck. He was on the short side, maybe five six or seven, nice face, and a slim build. We introduced ourselves and shook hands.

"Why don't you join us tomorrow night?"

"Sounds great."

Carlos looked to me for approval.

I nodded with a smile.

"Meet you here in the lobby around eight then. Say"—Jeff hesitated—"you guys don't ever swap, do ya? Ya know what I mean."

"We've only been together a few days," I replied.

"Wow, hardly time. But ya never know." He shrugged his shoulders and picked up the tray of dishes. He disappeared in the direction of the kitchen.

Carlos slid over and put his arm around me, and we kissed. "I love ya, babe."

Someone behind us cleared his throat loudly. "So you're the two guys on the bus."

We twisted around.

"Yeah," Carlos replied, "we're half brothers. Haven't seen each other in years." He snapped his fingers as if just remembering. "You must be the guy on the bus waiting while we fucked in the restroom."

The man's face clouded with distaste.

"We're a close family you know." Carlos grabbed me playfully around the neck.

"A little too close I'd say." He strode away.

"Hey, mister, wanta go dancing tomorrow night?" Carlos called after him.

The guy kept walking, shaking his head.

"You twit!" I laughed as we moved out into the lobby.

It was still before eight o'clock, but people were already checking out.

"What do you want to do?" I sensed we both needed some privacy. "Should we see if our room is available now?"

He gave me a sexy look as we moved toward the desk.

"I want a nice soft bed"—he lowered his voice to a whisper—"and have the daylights fucked out of me."

"And the favor returned." I squeezed his hand.

⁂

This was the first time we had really been alone, and we made the most of it, twice apiece, actually. As we undressed, Carlos noticed the black fish-shaped birthmark under my right arm. I confessed how I used to try to hide it in the shower room in high school. The guys used to say only queers had birthmarks. Carlos kissed it every time after that. He called it my good-luck charm.

We arose around eleven, showered, and dressed for the day, a very hot day. The suite we rented had a wonderful view of the city, and I was anxious to see it after dark. Although I doubted it would be more than fleeting.

The sun was high, and our sandals soon felt like flapjacks hot off the griddle as we hit the sidewalk. No one but mad dogs and Englishmen, as the saying goes. The shops chilled our hot bods as we popped in and out for respite with the welcoming rush of chilled air.

We pondered renting a car, but where would we park? Taxis were everywhere, but DART, the rapid transit, filled the bill best for us the first day. Carlos proved to be a trooper, and wherever I wanted to go, he was all for it, unlike Mike, who could be sullen if he didn't get his way.

Hunger settled in around three. Our dog-eared guidebook led us to Chip's Old Fashioned Hamburgers on Cole Street. The place was cool, light-filled, and noisy. It was well after dinner hour, so we got stools at the bar. Chip's classic cheeseburger with all the fixings tickled our Eastern fancy, plus cold draft beer. We took our drinks to a back table, where we could be more comfortable.

❧

I have a special affection for JFK; although he died ten years before I was born. We headed for Dealey Plaza and the Sixth Floor Museum. I felt a tear on my cheek as I peered out the window and imagined that horrible day so many years ago. Tourists spoke in whispers as though not wanting to disturb his eternal rest.

It was much as I had seen pictured, but the immediacy of being on the spot was chilling.

A half hour later, we snuck a kiss on the otherwise empty elevator as it noisily rumbled down to the first level. We headed for the West Village, the so-called historic district. Their history is a lot shorter than ours back east, but nonetheless interesting.

I spotted Wild Bill's Western Store on North Market Street, and an idea sprang to mind—a Stetson for Carlos. We walked into the store and were overcome with everything Western. I never knew there were so many styles and types of hats. Carlos put up token resistance because of cost and the newness of our relationship, but I was not to be deterred. He modeled several as a number of female clerks gathered around, giving advice and encouragement. We finally decided on white. I whispered that it really turned me on; that clinched the deal. He said no one had ever bought him anything so expensive before. I promised many more and gave him a big hug.

"Now it's time for me to buy you something." Carlos swung his arms around.

"Naw, I don't need anything."

"How about I take you out to a fancy restaurant?"

That had real possibilities. "You're on."

❧

Blowfish on Mckinney Avenue was highly recommended, and rightly so. We sorted through our luggage, and each came up with a pair of slacks, a real shirt and a tie. It was worth it; the setting was stunning, dim lighting, red and black décor with a wall of white stone.

We sat at a corner table. Carlos held my hand every so often. It made me a little nervous, yet it seemed so natural. We started with Pinot Grigio—my favorite—and moved on to a scrumptious seaweed salad with sesame sauce. The entrée tempted our palates—a roll of lobster katsu with avocado and cream cheese topped with crab and wasabi mayo. We barely made it through the mango cheesecake in a fortune cookie crust with something exotic dribbled over the top. The meal ended up costing as much as the Stetson!

"Worth every penny," Carlos happily replied.

The Patio Grill, not far from Blowfish, turned into a blast the next evening. Jeff and his date, as he called José, turned out to be interesting, but definitely not habit-forming. Around midnight, the crowd thinned as the guys hit the bar and tables.

Carlos turned to me, eyes twinkling. "Wanta give 'em a show?"

"Whatcha got in mind?" I asked a little nervously.

"Take off your shirt," he whispered, peeling his off and twirling it in the air over his head, shouting, "Yippee."

What the hell. I whipped mine off and pitched it into the melee.

The crowd gathered around, clapping and chanting to the music. Carlos, twice the dancer I am, made all the fast moves. The white Stetson clung to his sweaty brow as he quick-stepped and pranced around. I picked up some of the easier moves, and the crowd pushed back farther, giving us plenty of room.

Carlos whisked off his belt. I watched with anxiety as his shorts slid down to his hip bones. With misgivings, I followed suit. The crowd chanted "Take 'em off" as he slowly unzipped, lowering them a bit more, wiggling his hips, and then, with a quick yank, he was wearing the tiniest black briefs, clearly showing the outline of his "equipment."

The crowd turned to me, chanting, "Take 'em off."

I had a problem, no under briefs. I kicked off my sandals, hoping to divert the crowd. I slowly unzipped a couple of inches, and of course, it jammed in my haste, or perhaps modesty. Catcalls broke out along with encouragement. I hoped that damned thing would stay caught, but no such luck. The zipper sprang open. I gyrated my hips, hanging onto my shorts for dear life. Carlos whispered encouragement into my ear. There was no choice, the crowd egged me on; my shorts slid off. I snatched his Stetson to cover my crotch. It was the most daring thing I had ever done, and I was terrified the place would get raided. Maybe the drinks were loosening my nerves. Whatever. A strange feeling of liberation flowed over me. I gyrated my body and hips again, making my penis flop around. Carlos held my right hand over my head as I did a complete spin. A cheer went up as though I had won an Olympic event. Better judgment quickly prevailed, and I made a beeline for the men's room, grabbing my shorts on the way. Carlos chased after me and caught my arm, swinging me around into an embrace.

"Where have you been all my life, cowboy?" He nuzzled my ear.

We ended up near a stall especially reserved for what we were about to do. We ducked in. It was rather small and reminded me of the bus restroom. Our tongues met and then our lips. He eased his knees down while mine went weak. His arms encircled my buttocks. A tingle went up my spine as my penis touched the back of his throat. It was some of the most intense sex I had ever experienced.

Carlos held me in his arms after.

"I'm proud of ya, babe. You're out of your shell."

Someone tapped on the door and passed in the rest of our clothes. As he pulled his arm back, I noticed he was naked too. What had we started? We tugged and wiggled our clothes on and sauntered out into the crowd as though nothing unusual had happened. Someone had scribbled First Prize on a piece of cardboard and presented it to us with a bow. Our "prize" consisted of free drinks at the bar, paid for by passing the hat. Cheers rang out all around when we toasted the crowd. Several other guys were dancing around in their briefs, none so daring as me, or so I thought.

Later, after the racket died down some, Jeff danced a couple of times with Carlos, and I did likewise with José. Clothes clinging to his body, breathing hard, José clutched me; his hand wandered down to my rear, fingers wandering. A new song blasted out, and I broke into a twist and whirl. José wasn't able to get hold of me again. Carlos finally freed himself from Jeff and broke in on José and me. The three of us went back to the bar and caught up with Jeff. We thanked him for the intro and took our leave. It was around one thirty, but apparently the two guys were just getting revved up for the night. We noticed piles of clothes thrown around with plenty of flesh showing amid the whooping and hollering.

Back in our room, we laughed about what had started out as a rather tame evening at a gay bar and how it had ended. We lay naked in bed. Carlos rose up on one elbow, inspecting me.

"What?" I finally inquired, wondering if he might be a little pissed at my actions earlier on.

"You've got a nice bod, champ." He leaned down into a kiss.

I lifted my arms to his neck and met his eyes. "Champ?"

"That's what you are to me." He reached for his Stetson and ran his fingers around the brim. "I need you, Damon, and I always will."

He lay back down, and we hugged before falling asleep.

The next four days passed by in a blur. Museums, art galleries, shows, shopping, eating and more eating and more shopping—need I say more? The whole Dallas experience spiraled into an unforgettable visual and sensual odyssey. I was not to return for another five years, but under very different circumstances indeed.

❧

With reluctance and foreboding on my part, we started out for Fort Worth. Where would Ilka fit into this grand scheme? We decided to rent a Hertz compact car and struck out on Route 30, the AC maxed out. Carlos drove, but his Stetson rubbed on the headliner, so he finally tossed it onto the backseat.

I was surprised at how built up Fort Worth actually is. Nothing like Dallas, maybe a bit more intimate, but still impressive to my Eastern eyes. Large buildings ate up the skyline as we approached. We called ahead for reservations at a Best Western. The sky darkened with storm clouds, so we hurried our sign-in and got to our room before the sky opened. And open it did.

Weariness was finally catching up with us from the long bus trip and the time spent in Dallas. The room had two king-sized beds, and we each flopped onto one, for the first and last time, and slept well into the evening. I awoke first while Carlos slept soundly. The Stetson lay beside him, the string around his wrist. I was unabashedly in love, and it scared the hell out of me. Never in the six or seven days we had been together had there been anything about Carlos that gave me a moment's pause. Could we get it together with such differing backgrounds?

CHAPTER

2

Sleep escaped me most of our second night in Fort Worth, what with the reality of facing Ilka tomorrow. Boarding a bus and heading to California with Carlos seemed ten times more exciting.

I scrambled out of bed around 6:00 a.m. Temperatures in the upper sixties were extremely cool for Fort Worth. The sky was a leaden gray, and dollops of mist rose from the warm pavement.

I edged back in beside Carlos and elbowed him in the ribs. He awoke with a start, gazed around bleary-eyed, yawned, and then stretched. He elbowed me back when I reached to shut off the alarm. I tickled his belly, and he grabbed my neck in the crook of his arm, making snorting noises, and held on till I stopped. He kicked off the sheets tangled around our legs and rolled over, facing me. We wrestled some more, jumped out of bed, and chased each other around the room. He grabbed my arm and threw me onto the bed. Fumbling under the pillow for a condom, he tore off a corner of the plastic wrapping with his teeth.

His body enveloped me. He crushed me within his strong arms. Unaware of the passage of time or the world around us, our bodies were recklessly given and received. Later, sated, we lay ensnared in each other's arms. A tear suddenly trickled down his cheek and fell on my face as we kissed. I pushed his body up with both hands. A question burned in my mind. He eased back down beside me, silent.

It was unlike him to be so quiet. Something was eating at him. Dreading what might be on his mind, my tongue couldn't form any words. After the events of yesterday, nothing seemed untoward. These past few days were the best of my life. I wanted to shout from the rooftops, live today, throw away the chains!

He took a shower while I brewed coffee in the complimentary coffeepot. He reappeared, pecked me on the forehead, and poured orange juice from our cooler into a Styrofoam cup. He sat drinking it, lost in thought.

I poured a cup of coffee, pointed to it and then at him. He shook his head. I stirred in sweetener and powdered cream. He seemed oblivious to everything around him.

Unable to stand his silence any longer, I blurted, "Out with it, something's bothering you." A forced smile creased my lips. I wet them with my tongue, my mind conjuring a hundred unpleasant scenarios.

"Yeah." He set his cup down, rotating it slowly on its bottom, the remaining liquid undulating with the movement.

"About me?" My old pessimistic self breaking through.

"Yeah."

"You going to tell me?" A shiver of doubt skittered up my spine.

He studied me a moment, his face serious. "Damon, you were never supposed to happen."

Shock radiated through me. I clutched the side of my chair. He must have heard my heart pound.

"If anyone told me back in Boston that I would meet someone like you, I would have said they were crazy." He pushed his chair back, stood up, and moved over to the window, twisting a blind cord in his fingers.

"But I did happen. We can't undo that." My voice was hoarse.

"Damon"—he jerked back toward me, surprise registering on his face—"that's the last thing I want. We've had a great time together. I don't want it to end."

"So why do I think a *but* is coming?" I steadied my voice, dreading what the next words might be.

Ignoring my question, he continued, "I've always been footloose and ready to move on a whim."

Here comes the Dear John letter. What a gullible jerk I am. A guy picks me up on a bus, and I expect him to devote the rest of his life to me. I gritted my teeth, not trusting myself to protest.

"I've been thinking it over. My career path is going to be very demanding. I have a few contacts in Hollywood who I want to pitch a couple of my songs. Possibly even record them."

"That's wonderful," I managed, sorrow mixing with admiration. So he writes music. I rose and started toward the bathroom.

"That's the problem." He caught my arm and swung me back toward him. "I can't ask you to tag along on a venture this up in the air. Money will be tight for a while, and my time will be tied up, especially evenings."

"And I would be a drag, tagging along, I suppose. 'Gotta get home, or Damon will be pissed.'" I pulled away and retraced my steps to the john.

"Damon," he practically snarled.

I spun around, startled.

"How dare you take my affection in such a cavalier way? There isn't a thing I wouldn't do for you. Do you take what just happened between us over there"—he nodded his head toward the bed—"was a 'good-bye, see ya later' kind of fuck?"

"Then tell me, for Christ's sake, that it isn't. Where do I stand with you? You've been evading my questions ever since we got up. Something's wrong, and you won't tell me." I looked at him, tears blurring my vision.

"Okay, I'm scared. It's as simple as that. I've never met—"

"Scared? Of what? Me?" I laughed mirthlessly.

"Shut up and listen to me." His face was flushed. Sweat beaded his brow.

"I've been on my own since I was sixteen. No commitments, no schedules, do as I please, go where I please, when I please. Nobody gave a shit about me." He swung his hand dismissively. "I've been a jerk-off all my life. I'm almost twenty-six and still drifting. I've slid by on my looks." A hand quickly swept his eyes. "Then, out of nowhere, you come into my life. In all the places I've been, all the men I've been with, I'm scared shitless I'll screw up, make you hate me—lose you."

He glanced toward the bed then back at me; he grabbed a tissue and blew his nose. I didn't know what to say. I stood speechless, as I had with Mike.

"You put yourself down, Damon," he continued, his voice strong again. "You don't need to. It hurts me." Grabbing my palm, he traced my lifeline with his index finger. "I see a long and happy life ahead for you." He paused. "Why is it so hard for me to say I'm crazy about you? I don't want you out of my sight."

His eyes met mine. We hugged. I could feel his heart beating.

"I'm scared too, afraid you might tire of me," I mumbled against his chest.

Neither of us spoke for several minutes. No one else on earth existed. At last, I looked up at him.

"I'll get a job, we could rent a place, nothing fancy. Later, buy a house, maybe near the ocean."

Carlos broke into a grin and stood back at arm's length. "I've got some money saved, we'd be okay to start. You're really serious about this?" His hands were firm on my forearms. "It won't be an easy life for a while, you know."

"Yeah, yeah, teenage girls throwing their panties up on the stage and teenage boys…" I trailed off, and we looked at each other.

His expression clouded. "That ain't gonna happen, not with this bod waiting for me at home." He slapped me on the rump.

The emotional tension building between us from the day we stepped off the bus in Dallas had finally come to a head. Neither of us had made any move toward a commitment until now. My track record had been anything but sound. Was I on the rebound, swept away by Carlos's charismatic aura? Could I watch him walk away? Never!

With his arm around me, we moved to the window to look out at the weather. His limp penis pressed against my buttocks. With arms around my chest, our fingers interlaced, his warm breath in my ear. No doubts lingered in my mind. I reached back and squeezed his thigh like I had so many days ago on the bus. I turned to him.

"Remember this, on the bus?"

"You were checking to see if I was hard?" The corner of his mouth curved up into a grin.

"Were you?"

"From the first five minutes. You?"

"Three minutes flat."

We laughed, and I relaxed. Finally.

∽

With Carlos's arm on my shoulder, we checked out the Chamber of Commerce map. Yesterday we had decided to jog on Trinity Park Trails, starting at Heritage Park, beyond the Tarrant County Courthouse.

We showered and dressed in tank tops, shorts, and Nikes. Carlos was fired up for a good run. His access to a gym had been limited the past couple of weeks. The trail was quiet this time of day, just the *spit-spit* of our sneakers on the damp surface. Tiny animals rustled in and out of the bushes. My one high school sport had been track.

The trails were well laid out and covered more than thirty miles, the brochure stated. We headed out, loping along toward Forest Park and the Fort Worth Zoo.

Voices raised in argument issued from a thick growth of trees, and we paused to listen. Moving in closer, we spied a couple, the girl in a sleeping bag and a guy about my age pulling his pants on. He had a dragon tattooed on his left shoulder and another tattoo of a vine or chain around his neck. They had probably spent the night there. The girl looked young, maybe fifteen or sixteen.

"You gotta get up and get movin'," the young man said. "Get you back home before your old man finds where you spent the night."

"I don't want ta go back, I told you. I hate my father. He's mean to me." Her voice was choked with emotion.

"Now, now, darlin', there's nothing we can do about that yet. You're too young." He began rolling up the sleeping bag. "Did ya ever hear of statutory rape?" She gave him a vacant stare. "I'd be sent up for life."

"They wouldn't do nothing to you after I told them I forced myself onto ya."

"Dream on, little girl." He slid on a T-shirt, spit on his hand, and slicked his hair back.

We snuck back onto the trail. I didn't want them to think we overheard, so I started to run, like we had just happened by this minute.

I shouted over my shoulder to Carlos, "You'll never catch me this time."

He picked up on the ploy and set up chase.

"You're in for it now," he shouted.

Glancing over my shoulder, they saw us as planned, unaware of our spying. We ran a ways out of their hearing then slowed back to a jog.

"Bet he's gonna get her up and out of there, pronto." Carlos snickered.

We hid in a bend of the trail. A couple of minutes later we saw them sneak out, check both ways, and head back toward town at a full trot.

CHAPTER

3

With reluctance on my part, it was time to call Ilka. We packed our belongings, checking once more under the bed and in the bathroom for stray toilet articles or condoms. I'm sure the latex-rubber-industry futures had shot up since the two of us met.

We turned in the rental car and walked to the bus station. Calling Ilka from the Greyhound terminal seemed the best plan. She didn't need to know we'd been in Texas the past several days.

"Hi, sis, I'm calling from the Southwestern Greyhound Bus Terminal. We've had a great trip. I'm anxious to see you." I had conflicted feelings, more interested in being with Carlos than in seeing her. But it seemed only fair to see her a few days before going on to California.

"Damon, I can't believe you're finally here. I'll hardly recognize you. It's been, what, ten years?" She hesitated. "Did you say 'we'? I thought Mike wasn't coming."

"It isn't Mike, it's a new friend. I know you'll like him." I was picking up bad vibes already. How to tell her about Carlos? The line went dead.

"You still there?"

"Oh, Damon, how could you? We haven't seen each other in so long. I wanted to talk over so many things with you."

"This is a special friend." I looked at Carlos, frowning, my heart sinking.

He motioned for me to speak with him. I covered the receiver, and he said in a soft voice, "Let me stay at the motel. This is throwing her a real curve. I can't blame her for being upset."

"No way. We're together." I was now feeling angry. Foolish and impulsive or not, I had made up my mind. "Come over and pick us up, we can talk this evening."

She paused again. "You say it's a man?"

"Yeah." I gripped the phone cord and twisted it.

"Gay?" Disapproval sounded in her voice.

"So what?" I bumped my forehead with the heel of my hand.

"You picked him up on the bus, didn't you?"

"There's more to it than that. A lot more. I thought you were okay with it." I was on the verge of hanging up.

"Stay there, I'll be right over. I'd like to meet your friend." The receiver clicked.

I bet you would, I told myself. She had set me to thinking though. Maybe she had a point. We didn't know too much about each other; it had all been very sudden. We had discussed the future briefly, but the past? She's trying to look out for me. Nevertheless, my mind and heart were set.

Carlos paced, hands in his pockets. He turned and sauntered back to me.

"There's a Greyhound leaving for Dallas in a half hour. I'm going to be on it." He stuffed a bus schedule from a plastic holder in the waiting area back into his pocket and took me by the shoulders, staring me in the eyes.

"Then I'll be on it too." My jaw was firm as I stared back at him.

"I can't do that to you, or to her. Look, Damon, I'll go on to California and call when I get there. You can come out later. We can be together."

We stared at each other for several seconds. What he said made sense, and I struggled with a reply. He dropped his arms, turned and sat on a bench, tipped his head back, and studied the sky.

A rather nondescript thirty-something man, presumably waiting for the bus, eavesdropped as we discussed what to do.

"There's a Best Western a couple of blocks from here," he offered.

Neither of us looked at him. His face reddened, and he opened a paper again and faked reading.

"Thanks anyway," I finally said to him.

He nodded.

I went over and sat down beside Carlos. Our eyes met.

"You go, I go. It's as simple as that."

A smile spread across his face, and he shrugged his shoulders.

⁂

Ten minutes later, a tan Neon pulled up to the curb. Ilka got out. We both hesitated, came together and hugged, then stepped back and inspected each other. She looked older, never particularly pretty. Ten years had not improved her appearance. She had straight, dirty blonde hair with no makeup to soften her angular face. She was nearly as tall as me and very slender. Her clothes were ordinary, mostly in shades of tan and brown.

"You look wonderful, Damon. You were just a boy the last time I saw you. But look at you now."

"You look great too," I lied.

She turned expectantly to the man who was waiting for the bus and stuck out her hand. "I'm Damon's sister," she said before I could stop her.

"Sorry," I said to the man.

He looked embarrassed and stepped back. Carlos came forward and took Ilka's hand in both his. "I'm Carlos, Damon's friend. It's nice to meet you." He smiled warmly and continued to hold her hand. "I apologize for intruding on your reunion. You must have a lot of catching up to do."

Ilka appeared flustered and embarrassed, her face turned scarlet. I could tell she was impressed. She smiled back, cheek twitching. Her eyes roamed over him as he let go of her hand and gave her a casual one-arm hug. She didn't utter a word.

Touchdown!

We gathered our luggage, and Carlos opened the car door for Ilka then went around and opened the other front door for me. A smirk passed between us. He loaded our bags in back and climbed in amongst them.

After an awkward ride, the silence crackling with emotion, we arrived at her house. It was prairie-style architecture with a large front porch, wide overhanging roofs, and squat dormer windows. Wood shingles stained a dark brown covered the exterior walls. Houses were built quite close together but all well tended. Ilka had a nice front yard with exotic foliage plantings.

Carlos insisted on bringing our luggage in, nodding for me to go ahead, giving Ilka a chance to show me the house. It was Spartan to say the least, tidy but as plain as her clothes. The woodwork was a depressing brown from many layers of varnish, all but obliterating the graining. The wallpaper and curtains receded in their blandness. It was quite warm as a single air conditioner did what little cooling existed on the first floor.

She took me upstairs to show the bedrooms. "This will be your bedroom, and your friend can sleep in here." She indicated a smaller room with a sloping ceiling following the roofline.

"His name is Carlos, and we'll share this room," I replied with just a touch of annoyance.

"It only has a three-quarter bed," she argued.

"We'll manage," I said.

We looked at each other. Her tic returned. She let out her breath with a sigh of resignation and went back down the stairs as Carlos came up with our luggage. She paid him little heed as she skirted around him.

⚬

A cold shower felt wonderful after the unbearable heat of the day. Water coursed down my body, my head tipped back as I shampooed with my eyes closed. Carlos stepped in, and we finished the shower together, the water splashing over and around us.

We stepped out and toweled off. I flopped facedown on the bed to catch some shut-eye. Carlos eased down beside me, one arm over my back. He kissed me on the neck, the shoulder, and then nipped onto my ear. He rolled me over, his warm breath caressing my back. His lovemaking was exquisite, gentle, yet intense, passionate, and all consuming. Afterward, he held me as our breathing returned to normal; I could feel his heartbeat. We soon drifted off into contented slumber.

Sometime later, a tap on the door awakened us. We scrambled to cover ourselves. Sis wanted to know if we were hungry. Assuring her we would be down shortly, we arose and showered again. As we dressed, for some reason and from nowhere, a troubling thought crossed my mind. I studied Carlos's fluid athletic movements and ruminated about the intense way he pleasured me. It had never been nearly as erotic with Mike. Was it right for anyone to have what we had found together? Should it only be a man and a woman with the object to procreate?

Fuck that, I thought, at least we won't be crowding the world with more babies—one small contribution to an overpopulated world.

As we ate dinner, I had another lesson in how Carlos worked his charms on others. Ilka had been rather formal and cool with him from the time she picked us up. In his usual disarming manner, Carlos's appealed to her vanity as he hung on her every word. She was charmed. He even worked up to asking her blessing for me to continue to California with him. I kicked his foot under the table and mouthed "Later" but too late. Her face clouded, but she didn't protest.

After we finished eating, he insisted on helping clear the table and loading the dishwasher.

We retired to the living room, where she turned on the evening news. I glanced at Carlos. He made a face and shrugged his shoulders. After a half hour, she snapped off the TV. Now, we all had to sit facing each other. We all made trite remarks about traffic and the weather.

Carlos nodded at me and mouthed "Gift." I nodded my head. We had bought a beautiful, colorful serape for her in Dallas. He headed upstairs.

Ilka asked briefly about Mom and Dad, and then, to my annoyance, she started asking questions about Mike. I'm sure she figured I hadn't told Carlos about him.

Carlos reappeared. He handed her the carefully wrapped gift. As she tore off the wrappings, she seemed to be genuinely pleased. Her face reddened, and her eyes widened at the sight of the beautiful handcrafted garment.

"This calls for a toast," she declared, heading for the kitchen, insisting we sit down.

"She really seems pleased," Carlos whispered, delighted we had thought of it.

She returned with three delicate wineglasses and a bottle of sparkling grape juice. Carlos and I tried not to look at each other as we all clinked glasses. I was foolish enough to think this would sidetrack the interrogation. Not so.

She finished her drink, set the glass on an end table, and leaned forward.

"I thought you were going to have Mike come out with you." She watched me for a reaction then glanced at Carlos.

"We had spoken about it, but that was before he knocked me down and said we were through," I replied, annoyed at her prying.

She looked startled. "Knocked you down? My god, I'm sorry, I hadn't heard about that. You must have been very upset."

"It wasn't pleasant, but we'd been drifting apart." My anger was quickly spent, so I refrained from reminding her we had discussed this on the phone when I asked about coming out.

"You'd known him a long time. What got into him?" she pressed on. "Was it something to do with his being black and you being—"

Carlos, smiling, seated across the room, hitched himself into a more comfortable position and crossed his legs.

"Maybe from his point of view, it was never an issue with me," I replied. "Mike is a very complex person." Damage control was on my mind. "He had become uneasy and moody. I think he resented my college degree and bank job while he was a telephone lineman."

"But you had been together quite some time, hadn't you?" she persisted.

"It was over! Period! Let's talk about something else."

She kept pushing my buttons, damn her. She had inherited so much of Dad: the "innocent" question, the goad, the patronizing manner.

"It's just that I'm concerned about you," she replied, placating me like a child then glancing at Carlos. "Things are so different nowadays. You hear about such bizarre happenings. You being—"

Her voice faltered.

"Gay," I snapped.

"Ilka," Carlos broke in, reading my growing ire. He leaned forward, hands clasped. "I have past relationships too, and I don't need to talk about them. Damon and I have not discussed that part of our lives, maybe we never will. Our time together has been very special. Perhaps our former experiences have allowed us to appreciate what we have found together."

Ilka had been sitting rigid during the "interrogation." She now settled back, her face flushed, the tic playing at her cheek again. Carlos continued looking at her with the slightest smile.

"What about your love life, sis?" I asked, breaking the spell, her gaze returning to me. I knew it was mean and underhanded, but she had asked for it.

"Well, it's been a while since I got knocked down, so I must be doing something right."

Touché!

We were both tired and begged off playing Scrabble (for Christ's sake). Sleeping arrangements were no problem. Any wider bed would have been wasted space. The murmur of the ceiling fan and his body against mine soon eased us into dreamland.

A few evenings later, Carlos declared it was time for Sis and me to have some private time together. Ilka appeared charmed by his thoughtfulness. He winked at me when he said he wanted to get acquainted with the city. Sis even offered him the use of her car, which he accepted with appropriate reluctance. This was the first time we had been separated for the past ten days. He gave me a hug, Sis a peck on the cheek, and was off, dangling the keys on one finger.

Ilka and I faced each other, more strangers than family. The room deflated without Carlos's presence. I was only thirteen when she left for Texas ten years ago. Ilka, now in her early thirties, never married, a career woman. Always the loquacious one, she soon delved into further cross-examination.

"This new guy of yours is quite a stud," she led off with. "He's a charmer for sure, but he's going to break your heart someday, you know."

"No, I don't know," I snapped. "We may have only known each other for a few days, but I have never felt this way before. He's the one I have always looked for. I know this is the real thing. Feel happy for me."

"I've seen you look at him. You'd follow him to the end of the earth, I bet. What will you do for money? After the initial attraction is over, what then?"

I felt a little pissed with her, so I blurted out more than I intended. "I had a sugar daddy, and he left me some money."

Sis looked surprised then scrutinized me sharply to see if I was joking.

"I was about sixteen at the time, looking for after-school money, mowing lawns, and doing chores for the neighbors. Seth Porter

48

bought a house about a mile away. Remember the Hyer house?" She nodded. "Seth was a successful businessman, a bachelor, and needed help around his property since he was away during the week. I answered an ad he placed in the grocery store. We hit it off right away. He was forty something, well preserved, I thought, for an *old* man, and very friendly. He had a nice tan and spent most of his time only wearing shorts.

"One particularly hot day, I was mowing his lawn, had taken off my jersey, and was working in shorts. Mr. Porter called me in to have a cold drink and take a break. By this time I was pretty sexually aware and terribly frustrated. Girls did nothing for me. Mr. Porter set out a large pitcher of lemonade, told me to help myself and to call him Seth. He gave me a look I couldn't misunderstand.

"I took a few swallows of lemonade, but my mind was on what I had just seen. I went back to mowing, my mind on Mr. Porter, Seth. Try as I might, no matter what I turned my mind to, it would not go away. I was pretty sure Seth was watching from inside. I finished the mowing and put the equipment back in the shed. I was going to duck off into the bushes when Seth called out to me.

"'Come on in, Damon.' He was sitting in a wicker chair, but it was obvious he was hiding an erection. I was trapped. My heart pounded. My face burned. I knew what I wanted. I dropped my shorts. To cut to the chase, we both had an orgasm. I was excited and scared, but a window had opened. This was the real me. 'Damon,' he asked afterwards, 'do you mind if I kiss you?'

"I was horrified and didn't know what to say. He stepped back when he saw my reaction. It felt good while it was happening, and I liked having him watch, but I didn't know how to deal with it beyond that. He pressed some bills into my hands before I hurriedly dressed and ran. I looked after I was out of sight of the house, two twenties and a ten, double the usual price.

"Every Saturday after that, I did the lawns or whatever chores he needed, and then we would go into the house. He never touched me, and we didn't speak during or after relieving ourselves or discuss it later. Over the next couple of years, he became thinner and appeared tired and sick. One Saturday I went to do the weekend chores. When I went in the house to get paid and the usual, a man I had never seen before met me at the door. He said that Seth was seriously ill and would be selling the house.

"I was eighteen by this time and had become very fond of Seth. I was crushed. There was no further contact with him during the rest of his life, although I tried. Letters returned, name unknown. A year later, a letter came from an attorney. Seth Porter's will was to be read, and I was mentioned in it. Probably a few hundred dollars given as a remembrance. I had certainly enjoyed our rather innocent sex. I was always well compensated for my work, he certainly owed me nothing.

"We sat rather stiffly in the attorney's office for the will reading. There were several of Seth's family members present, but they ignored me. He left a large estate, mostly to charities and causes he had apparently cared about during his lifetime. Cousins, nephews, nieces, distant relatives [both parents were dead], each received twenty-five thousand dollars from his ten-million-dollar estate.

"'And to my Saturday friend and helper, Damon Duncan, the sum of two hundred [dollars, my mind conjectured] thousand dollars.' My attention had wandered, and I disbelieved my ears. All eyes turned on me. Looks of disbelief, anger, hostility, and outrage showed clearly in the room, now heavy with emotion. I sat like a zombie, stunned!"

"'Excuse me,' one of the relatives asked angrily, 'was Seth in his right mind when this was written? Sometimes things are wrung out of a dying person in a weak moment.' He gazed directly at me. 'As a matter of fact,' the attorney remarked, 'this will was written two years ago when Mr. Porter was still in good health. He had several witnesses verify it, so his wishes could not be contested. If you require names or addresses, they can be supplied.'"

Sis had been staring intently at me all during my narrative, occasionally leaning forward if my voice faltered. When I got to the part about Seth and me masturbating the first time, she looked startled then increasingly more curious. By the time I had finished, she was absorbing every little nuance of the story.

We fell silent; the room felt roasting hot. Damn, I had told much more than I intended, and I kicked myself for spilling it out. She finally rose, went to the window, and snapped a dead leaf off a plant as she stared out into the darkness.

At length she turned back to me.

"Do Mom and Dad know about this?" she asked rather acidly.

"No, you're the first person I've ever told."

"I'm glad this Seth is dead. I hope he died a painful death," she spit out, "corrupting a sixteen-year-old boy. Why didn't you tell someone?"

"I wasn't corrupted. I enjoyed it. I knew if I told anyone, he would have been arrested and sent to jail. I was glad somebody nice was gay too."

"Nice," she sputtered. "Nice my foot! He was a pedophile, he indoctrinated you! Don't you understand, he made you a sinner in God's eye?"

"I thought you understood. God made me gay! You're just like the rest of them," I shouted. "I should never have told you. I'll never tell you anything again."

I jumped up and stormed out the door. Carlos was coming up the walk as I bounded down the front steps.

He grabbed me by the arm as I brushed by him.

"Hey, Damon, it's me, what's wrong?"

CHAPTER

4

Carlos knew I was upset, but I managed to wriggle away from his grasp. My mind blazed with ill-thought-out fury. Images of Seth Porter and Mike Washington swirled before me. The old school-yard taunt rang in my ears, *Mike and Damon are queer! Mike and Damon are queer!* Hands clamped over my ears didn't still the ancient echo. I no longer knew who I was or what I was; life was being squeezed out of me. Running, the one thing I was good at, might give me time to think.

Ilka, the one person in my family whom I thought understood and accepted me, was no longer there for me. It was all a lie, a goddamned lie. She was worse than the rest. At least the others were honest. Ilka wasn't planning to disown me; no, she was going to reform me.

Winding back and forth from one street to another, distance my only goal, I set an easy pace and could have run all night. Everything turned to a blur. One street looked the same as the next. Attention to directions or where I would end up mattered little to me as I pushed on. There was no traffic or other hindrance to my blind and unplanned escape. Carlos was in full pursuit, but he couldn't keep up. Glancing over my shoulder, images of him flashed under streetlights, but he continued to fall behind.

I needed time to work out my feelings, discuss things with him, but not now, not yet. I ran up a dark alley. He didn't see me and raced by. Streetlights soon ended, and the inky blackness and fetid air enveloped me. No semblance of self-preservation or better judgment slowed my headstrong plunge into oblivion in the bowels of a strange city.

My mind flooded with hateful memories: my father's angry face when he disowned me, Mike's look of disdain as he slammed out of our apartment, Ilka's parsimonious expression as she castigated Seth Porter. A wave of self-pity swept over me. Bitter tears fell to the warm pavement.

What *had* my relationship with Ilka been? She was ten years older, so we had little in common. I was only thirteen when she left for Texas. The family heard little from her in the intervening years. Then, several months ago, a high school friend of hers saw Mike and me go into a gay bar in Boston. She couldn't wait to tell my sister.

Ilka called, and we had a long conversation. At the time, we seemed to bond, and we both ended in tears. Before she hung up, she said she loved me just the same. Just the same as what? As she would if I was retarded? As she would if I was convicted of a crime and imprisoned? As she would if I murdered someone in cold blood?

Had she planned to break Mike and me apart? Was this the scheme she had in mind all along?

Darkness disoriented me, and panic edged in. I came to a halt. Where to go next? Blackness surrounded me like a hangman's blindfold. I tramped around with my foot for the edge of a sidewalk, eased up onto it, then groped with my hands to find something solid. My fingers traced the outlines of what felt like a brick wall. I leaned gingerly against it and slid my back down the rough surface to a squatting position. Paper and broken glass assailed my hands, so I brushed a space with something flat and sat on the hot pavement, head in hands, shoulders shaking and racked with despair.

Too many things had happened too fast: my family disowned me, the breakup with Mike, and now my sister's betrayal. But tears can last only so long. Reality sets in. I eased to a standing position, brushed off my shorts, and started walking. Maybe this is a slum area. People get shot in dark alleys. Was I in danger?

The air was suffocating, the night still and black. Odors of garbage and human waste filled my nostrils. Stumbling on broken pavement, struggling to catch my balance, I fell. A link-wire fence broke my fall. It was quiet, eerie, the sounds of the city far in the distance.

I had gone into unknown territory. Should I wait until dawn to return?

A sound in back of me. Was someone following? I paused, no sound, imagination, nerves. I felt rather than saw the presence of the surrounding buildings. A lighted window ahead, burned a hole into the blackness.

I snuck cautiously forward, not twenty feet away. Shivers ran up my spine; my throat constricted with anxiety. A fight went on inside. A man and a woman were shouting and threatening each other. I stood as though glued to the spot. The man picked up a chair and held it in the air, ready to swing. The woman screamed an obscenity as she threw something at him. Glass shattered, and the man chased her into another room. A gunshot, a woman's scream, and then silence. The light extinguished. Blackness filled the void like a door slamming. The stark horror of the scene repulsed and rattled my senses. If a weapon had been available earlier in the evening, could a similar thing have happened with me? Even pondering such insanity shook me to the core. I had to get away from here.

Where was Carlos? Was he lost too? Had I endangered him as well, or had he given up and decided to wait for my return? I longed for his arm around my shoulders, his reassuring smile. He was the one bright spot in my life.

What time must it be? My wristwatch was no help as I twisted and turned my wrist. Even the luminous dial had gone black. I left Ilka's about eleven thirty; it must be the early hours of the morning by now. What was I doing in a strange city in the night, fleeing my past?

A sound behind me. My heart beat in my ears. No place to hide. Stop. Silence. Nerves. Try to stay calm. An irrational feeling of being stalked plucked at my nerves. But how could anyone else see better than me? Blackness might be my friend. I tested the theory. Several sprints forward and a quick stop produced nothing. Moving more slowly now, then a quick turn. A noise, indistinct, like a sneaker striking pavement, then stillness.

Motionless, pulse rapping in my ears, I flung my arms out in several directions; my hands touched nothing. The night air was suddenly torn by the screech of two cats attacking each other. My knees went weak with relief.

Tracking forward once more, something soft brushed my arm. I reached out gingerly, but nothing was there. Then the faint sound of something a few feet back. I froze. My body was covered with sweat, my breathing short and ragged. An uncontrollable terror seized me, all rational thought aborted.

An eternity in two seconds. I turned to careen forward, to run, to escape. Jabbing my hand out for guidance, mimicking a blind man's cane, I touched something warm, the contour of a human nose. I recoiled in horror.

"I'm lost," I rasped, "please help me."

Rough laughter erupted from all around. Unseen hands seized my arms; more hands grappled my torso. Terrified, I attempted to speak, to plead. My mouth went dry. I couldn't swallow. No words came out. A hand at my neck, then the ripping sound of my T-shirt. The mutilated fabric strangled me as it pulled by my neck. A quick, painful twist to my arm and elbow when my watch left my wrist. Rough hands yanked at my shorts. A knife slashed them off when they caught on my foot. Pain shot up my leg from the careless butchery. My wallet rifled, I could see by their flashlight, their backs to me, goggles shielding their faces. There were at least five of them. Money and credit cards pocketed, they pitched the rest into the gutter.

"The fucker's getting a hard on," the one still gripping me snorted, tightening his grip on my genitals.

Several voices laughed.

One shouted, "Cut it off and feed it to the cats."

I wriggled in desperation. My captor had problems holding onto my slick, writhing body.

Someone else approached me. Did he have a knife? I was naked and terrified; further struggle was useless. I was not strong. Of all the things I feared in life, knives and razors were the worst. Suddenly my body was pitched to the ground, the pavement rending my hands and knees. Warm blood oozed on my palms and gushed from my leg. A boot under my waist flipped me over onto my back. The cut in my ankle burned like fire.

"Fuck 'im first, Kirk," a voice cried.

"Get in line," another voice snarled. "We'll have a nice little gang bang here."

Conflicting emotions of terror and rage roiled inside me. I was nothing but a piece of meat to be violated and thrown aside. Was this some terrible, sick nightmare? Would I wake up? Would I even survive?

I was roughly yanked back onto my feet by the hair. My left arm violently twisted. I felt the bone break. The pain was excruciating as the ends ground together inside the flesh. I must have blacked out momentarily. The next thing I remembered was being rammed headfirst against a woven steel fence with sharp edges protruding against my defenseless body. My life must be near an end; tears of frustration trickled down my cheeks. Pain and terror momentarily interrupted by a sick thought. My naked, mutilated body would be found by the police, and Ilka would think I was murdered while soliciting sex.

Was Carlos nearby now? Would he be outnumbered and murdered as well?

My head and shoulders were slammed tighter against the fence as a rough hand clamped around my neck. Grabbing at his hands, his fingers, strong as steel rods, I noticed he had a thumb missing. He yanked his zipper down, cursing as it momentarily snagged, and rammed his erection against my buttocks, impaled me with one deep thrust, pulling me onto him, his arm like a vise. The intrusion was like a knife twisting, goring me. An unearthly scream issued from my lips.

"Shut your fucking mouth, asshole, or I'll slit your throat," my captor snarled, tightening his grip on my stomach. He pinned my torso against the fence with the pressure of his body and produced a knife held against my neck. Sticky blood ran down my chest where the knife slit the skin. He continued to pummel; one last lunge and he climaxed.

As the next rapist grabbed me, blinding headlights washed the scene. A police siren wailed, and my tormentors scattered, dumping me behind a bush. It all happened so fast it was impossible to identify any of them. The cruiser raced by, followed by an ambulance, screeching to a halt in front of the house where I had heard the gunshot.

In spite of complete exhaustion and injuries, the will to survive triumphed. My escape must be accomplished before my tormentors reappeared. Naked and bleeding, struggling painfully to my feet, I limped toward the ambulance, whose swirling lights illuminated the street. Gritting my teeth against the pain and nausea, I prayed not to pass out.

"Help me!" I croaked.

CHAPTER

5

Ilka stood motionless at the screen door for several minutes, shocked at what had just happened. Damon had never lost control like this before. No matter how he protested otherwise, he was obviously unhappy with his sexual orientation and with those who had used him. Her brow wrinkled, and she nodded. At last, the reason he had turned gay made sense. Seth Porter had started the whole nasty decline. Never mind all the drivel the gay community espoused. Once the root cause was discovered, most gay people could be cured if they wanted to be. She crossed the room to the bookcase, scanned the titles, and her finger rested on *Change Is Possible*. She had purchased it several months ago. Settling on the sofa, she opened the book and began to read. A smile crossed her face; she closed the book and impulsively held it to her breast, rocking back and forth.

Damon had ignored Carlos, a good sign. Maybe he was beginning to see the light already! Damon was always such easy prey, falling in with any bum who happened along. If it hadn't been for Carlos, Damon might well have turned from his gay lifestyle with Mike, gotten back to his right senses, found a nice girl, and gotten married.

He would return soon, embarrassed about his display of groundless anger, and apologize. She would be kind and understanding. They would send Carlos on his way.

Baking Damon's favorite dessert would please him, a nice chocolate cake. His birthday was only a few weeks away, so the cake must have candles. We'll have a little party. She had ice cream in the freezer too, butter crunch. He always loved butter crunch. She hurried to the kitchen and got out her cookbook. She set the oven temperature in preparation for baking, humming as she worked. Yes, nothing was too good for her baby brother.

As the aroma of the baking cake permeated the kitchen, a smile came to her lips. Ilka remembered sitting at the kitchen table on Damon's third birthday. His face and bib were covered with chocolate frosting. When Mother wasn't looking, she would pull the cake away from him, and he would cry. Then she'd push it back, and he'd laugh again. Yes, she had always gotten her way with him. But he seemed different now. Goddamn men.

After what seemed like hours of pacing and checking, she looked at her watch; it was nearly 3:00 a.m. The cake had long since baked and cooled. She was nervous in spite of her better resolve. Had Carlos found Damon and turned him against her? Damon would be very vulnerable at this point, and Carlos certainly had winning ways. Carlos, the bastard. Why doesn't he pick up some Hispanic slut and rut around like a normal man?

A thought came to her. She hadn't checked their room. She would go up and tidy it, change the bed linens. It would be something constructive to do.

The room was far tidier than expected. Clothes were hung up, and the bed was made. She dusted the top of the bureau with the side of her hand and adjusted the window shade, which had rolled up crooked. She was about to leave the room when she noticed Damon's duffel bag in a corner under the roof slant. She scrunched down, grasped the side handle, and pulled it forward. She'd put it in the closet. No need for him to bend down to get it. It was heavy and unruly as she tugged it forward. A small blue canvas bag slid out of the open end and onto the floor. She was about to slide it back when she noticed Property of Carlos Bravara scrawled in white letters on the side. So it was Carlos's duffel bag. She picked up the pouch and held it in her hand. Should she look inside? No, probably porn material. She slung it back into the duffel bag and kicked it into the corner.

She turned to leave, paused, swung back into the room. What harm if she took a quick look inside. If she found anything incriminating, she could warn Damon. The zipper slid back easily, and she reached inside. Her heart began to pound, and her breath quickened. What if Carlos or Damon should come back and discover her? Her fingers shook as she crammed the contents back in. A folded letter fluttered to the floor. Her face flushed as she saw the letterhead, State of Massachusetts Probation Department. She started to read: "Carlos Santos Bravara, this is to notify you that you have successfully completed your parole obli—"

A noise on the stairs.

In a panic, she pushed the pouch and letter down in back of the duffel bag.

He's a criminal.

She straightened up quickly, slamming her head on the low ceiling. Startled at the noise and her intrusion, she tried desperately to think of an excuse. How could she explain being in their room?

Had she left the door unlocked? Maybe it was an intruder. She paused, no further sounds. She needed a weapon. A quick scan of the room offered nothing except for a chair. She grasped it by the back, the legs projecting forward. All was silent except for the heartbeat drumming in her ears. She inched forward toward the door. Sweat beaded on her forehead and cheeks. She could feel it running down under her arms.

"Is that you, Damon?" she asked, voice quavering. She set the chair down, but still within reach, and peered cautiously out around the doorway. Empty, no one there. She eased to the head of the stairs and peered down. A pile of clean sheets and towels lay scattered on the floor at the foot of the steps. She exhaled in relief.

Being far too keyed up to go to bed, she returned to the living room and searched for the remote to turn on the TV. She settled in a chair and surfed a few channels then back to the local news. The usual police reports, national news, and then reruns of *Lucy*. Breaking news interrupted the regular programming.

> Police reported a fatal shooting on Linden Street at 2:30 a.m. A domestic quarrel ended with a man fatally wounded. The suspect claimed her husband attached her with a chair. He had been violent in the past, and she had obtained a handgun permit. The victim was DOA at Harris Methodist.
>
> In an apparently unrelated incident, a young white male was found nearby, lying in the street. Knife wounds on his neck and ankle as well as severe lacerations to much of his body were reported. He was found naked, severely beaten, and possibly sexually assaulted. He remains unconscious, according to police reports. This appears to be another gang-related attack. There have been two other such incidents in the past month. The police department is under heavy pressure from the community to bring this under control.

Serves him right, probably some homosexual, naked out on the street. No morals anymore. She shuddered and snapped off the set. A knock at the door lifted her spirits. A smile crossed her face as she hurried to answer it. He's back, thank God. She slid back the lock and threw the door open.

Her face hardened. Carlos stood outside, one arm braced against the door casing. He held out the car keys. She snatched them out of his hand and yanked the screen door shut.

"What do you want?" she snapped.

"Is Damon here?"

"You know dammed well he isn't!"

"No, I don't. I've been looking everywhere for him. I'm really concerned. I followed him as far as I could, and then he disappeared."

"Good going," she spit out. "So you chased him away."

"Chased him away, nothing. You saw him leave. What happened here that made him run out like that?" His eyes blazed, and his voice was harsh.

"For your information, we had a very frank discussion tonight. I think he's starting to see a lot of things a little more realistically." Her chin lifted, and she returned his stare.

"What kind of things?"

"A lot of things.

"About me?" Carlos looked questioningly at her.

"About you and your kind!"

"And what is my kind?" He clutched the handle on the door, moving his face nearer the screen. She noticed his right sleeve was torn, and he had a scratch on his arm.

"Troublemakers and worse. You don't care what happens to anyone else as long as you get your own way."

"The last thing I want is for anything to happen to him. He's the nicest guy I've ever met."

"And you've met a lot of men in your time too, I'll bet."

"I don't deny that, but with Damon, it's different." He paused, averting his face. "I...I love him."

"You don't know the meaning of love. It's not a quick screw on the bus or in the bushes"—her voice rose—"or up in my guest room." She indicated the staircase with her outstretched arm. She shook her index finger at him. "I don't ever want to see you again or have you see him!"

She slammed the door in his face.

Tears ran down her cheeks as she slumped against the door, head in hands. She finally straightened, wiped her eyes, turned the lock, and slid the chain in place.

He'd corrupted one too many men. I'm going to put a stop to that.

Her heart pounded as she paced the floor. She felt light-headed and weak in the knees. It was all his fault. She collapsed into a chair, resolved in her mind to end their relationship once and for all. She finally fell into an uneasy sleep.

Carlos had Damon tied to a chair, taunting him about all the men he knew. Her body felt heavy. She protested, but nobody paid her heed. Carlos continued to browbeat Damon with a barrage of accusations and insults. Damon pleaded with him to stop, but Carlos continued his harangue. Damon shouted, "I hate you, I hate all men, leave me alone."

Startled, Ilka awoke to pounding on the door. She struggled to shake the nightmare. Thank God, Damon is back. She struggled out of the chair, rubbing her eyes. She looked in the mirror by the door and brushed her hair back then threw the door open.

"Thank God, you're—"

Carlos stood at the door again.

"What do you want now?" A wave of cool night air wafted into the stuffy room.

"I'm worried about Damon, really worried," Carlos replied between breaths.

"It's a little late for that, I'd say."

"He's not back then?" Carlos looked up then down the street. "I've hunted all night, trying to find him. Something bad has happened, I feel it." He paused then turned back to her, his voice softer. "Can I come in?"

Ilka inched the door open. Something in his tone touched her. For a fleeting second, she felt almost sorry for him. He seemed so forlorn. But that was part of his game, wasn't it?

"Come in, I'll make some coffee, but don't let this give you the wrong idea."

He stepped in and followed her to the kitchen. She went to the counter and pulled out a Mr. Coffee. She opened the coffee canister, spooned in several scoops, and added water to the reservoir. They waited wordlessly until the pot sizzled, and the brown liquid slowly filled the glass pot. In the distance, a clock struck six times.

"I know you don't like me." Carlos paused. "But we both know something has gone wrong. It's getting light, and there's still no sign of Damon." He poked the curtain aside with his finger, peering out into the lightening sky.

"Where did you last see him?" Her voice was flat and low.

The coffeemaker stopped brewing and flipped onto warm. She reached for two cups, placed them on the counter, slid the sugar bowl forward, got two spoons from the drawer, then filled a pitcher with cream from the fridge.

"I chased him for eight or ten blocks, and then he just disappeared. It was around Linden Street, I think."

Her face turned ashen. "You said Linden Street? Dear God." Her hand trembled as she started pouring the coffee. The mug tipped over and spilled on the floor.

"What's the matter? You know something about Damon." He grabbed her by the forearms and gave her a little shake. "Tell me."

"Turn on the TV," she ordered, disengaging his hands.

"What for?" he snarled back. He righted the coffee cups and started to pour.

"Do what I say, dammit." She grabbed the pot.

He took the remote and clicked on the TV, eyeing her. A weather report droned on endlessly, then a string of commercials. Finally the national news came on: a seven-year-old girl missing in Mississippi; a liquor store holdup in Dallas, proprietor seriously injured; a downtown apartment building gutted by fire, thirty-three people homeless. Carlos paced forth and back, sipping black coffee. Then the local news.

> As reported earlier, a young Caucasian male,
> early twenties, brown hair, about six feet, small
> black birthmark under his right arm, was found

on Linden Street with knife wounds and badly beaten. He was taken unconscious by ambulance to Harris Methodist. Anyone able to identify the victim, please contact the Fort Worth PD.

Carlos banged his cup down. "Jesus Christ, Ilka!" He grabbed her arm again. "The birthmark. It's Damon. Let me have the car keys."

Her eyes darted toward the kitchen counter, but she said nothing. She had to divert him, get to Damon first. He'd have to break her arm before she'd give him the keys.

He strode over, scrambled through several boxes and vases, finally picking up a canister. Something rattled inside. He snatched off the cover, and keys fell out.

"I've got to go to him." He took a last swig of coffee. "He needs me."

"You?" she screamed, jumping up and wrestling the keys from his hands. "*I've* got to go to him."

Carlos caught her by the arm. She tried to shrug him off, kicking him in the shin. He held her arm firmly.

"Listen to me, I don't give a damn what you do, but I'm going to him."

She clung firmly to the keys.

"You're in no condition to drive. You can come along, but you wait in the car. Now let go of the keys. I'll break your arm if I have to!"

Their eyes locked. He tightened his grip. Tears ran down her cheeks, and her shoulders shook as she crumpled down onto her knees, the keys slipping to the floor.

Carlos scooped them up and headed for the door. Ilka struggled to her feet, wiped her eyes with her sleeve, and raced him out.

Carlos yanked the driver's door open and jumped in, stuck the key in the ignition, and raced the engine as soon as it kicked over. Ilka grabbed the passenger door handle. He paused long enough for her to get in. He jammed into reverse then hit the brake. A line of cars wove endlessly by.

"Shit, rush hour."

A break in the lineup came, and he backed recklessly out. Horns blew, and tires squealed. He jammed the car into drive and hit the gas then braked heavily as traffic tied up again.

"Directions, Ilka, I need directions."

She remained silent.

"For Christ's sake, what's the matter with you?"

He slammed on the brakes, ran the window down, and shouted to a man on the sidewalk.

"Hey, mister, how do I get to Harris Methodist?"

The directions were complicated; Carlos shouted thanks and gunned the engine.

He was in the wrong lane. He put on the directional and started squeezing over into the right lane. The driver beside him had no choice; his fender brushed the rear door of Ilka's Omni. Carlos glanced down at the instrument panel.

"Christ!"

The gas gauge registered empty. He chopped at the steering wheel with the side of his hand.

A Texaco sign loomed ahead. He swerved in, but all the pumps were busy. One finally cleared, and he squeezed in ahead of another car. The driver blew his horn and swore. Carlos jumped out and caught his arm in the seat belt. He untangled his arm, rifled through his wallet for the credit card, and shoved it into the slot. It refused his card, and a notice rolled along the screen, "Pay inside before operating the pump." He grabbed the keys out of the ignition and raced inside.

The line of people at the counter took forever. He was finally the next customer. He laid down a twenty and a five.

"Pump two."

"Pump two? There's no one at pump two, sir." Carlos glanced out the window; Ilka was at the wheel and accelerating out into the traffic.

"Bitch! She must have had another key," he snarled.

"Bad hair day, mister?" the clerk remarked.

66

"You have no idea. I've got to get to Harris Methodist. Is there a pay phone I can use to call a cab?" The attendant indicated a pay phone in the rear.

A man in back of him spoke up. "I'm going in that direction. Have to make a stop first, but that shouldn't take long."

"Thanks, mister, I appreciate it, but this is an emergency."

"Suit yourself," the man replied.

Carlos thumbed impatiently through the phone book, looking for a cab. His hand shook as he crammed a quarter in the slot and dialed.

A sleepy voice answered, "It's rush hour now, pal, where are ya?"

Carlos explained as best he could.

"Get there ASAP. A tough time of day though."

Yeah, right, every day's a tough day.

༄

Ilka stepped on the gas and checked the rearview mirror, looking for Carlos. Did he bum a ride? No sign of him. The directions he got from the stranger were the long way. She knew a shortcut; the damned gas gauge never worked right anyway. She wove skillfully through the crowded streets until the huge Harris Methodist sign appeared ahead. She parked in the farthest lot so Carlos would have a hard time finding her. She slipped the spare key back into her purse and headed toward Admissions.

A pleasant older woman stood at the visitor's desk. Ilka stifled a sob and blew her nose. Her mind was working again. Damon is in God's hands. Now I have the plan to end this whole sordid affair. Damon will thank me someday.

"I think my brother may be the unidentified man brought in last night. Would it be possible to see him?" She suppressed another sob.

"He's under police guard now, in case he's still in danger. Let me call the guard and ask if it's okay for you to go up."

"Tell him I may know his assailant."

The receptionist's eyes lit up. "Really? They'll be glad to hear that." She tapped in a number and waited, smiling as though she had just hit megabucks. "Hello, officer, we may have the sister of your mystery man." She listened and then replied confidentially, dropping her voice, "She may know the name of the assailant too." Another pause, then, "Yes, wouldn't it!" she practically purred. "I'll send her right up."

The receptionist accompanied Ilka to the bank of elevators and told her the floor and room number as they walked.

"Good luck, dearie."

The doors slid together. Ilka shivered with anticipation and also a little fear. Nothing must go wrong, but it would take some doing.

A guard stationed by the room alerted and rose from his chair as she approached.

"I think it may be my brother in there." She sniffled as the guard took out a pad.

"What is your name, ma'am? Where do you live?"

She gave her name and street number.

"Can you describe your brother?" He looked up from the pad, pen poised.

"Yes, of course. He's white, twenty-three, around six feet, light brown hair, blue eyes, and very sweet. His name is Damon."

The guard eyed her closely. "When did you last see him?"

"It was about eleven o'clock, I believe, last evening. Oh, and he has a black birthmark under his right arm."

He glanced up at her. "Hmm, that could be helpful." He tapped the pen against his chin. "Now, before he left, did he seem upset? Had there been a fight with anyone prior to his leaving?"

"He met a man on the bus when he came on from the East last week. The man has been stalking him ever since. Damon, my brother, told me yesterday that the man wanted to talk with him. My brother seemed alarmed but determined to have it out with him. They were to meet around midnight."

"Did you get a look at this stalker? Could you describe him?"

"Yes, he's tall, well over six feet, I'd think, dark complexion, Cuban, maybe. Slim but very muscular, black curly hair, nice looking."

"Did you get a name?"

"First only, Carlos. Wait, I think his last name is Barveto, something like that." She peered nervously toward the elevator each time the doors slid open.

"That can be very helpful." He watched her as they spoke. "You seem distracted, ma'am. Are you expecting someone?"

"I'm afraid he might appear here." She shivered and pulled her sweater tighter.

"Carlos?"

"Yes." She nodded and looked worried.

"Do you have reason to be afraid of him?"

"I don't know. He knows where I live and also that my brother was staying with me." She covered her mouth, and the tic reappeared on her cheek.

"Did this Carlos personally threaten you?"

"Not in so many words, but he was aggressive," she replied.

"Do you know if Carlos has ever been in trouble with the law?"

This was taking far longer than she had imagined. Carlos could arrive any moment.

"Damon thought he might have been in trouble in Boston a few years back." She was beginning to sweat; this was getting her in deeper all the time.

"One last question, ma'am, I have to ask, and I apologize. Is either your brother or this Carlos homosexual?"

The question startled her. She hesitated, confused as what to say. She lowered her head demurely and replied, almost in a whisper, "Carlos is."

"I thought maybe… Certainly could be a motive for that kind of attack. We'll put out an APB on him. We'll want to question you more later, ma'am." The officer started toward the door to Damon's room. "I will check with the nurse to see if you can identify the patient."

Ilka caught his eye.

"Ma'am, something else?"

She looked worried. "My brother has a considerable amount of money."

The officer nodded as he scribbled in his notes. "Did he have a large amount with him last night?" He stopped writing and looked up.

"I have no idea." She hesitated. "Can I see my brother now?"

"Let me check." He stuck his head in and spoke to someone. He nodded and held the door open. "Remember, he has been through a terrible ordeal and may not respond to you."

"I understand."

The guard took her arm to escort her in.

Damon lay partially elevated, his midsection covered with a sheet, bandages on his throat, chest, and left ankle, a cast on his left arm, large, puffy bruises on all exposed skin, his right eye swollen shut, and tubes everywhere. He was hardly recognizable. She rushed over to him. He grunted when she took hold of his hand but gave no sign of recognition. Finally, able to see how seriously he was injured, a chill ran up her spine. A sob erupted spontaneously.

"He's had a pretty rough go of it," the nurse said, a reassuring smile on her face. "You can stay a few minutes. I'll tell the doctor you are here." She patted Ilka on the arm.

"I need to get on this Carlos business," the guard said as he left the room.

CHAPTER

6

Carlos paced up and down the sidewalk, checking his watch every few seconds. Ilka knew the car better. There must have been enough gas. *Maybe she'll run out, and I can still get there first.* He ignored the people jostling him on the sidewalk.

Nothing made sense. The relationship with Ilka started out regrettably but improved as the days passed. When he left with her car last evening, everything seemed fine. What brought on the change three hours later?

He paced in the other direction. She must have told Damon something upsetting to make him run out like that.

Was it about me? It didn't make any sense. There's no way she could have known about Boston. Or is there?

He wiped his brow and squinted at the sky, eyes shielded by his hand. The relentless sun ate through his clothing. He needed to shower, shave, and change to lighter clothes. His duffel bag and toiletries were back at Ilka's. That could wait, plenty of time after he saw Damon.

But what about Ilka? She must have gone through his duffel bag when he was away yesterday. She had the chance; maybe that was why she let him borrow the car. He would be away, the perfect time to check him out. She must have found the papers. But why would Damon believe her?

Why didn't he ask me? I could have explained, and he would have understood. The bitch has been trying to drive a wedge between us ever since we arrived. What else could have made Damon run away from me?

He smacked his right fist into his left palm. I should have gone on to California then sent for him. I had a feeling his sister might be trouble. I almost convinced him to stay and come out later. I should have been stronger.

He checked his watch again, fifteen minutes. He could call the hospital, talk with the nurses' station. There must be some information they are allowed to give. He dashed into the station again and groped in his pocket for change. Nothing. He was out of change and had to get in line again, the damned line.

It was not moving forward. The clerk had charged the wrong price for someone's gas and needed help with the register. He finally pushed around the line and laid a dollar bill on the counter.

"Could I have four quarters please, I need to make a call."

"Sorry, sir, you'll have to wait your turn."

"It's an emergency. I've got to make a phone call." The clerk who waited on him earlier was nowhere in sight. The line at the counter drew back, and an older man motioned for him to go ahead. The girl finally took the bill and angrily slapped four quarters on the counter. They rolled and bounced onto the floor. He found three of them.

One pay phone was in use. An Out of Order sign hung on the one beside it. Carlos balanced from one foot to the other. He finally asked the caller, "Would you hurry please. I've got to make an emergency call."

"Sure, buddy, in a minute." The man chatted a bit longer and then hung up. "Everybody's got an emergency." He slammed the receiver back on the hook.

Carlos scanned the phone book, fingers shaking, finally finding Harris Methodist. He dropped a quarter in the slot, dialed the number, and drummed his fingers on the side of the phone.

"Come on, folks, come on, answer." Ilka's coffee felt like lead bolts in his stomach. The phone rang ten times before someone answered.

72

"Good morning, Harris Methodist, may I help you?"

"Hello, I'm calling about the fellow brought in last night, seriously injured with no identification. I may know who he is."

"I believe someone has been in here and identified him. She's gone up there now. Are you a relative?"

"Close friend."

"Where are you now?"

"Here in the city."

"Stop by then, he's under guard. Maybe you can discuss it with the police. I'm sure they would like any information you might have."

"Did you say there is someone with him, a woman?"

"Yes, I believe it's his sister."

His heart sank. Ilka had arrived and had had a chance to talk with Damon. Carlos pressed his fist against the wall. What now? The receptionist asked if he was still on the line.

"Yes, yes, I'm still here. Can you tell me his condition?"

"I'm sorry, only a family member can receive that information."

Carlos thanked her and hung up, keeping his hand on the receiver. At least Damon's alive. Ilka's gotten to him though. I wonder how much she's found out and how much she's told him. A man standing behind him jingled change in his pocket. Carlos stepped back. The man gave him a disgusted look, picked up the receiver, and dialed.

Carlos pushed his way back to the sidewalk, his mind in turmoil. He spotted a cab that had slowed for a red light. He rushed out to hail it just as the light turned green. He raced up and grabbed the door handle and rapped on the window. The driver slammed on his brakes, waved his arms, and swore something unintelligible.

Carlos kept his hand on the door handle and ran along beside the cab as the driver tried to accelerate. A middle-aged woman sitting in the rear screamed, pulled her pocketbook up to her breast, and retreated to the farther corner of the seat.

The driver ran down the window.

"What the hell's the matter with you, feller? You trying to get us all killed?"

Carlos yanked up the door lock and leaped inside.

"This is an emergency. I've got to get to the hospital pronto. A relative, severely injured. I've got money," he explained between breaths.

The driver eyed his passenger in the rearview mirror. The women nodded reluctantly, and the cabbie accelerated.

"Which hospital?"

"Harris Methodist."

The balance of the trip passed in silence. The driver wheeled around to the visitors' entrance. Carlos added twenty bucks to the fare, tossed it on the seat, and nodded toward the woman.

He strode into the reception area. A wave of fatigue hit, and his stomach rumbled as odors of food wafted out from the cafeteria. His first mission was Damon, however. A white-haired, motherly looking lady stood behind the desk.

"I called a few minutes ago about the unidentified man."

"Oh, yes, terrible things happen on the streets at night. I'm sorry about your friend. I'm sure they will take good care of him here. A policeman will be stationed outside the door and able to help."

Carlos thanked her as he hurried to the elevator. Damn, he didn't have the room number. He turned back to reception. He repeated the number she gave him and thanked her again. A bank of elevators lined the corridor; he wished he had asked which one. An up arrow lighted, and the door slid open.

Apprehension enveloped him when he stepped out of the elevator. Must have taken the wrong one. He walked along the corridor as casually as possible, checking room numbers and looking for a guard. The room must be down the next corridor.

There was danger in the air; he could feel it. Rounding the corner, he spotted a policeman leaning against the wall, sipping coffee from a Styrofoam cup. Another twenty-five feet brought them face-to-face.

"I believe the patient in there"—Carlos motioned to the door—"is my friend, Damon Duncan. I'd like to see him if I could."

The policeman alerted and stepped forward, a scowl on his face. "He's under protective custody until we know more about the case. You a relative?"

"No, a friend. A close friend."

The officer flipped open a spiral notebook. "Name and address."

"Carlos Bravara, just visiting a few days here in town."

The police officer's head jerked up when he heard Carlos's name. He flipped a page back, inspected it, cleared his throat, and stared at Carlos. "How long have you known the victim?"

Carlos paused. "About ten days, I'd say."

"Where did you meet him?" He nodded toward the door.

Carlos was immediately aware his premonitions were not wrong; the back of his neck tightened. This was beyond the usual questioning. "I met him on a bus trip coming over from Boston a few days ago."

"You make friends fast." The officer continued to stare at him, not waiting for a reply. "Where were you last night, say, after eleven?"

Carlos didn't like the tenor of the conversation now at all. What had Ilka told the police? It was potentially incriminating that he had been looking for Damon and was not accounted for until morning. He turned over in his mind how to answer. Best to tell the truth.

"I was out looking for him."

"Why were you out looking for him?"

"He ran out of the house just as I was going in. He seemed upset. He wouldn't speak to me."

"Did you threaten him?"

"Of course not," he snapped.

"Let's stay calm now, just stay calm," the officer repeated, his open palm making quieting motions downward. "Where was this house?"

"His sister's house." He gave the address.

The officer wrinkled his brow and pushed his cap back with the tip of his pen. "What happened next?"

"I ran after him, asking him to stop, what the matter was. He wouldn't answer. He kept running."

The officer wrote busily on his notepad. "When did you catch him?"

"I didn't. I couldn't find him. I looked all night."

"Did anyone see you?" the officer asked with a slight curl of his lip.

"No, it was dark. I couldn't see much of anything. Nobody was on the street."

"Somebody was on the street, and this feller in there met up with him." He went toward the door, paused, and then turned back. "Nasty scratch you've got there." He eyed Carlos's arm. "Want to tell me how you got it?"

Carlos put his fingers up to the torn sleeve then onto the wound and winced.

"I caught my sleeve on a fence. It didn't bleed much, so I guess I forgot about it."

He knew the excuse sounded weak and wished he'd changed the shirt back at Ilka's.

"You wait right here. We're going to have a lot more questions for you." The officer pulled out his cell phone.

"Am I under suspicion?"

His heart pounded, and he broke out into a sweat. The room started to sway, and he caught onto a table.

"Everyone's under suspicion. Right now, we need a lot more answers from you."

The officer punched in a number.

"Yeah, we got a suspect in the Arlington Heights assault."

He listened, nodded his head, and glanced at Carlos.

"Yeah, I'll read him his rights."

Carlos slid sideways into a chair and put his hand to his forehead. This couldn't be happening; everything was spinning out of control.

"Hey, you all right, fella?"

"Sure, everything's fine. I haven't slept or eaten since yesterday, and I'm concerned about my friend in there. Otherwise, everything's fine. Don't bother with the Miranda rights. I got nothing to hide. Now, can I see him?"

"Police procedure. I have to read your rights." He parroted off the words by rote. "Do you understand?"

"Yeah, yeah, now can I see him? He can identify me and save you a lot of trouble."

"Only one person at a time at this point, and his sister's in there with him now. I'll see what she has to say." He tapped lightly on the door then ducked his head in. A brief conversation ensued in hushed voices.

Carlos was aware it was Ilka, and she was upset.

The officer closed the door and approached Carlos.

"Turn around, hands on the wall, spread 'em."

The officer grabbed his shoulder and spun him around. Carlos shook his hand off but complied. The officer pulled Carlos's left arm behind him and snapped on a handcuff and then pulled the right arm around and cuffed it. He patted Carlos down, finding nothing. He grunted.

He took out his cell phone and walked up the hall out of earshot. He spoke briefly then walked back.

Carlos twisted his head and stared at the officer; his eyebrows lifted.

"Hey, wait a minute, I've cooperated. I'm not armed. I've answered all your questions honestly, even to my own detriment." Anger gripped him as he spit out, "It's the color of my skin and the black hair, isn't it?" He twisted his body and looked the officer in the eye.

"I ran a check on you, you've got a record. You've been in jail, right?"

"I served my time. I caused no trouble. Out on good behavior. I've been off parole for four years. It's the ethnic thing, isn't it?"

"It's nothing to do with race, Bravara, I have information that you're more involved than what you're saying. Now don't cause me trouble. I want you to stand right here, no funny stuff."

The officer paced around, his hand not far from the revolver on his hip. An elevator hummed to a stop, and the doors slid open. Another officer stepped out and approached. The two of them conversed in low tones for several minutes. He finally approached Carlos, took him by the arm, and led him back toward the elevator.

"We're taking you down to the station for some more questioning."

There was no use in protesting further. He held his head high and kept a defiant expression on his face as the humiliating trip to the squad car proceeded. People in the elevators and in the reception area eyed him with disdain and fear, talking in low voices, cupping their hands over their mouths, and murmuring to each other.

Carlos was herded into the backseat, hand to head, as two policemen escorted him to the station house for questioning. He felt like a caged animal behind the bars separating him from the officers in front. It seemed like Boston all over again, but no son of a bitch was going to do the same thing to him again!

CHAPTER

7

The walls were dirty gray. Footprints marred the lower walls where interrogators often stood, one foot on the floor, the other foot braced against the wall. The only furniture was a heavy rectangular table bolted to the floor with a steel ring in the center and three heavy metal chairs spaced around it. A lightbulb dangled from a cord in the ceiling, positioned to shine down onto the face of the person being questioned. The concrete floor had been painted at some point but was now worn and peeling. One-way glass spanned half a wall.

Carlos was led in, his mood as somber and depressed as the surroundings. A guard removed his handcuffs and left, jingling the keys. He slammed the door. Carlos felt light-headed from anxiety and lack of food. He was paradoxically aware that his whereabouts of the night before placed him in a very untenable situation.

A detective entered the room. He was a rather nondescript person, probably in his forties. About five eight or nine, Carlos judged, broad shoulders, probably an athlete in his younger years. The start of middle-age spread pushed the waist out on a brown pinstripe suit. He removed his jacket, slid it over a chairback, and dropped onto the seat.

"My name's Cochran. Let's see, your name's Bravara, Carlos Bravara. What kind of a name is that?"

"Cuban American. What about it?"

"Immigrant?"

"No. And you wouldn't be fucking with me if I had blue eyes and blond hair."

"Cut the shit, Bravara, race's got nothing to do with it."

Carlos could hear the detective's stomach rumble as the silence lengthened. The noise of the station and the outside world were muffled by the thick walls. It would seem more like another nightmare if it weren't so real.

"Coffee?" The detective tilted his head toward the coffeemaker, which periodically belched steam as it kept the pot heated.

"I'd rather have something to eat," Carlos replied.

Cochran nodded, pushed his chair back, and went to the door. He mumbled to someone outside then crossed back and poured himself a cup. It looked black and strong. He added three teaspoons of sugar, stirred vigorously, and took it without cream.

"I've sent for a sandwich and a Coke," he said between slurps.

Carlos shrugged. "I'm still not sure why I've been brought down here. I haven't committed a crime. I wish someone would tell me what the hell's going on! All you need to do is ask Damon Duncan to identify me."

"'S not possible now. He hasn't regained consciousness. The doctors say no visitors except for his sister."

Carlos was immediately alarmed. "He's going to be okay, isn't he? He's going to be…" He swallowed hard and leaned forward. "He's going to live, isn't he?"

Cochran grunted and nodded.

Stay calm, Carlos said to himself. *Don't let this bastard freak you out. He probably thinks if he waits long enough, I'll incriminate myself.*

He looked up and ran his eyes along the ceiling. It appeared like maggots crawling in circles. He blinked, and they disappeared. His stomach rolled, and he covered his mouth to keep from puking. The air was stale and felt raw in his throat. He coughed and almost puked again.

Boston, eight years ago, flashed through his mind.

Running, they were all running; cruisers blocked every escape route. He and the gang tried to flee between two buildings. Cops were everywhere. Rough hands caught him by the elbow. He struggled to get away. A policeman grabbed him by the arm and slammed him against a brick wall.

"It says here you've known the guy five days." Cochran looked up from his notes and arched an eyebrow.

Carlos jerked back to the present. "Ten days in all. Can't you tell me anything about his condition?"

"My information says five days."

"Ten. I told the cop ten days, back at the hospital." Carlos knew right off that Ilka had told them five, and they were using her information over his.

"You're from Boston?"

"Yeah. Can't you tell me anything?"

"How long?"

"The past eight years.

"Born in America?"

"I was born in Miami. My folks are Cuban-American. They immigrated here thirty years ago. They're back in Cuba now. My father was disabled, couldn't work." Carlos was becoming annoyed at this line of questioning. He stared at the detective emotionlessly as the questions continued.

"What brought you to Fort Worth?"

I was on my way to California. I can't stand the New England winters."

"Why did you stop in Fort Worth if you were headed for California?" He stopped writing and gave Carlos a sharp glance, one eyebrow raised.

"I met Damon Duncan on the bus, and we became friends. He asked me to stop and meet his sister, and then we were both going on to California." Carlos replied, trying to control the edge in his voice.

"What did his sister think of that?"

"She seemed okay with it at the time."

"At the time. Did that change?"

"She loaned me her car to see the town last evening. She seemed okay then. I came back around eleven or so just as Damon ran out the door."

"You're sure she let you borrow the car?"

"Of course I'm sure." Carlos struggled to keep his cool. He wouldn't let Cochran get the best of him.

"But now she doesn't like you anymore?" Cochran had a smirk on his face.

"Apparently not."

"Why do you think that is?"

"You tell me, then we'll both know." Carlos returned the smirk.

"What was the nature of your relationship with this Duncan fellow?"

"Friends."

Cochran consulted his notes. The only noise was the scratching of his pen on a yellow lined pad. He paused, looked at Carlos and then back at his pad. He cleared his throat, pushed his chair back with a loud scrape, stood up, and jabbed at Carlos with his index finger.

"Isn't it the truth, Bravara, that you met Duncan on the bus and started pursuing him?"

"It was a mutual attraction."

"Then we can say you were pursuing him."

"Depends on what you mean by pursuing."

"You're a big man of the world, you know what pursuing means. You were following after him, not letting him out of your sight."

"We were keeping close company. He was pursuing me as well, if you want to put it that way."

"I want to put it the way it was. Did he tell you he had a lot of money?"

Carlos looked startled. "We never talked about money."

"Did he pay for your meals on this bus trip?"

"No, we agreed to go Dutch."

"He never said something like, 'Don't worry about stopping in Fort Worth, I'll pay for the tickets'?"

"As a matter of fact, he did pay for the rental of the car we came to Fort Worth in. He insisted. It wasn't a big deal, something like forty dollars."

"So you didn't go Dutch, as you stated, all the time then?"

"Not that time, no, but I paid the rest of the rental when we turned it in."

Cochran paused then spit out, "Isn't it also the truth you have been stalking him ever since you both arrived here, and isn't it also the truth he tried to reason with you last night?" The detective turned away and then spun back, prodding his right index finger at Carlos's face again. "And you were outraged, chased him down, attacked him, and left him for dead."

"Jesus Christ, man, why would I do a thing like that? I...I love the guy."

Cochran made a hissing noise through his teeth. "These are all lies."

Carlos's head pounded, the pain ran down his spine; his eyes were smarting from lack of sleep and emotion. It was difficult to breathe in the stifling air.

"For his money, Bravara, for his money!" the detective snarled, enunciating the last three words slowly and deliberately.

"What money, what are you talking about?"

"Mr. Duncan's money. Just like you hustled that rock star in Boston till he threw you out."

"Where the hell are you getting all these goddamned lies you're accusing me of?"

A knock sounded on the door. A policewoman entered and set a sandwich in a plastic bag and a can of Coke in front of him. Cochran nodded at the policewoman, and she scuttled out. Carlos stared at the detective. He struggled to his feet, his chair slamming the wall with a solid thud.

"You take this fucking sandwich and stick it up your ass, you bastard! Every word you've said to me is a lie, a goddamned lie, and you know it. Either you charge me with something or get me out of here now!"

"Sit down, sit down. Eat the food," Cochran said in a calm voice. "I have testimony from a credible witness that you have been stalking this guy, and he was going to face up to you last night. What do you say to that?"

Carlos caught onto the little game being played, and his temper cooled as fast as it flared. He nonchalantly pulled the sandwich out and took a bite, made a face, and tossed it back into the wrapper. He flipped the tab on the Coke, and it foamed out onto the table.

"Got any napkins?"

"Don't worry about it."

Cochran got up, reached in back of the coffeemaker, grabbed a handful of napkins, and tossed them onto the table. Carlos took another bite from the sandwich.

So Ilka's been playing games. Fuck him, he wants the whole truth, well, buddy, here it is.

"Did your credible witness also tell you her brother is gay, and we have been sleeping together in her house since we arrived?"

He took a swig of the cola, wiped his mouth with the back of his hand, fished the sandwich out, and took another bite.

Cochran maintained a poker face.

Carlos swallowed and then continued. "And did she tell you I stopped twice at her house last night looking for Damon? And did she tell you why he ran out on me last night?"

He bit his tongue after the last remark. This was walking into a trap. He kicked himself for the foolish mistake.

"And you were furious when he wouldn't stop, so you ran after him."

"I was alarmed, not furious. I knew she must have told him something upsetting." He paused again, continuing to eat the sandwich.

"Could that something upsetting have been about your police record in Boston?"

Carlos looked startled. "There was no way she could have known about that unless she rifled my duffel bag while I was out with her car that she loaned me."

"Care to tell me where the scratch on your arm and the torn sleeve happened?" He glanced down at his wrist. "I cut around a corner too quick and caught my arm on a fence. Look at my hands, do you see any blood?" He held them out, turning them over and back.

"You're nobody's fool, you washed it off."

"That would be difficult since my clothes are still in your credible witness's guest room with Damon's, and she was in the house all night. If you don't believe me, ask her."

"How long was it between the time you say his sister left you at the gas station until you got to the hospital?" Cochran asked, starting to pace back and forth.

"A half hour tops."

Cochran tapped his forehead. "Plenty of time to wash your hands and get to the hospital."

"That's bullshit. If that was the case, why didn't I change my shirt as well? Besides, I don't have a car. It was morning rush hour. I took a cab from the gas station. You can ask the driver."

"You can bet your ass on that."

Carlos crumpled the sandwich bag and took a last drag on the soda. He stood up again, several inches taller than the detective. They stared at each. Cochran looked back down at his papers, gathered, and shuffled them on the table.

Carlos said in an even tone, "You know your credible witness will fold when you push her, and you know Duncan will clear me. In the meantime, you're welcome to test my DNA. Give me a lie detector test if you want."

"In good time, Bravara, in good time."

Cochran's face flushed. He stuffed the papers into a file folder. He started to say something then turned and headed for the door.

He swung back and warned, "Stay where you are, I'll be right back."

Carlos paced around the confined space. Every step was like dancing on ice. He knew enough about police tactics to know they needed a culprit, guilty or innocent. It made no difference which—get your conviction and go on to the next case. He fixed a bored look on his face as the door reopened.

Cochran stepped back in, flipping a folded paper in his right hand against his left. He pulled a pen out of his pocket and sat down.

"You're free to go, but stay in town, I'll need an address and phone number." He looked up, pen poised to write.

"I'll call when I have one. In the meanwhile, you can reach me through his sister."

The detective's head shot up. He started to say something then clamped his mouth shut. He rose out of the chair, rummaged in his jacket pocket, and extracted a card, flipping it to Carlos between his first and second fingers. He motioned Carlos out, anger distorting his face.

"Stay away from Duncan. If my men catch you anywhere near him, you'll be under lock and key before you can say 'Boo.'"

"By the way, detective," Carlos said with a sneer, "the sandwich was stale, and the soda was flat."

"Don't push your luck here, boy!"

"De carbron."

♋

Cochran watched the door close. His hopes of wrapping the case up quickly were now dashed. Why is the sister so damned sure Bravara is the perp? Something was going on here he couldn't quite figure out. Bravara's got a record, but it doesn't add up to an aggravated assault charge. He's a sly bastard, maybe too sly, and he isn't in the clear yet, but he's got the goods on Ilka Duncan at this point. Better call her in for some more questioning.

He pushed the squad-room door open. All faces turned to him. He figured they'd all watched through the one-way glass.

"He your man?" An officer looked at him, wrinkling his brow.

"Of course the cocksucker is," Cochran replied, trying to save face after the time spent. "You guys got anything else to do?"

"You let him go?" another officer asked, throwing his right hand up in question.

"Not enough evidence, but I'm putting a tail on him. He'll misstep, you can bet on that. Besides, I don't want the ACLU on my ass until we have proof. He pulled the ethnic bit, the prick, that's always supposed to work."

"He's kinda cute," one of the female detectives commented then feigned ducking.

"Yeah, right, fucking queer, he uses it to suck people in."

They all laughed at the unintended double entendre. Cochran colored and swatted his hands at them.

"Stevens, Maloney, put a 24-7 tail on him. I want to know his every move. He's a clever bastard, and he knows his way around. I don't want him to finish the job with Duncan. Keep watch of Ilka Duncan too. She's trouble."

CHAPTER

8

Carlos let his breath out in a whistle. This was only the beginning. He commandeered a shady park bench, tossed his jacket over the back, and undid several shirt buttons. It felt good to sprawl his body out. The day was going to be another scorcher. The sandwich and soda had barely sated his hunger, and he felt inundated with exhaustion.

He lapsed into a half-sleep. Unpleasant memories of Boston eight years ago clamored through his mind.

A police officer grabbed him and rammed him against a brick wall. His partner called out to the other gang members to halt. High-powered flashlights swept over them as they attempted to scramble up a fence. They were peeled off like so many climbing vines, grabbed by resisting legs, pants, jackets, anything they could get hold of. One gang member managed to leap over and run down the street.

"Halt, you little fucker, or I'll blow your brains out," an officer yelled.

The kid kept running. Shots rang out. The boy's body pitched forward and then crumpled like a stabbed balloon onto the sidewalk.

The rest of the boys were now in handcuffs. One yelled out, "You fucker, you killed him!" Another started to sob.

"Shut the fuck up, you murdering piece of crap!" the officer ordered, grabbing the boy by the scruff of his neck and shaking him. Next, they were lined up and searched. Carlos, still pinned to the wall, an arm to his neck, felt the officer's other hand pat him down and then squeeze his crotch, his hand like a vise. Carlos doubled over, retching.

"Stand up, you little prick, or I'll tear 'em off," the officer spit out.

A man's voice propelled Carlos back to the present. A couple of police officers leaned on the back of the bench.

"Hey, buddy, move along. This is no place for a nap!"

"I was just crashing for a few minutes, for God's sake." He grabbed his jacket and swung it over his shoulder. Sauntering down the sidewalk, he sensed being followed and whirled back.

"Is there a Y in the area?"

Startled by his quick move, the officer was rattled for a second and started to reach for his gun.

"Yeah, over on Eighth Street. I'll give you a lift."

"Right, like a hole in the head."

"Suit yourself, big shot."

"How long do you guys have to tail me anyway?"

"You know all the answers, you tell us."

Carlos bought a newspaper and a city map at a corner newsstand, checking his cash as he paid—seventy-eight bucks and a few coins. He'd have to try the credit card again. Shouldn't be a problem. Still, it hadn't worked at the convenience store gas pump. There was a savings account he could access as well.

He ran a hand over his chin; he needed a shave and a shower. At the moment, however, a pancake shop down the street beckoned. A decent cup of coffee and scrambled eggs would hit the spot. Crossing over, he noticed a man loitering on the corner. Carlos glanced in his direction, and the man looked away, pulled a cigarette out of his pocket, snapped a match with his thumbnail, and cupped the flame with both hands.

The AC in the restaurant was a welcome relief from the heat. The blonde at the counter took his order and gave him an appreciative once-over. She made skin contact handing him the coffee and watched him take a booth. Her elbows were perched on the counter, hands cradled her chin. Carlos took a sip of coffee and smiled in her direction. She met his glance and smiled back. She started around the counter, but a customer stepped up to be waited on. Thank God.

With a street map laid out on the table, he ran a finger along to Ilka's street then back to the Y. Opposite directions, of course. It involved a lot of walking, but he had the time. Hell, that was the only thing he did have. With the coffee and eggs consumed and the remains thrown into the trash, he glanced out the window. The man still lingered across the street, leaning against a tree. He looked up and down, lit another cigarette, and changed positions from one foot to the other. He glanced over at the restaurant every couple of minutes.

Carlos slipped out the side entrance, cut across an alley, and walked up a narrow side street. Apartment buildings of several stories lined the sidewalks. Old newspapers and other debris eddied around in the hot breeze. A derelict sat with his legs doubled up, his back against a building, too drunk to even panhandle. Several ragtag boys raced in and out, challenging drivers to hit them. A woman leaned out a second floor window and cursed in Spanish at one of the boys. He gave her the finger.

"Hey, dude," another boy shouted, "catch." He tossed a football.

Carlos turned, clutched the ball, and heaved it back. The kid jumped to catch it, but it bounced out of sight. The boy scaled a fence. A dog stood over the ball, growling low in his throat, daring the kid to grab it. Carlos turned away, let the dog and kid fight it out. He had his own devils to deal with. He moved along several more streets and then cut back onto the route he plotted to Ilka's. No sign of the tail.

His shirt clung to his body in a sodden embrace, the jacket he wore the night before now an albatross clinging to his shoulder. Ilka's house finally came into view. There was certain to be an imbroglio, at best, when he arrived. If she were there, would she share any news of Damon's condition?

She had to have gone through his things to find those damned papers. Where was Damon when she was rifling his belongings? Maybe she confronted him with it and he became angry and raced out. There had to have been something bad.

A black Crown Vic stood in front of her house. He hadn't seen it in the neighborhood these past few days, probably plainclothesmen watching for his return. All he wanted was his damn bag. If he circled around a back street and eased up to the kitchen door, maybe they wouldn't spot him. Too late. Two men got out and approached.

"Police. Are you Carlos Santos Bravara?" one of them asked, stating his name and flipping out a badge.

"Yeah, what of it?" Apprehension and a sense of foreboding swept his mind in spite of blowing them off.

The second man flipped his badge and drew an envelope out of his pocket. "We're serving you with a restraining order. You are not to come within five hundred feet of this property or the persons of either Ilka Duncan or Damon Duncan."

Wordlessly, Carlos took the papers and perused them, grunted, and passed them back.

The first man added, "Sign there at the bottom." He indicated the spot with his finger. "And date it. Violation of this order will bring criminal charges. Do you understand?"

"No, I don't understand." He leaned forward, scribbled his name, and tossed it back onto the car hood. "I haven't done anything wrong. I need to hear it from Damon Duncan himself that he doesn't want to see me. Besides, all my clothes and personal things are in there," he exclaimed, pointing toward Ilka's house. "How do I go about getting them?"

"You'll have to go to the precinct station and fill out a form. They'll be picked up and held. Come by tomorrow. They should have them by then."

They both got into the car. The driver ran the window down.

"We've warned you now about further contact. Five hundred feet, remember that, Bravara."

Carlos leaned his body against the driver's door.

"The papers I signed, I'm not admitting to anything."

"Police procedure, Bravara."

"You don't give a shit whether I'm guilty or not."

Convulsed in pent-up anger, he banged his fist against the door, eyed the two men, and twisted his body away.

The detective, annoyed, touched Carlos's arm.

"I'm following orders. I suggest you move along.

∽

The heavy door of the Y swung open, and a surge of welcoming cool air wafted out. Taking a moment for his eyes to adjust, he glanced around for a registration desk.

"I need a place to sleep tonight," Carlos told the attendant, heat and dehydration making him unsteady on his feet.

The man was probably in his fifties, dressed in sweats with the name Lou embroidered on the chest. A band around his head partially covered a half-moon of hair. He was pudgy and rather short, probably a volunteer. He had a friendly face. The corners of his mouth tipped up, and his smile was easy. As he inspected Carlos, however, he became serious.

"You been drinking, young man? We can't allow anything like that here."

"No, I've been out in the sun, walking for the past two hours. This Texas heat is something else."

"Two hours? Good God, you could get heatstroke." He scratched his head. "Not from around here, I take it?"

"Boston, for the last several years."

"I used to live in the East. Quite a culture shock," he replied, the smile returning.

"That's for sure."

"Looks like you need a shower and change of clothes." He peered over the counter and down at the floor. "I don't see any luggage."

Carlos struggled for a reasonable answer. "The people I was traveling with have gone on to California and took my bags with them by mistake. I need a place to rest and clean up." A half-lie was better than a whole one, he figured. He stuck out his hand. "Hi, I'm Carlos."

The man nodded, shook hands, then patted "Lou" on his sweatshirt. "Get yourself a drink over at the machine. I don't want no one passing out from dehydration. I'll see what I can do for a room and a razor. There's a shower down by the pool."

"Is there an ATM nearby?"

"There's a bank a couple of blocks down, a machine's there. But you be sure to sit down and drink something before you go out again. Dehydration's nothin' to fool around with."

Carlos put a dollar into the slot, and a plastic bottle of water dropped down. He straddled a folding chair, hunched over, and rested his elbows on the wooden back between sips. The cold drink, the refrigerated air, and the rest revived him somewhat for the afternoon ahead.

Carlos leaned his left elbow against the polished stone surround of the ATM machine, pushed his card in, typed in the password, and clicked on a hundred dollars. A message came back, "Insufficient funds," and the card popped out. He tried the same procedure again—same results. He shook his head in disbelief. He had a five-grand credit limit.

He was met again with a blast of cold air as the revolving foyer doors on Texas Bank and Trust spun effortlessly at his push. The dampness of his clothes gave him a momentary chill. Polished stone floors glistened from the slanting afternoon sun. The main lobby was elliptical, the walls paneled in a dark-grained wood. Heavy draperies with tasseled tiebacks fell from the tall windows to the floor. Groupings of leather chairs were arranged around kidney-shaped, polished wooden desks for customer service. He approached one of the teller windows and presented his credit card.

"I seem to be having a problem with this card. I'd like to draw out some money. My cash-advance limit is two thousand dollars, I believe. Two hundred would be fine."

"Certainly, sir."

She took the card and ran it through the machine. He punched in the numbers. Account cancelled. It couldn't be. No late payments, nothing. In a low voice, she consulted with another teller, who also slid it through.

"I'm sorry, sir, that account has been cancelled." The young woman looked perplexed. "Three days ago. Are you the only one on the card?"

He ignored her question.

"That can't be. There should be a five-thousand-dollar limit on that account."

Nothing was making any sense. He'd paid the card off before leaving Boston. He pulled a savings withdrawal slip out of his wallet, scribbled off the numbers, and entered a thousand dollars on the amount column. He slipped this along with his photo ID driver's license back across the counter. She punched in the info, and he could see unfavorable news by her expression even before she spoke.

"I'm sorry, sir," the teller looked troubled. "This account has a balance of fifty dollars. It appears that you or another party to the account drew out twenty-seven thousand dollars three days ago."

"There has to be a mistake. A week ago there was practically twenty-eight thousand dollars in that account. I haven't drawn anything out."

Anger strangled in his throat. Everywhere he turned, something went wrong. That prick of a Jerry Haines has done this to him.

"Oh sure, Carlos," he had said, "put my name on your account, and I can withdraw for you and wire you money when you need it."

Haines he could deal with.

The slimy bastard, he'll be sorry he ever knew me before I'm done.

He thanked the teller and headed out.

Across the street a sign caught his attention, Warm Beer, Lousy Food and All That Jazz.

Intrigued, not knowing his next move, Carlos crossed the street and read a small sign written with a black felt marker on a piece of white paper taped to the window, Piano Player Wanted.

Carlos stepped down the three granite slabs to the entrance. It was gloomy inside, only a few dark shaded lamps illuminated the area. A bar ran along the back wall, and a couple of dozen or so round tables with bentwood chairs were spaced around the room. As he became accustomed to the dim light, he spotted two or three patrons seated at the bar. An old upright piano stood in one corner lighted by a grouping of candles. Overhead fans twisted the flames in a circular motion.

Carlos strolled to the piano, seated himself, and fingered out a blues song. It was a great feeling to play again. Memories of the two songs he had composed at another piano flooded over him.

I'm down, but I'm not out.

A skinny young blond guy about his own age, he figured, appeared from the shadows, holding a saxophone. "Y'all know 'September in the Rain'?"

"You know it, brother!" Carlos played the opening bars.

"Hit it."

They broke into an improvised rendition, becoming more in sync as they played. The patrons at the bar worked their way over humming and slapping their thighs to the rhythm. When they finished, everyone had gathered around, and applause broke out.

"You done this long?" the bartender asked.

"Yeah, a number of years in my folks' restaurant back in Miami."

"Consider yourself hired," the bartender said, both as a question and as an offer. "How about a beer?"

"Yes, on both counts," Carlos replied.

CHAPTER

9

The room pitched and careened like a circus ride as Carlos's fingers flew over the keys. A tapestry of pieces from the past ran through his mind like ten movies spliced randomly into one film. Threads of ambition, regret, hope, and despair were intricately interwoven into the present state of his existence. So many of the things that were important at the time were now gone. The good times at the family restaurant in Miami, the promise of a career in music, the two songs he had written, the love he felt for Damon—all appeared to be gone. He couldn't recall ever being more tired or emotionally drained.

Customers on the street, returning home from work, hearing the music, filtered in. Lenny offered him fifteen bucks an hour plus tips, starting tomorrow. By the time he quit, thirty-five dollars had collected in a bowl on the piano.

With the sun set and the somewhat cooler evening air, it made the street a little more bearable as he emerged from the club. An occasional breeze wafted heat up from the steaming asphalt. At a drugstore, Carlos bought a razor, shaving cream, soap, shampoo, and deodorant.

He spotted a health bar and entered from habit. Carrot juice, green salad with grilled chicken, and a banana comprised the meal. The other patrons were arrayed in a rainbow of colored outfits, tie-dyed T-shirts, fringed scarves, baggy, drawstring pants, and sandals. Oriental music issued from somewhere in the walls. No one paid attention to his jeans and sport shirt or his Eastern accent. In spite of the calm atmosphere, his temples throbbed, and he wished he had bought some aspirin.

The envelope containing the restraining order felt heavy in his pocket, as did his feet on the sidewalk as he emerged into a hot, noisy Southwestern evening. As luck would have it, Lou was still at the Y. His face lit up when he saw Carlos.

"Glad ta see ya back, young feller, I was about to close down." He reached behind the counter. "Thought you could use these for tonight." He held up a shiny white jersey with Fort Worth arched across the front in large black letters and a pair of gym shorts.

"Thanks, Lou," was about all he could squeeze out for conversation.

He paid for the night and got directions to a room. It proved to be sparsely furnished but clean. It contained three cots, a couple of chairs, a desk, and a lamp. A ceiling fan rotated unevenly, causing a wheezing sound. Two rather nondescript roommates, one sitting on a cot, the other one sprawled on the floor, argued back and forth about who could ride a steer the longest. Both were skinny, almost emaciated. They wore typical Western gear, worn fringed shirts with brass snaps, tight faded jeans, scuffed cowboy boots, and broad-brimmed hats carelessly flung on the floor. They looked up, gave him the eye when he entered, then continued.

Carlos introduced himself, holding out his hand. He felt empathy. They both looked down on their luck.

"My name's Slim, and this here is Ferdinand, Ferdy," one said, pointing to the other young man lying on the cot.

"Where, y'all from?" Slim questioned, returning the handshake.

"Born in Miami, spent some time in Boston."

"Yowee, them winters are some all-fired cold in Boston, so I hear tell," Ferdy said, tucking his shirt in and brushing his long, disheveled hair out of his eyes. "Where ya headed?"

"LA in a few days."

"What y'all gonna do out there?"

"I'm hoping to break into the music business."

"No kiddin'? Good ole California, the land of pretty gals and earthquakes."

"Sometimes one and the same," Carlos replied, shaking his head.

Buck slapped his knee and guffawed in appreciation. He moved in close to Carlos, looking him up and down.

"Say, y'all are one fine-looking dude."

He had been through this enough times in his life to know what was coming. It was not going to be a comfortable night; he could sense that. Buck was now standing so close Carlos could smell his garlicky breath.

He stuck his hand out, palm up.

"Hey, Carly, I'm kinda down on my luck. Could y'all spare me a coupla bucks?"

Carlos shook his head. Buck pulled his hand back, hesitated, and then reached for Carlos's crotch. "How's about a good ole ten-dollar Texas blow job?"

Carlos grabbed Buck by the wrist and snapped his hand up to the boy's chest.

"Keep your hands to home. The name's Carlos, and don't you forget it."

Carlos pushed him back to the cot and set him down. He reached in his pocket, pulled out a ten, and tossed it on the cot beside Buck.

"That's not my game, Bucky, get yourself something to eat and leave me alone, understand?"

The shower room located down by the pool was nearly empty. Carlos stripped and got under the water, running full force. The cold needles stung his skin. It felt good though, after the past twenty-four hours, to get cleaned up. Most of the swimmers had come up, showered, and left. He took his toilet articles and shaved. Next he took his shirt, underwear, and socks and washed and rinsed them. He put on the jersey and shorts Lou had given him and headed back to the room. Slim and Ferdy were gone.

He draped his wet clothes over a couple of chairs and stretched out on a cot. In spite of his weariness, sleep escaped him. Visions of Damon's attack invaded his thoughts, the terror, the pain, the utter submission to another's act of violence. Carlos tried, without success, to wipe the image from his mind.

"God, Damon, how I miss you," he murmured.

Bits and pieces of last evening flashed through his mind: Damon hugging him in the hall, thanking him for a private time with his sister, Ilka offering her car keys, probably glad to get rid of him. On the other hand, how did she know about his problems in Boston?

Carlos swung his feet onto the floor, leaned his elbows on his knees, and messaged his forehead. Why did Damon run out? What had happened between them? If he had caught Damon, could they have talked it out?

He finally stood up and paced the floor, stopped, braced one arm against the window casing, and peered out into the night. Texas sure comes alive after dark, he thought. The traffic and the buzz of people on the street talking and laughing forged into his brain. He flopped back down onto the cot. Neon lights flashed through the windows, splashing garish colors onto the ceiling. He closed his eyes, head pounding.

Tears of frustration tempered by growing anger slid down his cheeks. He finally turned onto his stomach, face buried in the pillow.

Sleep and dawn finally returned.

⁓

The policewoman stood behind bars imbedded in bulletproof glass. Her steely eyes pierced the barrier like a laser beam. Middle forties, he figured, she must have seen every kind of emergency and listened to thousands of stupid and hysterical people.

"There is a restraining order against me," Carlos stated matter-of-factly. "All my belongings are in the woman's house. Is there some way I can get them?"

"Name?" she asked in a brittle voice.

"Carlos Santos Bravara."

Spell the last name."

"B-r-a-v-a-r-a."

The woman gave him a sharp look, turned, and searched through a file drawer. She took her time perusing them, saying "Hmm" every so often.

"Address," she finally asked.

"Probably the Y, for tonight anyway, or a park bench."

She studied him as though trying to determine if he was being truthful.

"You'll have to fill out this form then sign at the bottom. I'll need some identification."

The area smelled of dirt, tobacco smoke, and sweat. The window AC did little to alleviate the heat and humidity. A Venetian blind with bent slats undulated lazily in the window. A young woman sitting across from him, her skirt only covering the upper portion of her thighs, ran her eyes up and down over him, an invitation intended. The sound of police business filtered through the walls. Sirens in the distance brought untimely memories of Boston seven years ago.

The eight of them were all pushed into police cruisers and driven to the station. Carlos rode alone in the backseat. Two officers were in the front. The one who'd frisked Carlos drove. They were talking to each other, but he couldn't make out what was being said. They glanced back at him once or twice and snickered.

"Hey, boy, how old are you?" the driver asked, observing him in the rearview mirror.

"Eighteen," Carlos lied.

"How'd ya like to beat this rap, kid?" the other officer inquired.

"Yeah, how?" he asked, not daring to hope.

"I seen you around. You're queer, ain't ya?"

What the fuck do you care? That's my business."

"Oh, we got a wiseass here. We're gonna take a little side trip."

"A little side trip where?"

Carlos was suddenly nervous. He broke out in a sweat. He'd heard of police brutality. Fags were hated by the cops. They patrolled the gay bars after midnight, fingering their nightsticks and making crude remarks.

The cruiser finally pulled off into the bushes, skirting a deserted ball field. The moon shone dimly through the branches. The driver strode around to the back door and dragged Carlos out and slammed him against the side of the cruiser. He released one of the cuffs, ordered Carlos to turn around and drop his pants. Carlos shook his head no.

"Come on, buddy boy, drop 'em. Make it fast!"

He rammed Carlos's left hand through the cruiser's rear window, his right through the front window, and snapped the cuffs back on. He yanked Carlos's pants down around his ankles.

Carlos heard the trooper's zipper open and felt his spit-covered hand massage Carlos's ass, ready to enter. The man was brutal. He gripped Carlos by the hair and yanked his head back with each thrust. His partner stood to the left of the driver, fly unzipped, fondling Carlos's penis with one hand and himself with the other.

"I'm only seventeen. You're raping a minor."

The officer yanked out Carlos's wallet and spotted the age on the driver's license.

"You little bastard," he snarled. "You're not going to get away with this." He uncuffed Carlos's hands and told him to run.

Carlos pulled his pants up, hands shaking, and struggled with the buckle. "You're gonna shoot me in the back, escaping, aren't you?"

"You can bet your pretty little ass, I am. Now run."

"Do you have the form filled out yet, Mr. Bravara? I've made some calls and explained your problem."

Carlos looked up, startled when she spoke. He stepped across to the wicket and slid the papers through. She glanced over them and passed them on to another officer. They conversed out of earshot, and then she turned back to Carlos.

"Stop by here tomorrow after ten in the morning. Your things should be ready."

The corners of her mouth tipped up slightly in a mirthless half-smile.

"The same thing happened to my son a few years ago." She spoke in a hushed tone. "You kinda look like him." Her smile faded, and her face grew grim again.

Carlos was taken off guard by the change in her attitude. "What happened?"

"He was out in San Francisco, a wild kid, but he never did any harm to anyone." She looked sad. "I don't hear from him anymore. I don't know if he's even alive."

Carlos tipped his Stetson up with one finger. Their eyes met.

"I'm sorry. You'll hear from him, count on it. Thanks for the help."

"Shush, along with ya now." Her face returned to its former frown.

Back on the street, he headed for the Pancake Shop. The blonde from yesterday was behind the counter. She took his order for coffee, pancakes, a side order of ham, and hash browns. He needed a good breakfast for the day ahead. The morning rush hour was over, and there were only four or five other customers.

She capped the Styrofoam coffee cup and handed it to him. "Cream and sugar over there." She pointed to a side bar. "I'll bring the rest over when it's ready," she added, smiling, laying out a tray with his order slip.

Carlos took a table near the front window. He sipped his coffee and glanced up and down the street.

The blonde came out from the kitchen and set the rest of his breakfast in front of him. She perched on a stool a few feet away, nursing a cup of coffee.

"My morning break." she said, setting her cup down. "You looking for someone?" She glanced out the window, spotting a man across the street.

"More like someone's looking for me."

"You in some kind of trouble?"

"In a manner of speaking."

"I don't mean to be nosy, but do you want to talk about it?"

"A shoulder to cry on?" he said without rancor.

"Whatever, it's my break, and I like to talk with the customers. Say, you're not a movie star, are you?" She gave him the once-over.

"No, nothing like that." He poured syrup on his pancakes and watched it run over the edge and down into the plate. He cut off a piece with his fork and twisted it around in the puddled syrup. "I came to town with a friend a few days ago. It seems like everything has gone wrong since then."

"Police tailing you?" She nodded her head toward the window.

"Yeah, there's a restraining order against me. My friend is in the hospital, and they think I had something to do with his mugging. They can't prove anything, but they want somebody to arrest, make them look better."

It felt good to have someone sympathetic to talk with.

"You're not from around here." She said it as a statement, not as a question.

"Boston, the past eight years. I've written a couple of songs. I'd like to get into show business."

"You've got the looks," she said unabashedly, looking him over.

He nodded; their eyes met.

"I was headed for LA. Then this happened, to my friend, I mean. He was mugged. He's in tough shape."

Carlos paused and took a couple of mouthfuls of pancake.

"Good," he said, pointing to the plate. "Sorry, guess I'm kind of running on. It's nice to have a friendly face."

"I'm a good listener. Maybe I can help. My name's Shirley. They call me Shirl."

"Nice to meet you, Shirley, Shirl. My name's Carlos, Carlos Santos Bravara."

"Nice to meet you, Carlos Santos Brav…whatever. That's a mouthful. Can I get you another cup of coffee? It's on the house."

"Sure, thanks, but I can pay."

She laughed, slid out of her seat, and went behind the counter, returning with another steaming cup. She pushed his money back.

"No, it's on me. Besides, it's a refill."

"Thanks, maybe you can give me some advice. I need a place to stay. The Y is not the greatest accommodation." He spoke louder as she went back behind the counter to pour herself another cup. "It won't be long-term, just a few days."

She returned with her coffee. "I've got an extra bed. You could bunk in with me."

Carlos took another sip of coffee and cut off a piece of ham. He was unsure how to answer. It all sounded too weird. Could this be another setup? He turned to her; she looked serious.

"Are you sure? How do you know I won't mug you?"

"You wouldn't ask me if you planned to. I'm a pretty good judge of character. Besides, I keep a gun under my pillow."

"Smart girl."

"Still alive at least."

"I'm playing piano down at the warm-beer place, evenings," he said, changing the subject.

"That's great. Lenny's been looking for a piano player since the last one ran away with his wife."

"No kidding."

"Lenny was more upset about losing his piano player than he was about losing his wife."

Carlos gave her a quizzical glance to see if she was being facetious. "You're puttin' me on."

"Well, maybe a little. How about I stop by after work, have a drink, and then we can go to my place after for some shut-eye? When do you get off?" She slipped off the stool and crushed the sides of her Styrofoam cup.

"About midnight."

"That's a little after my bedtime, but hell, I need a night out."

"You're positive? You don't have a boyfriend that will pop in and bust me up?"

"Nothing like that, my nearest relatives live in Tennessee. Anyway, you look like you could handle yourself."

"See ya later then, Shirl."

Carlos collected the breakfast things onto the tray. He started to give her a hug, but a customer came up to the counter. Shirl hesitated for a beat, but the moment passed. Carlos dumped the tray contents into the refuse container, waved to her, and left.

Shirl appeared at the nightclub around ten thirty. She had slipped into a dark blue one-piece sheath with side slits. Several gold chains dangled around her neck, and she'd put her hair up in a bun.

The place was packed. Lenny poured the drinks while young women in abbreviated Western costumes waited on the customers. Shirl wove over to order a Manhattan.

She had to shout over the din.

"A new piano player I see," she said, smiling.

"Yeah, would you believe, he just walked in off the street yesterday and headed for the piano. He sure knows his stuff."

"Know anything about him?" she asked.

"Not a thing, he clams up about himself. The women love him. He'll be rich from tips."

Shirl took her drink and moseyed over by the piano. Carlos spotted her, his face brightened, and he nodded. She tossed a five-dollar bill into the bowl. He shook his head no and then tipped it sideways in resignation.

"Hey, you're good," she mouthed.

"You're not bad yourself," he mouthed back.

She slid into a table near the piano and sipped her drink, watching the crowd. A young couple drifted up and asked if she minded whether they joined her. Shirl smiled and nodded. The young man drew the chair out for the girl and gave her a kiss on the cheek. A waitress came to the table, and the young couple ordered beers. Shirl ordered a gin and tonic.

"Say," the young woman remarked, "looks like Lenny's got a new piano player. He's a hunk. I wouldn't mind having a piece of him."

Her male companion smiled. "Sure, you used to say that about me."

The young woman sighed. "You're still okay, and I love ya," she said, but her eyes were on Carlos.

The waitress brought their drinks. The guy threw out a twenty. Shirl reached for her purse, but the guy shook his head. Shirl nodded thanks.

Carlos played a couple more numbers then took a break. He juggled in and out among the tables with pats on the back and compliments from various patrons. He spotted Shirl at the table where the three of them sat.

"You're here. I didn't know if you'd stay or not." He gave Shirl a peck on the cheek.

The young woman looked embarrassed. "I'm sorry, I didn't know you two knew each other. As usual, I put my foot in my mouth."

Shirl laughed and introduced them. They chatted for a bit, then the couple left.

Another hour back at the piano and Carlos tried to call it a night. The patrons induced him to play a couple more numbers. After that he was firm about leaving. The bowl was stuffed with bills. He crammed them into his pocket and piloted Shirl by the arm through the admirers.

It was a short walk to her rather ordinary apartment building. When they reached her flat on the fourth floor, Carlos was relieved to find the AC chugging away. Her apartment was a tastefully decorated, compact two-bedroom space. The rooms were small, the walls pale beige, and the upholstery soft and inviting. Splashes of color appeared in artwork and accessories.

"Nice place," he complimented her.

"Thanks, I'm a frustrated decorator." She went to the fridge. "Like a drink?"

"A glass of water would do just fine."

"Ice water's in the fridge door. Glasses over the sink." She reached for one and turned back to him. "Say, you don't have any luggage. You must travel light."

"Not by choice, but that's another story. Maybe tomorrow."

"The bathroom is down the hall on the left, plenty of towels, soap, shampoo. Make yourself at home."

The shower full-on massaged his exhausted body. He was looking forward to hitting the sack. His head was tipped back, shampooing, when a tap came on the plexiglass door.

"Mind if I join you?" She slid the door open, naked. "It saves water, I hear," she said, her face flushed.

Carlos turned toward her as she spoke. Her eyes widened.

She was strikingly attractive with firm, full breasts, slim waist and hips. Her legs were long and shapely. It had been at the back of his mind he would probably have to fuck for his bed. Now it was happening, and he felt somewhat panicked. He'd dated a lot in high school but had never been intimate. How do you make love to a woman? he pondered. Maybe the same as a man, only more gentle.

"Sure," he said as firmly as he could muster.

He moved back so she could step in. The stall was small, so they had to stand close together. They were awkward with each other. She tried not to stare at his penis, but it was a no-go. Her nipples pressed against his chest as he pulled her into a clumsy embrace. She was considerably shorter, so he couldn't kiss her in their confinement. He ran his mouth over her hair. They played at soaping each other.

"One of us has got to leave, I can see that clearly," she said.

"I was here first, so I'll get out."

"This wasn't a good idea to start with. I embarrassed you, and I'm sorry."

"No, not a problem. You're okay, more than okay."

He toweled himself off and then wrapped it around his waist. She slipped out. He wrapped a towel around her and stooped to give her a kiss. She put her arms around his neck and pecked him on the cheek.

"You're the most gorgeous man I've ever met, too handsome to be straight."

Carlos swallowed and looked at her with a quizzical expression.

"You're the first man I ever showered with that didn't get an erection."

Carlos colored. "Shirl, you're a remarkable girl, most women don't pick up on it."

"Maybe they don't want to," she said with a sigh. "I won't lie, I wish you weren't, but you're a nice guy. I've dated some real creeps. I wasn't lying about the gun under the pillow."

"That makes me sad. When I leave in a few days, I'll think about you. I mean, I'll worry that some scumbag will try something with you."

"You're sweet." She paused momentarily. "But I'm tough. You get that way around here." She finished toweling off and reached for her robe.

"Wait, let me look at you, I've never seen a girl as pretty as you. You're like a statue."

"Are you getting hard?"

He hesitated. "Well, no."

"Hand me my robe," she said lightly. "That friend you were speaking about, the one who got mugged. You're lovers, aren't you?"

Carlos's frowned. "Yeah, believe it or not, I've only known the guy like ten days, but I'd do anything for him."

"He's a lucky guy." She took him by the arm. "Come back out to the living room, you need to talk."

"But you've got to work tomorrow."

"It's my day off."

"You're sure?"

"I'll call in sick, I've worked too much anyway. Six days a week, sixty hours."

Carlos whistled. They settled on the sofa, and he pulled her against his chest. Her hair smelled clean, and some of her perfume had lasted through the shower. She tipped her head back onto his shoulder, and he leaned over and kissed her. She snuggled closer, and they talked into the early dawn.

CHAPTER

⧏ 10 ⧐

A woman's touch was a whole new experience for Carlos and certainly not an unpleasant one. Pillows and crumpled sheets littered the bed and floor in a tangled heap. They were both out of breath. He needed sex as badly as she, the great equalizer.

They lay back together afterward. He pulled her close and kissed her warmly on the lips. Caught up in the moment, her body warm and responsive, he felt grateful to her for trusting him. She returned the kiss and snuggled against him. Her arm slid across his chest. She was soon asleep, but he remained wakeful. The night sounds of the city, although he was becoming used to them, seemed somehow foreign here in Fort Worth. The city came alive after dusk; life inverted during the heat of the summer. When would his own inversion end? This town had much to offer yet was so alien to his present state of mind and predicament. Sex with Shirl was just that, sex. Sex with Damon was like nothing he had ever experienced before. What had come over him? Damon lay critically ill in the hospital, and here he was, having sex with a woman.

Sleep came at last, so did the nightmare. Again. A dream that had haunted him for the past eight years. It would disappear for a while and then reemerge during times of crisis.

Punky the Panhandler, they called him, an ex-boxer in his sixties, a legend on the streets of Boston, morphed into his nightmare.

"Leave me alone, you goddamned hoodlums," Punky shouted.

The street gang gathered around him. Tony, a tall redheaded thug, a scar marring his left cheek, slammed both fists into the old boxer's gut, staggering him backwards against a brick wall. He lost his balance and fell. Greg, a tall, angular boy, his black hair knotted in a ponytail, kicked him in the stomach. The old boxer grunted, rallied, and caught him by the leg. Greg fell spread-eagle to the pavement, hitting his head. He lay there dazed for a few seconds. Tony stepped over him and grabbed Punky by one arm, pulled him to a sitting position, and slapped him in the face, first one side and then the other. The old man spit at him; Tony punched him under the chin, knocking his head against the bricks.

"Y-you're a f-fuckin' b-bag of s-shit," Sonny, a pimply youth, stuttered, kicking the old boxer in the groin. Punky writhed in agony.

Carlos watched in horror as the five other teens in the gang proceeded to beat Punky with sticks. Carlos grabbed at them, trying to stop them, but to no avail. The victim drew his knees to his chest as they clubbed him again and again. He tried in vain to crawl away, his body slipping in the blood.

"Let's get the fuck outta here," Sam, the youngest of the gang, hissed. He yanked on Carlos's sleeve, trying to pull him away.

The old boxer moaned and started to roll over. Greg crawled away and found a length of iron pipe. His face twisted in anger as he whacked Punky beside the head. The metal against flesh made a dull thud. Punky crumpled over and lay still.

"Shit, you've killed him," one of the boys said in alarm, stooping to inspect the mangled body.

"You're all crazy," Carlos said in a husky whisper, looking toward a neighbor's window where a light had flipped on. The rest of the boys dispersed. Carlos knelt by Punky's grotesque body, feeling for a pulse. It was faint but steady. This was never supposed to happen. They were only going to rough him up a little. Tears rolled down his cheeks at the enormity of the crime. A man appeared at the screen door and flashed a light out onto the sidewalk where the body lay, then onto Carlos, his hands and knees covered with blood.

Carlos rose slowly, his legs shaking. He felt like throwing up. He approached the door where the neighbor stood. The man slammed it before Carlos could ask for help.

Tony snuck back and grabbed Carlos from behind.

"What the fuck you planning ta do, Bravara, rat on us? You're in this up ta ya ass like the rest of us. Get the fuck outta here." He yanked Carlos by the arm.

"What a we got here anyway, a snitch?" Greg snarled, materializing from out of nowhere and seizing Carlos's other arm.

"Fuck, fuck," Carlos snapped back, struggling to free himself. "We were just going to scare him a little, remember? What the fuck did ya have to kill him for?"

He was quickly encircled by the rest of the gang, fists and clubs flying. He ducked, narrowly missing the iron pipe.

A police siren sounded up the street. The boys exploded and fled. More sirens wailed. The streets were quickly sealed in all directions by troopers, their guns and nightsticks drawn.

The shrill sound of an ambulance split the night air as it roared up the street.

An emergency vehicle followed, siren on full blast.

Carlos awoke with a start. His breathing was constricted; sweat seemed to ooze from every pore. It took several seconds for the nightmare to leave and reality to seep in. Carlos pulled the sheet back and twisted into a sitting position, the cool floor felt good on his feet. He stood, gathered himself, stretched, and went to the window. The day promised to be another scorcher. The sky was clear. The sun streamed mercilessly in the windows. He pulled the shades against its onslaught.

Damn, nine fifteen. Gotta get going.

This was the morning he was to retrieve his belongings.

Shirl stirred, yawned, sat up, and reached for her robe.

Carlos padded out into the kitchen. She appeared at the door.

"I haven't gotten up this late since I was in high school." She laughed. "Let me scramble some eggs. Do you like bacon?"

"Let's eat out. My treat," he replied.

"I'll make some coffee first though."

"I'll take a shower and be right with you," he said.

They looked at each other and smiled, thinking of last night. His smile bittersweet, hers he could only imagine. A concern was already building about this new relationship with Shirl. Uneasiness crowded the back of his mind. If this were to go on for too many days, she would expect more from him than he would be able to return. Abstinence, due to circumstances, had allowed him to perform last night. Could he again? Was he being fair to her? Maybe he should cut and run. But where? He needed to be near Damon.

∾

Shirl floated down the three flights, slightly in front of him. Blonde hair spilled down over her freckled shoulders. She wore a pale lavender tank top, low cut in the back, over slightly darker midlength shorts. A black, gold, and beige band was tied casually around her waist. A gold neck chain matched gold hoops in her pierced ears. Her feet were bare in woven sandals. Quite a figure of a woman, he mused. They made a striking couple as they loped along the street to a place Shirl recommended.

An intoxicating aroma of coffee brewing wafted around them as they entered. It was after rush hour, so the place was half-empty. They picked a table overlooking the street and ordered coffee. They sat sipping the steaming brew and perusing the menu. Shortly after they ordered, the waitress returned with steaming plates of eggs, sausage, and pancakes. Carlos ate more from instinct than appetite.

He sat facing the entrance in order to view the customers coming and going, a habit he had acquired back in Boston. A man, somewhat familiar, glanced their way from time to time. Carlos couldn't pin down who he was, probably a plainclothesman.

Shirl noticed his preoccupation.

"You're thinking about him, aren't you?"

He brought his attention back to her.

"At the moment, I'm curious about that fellow near the door. Ever seen him before?"

She glanced over, studied him a moment, then shook her head. Carlos sighed and continued.

"Yeah, I guess Damon is on my mind. We were supposed to be going to California last week. Afraid I'm not very good company."

She put her hand on his. "It's okay, you've been honest with me, I understand."

"I'm so damned frustrated. I can't get near the guy. It's driving me crazy."

"There's nothing to stop me," she replied, looking into his eyes.

"I don't see how." His hopes elevated for a moment, then reality rushed back in. "They won't let anyone but family go in." He reached over and patted her hand. "But thanks for the thought."

"No, I really can get someone in. I have a friend who's a nurse there, he has connections."

"Sounds like he's more than a friend," he said with an anxious smile, hopeful it could take some pressure off him.

"He's a sweet guy, that's all," she said.

He nodded. "You don't know how much it would mean, Shirl."

"I kinda sensed that."

The familiar looking man across the restaurant perused a newspaper. Carlos noticed him continue to glance their way. The man held the unfolded paper in a strange manner, like he was missing a finger. Who is that guy? Feels like I should know him.

They finished eating in comfortable silence. On leaving the restaurant, Carlos made a point of walking by the stranger. What was it about him?

"I've got to make a side trip," Carlos said, catching up with her. "My belongings from Ilka's are supposed to be at the precinct station this morning. Ilka probably went through 'em and tossed half of them away."

"Is she that mean and vindictive?"

"And then some, to me anyway."

They walked back to Shirl's and got her car. She dodged through the heavy midmorning traffic, let Carlos off at the precinct station, and circled the block while he went in. The same woman as yesterday was at the window. He spotted a flicker of recognition but identified himself anyway. Her face reflected the same stress of the job.

"I'm sorry, Mr. Bravara, but we weren't able to find anyone at home. Are you sure you gave us the right address?"

He repeated it to her, and she nodded in the affirmative. They would try again tomorrow, and he could come back. Carlos sensed she wanted to ask him something. He waited for her to continue, but she remained silent.

"Call your son," he told her. "He may be waiting for you to make the first move."

"I wouldn't know where to start."

"You must have connections out there."

"I've used all of them. He's vanished."

"Keep trying, he'll show up."

"You're a kind young man. Most people wouldn't care. I hope we'll have your things tomorrow."

This time she smiled.

"I'll be back, don't give up, on your son, I mean." He felt sympathy for her, probably stuck in a difficult job, having to hold on now at this age, retirement her only hope for the future. He could have been like her son, lost in drugs, rootless, delinquent. Jerry Haines tried to send him in that direction.

He pushed the door out into the relentless sun. He was wet with sweat and had forgotten his sunglasses back at the apartment. He squinted and spotted Shirl a distance down the street. If he could only keep her at a distance, but he couldn't have it both ways. She pulled up into a twenty-minute parking space.

"Didn't get your things?"

"They couldn't find her at home." He swung into the front seat. "I'm not surprised, but I want my things back. I have a couple of songs that may be valuable to me someday."

"I bet they're good." A smile lit her face. "Looks like we've got the day to ourselves. What would you like to do?"

"There's one thing I really need to do, make a phone call. Can we go back to your place? I've got a phone card, if it hasn't been cancelled."

Back at Shirl's, Carlos mounted the stairs two at a time. He caught his breath on the landing as Shirl appeared, panting. She unlocked the door, and he pushed in past her. She pointed at the phone beyond the fridge. He clutched the receiver while his breathing eased. He sighed with relief when the phone card worked. He dialed the number from memory. The phone rang a number of times. Carlos twisted the cord impatiently in his fingers. He was about to hang up when a groggy voice answered.

"What the hell do ya want this time in the mornin'?" an unfamiliar voice slurred.

"Hi, this is Carlos. Is Jerry in?"

There was a long a pause. Carlos could hear arguing in the background.

"Jerry's madder than hell. Where the fuck you been, man?"

"Who the fuck wants to know?"

"Look, smart-ass, you'll be lucky if Jerry doesn't turn you in, ya hear?"

"Is he in or not?" Carlos demanded. It sounded like a fistfight going on.

Jerry finally came on, out of breath. "You have one hell of a nerve, running out on me like that."

"I didn't run out on you. I told you I was going. I'm not your slave."

"We had a verbal contract, if you recall, and you've broken it. The *Boston Herald* ate the story up."

Bastards, Carlos thought. "Look, Jerry, I know there's been some bad blood between us, but I need the money. It's mine, I earned it."

"What money are we talking about?" Jerry questioned, all innocence.

A shiver ran through Carlos in spite of the heat. "The twenty-seven thousand I had in my bank account. The one you opened with me. Remember, you said to have your name on it too so if I needed money, you could wire me."

A long pause ensued.

He finally replied, "That was my money. You'd been living off me. You can't expect to break our agreement and take my money too."

"I earned that money fair and square. Half of it was for playing piano at Albert's Bar."

"I took my share as your agent. I was making you into a star, and you ran out on me. You're finished, I'll see to that."

"I trusted you, Jerry, I trusted you, and you've fucked me over." Silence.

"What about royalties on the two songs I wrote?"

"What about 'em? You were to get 10 percent of the profit above fifty thou. We're not even halfway there yet."

"I have to take your word on that, for what it's worth." He used the only card he had left. "I've written a couple more songs I was going to send to you. No way now, no fucking way."

The silence on the other end indicated he'd struck a nerve.

"Now let's think this over, nothing rash. How about I send you five thousand and get us a gig in Miami? Then we can see about the rest. What d'ya say?"

"The goddamned money is mine, Jerry, all of it. A verbal contract isn't worth shit, and you know it."

"I guess we got nothing to talk about then."

Carlos knew Jerry wanted the songs as much as Carlos needed the money, and Jerry had to know it.

"Okay, deal," Carlos countered. "You agree the money's mine. You send me ten thousand now. I'll meet you in Miami in three months, and we talk about the gig, and you give me the rest of the money."

"I'll send you five thousand, you be in Miami in one month, we talk about the gig."

"Seventy-five hundred, two months. I'll meet you in Miami. You bring the rest of the money. I can't come any sooner. I've got things to see to here."

"You sign a one-year contract and we've got a deal."

"I sign a contract, you give me the rest of the money. Deal?"

"Deal," Jerry said. "Send the songs."

"Send the money."

They agreed the money was to come to Shirl's address, registered, overnight mail. The line clicked dead. Carlos was dripping with sweat from the ordeal. Shirl poured him a whiskey on the rocks. He bottomed it and held out the glass for another. He chugged that one down too then jumped up and spun her around the room. And then he felt the emptiness. This should have been Damon.

But what if we had started for California with no money?

The next several days creaked by. Carlos checked the mail each day. No money from Jerry. He checked the police station; they had made no contact with Ilka.

His night job brought some continuity and bread, but he was absolutely adrift. The tips continued to pour in, and though a larger nightspot offered him a much better deal, he stayed with Lenny. No contracts, he needed to be able to move fast.

As the days dragged on, Shirl was becoming more of a problem. She insisted they sleep together and snuggle. He was unable to perform, and she became petulant.

༅

"I've spoken to my friend, Adam, at the hospital," Shirl said one night when they were both off.

"Great, will he do it?"

She looked dejected. "He tried a couple of times, but Damon's sister was there both times. He said she stays with Damon most of the time."

"Did he say how Damon appeared? Is he conscious, able to eat?"

"He said Damon seems to be coming along, but he's banged up pretty bad. Adam can't go up there anymore. He doesn't want to get questioned by the hospital supervisor. Damon is due to go home in a couple of days anyway."

"Tell him thanks,"

Carlos pondered the chance of catching Damon alone. Ilka would have to go out sooner or later. It would be dangerous if he got caught, but he had to risk it.

I'll tell Lenny I have to get away a couple of hours every so often."

Business was slow one evening, and Carlos decided to knock off at nine. He walked back to Shirl's, took a shower, put his briefs back on, and slid into bed. Shirl turned over and reached for a kiss and snorted when her hand touched his briefs. She rolled over back to him. He lay awake a long time, pondering the future. It didn't look hopeful. He needed to make a move, take action, get away from this apartment, and see Damon one way or another.

CHAPTER

11

It was another hot, steamy evening. Crickets chirred their summer rhythm in the dewy grass. The night, black and starless, was only lit by the eastern skyline from the city beyond. Carlos leaned against a locust tree several hundred feet down the street from Ilka's house. Her car was not in the driveway or the garage. His luminous watch registered nine thirty. He stubbed out a cigarette on his shoe sole, mentally castigating himself for returning to the nasty habit. Tonight was his last chance to speak to Damon for tomorrow he must leave for California.

With Ilka away, he decided to take the risk. He noted the irony in the situation. She accused him of stalking Damon. Well, so be it, she can't guard him every minute. He'd waited after dark in the vicinity for several nights now, ostensibly out for a walk, looking to catch Damon alone now that he was out of the hospital. This was his last chance.

Nervous determination propelled Carlos up the walk. In spite of the restraining order forbidding his contacting or speaking with Damon, Carlos had to find out face-to-face where they stood with each other. It had been three exceedingly long weeks since Damon's assault. Carlos could wait no longer to see him.

He tapped lightly on the door. Damon, visible through the window, scrambled for the phone. His heart sank. Damon was calling the police for sure. He took a chance. "Damon, it's me, Carlos, will you let me in," he called through the door. "I'm alone, I need to speak to you."

Damon paused, the receiver in his hand, and then he slowly put it down. He hobbled to the door. The dead bolt turned with a metallic click. The door slowly opened on the chain. They stood, peering at each other, then Damon slid back the chain. Damon had changed so much. Carlos scarcely recognized him. His face was ashen, making the red scars still angrier. His throat was bandaged, and a sling supported his left arm. His left foot was heavily bandaged with the pajama leg hiked up above the tape. His face and neck were thin and haggard, the sparkle in his eyes replaced by a haunted look. He peered over Carlos's shoulder toward the street and gestured with his right hand for Carlos to enter.

Carlos reached for Damon, to crush him in his arms, to tell him how much he missed him. To tell him how much he loved him.

Damon pulled back, holding up his right hand as if to repel Carlos's approach.

Carlos, heartsick, retreated as if stung. An awkward silence fell as they sat, several feet separating them. The monotonous tick of the cuckoo clock and a siren wailing in the distance the only sounds.

More taken with Damon, he hadn't noticed the room much before. It had a musty, unused feeling. Pictures of people, probably family, were hung around the room and cluttered the piano and windowsills. Damon's high school picture, he guessed, hung over the mantel. Another picture of Damon and Ilka seated in a porch swing hung below. Damon was probably eleven or twelve. What he would give to have known him then. The walls, papered with nondescript beige and rose wallpaper, matched the draperies. Damon sat on a worn velvet club chair, the arms shiny from many hands.

Damon coughed, bringing Carlos's attention back to him. Time was passing. Ilka could return anytime. He struggled for words. So much had happened. He dreaded to tell Damon of his departure tomorrow and secretly hoped Damon would be concerned. Damon sat, his face a solemn mask, apart, it seemed, from everything and everyone.

"Ilka will only be gone half an hour," Damon finally said. "You must have been watching the house and saw her leave."

Carlos reddened, whatever receptions he may have had in the back of his mind, this was not one of them.

"Yeah, I guess I have turned into the stalker your sister thinks I am. I have wanted to see you, to be with you." He stretched his right arm toward Damon, an anguished look on his face. "There is so much I don't understand."

"What's to understand? I was beaten, raped, and left for dead. I shit blood for a week and have probably contracted AIDs." His voice shook, and a tear ran down his cheek. He brushed at it angrily.

Shock registered on Carlos's face. He mouthed the word *AIDS*, grasped again for Damon's hand, but Damon pulled away. AIDS was a complication Carlos had not even thought of.

He's slipping away from me, and there's no way I can stop it.

A helpless fury gripped him, and his hand tightened on the sofa arm.

"I'm terrified to go outside, even in the daytime. They will figure out who I am and be after me. Ilka is the only one I have now." He sighed and looked out the window.

"You have me."

"You knew where I was." His mouth tightened, and he stared at his hands.

Carlos looked startled. "You didn't know I tried to see you as soon as I heard? I was handcuffed outside your room the next morning, for God's sake. Or about the restraining order Ilka had placed against me, the questioning by the police? Hell, if they knew I was here tonight, I could get arrested."

"Why would she do that? You two seemed to be getting your act together." He shook his head. "You're trying to turn me against my own sister. She said you'd try this." He sighed and put his head back. "I'm very tired now, please leave." His voice was flat. The words were mumbled. He shifted his position in the chair, wincing noticeably, reaching for his left foot.

"I'm leaving for California tomorrow and needed to see you before I left."

Damon evidenced no reaction, no protest.

"Some bad things have happened. I wanted to explain, to have you understand. I would never do anything to hurt you. I hoped you might even miss me a little."

"Why don't you tell that to Jerry Haines, your shack-up out in Hollywood. That's where you're headed, isn't it?" It was more a statement than a question.

Carlos was startled. "Who told you about Haines?"

Where was this information coming from? Ilka, of course, what she couldn't find on her own, the police supplied.

"What difference does it make? It's true, isn't it?"

"No, dammit. Everything Ilka fed you is a lie. We're not a shack-up, as you put it." His mouth twisted in anger. "Sure, I worked for the guy. I tried to quit, but the bastard tied up all my assets. He promised to release them if I came to back to Boston. I wrote a couple of songs he later recorded. I was foolish enough to believe he would pay me the royalties I was promised. I've got no real job, no money. I've got no choice."

He paused, looked at Damon, then at his watch. He moved to the window and peered wordlessly out into the night, struggling with his emotions. He turned back to Damon.

"I've been wrong about too many things in my life."

"About me?"

"Have I? You tell me."

"I suppose I could write you a check, say, for past services."

A blood vessel pulsed on Carlos's forehead. His jaw tightened; he turned and paced the room, fists clenched in his pockets, finally stopping in front of Damon, staring down angrily at him.

"Goddammit, Damon, goddammit! That's the cruelest, most patronizing remark anyone has ever made to me. You weren't a trick in my mind—ever. Rockets went up when we first met on the bus." He swung around the room with his arms in the air. "You were yin to my yang. I could feel it. I know you did too. We were two halves of a whole. I don't give a damn what Ilka or the rest of the world thinks. Damon, we were meant to be together. Ask me about myself, anything, everything, find out from me, not some warped story from the police."

He knelt in front of Damon, holding his hand out.

"I don't know what happened that night, it's all so fuzzy. Ilka and I argued about something. I ran out of the house. I had to get away. It was black. I was lost. The rest is a blank. Then I woke up in the hospital. Ilka was there. I asked for you. She said you had gone. I blanked out again."

"Gone?" Carlos looked at Damon, and Damon caught his stare and then looked away. A chill ran through Carlos's body. "You don't think I had anything to do with it?"

"I don't know what to think. I can't remember."

Carlos turned away heartbroken. Damon's words were like a body blow. He headed for the door, held the knob in his hand, turned back to Damon. He started to say something; no words came. With a quick twist, he threw the door open. Hands grabbed him; an officer stepped in.

"Sorry about this, Mr. Duncan. We had to catch him in the act."

CHAPTER

⊰ 12 ⊱

Strong arms gripped him from both sides. Carlos's first inclination was to disentangle by force and speed then run. A third officer stepped inside and apologized to Damon for something. He was surrounded by police. It was obvious Ilka was in cahoots with the police and this was a setup. And what about Damon, was he involved? That would be too much.

The initial scuffle subsided, and handcuffs were roughly applied. He felt his spirit was broken; his soul lay bleeding in front of a house of horror in Arlington Heights, Fort Worth, Texas. For three long weeks he hoped and despaired. Tonight, despair won.

Once more Carlos rode alone in the backseat of a police car, shackled, his destiny to be determined by forces beyond his control. The rape of the soul is no less devastating than the rape of the body.

Damn you, Damon. The steel edges of the handcuffs dug satisfyingly into his wrists. He bit his lip till it bled. The pain extracted satisfaction in a perverse way.

Maybe I can escape and they'll shoot me this time.

Every face on the sidewalk melded into disdain and recrimination. The sounds of the night were cacophonous in his ears.

At the downtown precinct station, the desk sergeant booked him for violation of the restraining order and resisting arrest. Carlos stood mute, head lowered, but not from shame. Paperwork was completed;

fingerprints were taken. He refused to let his mind grapple with what has just happened. He must hang on with no further fight. Yet his mind was not to be stilled. Why did he react so foolishly? The charges would be compounded. The web was tightening around him. Each step was lowering him deeper into the quicksand of circumstantial evidence. There must be a thread here, something he couldn't quite grasp. He felt his mind reaching, but for what?

Then slowly the picture of his father entered his mind. His father seemed to be saying something. Carlos is a little boy. His father is angry; his father is always angry. What is his father saying? Why is the boy crying?

No, Dad, please, I'll do better, I promise.

You promise, and you lie.

"You are allowed one call, Mr. Bravara," the sergeant said out of the fog. "Your bail will be set by the judge in the morning. A bail bondsman will be summoned. If you have an attorney, he can be contacted. Otherwise, you will be assigned a public defender."

The sergeant and Carlos stared at each other. The sergeant, impatient, raised an eyebrow in annoyance.

"I have no one to call," Carlos replied.

"Very well, you will be placed in a holding cell for the night. Follow the guard,"

The sergeant dismissed Carlos with the wave of a hand and called the next case.

A somewhat familiar-looking young man, apparently with his attorney, stepped forward.

Jesus, Carlos said to himself, *that's the kid in the woods with the underage girl. They're gonna hang him. Daddy will see to that.*

Carlos was escorted to a holding cell with a bunch of miscreants to spend a mind-bending night of despair.

The next morning, after bail was set, he was frisked, his personal belongings were confiscated, and he was ordered to strip and shower. He had no dignity left, no privacy. He was treated like a caged animal, was handed prison garb, a blanket, and was assigned a cell. The cell door closing reverberated in his skull.

His cellmate was a scruffy character. His head was shaved. An ugly scar veered down his right cheek, ending by his mouth. His face was florid and pockmarked, and prison uniform strained over a protruding stomach. His mouth was busy chewing gum, or more likely tobacco that exposed stained and snaggy teeth. He spat into the toilet every so often then strode restlessly around the perimeter of the cell, cracking his knuckles.

"Well looky here, someone's tangled wif a wildcat." He laughed, inspecting Carlos's face and arms, a deep cough resounding through the cell. "Whatcha in for?" He wheezed.

"Restraining order violation."

"Me too. This your first time?"

"Yeah."

"I been in once before. Ain't bad the first time. They get pretty fuckin' pissed the second time. I knocked the old lady around a little. She had it comin', the bitch. Been humpin' the mailman. I'm gonna kill the son of a bitch when I git outta here."

"The mailman or your wife?"

The man broke into a toothless grin. "The both of 'em, wif one bullet."

"I get your drift."

He held his hand up to Carlos's ear and whispered, "Ain't got any fags, have ya?"

"I beg your pardon?"

"You know, ciggies, smokes."

He put his hand up to his mouth pantomiming inhaling a cigarette and then blowing out smoke.

"No, I don't smoke," he lied.

CHAPTER

🖙 13 🖚

Questions raced through my mind. It was hard to concentrate, and decisions tired me. Ilka wouldn't have placed a restraining order on Carlos, would she? I settled down and tipped my head onto the back of the chair. It felt prickly. Everything felt prickly; my whole body felt like raw meat.

Ilka came in the front door, humming a tune from *Oklahoma,* which was not like her. Something about a beautiful morning.

"You look sad, Damon. Ready for more pain meds?"

I shook my head.

She turned and carried several bags into the kitchen. I could hear things being put away—drawers and the fridge door opened and closed several times. She appeared in the kitchen doorway with a piece of chocolate cake on a plate.

"I have a special treat for you," she enthused, depositing it in my lap.

I set it aside; the plate rattled on the side table. A question burned in my mind.

"You put a restraining order on Carlos, didn't you?"

Surprise and hurt spread across her face.

"Why would you think such a hateful thing of me, Damon?"

"Somebody has, who else would do it?"

"Why do you think it's me?" she asked, wrinkling her brow.

"Then you know there is one."

Ilka reddened as she bent over and straightened magazines on the coffee table.

"You just said there was."

"But you didn't ask how I knew. You did it, damn you."

"Damon Duncan, I'm your sister. I won't have you talk like that to me."

"Then tell me the truth."

"If you're going to be rude, I'm leaving you alone."

She strode toward the stairs.

Now I knew she did it. In my selfishness, I had not considered anyone else's feelings, only my own. I had thoughtlessly put Carlos in danger. Ilka set him up, and I sprung the trap. If I had only known the police were waiting outside for him.

I needed time to be able to think straight. Too late.

"You're lying to me. You hate Carlos, don't you?"

"I don't hate him, he's a felon and a dangerous man," she said from halfway up the stairs.

"Bullshit, Ilka."

"If you weren't sick, I'd slap your face."

She stomped back down the stairs.

"You hate him, don't you, sister dear? Admit it," I taunted her. I was sweating all over, exertion sapping my strength. The pain in my arm now jabbing with each heartbeat.

"You would too, if you would accept the truth." Her face was scarlet with emotion. Her temples throbbed; the tick in her cheek danced.

"So you got a restraining order to keep him away?" My mind, slowed from medication, struggled to accept she would do such a thing.

"I did it to protect you, he's dangerous."

"Dammit, Ilka, you don't know him like I do. Call the police. Tell them it was a mistake."

"I'll do nothing of the kind. You don't know him as well as you think you do. He's got a police record. Did you know that?"

"No, I don't." I stared at her, my mind in turmoil. "Where are you getting all these ideas from? What kind of a police record?"

Ilka made no comment and would not make eye contact.

"I'm calling the police. I want him released, and I want to talk to him."

I reached for the phone. She grabbed it out of my hand. I lost my balance and fell forward. The pain in my arm was so intense I thought I'd pass out.

"Give...it...to...me," I whispered through clenched teeth.

She made a feeble attempt to help me back up. I shook her hand off.

"All right, I'll call, but you'll regret it."

I noticed she didn't need to look up the number but dialed as she watched me. She explained that her brother was demanding the restraining order be dismissed and Carlos Bravara released. She nodded, and a wisp of a smile played momentarily on her lips. My body felt hot, and each breath tore at my arm. As I slipped into semiconsciousness, she said something about my being afraid of Mr. Bravara. I attempted to snatch the phone again, but she turned and walked into the kitchen. She continued talking, but I couldn't make out any words.

She walked back in. "I'll be down to sign the necessary papers in the morning." Her eyes were on me as she hung up.

I mimed sleep. The one thing I knew for sure, Carlos had been wronged. Why would he have been involved in my attack? It made no sense. Carlos would not have come to see me, plead with me to believe him, if he was culpable. He wouldn't. I also felt in my heart Ilka wouldn't go to the police station in the morning. The room started to spin.

I came back to consciousness with Ilka injecting my good arm with pain meds. I stirred restlessly, feigning grogginess. She had become very proficient at injections. I wondered if she could do it while I was asleep. She returned to the kitchen and shortly disappeared outside; the door closed.

I must get away from her. But how?

The only thing to do was to struggle upstairs and lock my bedroom door.

It was a slow climb. I clutched the rail with my good hand and inched up step by painful step and limped across the hall. The doorknob served as a crutch while catching my breath. Stepping inside, I leaned against the door, twisted the lock behind me, and collapsed onto the bed, exhausted. I fell into an uncomfortable sleep. A loud bang awoke me with a start, wrenching my shoulder and arm with the movement. Was the noise outside or part of the continual nightmares conjured in my sleep? The travel clock showed eleven thirty, three hours since coming upstairs. The house seemed strangely quiet.

A bottle of pain pills came into focus on my nightstand. It almost seemed to beckon. I reached for it and held it in my hand, running my fingernail around the label.

"Keep out of the reach of children, no more than ten in a twenty-four hour period."

I counted thirty-five on one side of the bottle; there must be more than a hundred in all. How many would it take? I broke into a sweat. Why had she left them in my reach?

I lay back on the pillow. Tears welled in my eyes. How did I really feel about Carlos? I love him, dammit, Ilka, I love him! I rolled the bottle in my hand. Why is Ilka doing this to me? She's as bad as Dad.

I slowly unscrewed the cap.

Seth Porter didn't make me gay. He was a nice man.

My arm pained me unbearably as I gritted my teeth and poured out a handful. Tears now rolled down my cheeks. I had trouble breathing. I took two in my mouth, held them there, my head pulsing, then swallowed. The pain seemed to increase. Two more shouldn't harm.

What have they done with Carlos tonight? He must be in prison. It's my fault. He wouldn't have been caught if it wasn't for me.

Sleep overtook me. The dream again, it was pitch-black, someone grabbed me.

"No, not again," I screamed, waking up. I ached all over, and my heart pounded.

The room was in shadows as my mind cleared. Ilka's footsteps sounded on the stairs. She tapped on the door, twisted the knob, then shook the door and shouted.

Ilka, go to hell. I hate you, bitch.

Had I taken my pain pills? It must be time. The bottle was still in my hand. When did I take the last dose? Take three this time to catch up. It was difficult to swallow, but I managed. Sleep overtook me again.

It was dark in the room. Kirk's presence was inescapable. If I moved, he would know where I was. He was going to kill me. I started to sob. I heard a rustle. My body was wet with sweat; I was drowning. My friends were the pills. They would save me. Kirk's breath was on my face now.

Take more pills, it will be easier.

He was shaking the door now and screaming. The pills slid down easily this time. His voice faded away.

Carlos and I were on a bus again. He was smiling at me. I reached for him, and then his face twisted in anger. He grabbed my arm and wrenched it behind me. I pleaded with him to stop. He laughed, a hideous laugh. Then I noticed a thumb missing as his hands closed around my throat.

I bolted upright in bed, gasping for breath. The sound of the door breaking had awakened me. Ilka pushed through the splinters and rushed to the bed.

"Damon," she screamed, "the pills, how many did you take?"

"Two," I lied.

"You're sure?" she prodded.

I nodded.

"I'm calling 911."

She ran for the phone.

I stared at the ceiling, counting the number of squares. An ambulance siren sounded in the distance. It's coming for me. I'm going to die; they're going to kill me.

"Thirty-seven, thirty-eight, thirty-nine," I'll keep counting, mustn't let them know I'm scared. "Forty, forty-one, forty-two."

A hand was on my forehead. I must strike back, use all my strength. But if I lay perfectly still, they might think I'm dead and leave.

Someone is in the room. A man's voice. Carlos?

"No," I scream, but no sound comes out. My body will not move. Someone is pushing something down my throat. I'm gagging and heaving. I want to die. Please, God, make them stop. I feel like my guts are being sucked out.

CHAPTER

⪤ 14 ⪥

The morning sun requisitioned a narrow path across the floor then lazily crawled up the front of the bureau and continued up the fabric of a folding screen. I watched the slow performance with detached interest. Where was I, and what was I doing here? My left arm was encased, my left ankle bound. I traced bandages on my neck and cheeks with my fingers. I must have been in an accident. My mind could not focus.

"Damon, I need to take your temperature and blood pressure," a nurse in a crisp white uniform said in a perky tone.

The room was now full of light, the curtains open. Ilka sat in a chair watching me. I had a faint memory of climbing stairs in her house. She arose from the chair and floated toward me. I was angry with her, and she was crying, but I couldn't remember the reason. Mom and Dad waxed into my consciousness. Mom looked sad, and Dad looked angry.

Mom and Ilka whispered. I drifted off to sleep and nothingness.

The room was dark. The night sky was clear, and the lights of the city shone in the distance. An IV bag dripped liquid into my arm. A tube had been inserted into my bladder. The last day at Ilka's seeped back into my mind. There was still a disconnect between climbing the stairs and waking up here in the hospital. Just sketchy flashbacks of the bedroom door being smashed and then a ride in an ambulance.

Carlos—what happened to Carlos? Alarm and foreboding crept into my mind. In prison? I tried to rise up.

"Ilka, somebody, I need to see Carlos."

Ilka eased up from a chair and approached.

"I need to see Carlos. I need to talk to him."

She massaged my right shoulder then stepped back and reached for her pocketbook. She shuffled through the contents and produced a folded paper. She unfolded then refolded it several times, as if in a quandary. There was writing on it. It must be a letter. For me? Why did she look sad yet not sad? She could have cried or laughed. I would not have been surprised at either. She held it out to me then pulled it back, as though thinking better of it.

"What is it?" I demanded. "Is it for me?"

"Yes," she said, but no more. She checked her wristwatch while holding the letter in her hand.

"Who is it from? What does it say? For God's sake, tell me or let me read it."

She reluctantly handed me the letter. "I'm sorry."

The letter was handwritten on a plain white piece of paper, probably from a copy machine. Large, masculine script scrolled over the page. The writing was careless, as if written in a hurry. My eyes scanned rapidly to the bottom, and I saw Carlos's signature. My heart raced as I read.

Dear Damon,

I will be on the way to California when you read this. I was released from jail this morning after your sister explained to the judge what had happened. I was wrong about Ilka. She really tried to help. I think she truly thought the restraining order was necessary after she and I talked it out. I asked her to wait about delivering this until I was on the plane and gone.

Believe me when I say I enjoyed our time together, short as it was, but it is useless to try to put things back together. You have family here in Fort Worth, and I have my career to pursue.

Please don't try to find me or get in touch. A clean break is the best thing for us both. It may seem hard now, but we'll both get over it and go on.

I forgive you for thinking I had any part in the attack.

Godspeed on your recovery. I hope they find the bastard who did it.

Take care of yourself.

Yours always,

Carlos

I reread it in disbelief. Gone. He wouldn't go without seeing me. But he did try to see me. My body was wrapped in sweat. The lump in my throat was choking me. Why couldn't I have died that night? Why did the police have to appear? I struggled with every particle of strength I had to get out of bed. I needed to run. I yanked at the damn IV tube and managed to get it out of my arm and tried to pull out the catheter. My arm was bleeding, and the pain was intense. Ilka rushed to hug me. Her hand shook as she squeezed the alarm button for the nurse. I overpowered her and sat on the edge of the bed, but all my strength soon departed. I crumpled back down. Tears of anger trickled down my face. I had sent him away, and he thinks I helped to entrap him. I wanted to die. Had I been wrong about Ilka? Did she try to help?

I lay flat on my back the next several days, speaking to no one, only nodding or shaking my head when spoken to, and refusing to take my pain meds. The stronger the pain, the more intense my inner sense of worthlessness became. Pain was my retribution for sins performed and a valueless life lived. In spite of best efforts to the contrary, the scene with Carlos on that last fateful evening bombarded my mind much of my conscious hours. I was struggling to remember what was said. Why had I let him go?

The danger to himself by his visit was unknown to me then. His plea for understanding and the parting looks we exchanged ground through my body like corn between gristmill stones. Days passed. No pain, no heartbreak, no despair can last forever. My inactivity had allowed repair to commence on my physical body. As the pain eased and strength returned, my catatonic period came to an end.

In my selfishness, thoughts of others' concerns for me had been ignored. I must now live for them, if not for myself. Or so I thought. Damon died a month ago on an unnamed street in Fort Worth, Texas. A new person now inhabited my body. I felt like a voodoo doll stuck full of pins.

My left ankle returned to near normal, so I was at least able to hobble short distances in the hall several times a day. It was time for me to be released. Ilka parked at the exit, and I was delivered by wheelchair into her custody. The beginning of the ride back passed well enough. I smiled a lot and said "Yes" and "Good" as often as it seemed necessary. Ilka chattered on, often glancing at me, changing the position of her hands on the wheel, braking for potholes, and apologizing for the roughness of the highway. It made little difference to me.

"You okay, Sonny?" she asked.

I hated being called Sonny. I nodded. She drove slower. A sense of extreme danger enveloped me for no apparent reason. Exhaustion grasped at every muscle in my body.

We finally pulled into Ilka's driveway. The door handle was difficult to open, and it felt heavy. The sun beat down menacingly onto me. This was the first time I had been outdoors in a month. My teeth chattered, and speaking was difficult. Mom and Dad greeted us at the door, waving and smiling. Mom was anyway. I thought their presence at the hospital was a hallucination from the meds.

I staggered into the house, fumbled into the bathroom, and emptied my stomach into the bowl. I flushed and put down the cover. Sitting on it and resting my forehead on the cold porcelain sink allowed the nausea to abate somewhat. After several minutes, Ilka tapped on the door and asked if I was okay. Rising slowly, the thought of running the gauntlet lay before me. I settled into the chair where Carlos had beseeched me for understanding just a few short—no—long days ago. The man I had always called Dad, out of habit, sat across from me. What did I feel for this man taken for granted as my father? Had I gone home with the wrong parents after my birth? The thought struck me as funny and weak laughter spewed out. Mom had tried her best to love and care for me, but it always ended in recriminations from my father.

You're spoiling the boy, Liz. Do you want him to grow up a sissy?

"So you've been through quite an ordeal," iterated the man whose namesake I bore and who contributed his sperm to my creation.

"Yeah, I guess."

"Filthy pig."

"Who?"

"The bastard who did this to you," he replied, his arm motioning in the air, the meaning of which I had not the slightest clue. The vision of his disowning me slid like brackish slime before my eyes. The fantasy of him crawling around on the floor in his den, trying to glue the pieces of the vase together, brought another brief bout of cynical laughter.

"Why don't you tell us what's so damned funny so we can all laugh, boy."

"Dad," Ilka said, "Damon's weak and tired. Give it a rest, for Christ's sake."

Mom looked startled and then checked her husband to see how he was taking the rebuke. His face turned red, and he scratched around in his breast pocket for a cigar.

"If you're going to smoke, go outside. I got enough secondhand smoke growing up."

Mom took Ilka's hand and patted it. "Go easy on him, dear. He's upset and worried. He just doesn't know how to show it."

"Bullshit, Liz, she's always got to run things. Neither of 'em ever listened to me, and you always defended them."

He sprang up and headed for the front door. The screen door slammed behind him. He scratched a match on the porch railing, cupped his hands around the cigar, puffed a couple of drags, tossed the match into the bushes, and strode down the walk.

As soon as he left, Mom came over to me. She got down on her knees and took my hand.

"I want you to know I regretted everything your father said to you when you left home last time. He was hurt and disappointed. He always wanted a son to go hunting and fishing with. He couldn't understand why you weren't interested."

"He never understood anything about me." I looked at her sadly. "Why don't you stand up to him, Mom? He treats you like dirt."

Her face seemed to cave in. "He has his good points. We've had good times together, a lot of good times. I learned early on though not to upset him, or we would have fought all the time."

Her eyes betrayed her weak protest.

Ilka turned to me and inquired, "What were you snickering about?"

I looked up at her and chuckled again.

"I visualized him crawling around on the floor, trying to glue Grammy Duncan's priceless vase back together after I smashed it."

Mom looked back at me, one eyebrow raised.

"How did you know that's what he did?"

"Just a lucky guess."

We both laughed. Ilka remained still; a deep frown creased her forehead.

"I hated that ugly vase from the first time I saw it," Mom went on. "Years ago, I got so mad I threw it at him." Tears ran down her cheeks from laughing. "But he caught it."

"He didn't this time."

CHAPTER

⊰ 15 ⊱

Dad came back up the walk, and the smile melted from Mom's face. She and Ilka headed for the kitchen. The brief respite fell away, and the world crowded back in once more.

He seated himself across from me again. His eyes bore into me like a needle pricking a boil.

"I've been reading up on this queer business you've been involved in. You can get over it, you know." He paused. "If you want to, that is."

"Why would I want to?"

Dad looked outraged, like I had punched him or kicked him in the groin. His face turned scarlet, and each breath became a wheeze. I thought he might be having a heart attack. He clutched the arms of the chair and hoisted himself to his feet.

"Who in hell would want to live like that if they didn't have to? Have you ever had one happy day in your life since this foolish notion filled your head?"

He lumbered over to the piano and studied the family pictures arranged three deep on the flat surface. He picked up a portrait of an elderly lady bearing a striking resemblance to the person holding the picture.

"What would Grammy Duncan think of such actions?" He set it back down carefully as though he might injure her memory. He stared out the window. "It's not normal. It's a sickness."

I stared at him. Reasoning would not work with him—it never had.

He turned back to the center of the room, just a few feet away from where I sat.

"There's help, you know. Find it before it's too late." He spread his arms out like angels' wings. "Repent and God will listen," he spouted unctuously.

What a bunch of bullshit. Who does he think he is, some kind of a fucking saint? Hardly, since I knew the reason Ilka left home ten years ago. I hated this man, my tormentor from birth. But his words echoed in my mind. How happy had I been since I acknowledged the truth about myself? The endless charade, the lies, the denials, laughing at gay jokes, never really being part of any group, the token dates with girls looking for a little action and then receiving excuses. Was he partially right?

"This foolish notion, as you call it, isn't something I thought up one day and decided to try. Have you ever attempted to understand what homosexuality actually is?"

"I know about those guys. They go down to some warehouse in Portsmouth and dance together and take off their clothes and do foul things to each other. It makes me sick to my stomach to think my own son is doing…"

His voice trailed off as he reached for a chair.

He gripped the spindles in his muscular fingers, swung it around, its back toward me. He straddled it, chin forward and hands clutching the side rails. He was only a couple of feet away, and the nearness made me uneasy but rebellious. How many times had he used this tactic when I was a boy?

"No son of mine is going to be gay." His lip curled. "I won't have it."

There, he finally said it!

His fingers flexed around the chairback, opening and closing around the wood like a vise. My rapist's hands a month ago flashed across my mind, the sensation almost palpable. He tipped forward, just inches from my face. He probably felt he had the advantage since I was in a weakened condition.

"Do you understand me? You can be cured, and you will be cured, by heaven, or I'll know the reason why."

I had never seen him this angry and out of control before. My chest ached; blood raced through my body. A tremor started in my shoulders and telegraphed down to my toes. I was suffocating. I struggled to get up and away from his venomous tongue.

"No," I cried, dropping back into the chair. "You don't know what you're talking about. Sure some of them do, and some men cheat on their wives."

"Goddamn you, boy. I never cheated on your mother."

"That's not what I meant, and you know it, you—"

Ilka appeared at the door.

"What the hell's going on between you two?"

Dad stood up and swung the chair back in place.

"Just trying to knock a little sense into his brain, if he's got one. I can't do anything with him. Maybe you can."

"Dad, he's just home from the hospital."

"Sure, sure, there's always some fucking excuse for him."

Ilka and I, startled, looked at each other. I had never heard him use that word before. Rethinking what he had just said, in some perverse way, his accusations struck a deep note. How happy had I been? Except for the days I spent with Carlos. But that part of my life was over. I had it all too briefly and threw it away.

Later, as we sat eating dinner, all of us seemed to be in our own worlds. The only noise, the clinking of silverware against plates, like chains scraping on a prison floor. I had no appetite. The food all tasted bland anyway.

Dad, the warrior king, sat at the head of the table, ruling his subjects with an iron hand, oblivious to the needs and hopes of those around him. He was the epitome of cynicism, obstinate, opinionated, and overbearing, with a real streak of cruelty thrown in.

Mom sat across from me, she with the Edith Bunker personality, forbearing, idealistic, kind, loving, but unable to stand up against her tyrannical husband.

Ilka, now in her thirties, sat implacably at the other end of the table in an unspoken battle with the father she both adored and loathed in equal quantities. She was driven from home at twenty-three by an abusive father and a mother who had no real control over events.

And then there was me, weak, ineffectual, pessimistic, and dull, living a false life, always on the sidelines, never wanting to come forward and be judged. The one real chance for happiness tossed aside in a fit of depression.

We finished the main course, and then Ilka brought on a frosted chocolate cake and butter crunch ice cream. She remembered my favorites, and a rush of sadness temporarily swept over me. She was good in so many ways, yet she was obsessive like Dad. Talk about a dysfunctional family. What a fucking bunch of misfits we all were.

With genuine affection and gratitude, I thanked Ilka for the nice meal and all she had done for me. Mom and I stood simultaneously. She came around the table, and we hugged awkwardly. She never divulged any of her joys or heartaches. I hardly knew her as a real person. Her acquired persona was as peacemaker and referee. I had ached to have a real heart-to-heart talk with her on so many occasions during my growing years. She surely must have understood the nature of my relationship with Mike, but we always skirted the issue.

Mom, Ilka, and I arranged ourselves in the living room with only the sound of the clock and distant, muffled traffic noises. Dad had retired to the porch before the rest of us left the table. The glow of his cigar when he inhaled jabbed the darkness.

The heat of the night, unappeased by a breeze, hovered over us. Ilka closed doors and windows and revved up the AC. Her small-screen TV perched on a slender pedestal allowed us to avoid conversation of any depth. We watched a half hour of *Designed to Sell* on Home and Garden TV. My eyes roamed the room as I was thinking of what a challenge this house would be to put on the market. Picturing Ilka with a paint roller seemed as ludicrous as putting herself in the hands of the host of the show.

After a half hour, I pled weariness and the need to go to bed. Ilka jumped up to accompany me up the stairs, but my reassurances sent her back to the couch. I made a show of nonchalance about climbing the stairs, making it more painful.

I dreaded entering the bedroom again. It had been only a week since I was hauled away. The remains of the smashed door had been removed; only the hinge halves hung uselessly on the casing. Ilka was not leaving me behind a closed and locked door again. I hit the switch and hobbled around to light the lamps. Ilka had kindly put my overnight bag from the hospital on a chair. My duffel bag lay in the closet. Carlos's was gone. He must have picked it up. But when?

The bed was nicely made and turned back. I sat down to work my shoes off, toe against heel. Papers rustled under my hand. Tossing the spread back revealed ten or so brochures on overcoming homosexuality.

I pitched them as far as they would go. They hit against the wall and slid uselessly to the floor. Depression and hopelessness grabbed at my gut. I was trapped in a damaged body in a web of family intrigue. Ilka and Dad were in cahoots, and Mom was complicit in her inability to stop or impinge on their plans.

After consigning them all to the hot place, I got up and kicked all the damnable booklets under the bed. I considered torching them in the metal wastebasket but knew that would set off the smoke alarms. My family had now become my nemesis and tormenters.

My laptop sat on the desk across the room. It had a wireless connector to the Internet, so I fired it up, hoping it would connect. It did so with no problems. I surfed a couple of porno sites and found sexual relief in viewing some hunky guys in action—the first time since Carlos left. My spirits lifted as I thought of the reaction the "enemy" below would have if they knew what was going on above. If anyone should appear, I could slam the cover down.

Next, I typed in *homosexual cures*, and ten pages of links popped up. My eye was immediately struck by "My Gay Therapy Session." It went on to quote a young man who went for a preliminary counseling interview.

Jack was referred to Dr. Tunis by a conservative Christian group, the Family in Crisis. They claim on their website homosexuality can be treated and prevented.

The Bible explains that homosexuality runs contrary to God's plan; those who struggle are still God's children in need of His forgiveness and healing.

CHAPTER

ᗷ 16 ᗴ

The brochures were never mentioned in my presence. Their invisible power hung in the air like a toxic compound eating away at my soul. We spent the next several days avoiding each other: Ilka back at work, Dad smoking on the porch, Mom watching TV, and me upstairs clicking away on my laptop.

Dad returned to the living room as the day heated up, each time complaining, "Nobody but a damn fool would put up with weather like this year-round." At ten thirty sharp each day, he strode down to the corner convenience store for the new *USA Today*.

Mom was a lost soul, out of her element. She was a neatnik by nature, so Ilka's house presented almost insurmountable problems to her. Everything was dark colored, so cleaning showed little positive effect, although she made heroic attempts. Nobody had much appetite, so fancy cooking was futile. Mom and Dad rarely spoke to each other, avoiding even being in the same room.

Ilka hired a local handyman to replace my bedroom door. The guy was tall and husky, average looking but definitely the macho type. I was unnerved all the time he was in the house. I half-expected he might grab me at any moment. He was wearing a wedding ring, which gave me scant comfort. They could be the worst kind.

Dad helped him carry the door upstairs, and they talked about sports and deer hunting, the latter quite a new subject to the fellow.

Dad expounded on the great New England sport as though Texans had never heard of hunting.

While the carpenter was in the house, I stayed downstairs with Mom, and we watched the tube. We had little to talk about, and isolation further engulfed me. She reached for my hand once in a while, and her fingers felt like cold claws. She had suppressed feelings so long she had lost all ability to convey them. I couldn't visualize her as the bright and vibrant woman Aunt Emma claimed. I hated Dad even more for what he had done to her.

With the door back on, albeit minus a lock, privacy became less of an issue. I spent many hours on the Internet jumping from link to link on the homosexual discussion pros and cons concerning "cures." The more I surfed, the more confusing it became. An impartial mentor was what I really needed.

My body was healing rapidly, and I felt stronger each day. Exercise was what I needed, but going outdoors without someone I trusted to accompany me was out of the question. Between sessions at the computer, I lay for hours, staring at the ceiling with no ambition. Nothing interested me.

On my infrequent trips downstairs, Dad handed me the crossword puzzle from the paper. In his own warped way, he was trying to be kind since he knew I liked working them. We seldom exchanged words. I piled the puzzles, untouched, in the corner of my room.

I grew a moustache and changed the way I combed my hair as a disguise in case Kirk tried to find me. Neither my picture nor address had been in the paper, but logical deduction was not wasted on me.

Several nights later, Ilka's voice interrupted my halfhearted Internet research.

"Damon, somebody wants to speak to you on the phone."

"Who is it?" I called down.

"She didn't say. Pick up the phone." She sounded annoyed.

"I don't want to talk with anybody."

I shut the bedroom door, but she pounded up the stairs. I thought of putting a chair under the knob but decided against it.

She knocked and opened it. She had a portable phone, the receiver under her arm. She thrust it into my hand.

With great reluctance, I took the phone.

"Hello, who's calling?" I asked in a dead voice.

"This is very awkward," a female voice replied. "But I had to give it a try. I'm a friend of Carlos, Carlos Bravara, and I'd like to get together and chat sometime."

I was struck dumb. Did she really know something about him, or was this some kind of cruel joke? The room seemed to change around me; the walls started to tip. I had to sit down to curb the vertigo.

"This is Damon Duncan?" she asked in a guarded voice.

"Yeah," I squeaked out. "What's this all about?"

"I've pondered calling, but as the days went by, I felt compelled to contact you. My name is Shirl. Carlos stayed with me while you were in the hospital."

I couldn't believe my ears. I waved my arms in agitation at Ilka to leave the room. She was reluctant but left. I knew she would head for the extension downstairs. I didn't want her to overhear and thrashed around in my brain on how to prevent it.

"Where are you calling from?" I needed to talk fast.

"Right here in Fort Worth. If this is a bad time, I could call you later."

"No, this is fine, but I need to do something first. Could you hold the line a minute?"

She assured me it would not be a problem. There was anxiousness in her voice. If I could get Mom to keep Ilka busy, she couldn't eavesdrop. In spite of Mom's weaknesses, I trusted her implicitly. I scribbled a note and went downstairs with it. Ilka was sitting in the living room near the phone and raised an eyebrow as I passed. Mom was in the kitchen, watching *Jeopardy*. I pressed the note into her hand and held a finger over my lips. She scanned the note then nodded. We smiled at each other. Maybe she could see by my body language I'd turned a corner.

"Who was that on the phone, Sonny?" Ilka inquired as I passed back by.

She knew the name pissed me off, but she used it to keep me in place as the baby brother.

"Just a girl I knew back in New Hampshire."

"She doesn't have much of a Yankee accent." I visualized Ilka's ears growing into giant antennae.

"She's originally from the South."

"Ilka," Mom called as I started back up the stairs, "come out and watch *Jeopardy* with me."

I was out of breath by the time I got back to the phone, more from anticipation than exertion. Suddenly, a ray of hope came back into my life. I clutched at it.

"Are you still there?" I asked, afraid she might have hung up.

"Still here." She had a Texas drawl and a pleasant, soft voice. "Was that Ilka who answered?"

"Yes, that's my sister, actually my jailor."

She paused. "Damon, how is your arm? It's the left one, isn't it?"

I knew immediately she was for real. I struggled to keep my voice steady.

"It was a clean break, and it's coming along well, thanks."

I wiped at my eyes and waited for her to continue.

"But you want to hear about Carlos. We met at the restaurant where I work. He was staying at the Y, and I encouraged him to stay with me. I have an extra room. We talked into the wee hours that first night. He was so worried and angry he couldn't see you."

"He really tried though, didn't he?"

"Damon, he tried everything. The police had an iron curtain around him. They watched his every move. You knew about the restraining order?"

"I'd guessed, then found it was true."

My mind jumped from one thought to another, like skipping stones across a pond. What happened here the night I was attacked? It must have been bruising, but why did Carlos excuse Ilka in his note?

"When we were all together earlier that evening," I continued, "everything seemed fine. She even let him take her car. Did Carlos tell you what happened between him and Ilka?"

"He finally went back to Ilka's after he lost you in the dark. They got the news on TV of an attack in the early morning hours. The description of the victim matched you. You have a birthmark under your right arm?"

"Yeah, it's shaped like a fish." My voice cracked, everything reminded me of our time together. "He liked to kiss it."

"They made a rush to the hospital. Carlos had to stop for gas, but Ilka took off while he was inside paying. When he finally got to the hospital, an officer stopped him at your door. There were heated questions and denials. He was finally taken to the police station in handcuffs. They didn't have enough to hold him, but they kept a tail on him."

I had trouble following her monologue, but I urged her on.

"Wow, did he say anything else about Ilka?"

"He said you and she had had a long talk about the situation and you were through with him."

"Through with him?" I thought my head would explode.

"That's what he said. Later that morning, when he went back to get his possessions, he was served with a restraining order. He never did get his things."

"You're kidding." I couldn't believe my ears. This woman had no reason to lie unless Ilka had gotten to her. But what could tie them together? "So Ilka told him I was through with him and practically threw him out.

"Are you still there?"

"Yeah, just thinking."

"Can we meet somewhere, maybe while your sister is at work? I could pick you up."

"I haven't left the house since I got back from the hospital."

My heart was pounding and my spirits were lifting by the minute. Could she and I find Carlos?

"Maybe it's too soon. Do you want to give it some thought?"

"No, I need to see you. Ilka leaves for work at seven thirty. Shit, I don't want Dad to know. He goes for the paper at ten thirty."

"I'm off work tomorrow. I can park up the street and watch for a man to leave. Will there be anyone else in the house?"

A chill raced through me. Is this a setup? Were she and Kirk in this together? I started to sweat and felt nauseous. Maybe Kirk knows where I am now. Stall for time, ask questions, draw her out.

"Yes, my mother is here in the house, and my father is most of the time as well. He's an ex-policeman. He's downstairs now."

"And you don't want them to know what's going on?"

"No, they mustn't know, at least Ilka and Dad."

"You trust your mother?"

"Yes."

"But you don't trust me."

"Should I?" Questions, I need to flush her out. Think. "Does Carlos have any tattoos?"

"No. Yes, yes, he does. A rosebud over his left nipple." The phone was silent for several seconds. "This was a rotten idea, I should never have called. I'm going to hang up now."

"No, don't hang up. Please understand, the attack, the beating, no one knows who did it. I'm terrified he may be trying to find me. Give me your telephone number."

I could check her out. There was no reply. Gall rose in my throat. My stomach started to convulse; I swallowed it back. The room was spinning. Sweat dripped off my right elbow holding the phone. A scratching sound at the window. The phone flew out of my hand. A weapon. There must be something I can club him with. Turn off the light so he can't see me.

"Damon, are you all right? Why are the lights off? My God, Damon, what's the matter?"

Ilka touched my arm, and I whirled and struck her with a phototube. She ducked and lost her balance.

"They're after me. They know where I live. They're going to kill me this time."

The phone lay on the floor beside Ilka.

A voice was saying, "Hello, hello, are you all right?"

I made a dive for the bed and rolled up in a blanket, my body shaking so badly my teeth chattered.

My next awareness: lying on my back on the bed, something cold on my forehead, Mom and Ilka standing by the bed, Dad in the doorway.

"The boy's gone crazy. We've got to have him committed," Dad said.

My breathing was labored. It was hard to speak.

"Don't you understand, any of you? They've found me. They're going to kill me," I whispered.

Mom sat beside me and plumped the pillow.

"You have every right to be scared, Damon, but we're here, and no one is going to harm you again."

She took my hand; hers felt warm this time.

"Call the police," she said to Ilka in a firm voice.

"No, Mother, I don't want them to screw anything else up."

"Call the police, Ilka."

"No, Mother. I know a private detective down at work. I'll call him. No police."

"Ilka," Dad said, "see if the call can be traced."

CHAPTER

17

Heat and humidity clamped its claustrophobic spell on the top of the fourth-story stairwell. Damon Duncan Sr. leaned his forearm against the wall and rested his head against it, his breath rasping after the long climb.

They had luck the night before tracing the call. Apartment 428 was etched in brass letters on the door just a few feet away. He waited for the dizziness to subside and his heart rate to slow. It had been foolish, he now realized, not to rest partway up, but anger had thwarted his better judgment. He was about to meet this woman, known only as Shirl, face-to-face and put an end to her little game.

He mopped his brow, stuffed the handkerchief into a rear pocket, brushed his hair back, and pressed the doorbell. A muffled ring sounded somewhere within, but no one responded. He hammered on the door. Footsteps and a rustle on the other side of the door were followed by a woman's voice.

"Who's there?"

"Damon Duncan."

The door opened on the chain.

"I didn't expect you to come over. What's going on here?" Alarm sounded in her voice. "You're not Damon Duncan."

She attempted to slam the door, but he had jammed his foot in and grabbed the edge of the door simultaneously.

"I'm Damon's father, Damon Albert Duncan. Let me in, young lady. We need to straighten some things out."

"You get away from the goddamned door, or you're gonna have a bullet between the eyes, whoever you are."

"Okay, young lady, your name is Shirl, I believe, you're wise not to take chances with strangers. I came on strong, but I need to talk with you about my son."

His voice was placating, but his mind raced with anger. Nobody spoke like that to Damon Albert Duncan.

"How do I know you're really Damon's father?"

"Damon is staying with his sister, Ilka, over in Arlington Heights. We're from New Castle, New Hampshire. Damon is twenty-three, five eleven with brown hair and blue eyes. Is that enough proof?"

Uncertainty replaced alarm on Shirl's face, but she released the chain and stepped back. Damon Senior pushed the door open, stepped in, and grabbed Shirl by both forearms. She threw back her head and let out a piercing scream and struggled, attempted to knee his groin, but he twisted away.

Duncan Senior deftly swung her around back to him, held one hand over her mouth, and crushed both her arms to her chest with his right arm. Her body felt soft and warm against him. Essence of an expensive perfume filled his nostrils; a wisp of her hair fluttered against his cheek.

"Now, where's this Kirk fellow you're in cahoots with?"

She continued to protest, but her words were garbled by his hand.

"Shut up your screaming and I'll let you go."

He kicked the door shut.

She wrenched his hand off, digging her nails into his wrist.

"I don't know what the hell you're talking about. Kirk who?"

"The one who attacked my son, left him for dead, and is still on the loose, that's who."

He swore under his breath but let her go. Blood oozed around the scratches. He held the wound up to his mouth and sucked the blood.

"You can't think I had anything to do with that? I never even heard the name before. Why would I want to harm Damon?"

"Why did you call him last night?" he inquired in a calmer tone.

Things had gotten out of hand; his temper had gotten the better of him. He would try a new tactic.

She rubbed her red-splotched arms and faced him.

"I called him as a friend." She backed away and ran a hand through her hair. "But I didn't expect to get attacked by his father." Emboldened, she moved closer. "Now get the hell out of here before I call the police."

"How did you get Damon's name?"

He was unperturbed by her threat; he could deal with the police if he had to.

She glared at him defiantly.

"From Carlos Bravara, if you must know. He mentioned Damon's address before leaving here." She paused before going on, rubbing her wrists. "You see, Damon and I are both good friends of Carlos. I have no idea where he is now, and I thought Damon might know."

"Yeah, Carlos, the son of a bitch."

"What do you mean 'son of a bitch'? Have you ever met him?"

"I've heard enough about him."

He twisted his body and leaned against the kitchen sink cabinet. Spots swirled before his eyes, and pain shot down his left arm. Sweat beaded on his brow, and his lips felt numb.

She held his gaze.

"You have no right to be making judgments about someone you've never met. I'll bet Ilka's poisoned your mind against him. He's a sweet guy. He stayed here with me while Damon was in the hospital."

"So you fell for his line too, just like my son did. The bastard fucking both of you then."

"For your information, you foul-minded piece of crap, Carlos and Damon were crazy about each other until Ilka started stirring the cauldron."

"You keep my daughter out of this. She's got nothing to do with it." His strength was returning.

She peered at him, her lip curling.

"She's got everything to do with it, something she said, something she did, I don't know, but Damon had to get away from her. She ran him out that night, or his attack would never have happened."

She leaned forward, eyes flashing.

"You seem to know a hell of a lot about it for someone who wasn't there. Or do you know something the rest of us don't?"

He watched for any sign, but her demeanor never cracked.

"Carlos stayed here for three weeks. I've pieced a lot of things together from what little he told me. He said something about meeting Damon on the walk at Ilka's that night. Carlos tried to stop him, but Damon raced by like a madman and kept running. Carlos put up chase but lost him in the dark."

"Oh sure, Carlos, he's just like all the other fags preying on my boy. They got him indoctrinated. He doesn't know any better. A black fellow back in Portsmouth hung around him, getting him to do all kinds of perverted things. Then some damn pedophile gave him a lot of money for sex. That kind doesn't give a damn what they do."

"Where have you been hearing all this garbage?"

"Ilka told me all about it." Half-turning, he followed her as she moved across the room. "They had a real frank talk the night Damon was ra—he was attacked."

Shirl thumped her forehead with the palm of her hand.

"Now this is beginning to make sense. Ilka gave Damon the third degree, they quarreled, and he ran out in a rage." Her expression hardened. "That bitch, she's the one responsible." She sidled over to the counter, and extracted something from a drawer in the counter.

Damon Senior's face twisted in anger.

"You shut your lying mouth, talking about my daughter like that, I won't have it."

He grabbed her left wrist and yanked her toward him.

A sneer came over her face.

"What are you going to do about it, old man, rape me? I've seen the look in your eyes."

He dropped her wrist like it was red-hot.

"In your dreams," he snarled.

"Caught ya with ya pants down, huh?"

"You come anywhere near Damon and I'll—"

"You'll what, you big, fat bag of wind." She moved up close to him, staring him in the eye. "Now that you've broken the ice, I'm coming over to see Damon at his sister's house, and we'll let him make the choice whether he wants to talk with me or not."

"Over my dead body." He backed toward the door.

"Now that will be your choice, won't it?"

An evil grin spread over her face.

"We'll just see how much he wants to see you after I tell him what you're like."

"Out of here, you bastard!" she screamed, drawing a butcher knife. It flew through the air and stuck quivering in the door casing near his head. "The next fucking time, I won't miss."

He grabbed the knob, threw the door open, darted through, and slammed it behind him.

She yanked it open, came to the banister, and shouted down at him, "Don't you ever come near me again, or I won't miss."

Duncan Senior eased his bulk back down the three flights. She was certainly a nice-looking piece, he told himself.

❧

"Where have you been, Al?" Liz Duncan inquired when he got back to the house, concern clouding her face. "I was getting worried. It's after eleven."

"I had an errand to take care of."

"An errand? What kind of errand?"

"I went over to confront this Shirl woman."

"You did what?"

"I didn't want to get talked out of it."

"Well, how did it go?" She brushed his sweaty forehead with a tissue from her pocket. "You look exhausted." He pushed her hand away. "Do you think she's dangerous?"

"Slow down with the questions, will ya. I need a cup of coffee."

Her eyes snapped, and she turned and stalked into the kitchen. He trailed behind.

"Where's the boy?"

"For God's sake, Al, why can't you ever call him by his name? Boy and Sonny sound so demeaning."

She set the kettle on, got a cup down from the cupboard along with a jar of instant coffee.

"When he acts like a man, I'll speak to him like a man."

"Damon is upstairs. He's finally resting."

He slumped down at the table.

"Well, do you want to hear what happened, or do you want to nag?"

The kettle whistled. She scooped out a teaspoon of coffee into the cup and poured boiling water over it. She thumped the cup down in front of him and dropped into a chair across the table. He reached for the sugar, measured out two heaping teaspoons full, and stirred.

"I wish you'd go easy on the sugar. You know the family history of diabetes."

He scowled at her and took a sip.

"This coffee tastes like shit. Can't you brew me some of the real stuff?"

She grabbed his cup, slopping some on the table.

He jumped up and snatched the roll of paper towels.

"Can't you do anything right, woman?"

He went to the trash bucket and threw in the wet towel, glaring at her.

"So now I've lost my name too, I see," she snapped. "Sit down, man, and I'll make some real coffee."

She measured two cups of water, dumped them into the Mr. Coffee, and added a coffee pack.

He half-fell back onto the chair.

"There's no reason to get nasty about it. I just asked for decent coffee. What's eating you? You've been on the hog ever since we got here. If anything needs to be done, I have to do it."

The room spun again, and he clutched the table edge to steady himself. A strange numbness returned to his left arm. It had occurred several times the past few days.

"Well, tell me, what did she have to say?"

"She's a feisty bitch, but I don't think she had anything to do with Damon's attack." He ran the scenario back over in his mind, but things were starting to jumble. "She didn't want to let me in. I had to reason with her to open the door." He broke out into a sweat and ran the back of his hand across his forehead. "She acted crazy, kicking and screaming."

"What do you suppose got into her?"

The coffeemaker finished brewing. Liz went to the cupboard and took out two cups.

"Watch it," he said, "you're going to get it on the floor."

"You want your coffee? Here it is."

She set it daintily in front of him.

He stirred in two heaping teaspoons of sugar.

"Well, where's the cream?"

She whirled, snatched the refrigerator door open, and grabbed the cream pitcher.

"Over here." He gestured at his cup.

She turned and threw it at him. "Here's your damn cream."

He jumped up, tipping over the cup, and raised his arm as though to strike her. "Goddammit, Liz, what's gotten into you?" He brushed himself off. "This whole family has gone crazy. I don't know what to think of anybody. I go over to see this Shirl person, and she throws a knife at me."

"I don't wonder," she muttered.

CHAPTER

⚜ 18 ⚜

"What the hell is going on, you two?" I confronted them from the doorway. "I could hear you upstairs."

A cup lay on its side, coffee running onto the floor. Dad's face, shirt, and pants were soaked. I stifled a grin and caught Mom's eye. She turned and moved away. Her shoulders shook as she clutched the rim of the sink. I hurried over and put my right arm around her shoulder. She stood motionless.

"Come into the living room and sit down. You'll feel better."

"I don't know what got into me. Something just snapped."

"Don't you leave this room, either of you. We're going to settle this right here and now. Do you hear me?"

We ignored Dad's orders, and I led Mom into the living room. His words became slurred and made no sense.

Mom had taken a small step, maybe very small, yet it was a start. She gave in to him thirty-five years ago. Perhaps this was a new beginning. I was proud of her. She sat by the piano. I perched on the chair arm, my hand on her shoulder. Her eyes veered toward the family pictures Ilka had arrayed across the shiny surface. She picked up a framed photo of the four of us taken a good twenty years ago—Dad, slim and handsome, Mom, seated, beautiful, holding me on her lap, and Ilka by Dad's side, looking up at him.

I had never studied the photo much before. There was sadness in Mom's eyes, as if her mind were somewhere else. She ran her fingers along the top of the frame, angling the picture to better see our likenesses.

Dad suddenly stopped raving in the kitchen, and it was ominously quiet.

A loud crack, then dishes breaking, followed by a heavy thud, resounded from the kitchen. The picture slid from Mom's hand and clattered to the floor. We glanced at each other, panicked for a moment. I recovered first and rushed to the kitchen door. Dad lay on the floor, head slightly bent, blood oozing from his nose.

God help me, my first thought was, *It's over, my hell is over.* That lasted about half a second. I rushed to his side and knelt. The tablecloth was clutched in his hand; everything on the table had shattered around him. A chair lay smashed nearby.

I held his hand for a moment after disengaging the tablecloth from his grip. This was the first time I had ever seen my father vulnerable. His fingers looked pudgy, and his wedding ring strangled the finger beyond. Mom stood at the door, motionless.

"See if there's a bottle of aspirin in the medicine cabinet, Mom."

I'd heard it helped to survive a heart attack. At least I thought it was a heart attack. Mom turned as if in a fog and headed for the john. Dad appeared to have broken his nose when he hit the floor.

I struggled up, knees shaking, and went for the phone. Thank God for 911. The dispatcher asked me to describe the patient's present condition.

"My father has fallen and is unconscious. I'm afraid he's had a stroke."

"Does he appear to be breathing?"

"It's hard to tell."

"See if he has a pulse."

I put my hand around his wrist, index finger on the vein. No sign of a pulse.

"I can't feel anything!" My voice shook, and I felt faint. The dispatcher told me to stay calm, take a deep breath, and try again.

"Yes, I can feel it now, it's rapid but steady."

"What is your address?"

She asked me to repeat it twice.

"Stay on the line. An ambulance is on the way."

Dad twitched slightly, moaned, and appeared to regain consciousness. He struggled to tap his chest with his right hand and whispered, "Pain."

His face contorted, and he made grunting sounds. The left side of his face appeared to sag. My mind froze. Partially paralyzed?

"God no!"

Mom reappeared at the door and handed me the bottle of aspirin. She held a glass of water in her other hand. The dispatcher didn't mention aspirin but it seemed worth the risk. The two of us attempted to turn him enough so he could swallow. What if his neck was broken? Dare we move him any further? I gently slid my right hand under his head. He didn't protest.

Mom slipped an aspirin into his mouth. He managed to swallow it with some water then choked. She gave him another sip. He swallowed. She tried the second one. He managed this one better. We looked at each other; Mom's eyes were dull and lifeless.

I hadn't physically touched Dad since I was seven or eight years old. If only it could be under better circumstances now. He tried to speak. I put my ear down to his mouth. I caught the word *sorry*. The rest was garbled.

There was fear in his eyes, something I had never seen before. I hunkered down beside him and held his right hand. His grip was firm—a good sign. In spite of our many disagreements and hard, hurtful words, there was still something there. I was ashamed of my first reaction. I prayed it wouldn't jinx his recovery.

It seemed like hours passed before the ambulance, siren screaming, arrived. I checked my watch; it had been less than five minutes. Mom stayed with him while I opened doors and made a path for the stretcher. They tested his vital signs, felt gingerly for broken bones, and conferred with the hospital on their two-way. He was given an injection and eased onto the stretcher with its legs collapsed to the floor. Dad's face was gray, and he stared blankly at the ceiling. It was a daunting task for the paramedics to lift him and lock the wheels, but they were trained, and he was soon rolling toward the front door. For the second time in less than a month, an ambulance sat in the driveway, lights whirling and flashing. A small crowd gathered on the sidewalk, silent witnesses to another family crisis.

Mom stood like a lost soul. She had blood on her skirt and one leg. I hugged her, and she put her arms around me but no other show of emotion. She acquiesced wordlessly and without protest when I encouraged her to ride to the hospital with him. If he died on the way, she would at least be with him. She was a forlorn figure stepping up into the passenger side with the assistance of a paramedic. The wailing ambulance pulled out of the drive, and I stood alone on the porch. Tears rolled down my cheeks.

He was always such a commanding person, always in charge. He was now a helpless figure with the future, if any, unknown. I closed and locked the door and headed for the kitchen. It was a mess. The tablecloth and broken dishes lay about on the floor. A mixture of coffee and blood spattered the area around the table.

He must have tried to save himself with the chair; both front legs were splintered. It lay by the table like a broken body. Keeping busy at this point was important. My first self-imposed task was to clean up the place. I needed to call Ilka but felt it best she not be at the hospital when Dad arrived. Ten minutes and I'll call. The tablecloth and broken dishes rolled up easily and went into the trash. The chair was beyond repair and went out onto the back porch. I got a mop and pail, filled it with hot water, and shook in some soap. I maneuvered the mop the best I could with my right hand.

I looked at the clock and decided it was time to call my sister.

"Ilka, Dad has had a heart attack."

It was terse and to the point. Again, not kind of me, but I didn't know of any easy way.

"Oh my God, Damon, have you called the ambulance?"

"He must be at the hospital by now."

Anger roiled inside me, and I felt like saying, "No, do you think I should?"

"He collapsed here in the kitchen about half an hour ago."

"Where are you and Mom now?"

"I insisted Mom go with him. I'm at the house."

"Are you okay? I'll be right over and pick you up."

"No, you go ahead. Mom needs you more than I do."

The remaining kitchen cleanup was time-consuming. At this point, time was the one thing I did have. My mind was involved with the job at hand.

"Don't think about what's happened," I said.

Tired and dizzy, my body still far from normal, the recovering arm was only a small part of my problems.

The cleanup finally done, I surveyed the room. Not perfect, but it would do. Exhaustion overcame me as I staggered into the living room and flopped onto the couch. My mind was so consumed with the events of the past hour, I was startled to hear a knock on the door. I peered out through the mesh curtains and saw an attractive blonde. Was she a crisis counselor sent from the hospital? I decided not to answer. She knocked again then stepped back. A white convertible was parked by the sidewalk, top down. No one was in it unless they were scrunched down. My eyes moved back to the blonde; she was about to knock again. I tiptoed to the door, my fingers curled around the latch.

"Who's there?"

"Damon. Is that you? I'm Shirl, Carlos's friend."

"How do I know that?"

"Carlos is Cuban-American, six foot four, black hair, the most gorgeous man on earth."

The smile in her voice when she said the last few words swayed my assessment of her. I slid the bolt and opened it onto the chain.

"May I come in and apologize?"

"For what?" I anxiously peeked over her shoulder at the convertible and then glanced up and down the street.

"For upsetting you last night. I called on impulse, not really sure if it was the right thing to do. It was stupid of me to ask if you would be alone."

Against my better judgment, I shuffled to the door and released the chain.

She stepped in, attempting to give me a hug, but I pulled back, so she took my hand. Her skin felt soft and warm, and her handshake was firm. She was dressed all in white, a woven mesh sleeveless top, a straight, rather short skirt and midheight sling-back sandals. Her hair was shoulder length, curling out at the tips.

"Have I come at a bad time?" Seeing the blood on my bathrobe, she stepped back toward the door, uneasiness registering on her face. "I should have called first."

I looked down at my robe and half-smiled in spite of myself.

"As a matter of fact, my father just went by ambulance to the hospital."

"Oh, Damon, you didn't—"

It took a second for me to realize what she was thinking.

"Oh, no, he had a heart attack and collapsed on the floor, he had a terrible nosebleed."

"I'm so sorry." Relief was mirrored on her face. "What can I do to help?"

I struggled to think of an answer. I was silent for several moments.

Her cheeks reddened, accented against blonde hair.

"I hope I didn't have anything to do with it," she said with a sigh, watching my face for a reaction.

"Why would you have anything to do with it? Oh, you mean the phone call last night? Dad was aware I was upset but nothing more."

It was obvious she was holding back, and there was more to tell. I gave her a look like, "What gives here?"

"He came to my apartment this morning."

"No way. Really?"

"I was amazed myself. He practically forced his way in and accused me of being in cahoots with Kirk." Her flush deepened, and a touch of anger wrinkled her brow. "Who is Kirk?"

"He's the one who attacked me."

Kirk's name again, Dad's illness, Shirl's connection to Carlos, it was all too heavy. I crumpled into a chair and dissolved. She knelt beside me and put her arm over my shoulder. She somehow brought a connection with Carlos. I could feel her tears as she gently pressed her cheek against mine.

I straightened up and blotted my eyes with the back of my hand.

She pulled back, speaking through a tightness in her throat.

"And you both thought I had something to do with your attacker." She stood up and circled the room, pausing before me again. "That must have been horrible for you." She dabbed at her eyes again. "I wish I could do something to help. Could I drive you to the hospital?"

"No," I snapped.

She recoiled like I had slapped her face.

"No, thank you," I said more gently. "The only time I've been out since…since…well…from the hospital, coming home with Ilka. It was horrible." I hung my head and looked at the floor then slowly back up to her. "Sometimes I feel like I'm going nuts."

The telephone rang. Shirl reached for it and handed it to me. I said thank you with my eyes. It was Ilka.

"Dad has had a heart attack and stroke," she said.

"How bad?"

"Bad."

"How bad?"

"He's going to live, but his left side is paralyzed. His speech is impaired. He may recover most of his faculties, but it will be a long struggle."

"And Mom?"

"She's in la-la land, Damon. Maybe you can get to her." There was anger growing in her voice now. "You've got to straighten out from this funk you're in and help."

"Jesus Christ, lay it on. You've always been the strong one, and I've been the sissy brother," I said in a singsong, mocking tone.

My hand shook on the phone, and I felt like puking. I put my hand over the receiver to contain my anger.

"What other fucking thing can go wrong with this family?" I said under my breath.

"Are you still there?"

"Yes, what do you want me to say?"

"You needn't be snippy with me. I'm coming home to bring you down."

"Stay where you are. I'll get down on my own."

I glanced at Shirl, and she nodded.

"How are you going to do—"

I slammed the receiver down and looked at Shirl.

"I'm sorry you had to see this," I said with resignation. "You must have already seen enough of this family to last a lifetime."

CHAPTER

19

The thought of going out into the world again scared the hell out of me. Thinking logically, however, I realized the time had come to face my demons. After procrastinating, I started the shower water and stepped in. Steam assailed my lungs; I twisted the valve to cold and grasped the chrome bar for balance. "Get a grip on yourself," I chanted in a whisper. I stepped out and reached into the linen closet for another towel to dry my hair. A medicine vial, hidden in the back, rolled out and fell to the floor. It was Valium. Why not take one? The dosage seemed low, so I swallowed two.

It was difficult to dress with the cast still on my arm. With luck, only five more days! A narcissistic anger rose in me when I viewed the slight scar on my neck while shaving—a constant reminder of my attack. The scratches on my cheeks had healed but not the wounds to my psyche. A rush of remorse jolted me back to reason. Dad was now in a perilous condition, and here I am feeling sorry for myself.

I had learned to button my shirt with one hand: one small step for man. Long trousers, in spite of the heat, somehow afforded more protection. I slid the Valium bottle into my pocket—just in case.

Shirl was seated in a chair, leafing through a *National Geographic*, as I clumped down the stairs. She laid it aside, jumped up, slid by me, and opened the door. My knees were a little shaky going down the front steps, but I felt more confident approaching the car. She ran the top up at my request, not telling her it provided me with a modicum of safety from the outside world.

Traffic was light this time of day, and Shirl was a pleasant conversationalist. We drove by her workplace, just a small restaurant. She mentioned in an offhand manner it was where she had first met Carlos. My guard immediately went up. Was it necessary to have taken this route? Was this testing me? When she showed me the pub where Carlos played piano, it became clear, she definitely had an agenda: Carlos.

How raw my heart remained. It was still hard to believe—after the promises we made to each other—that it was over. He and I spent ten wonderful—no—thrilling days together. He and Shirl spent three weeks together. Was Carlos taken by her charms? No, that didn't make sense. Why would he try so hard to reunite with me?

Yet Shirl was certainly attractive. Her white skirt had slid provocatively up her thighs as she drove. Her polished fingernails tapped idly on the white leather-wrapped steering wheel as we stopped at a traffic light. She wanted to talk about Carlos; that seemed certain.

"I was just going to—" she started.

"Did you—," I said at the same time.

We both laughed, and I insisted she continue. The effect of the Valium was settling in and loosening my tongue.

"I was going to say, it must be difficult for you now that Carlos is gone."

"I'm in agony every time I think about it," I replied.

She made a clucking sound in the roof of her mouth.

"Be honest with me, Shirl. Did you sleep with him?"

She glanced at me then straight ahead. Her cheeks reddened as she ran her left hand up into her hair. She didn't need to answer; I knew.

"I take that as a yes."

I gazed out the side window, biting my lip. What difference did it make now? It's over. He's gone, end of story.

The light changed, and we eased forward behind a city sanitation truck. Shirl was silent for a bit.

"I'm sorry, I would never have said anything if you hadn't asked." After another pause, she continued. "I really think he's bi, Damon. That's not what you want to hear, but Carlos is a passionate person. I really miss him."

I stared straight ahead. Her hatchet had hit the intended target. Was this some kind of cruel joke? Why do I persist in asking questions that have such painful answers?

I turned to her.

"Have you ever spent ten days with someone so blissful you never wanted them to end? That you—that the two of you thought with one mind? That you would do anything for, go anywhere with? He and I had that for ten days, Shirl, ten fucking days, and now it's all over. I miss him like crazy."

We continued on in silence. I knew her game.

✌

As we pulled into the hospital parking lot, I spotted Ilka leaned against her car, smoking. When did this all begin? Shirl pulled up beside her at my request. Ilka observed me get out of the car, her brow wrinkled, and her head slightly inclined toward my "chauffeur."

"How's things going with Dad?" I asked.

She exhaled smoke into the air.

"I thought you didn't smoke," I snapped.

She ignored my jab. "They have him stabilized now and are evaluating for possible long-term damage."

"Shirl, this is my sister, Ilka."

They shook hands without smiling.

I turned to Ilka. "Shirl is a friend of Carlos. He stayed with her while I was in the hospital."

I stood back to watch the reaction.

"I suppose you were taken in by him too, just like Damon." Ilka tapped the windshield impatiently with her fingernails.

"What do you mean 'taken in by'?" Shirl's face reddened.

"What you both want to overlook is his background. He's been in jail and Lord knows what else."

"I suppose that means he's a bad person and can never be trusted again." She challenged Ilka with her eyes as she stepped closer. She nonchalantly pulled off her sunglasses and slipped them into her shoulder bag.

"I would say that about sizes it up." Ilka leaned back against the car, a smirk planted on her face.

"Carlos stayed three weeks with me and was a perfect gentleman. He got a job playing piano evenings in a nightclub."

"It fits his MO. He's from Boston and had some kind of run-in with a rock band, Harry something. Carlos ran out on him and took a mess of money." Ilka colored, and the tic in her check twitched. "And that's what he wanted from you"—she turned to me—"money."

"Money, what money? We each paid our own way."

"The money you inherited."

"You're the only other person who knows about that money."

"I'm not a fool. Of course you told him about the money."

"Lies, half-truths, twisted facts to suit your own purposes." I wanted to strike her, smash that pious look off her face. My right hand was deep in my pocket, fingers clenching and unclenching.

"Damon, you poor boy, you meet a guy on a bus, spend a couple of days with him, and you're completely hoodwinked. That's not love, that's deception. He's a master at that. Why else would he hang around if it wasn't the money?"

"Well, thanks a lot. All I'm good for is money, huh? We went Dutch, and for your information, we spent ten days together, if you can deal with the truth."

"More like five days total, by my figuring." She shifted her weight and leaned an elbow on the car to better enable confrontation with me.

"We spent four days in Dallas and two days here in Fort Worth before we met up with you. Six of the best days of my whole fucking life. I wanted to get back on the bus and go to California with him, but he talked me out of it. I kick myself every day for not going." I was breathing hard, and I had twisted my arm, so a dull ache gnawed at me.

"Damon, wake up and look at the world. You've always had to lean on someone. Dad tried to put some steel in your back, then you had Mike to wipe your nose, and now Carlos. Dad finally gave up, and the other two dumped you."

She grabbed my shoulder as if to shake me. I slapped at her with my good hand. She recoiled like a rattlesnake, ready to hit me back.

Shirl grabbed her arm. Ilka doubled both fists, her elbows bent tight to her side to repel the interference. She rotated and caught Shirl in the stomach. I don't think Ilka intended to hit Shirl, but the damage was done.

"Don't you ever touch me again, bitch, or you'll regret it. I don't take shit from anybody, not you or your father or anyone else. Do we understand each other?"

"What do you know about my father?" Ilka's eyes gleamed, her breath coming in spurts, staring at Shirl.

"He came to see me this morning, accusing me of being in cahoots with the creep who assaulted your brother."

"And he came home and had a heart attack. What did you do to him?" Ilka's voice rose in anger.

"What did I do to him? What did he try to do to me?" She held her arms out. "See these bruises? That's where he grabbed me when I opened the door."

"What did you do to provoke him?"

"Right. A three-hundred-pound slob against a hundred-pound woman."

"Don't you call that man up there, on life support, a slob."

Ilka grabbed Shirl by the shoulder. They glared at each other.

"Then don't you imply I had anything to do with it."

Shirl jerked her hand up to knock Ilka's arm off her shoulder.

Ilka snatched a handful of Shirl's hair and yanked, twisting her head. Shirl gave Ilka a chop against the wrist and at the same time kinked her right leg in back of Ilka's knees. Ilka pitched sideways then slid down onto the pavement with a thud.

"Whore!" Her skirt had slid up, and she tore her sleeve on the rearview mirror.

"Bitch."

Everything happened so fast. I watched openmouthed. Ilka struggled to get up. Shirl was waiting, fists doubled up.

"Stop it, you two. Stop it!"

I was horrified and shaken. I looked first at one and then the other.

"You get to hell outta here, you understand?" I snarled at Ilka. It took every bit of strength I had.

She got up, brushed at her torn sleeve and the scratch on her arm. She started to say something, snorted, and strutted away, head in the air.

"I can't go back to that house. She's sucking the blood out of me. Now I've got to see my father." I rubbed my left arm and tried to push the girl fight out of my mind. "Poor Mom, I don't know if she can stand the strain." I was short of breath and had a pounding headache.

"Damon"—Shirl brushed her hair back and adjusted her skirt—"come stay a few days with me. Let your sister cool off."

CHAPTER

20

If I ever pondered what hell was like, the hall and stairway leading to the third floor of King's Arms first springs to mind. The outside temperature here in Fort Worth had remained over one hundred degrees for better than a week, dropping only to the midnineties in the early morning hours.

After staying six days with Shirl, I heard about a vacancy on the third floor and rented it on impulse. It was a living hell at Ilka's, and staying with Shirl was not that much better. She meant well, but the last thing I needed was another interceder. It was time to make a move, declare my independence. Ilka, in anger, said it so well: Dad had tried to toughen me. The other men in my life had dumped me. Now I needed to make it on my own.

The cavernous hall yawned before me as I swung around the newel post. Several doors along the passageway led to efficiency apartments, probably much like mine. I rested a moment; the weight of my duffel bag and suitcase had winded me. Several dim fluorescent lights spotted along the ceiling helped me find apartment number 310. A TV wailed in the distance, and street noises penetrated the flimsy walls.

My shirt was streaked with sweat, and my head pounded. The escutcheon surrounding the keyhole on the entrance door was scratched and worn from many fumbled attempts at unlocking the door. A half-circle of darkened woodwork encompassed the latch. I sucked in my breath. Could this be another mistake?

The key slid easily into the lock. The door swung into a narrow passageway between two rooms. A welcoming rush of cooled air issued from a compressor rumbling in one of the windows. The odor of Lysol and Sani-Flush tickled my nostrils. The place was clean but Spartan, which suited my needs perfectly. I exhaled in relief.

I dropped my duffel bag in a corner of the bedroom, kicked off my sandals, and ran my eyes around the room. The walls were painted a pale green, the woodwork a streaky white. Tiny holes dotted the upper walls, the paint a shade darker in squares around them. A roller shade was pulled to the sill. A bare curtain rod dangled from a single bracket. An aluminum rack with a pole across the top served as a closet; the metal hangers clanged as I ran my hand along them. The floor was covered with a stylized leafy, blossom-patterned linoleum; a flatiron-shaped burn marred the center. An inflated air mattress pushed into a corner would serve as my bed. I would continue to sleep alone, no warm body next to mine. I swallowed as I plodded on.

The living room furnishings consisted of two folding chairs, a card table, and a worn piece of sage green carpet covering most of the hardwood floor. Two windows, sparkling clean, looked out onto the busy street below. The air conditioner, making the space more or less livable, was perched half in and half out on one of the sills. I held my hand in front of the cool air issuing through the grill. It sent a chill up my sweaty arm.

Faux painting did little to disguise vertical lines at four-foot intervals along the walls from a hasty Sheetrocking job. My suitcase placed near a blank wall was almost sculptural against the stark canvas.

The kitchen, if it could be called that, comprised little more than ten square feet of floor space pushed back from one wall of the living room. A wine-colored Formica countertop contained a tiny sink, its white enamel surface nicked and dull. An under-counter fridge was tucked on one side. I bent and opened the door. A light came on, and the tiniest ice cube tray I had ever seen sat proudly on an equally tiny wire rack. A faded curtain shirred onto a round pole concealed the space around the sink. Open shelves above stared back at me with a toothless grin. Fresh shelf paper edges stirred in the breeze from the AC. A tiny gas range projected into the main room, its only amenity, an exhaust fan screwed to the wall above.

The bathroom was literally squeezed between the living room and the bedroom. An abbreviated tub on legs stood against one wall, stool and sink on the opposite wall. A large beveled glass mirror hung over the lav; a jagged crack ran partway down one side. Leaning closer, I noticed my hair looked disheveled, and the stubble on my jaw was accentuated. The water lily wallpaper, in remarkable condition despite mismatched patterns, testified to a recent application. I was to spend many occasions sitting on the can, observing a half swan floating beside a half water lily while their rear portions happily drifted several inches below.

If I still had the capacity to be content, this could be the place. The bare walls and near-empty rooms were akin to having the cobwebs of the past swept from my mind. There was no baggage from the past here, literally or figuratively, no one to look over my shoulder or remind me of what a fuck-up they perceived me to be.

After a final look around, I flopped onto the mattress, the plastic body shifting under my weight and farting against the slick linoleum floor. I threw my forearm over my eyes, sighing with a feeling of freedom.

As I lay there, thinking, the events of the past two weeks stabbed at me like spikes being driven into a plank, the bitter scene at the hospital when I told Ilka I wasn't going back to her place.

"What do you mean you're not coming back to stay at my house? Where will you go?" Her face flushed in anger, the tic in her cheek twitched.

"I'm finding an apartment." No need for her to know where. She stood appraising me like a farmer deciding how much his prized heifer would weigh out at the slaughterhouse.

"You're going to bunk in with that blonde bitch, aren't you?" It was a statement more than a question.

I ignored her bitter words. "Face it, Ilka, we're like oil and water together. I'm not the thirteen-year-old boy you knew ten years ago. My choices have not been the best, I'll concede, but I have to live with them." A jot of strength seeped through me as I stared her down.

"Suit yourself, but you'll be back, mark my words." She turned dismissively, her flat-heeled shoes clicking on the tile floor as she disappeared around the corner towards Dad's ward.

I awoke from an uncomfortable half-sleep. Darkness had settled in. Lights from across the street cast elongated patterns across the walls. Strobe-light effects danced across the ceiling from side to side when a vehicle swung around the corner onto the street below. Although I wouldn't consider going out on the sidewalk after dark even if the building were on fire, the invidious shadows around me inside seemed rather pleasant. The only illumination came from a wall light over the sink and a bulb hanging from the ceiling in the bath. I crawled across the mattress to the window. Many coats of paint clogged the lock, but I managed to wrench it open. Pushing up the sash, I peered down to see if it was possible for someone to scale the walls. I pulled back in and swung the lock back into place. Would the lingering feeling of personal danger on a dark street ever leave me? I doubted it.

I stretched and yawned, and my stomach grumbled. Energy bars would have to do for tonight. I pawed through my duffel bag for the bars and a package of Styrofoam cups left over from our last night at the motel—Carlos and my last night together.

Carlos's face materialized before me. A torrent of images raced through my senses: Dealy Plaza in Dallas, buying fruit at the farmers' market, the white Stetson, jogging along Trinity River Trail here in Fort Worth, his fingers touching my arm, pointing with his other hand at a strange bird in the tree, the incredible animals at the zoo, later, our bodies bonding in passion and commitment.

With a fist against my forehead, I paced into the living room in a trance, willing myself to blot out the vision. I returned to the bathroom and scratched through my black zipper case for aspirin, when my fingers fell onto the vial of Valium. The bottle was two-thirds full. Surely enough! Tears ran down my cheeks. His voice echoed through my mind, *We're partners now.* I clutched the rim of the sink with all my strength, my fingernails white from the pressure. I prayed for the pain to ease.

My hands shook as I reached for the cursed bottle and rolled it forth and back several times in my palm. The pills rolled and tumbled until I gripped the bottle in my fist. My fingers slowly opened and uncapped the top. I sobbed audibly while pouring out a handful. I stood, mesmerized, staring at them. My throat ached from emotion and the thought of what might lie ahead.

In a moment of clarity, I realized I couldn't do it. My hand poised over the toilet. I dropped tablets into the hopper, one blip at a time. When they were half-gone, I closed my fist over the rest. Sweat broke out on my brow; bile pushed up from my stomach. I fell to my knees and purged into the pill-strewn water.

"God, please help me, take away the pain," I pleaded.

Almost against my will, my hand opened, and the remaining pills splashed into the bowl. I pitched the bottle in as well and hit the flush valve. Half-walking, half-crawling into the bedroom, I fell onto the mattress. By sheer willpower and from exhaustion, sleep finally came, a restless but dreamless sleep.

Sunshine peeked through a tear in the window shade the next morning, awakening me with its hot hand on my face. I had slept in my clothes on the bare mattress. My mouth tasted like shit, and my stomach reminded me I hadn't eaten anything of substance for twenty-four hours. The AC rumbled, and my skin felt clammy. I turned over onto my back and stared at the ceiling.

I felt completely adrift. Like the swans on the bathroom wallpaper, I was dissected, one part involved with a dysfunctional family, the other with a physical and emotional need far out of my reach. It was disquieting to think I had no reason to get up. It would make no difference to anyone if I arose or not, or so it seemed. The longer I lay there, the stronger my resolve became. I was not going to cave in or curl up and die. The past must remain that—the past.

I crawled off the floor mattress, stood up, and stretched. The cast was now off my left arm. First, a bath and change of clothes.

As the tub slowly filled, my fingers dangled in the swirling water, just warm enough to take the chill off. With Irish Spring in hand, I lowered myself into the water. My body, if not my soul, rejuvenated. I forced myself not to think of him.

My mind turned to Dad. He was home now, *home* meaning not in the hospital. Ilka's house could never be home to me. Not anymore. Dad spent much of his time in a special bed in Ilka's living room. My offer to help daytimes was promptly rejected by Ilka. She hired a nurse to help with meals, bathing, and general care. Dad was different now. He seldom spoke—embarrassed by his twisted mouth—nor was he confrontational or obstreperous. His spirit seemed crushed. His old body needed a new engine.

I stepped out of the tub and dried off, encircling my waist with a towel then shaving and brushing my teeth. The mirror reflected how gaunt my body remained. Twenty-five less pounds and not overweight to begin with. My body felt cool as the moisture dried on my skin.

Over the sound of the AC, I heard a knock on the door. Probably Shirl, since she lived on the floor above. I padded over and spoke through the door.

"Who's there?"

"It's me, Shirl."

The two added locks took me several seconds to undo. She swirled in like Loretta Young in TV reruns, holding two bags. Her eyes seemed to take in every detail of the room. Wrinkling her nose derisively, she shrugged her shoulders then threw her arms around my neck, pressing herself against me while dangling the bags behind my shoulders.

"I've brought you a housewarming gift. Got some glasses?"

"To drink out of or spy through?"

"Oh you," she said, setting the bags on the floor and cuffing at me. "My god, it doesn't look like you have either." She surveyed the emptiness. "We've got to get you some furniture and dishes and curtains and bedding and—"

"Hold it right there. This is the way I want it."

"But you've got nothing decent to sit on."

She eyed the two folding chairs then walked over to the sink, ran her fingers along the counter, glanced up at the empty shelves. She turned back to me, raised her eyebrows, and shook her head slowly.

"Stinks, doesn't it?"

She returned to the sink counter and noticed the damned Styrofoam cups. "These will have to do." Shirl wrinkled her nose. "They look like they've been crushed. Where'd you get 'em?"

"Some I had."

"Get rid of them." She looked for a garbage container of some sort.

"No," I snapped. "I want to keep them."

She turned back to me, surprise on her face, and then started to nod like a fog had lifted.

"Carlos?"

"Yuh" was all I could say, my throat constricting.

She laid them carefully beside the sink and came back to me. A tear ran down her cheek. She put her arms around me, and we wept several moments together. My towel started to slide, and I made a grab for it, but she kept her arms around me. I was naked against her. She hugged me closer. The odor of her perfume, her soft kiss and warm body against me were too much. To my amazement, I was developing an erection! Embarrassed, my face hot, I tried to turn away.

"Damon, don't."

She grabbed me by the arm and gazed at me. I felt like a tongue-tied teenager having his first sex.

"I was attracted to you from the first day."

She ran her hands down my hips then up onto my back. She knelt and gently held my penis in her hand and kissed the head. Taken off guard, a tremor ran through me, and my knees felt weak. I eased her back to her feet, and we kissed.

"Carlos told me so much about you."

Her eyes glistened, and a fresh tear ran down her cheek. I hesitated then pulled her into my arms.

"Let me love you," she mumbled into my shoulder.

"I can't, it isn't fair, to you, I mean."

I pulled back. Strange emotions crowded my mind. Did I feel a real physical attraction? Just the thought of her and Carlos... Shirl seemed to be my last tie to him. A dull ache stirred in my neck. Something played in my mind; a door was opening. Dare I step through?

"You can be cured," the pamphlets said.

We moved side by side toward the bedroom, arms around each other's waists. Excitement yet a bit of apprehension showed in her eyes. I was embarrassed about the bed we would be using. I knelt awkwardly and drew her down beside me. I tugged at the back of her jersey as she pulled it over her head. It caught in her hair, and we both worked at untangling it. Her breasts were large but firm. I smoothed her hair back and kissed her cheek then helped slip down her shorts. Don't women usually wear a bra and panties? She wore neither.

We eased down side by side, caressing each other's bodies. I fondled and kissed her breasts as I had read about in novels. Her hand on my penis was tentative, and my erection softened somewhat. What if I disappointed her? I kept my eyes closed and fantasized about Carlos. We lay facing each other, our legs entangled. I slid against her, marveling at not using lubricant. I'm sure she mistook the sweat on my brow and my shakiness for passion. Yet that element was there somewhere in the mix.

As our bodies moved together, the all-encompassing sensations of preclimatic ecstasy racked my senses. My mind fled to the Greyhound bus restroom. Animal instincts instead of sentiment goaded me on. "A woman deserves an orgasm," ran through my mind from somewhere, so I postponed mine as long as possible. Her breathing grew swifter. Her fingernails brushed my back. With eyes closed, she moaned and undulated against me. I was nearing climax, when Shirl's body suddenly morphed into Carlos for a split second. No longer able to prolong my compulsions, I erupted inside her.

"Carlos," she whispered.

I was shaken. We were both fantasizing about him. I propped myself clumsily on one elbow. Her eyes slowly opened; her face flushed. I withdrew and lay back beside her. We hugged, and I massaged her back and spine. She smiled then closed her eyes again. I carefully slid my arm out from under her neck as she continued to doze.

I was able to perform with a woman. What did this all mean?

CHAPTER

21

The setting sun smoldered in the western sky as it slowly burned itself into the parched horizon. Brush fires dotted the landscape, lighting the skyline like giant torches mimicking the sun. The early evening traffic slithered snakelike over the torrid pavement. "Red at night, sailor's delight," an old tale foreshadowed yet another day of staggering heat.

I pulled back from the window and sprawled naked on the unruly air mattress. With a brochure held open in one hand, I slid the other arm under the pillow propping up my head. Several other dog-eared pamphlets lay around on the linoleum floor, most of them read and reread a dozen times.

Shadows invaded the room as I tossed the printed matter aside and stared unseeingly at the ceiling. Despite many misgivings, now was an opportunity to put the memory of Carlos behind me and move on.

A commitment of ninety days was required, the registrar informed me. It did not seem unreasonable, for a start at least. Shirl was the only one who knew my true agenda. Best that Ilka and my folks not know or even suspect until results warranted it.

Rolling off the mattress, I yanked the duffel bag from under several misshapen pasteboard cartons. Sorting through my clothes and stuffing those that would require little care into the canvas bag,

I was done packing. I leaned back on my haunches and surveyed the room. No memories had been constructed here. The rooms remained the same blank canvas as the first day.

Yet was this really true? Shirl had happened here, at least for a few days. We seldom saw each other now. Hard words over Carlos had passed between us. Since somebody should know where I was for the next ninety days, I entrusted Shirl not to tell. She readily agreed since she disliked Ilka so much. Was she so different from Ilka? Both were capable of leaving me a mental quadriplegic.

Elbows on the windowsill, chin in hands, I watched darkness settle. It would be so wonderful to run out into the night, unafraid of the shadows, ready to plow under the past, plant new seeds, and pull any lingering weeds from my former life. Would this new garden flourish? Only time would tell.

∽

The flat, monotonous Texas landscape crawled languidly by the bus windows. Dialogue from a movie seen long ago, "Texas, flat and beautiful," so ironic to an Easterner, pulsed through my head, as difficult to extinguish as pulling porcupine quills out of a dog's mouth. With a sandaled foot up on the seat ahead, I stretched out on the double seat of the nearly empty bus. Filled with both anticipation and anxiety over what the next days and weeks would bring, I tried not to think too far ahead. Although the sharp edges of sadness and abandonment had sloughed off, I realized that a little part of Carlos would always stay with me. What of Mike? Six months ago, he'd confronted me with a reality that I did not want to accept. Had Carlos done the same thing?

By midafternoon, the Blueline bus arrived in an abysmally flat, nearly deserted small town. Fences stretched to nowhere; a few flat-roofed buildings hovered against the wind and infrequent twisters.

A dusty Chevy Blazer, engine idling, waited in front of a small store / post office, the idling engine and AC compressor clicking on and off the only noise, save the low murmur of the pervasive wind. A sandy-haired young man around my age hopped out, circled the vehicle, and projected a scrawny hand.

"You must be Damon." His mouth spread into a friendly grin. A prominent Adam's apple traveled his throat when he spoke. "People call me Randy, short for Randolph," he continued in a pleasant, mush-mouthed Texas drawl.

"Nice to meet you, Randy."

His handshake was firm but not daunting. He leaned back against the Blazer, his Western-style plaid shirt open several buttons, and worn jeans hugged his legs. A broad-brimmed straw hat shaded his eyes from the sun. He traced a square in the sand with the toe of his pointed boot.

He looked back up, studying me for a moment, as though trying to read my mind. A pensive expression crossed his face.

"We're out in God's country here, it helps to deal with the demons we've been struggling with, seems like."

I nodded, suppressing a shudder, glancing about apprehensively at the open prairie, barely an undulation in sight. No trees, just a few tumbleweeds rolling here and there. A life could be taken, the body buried in the endless desert. Who would know? A couple of hundred dollars in cash and two blank checks were stashed in my pocket. People had been murdered for less. Foreboding arose with a rush, raging unchecked through my body. Difficulty in swallowing and light-headedness caused me to grasp the antennae for balance and lean against the Blazer to steady myself.

Randy grabbed my forearm, concern on his face.

"You okay, pal? You look like you've seen a ghost."

I nodded, touched Randy's hand, then pushed it away. "Yeah, just trying to catch my equilibrium. Nothing prepared me for this." I swung my hand at the horizon. "Things are so busy back in Fort Worth." My voice trailed off.

Randy nodded. "If you're all right, we better get moving. Looks like a storm building. They come up fast around these parts."

He swung the tailgate open and tossed my duffel bag into the rear compartment. The smooth action of muscles in his arms and shoulders belied his slim build. Both Mike and Carlos were strong and well built, one of the reasons they had attracted me. Randy moved to open the door but pulled back. Instead, he nodded to me and retraced his steps back to the driver's door. Dust still rising from the departed bus lingered on the horizon. At this point there was no turning back. We rode in silence for several minutes.

"You like country music?" Randy flipped through several stations, each worse than the one before.

"Not particularly."

"Good, neither do I. Mostly classical at the house."

I nodded, and we made brief eye contact. Randy, at this point, was a blank page. Was he shy or just quiet? A hundred questions hovered in my mind.

A large, dark angular building slowly emerged in the distance. Gables and balconies sprouted out asymmetrically, the roof topped by a massive cupola. Drawing closer, a swath of green encircled the house like a skirt encircling a Christmas tree. Sprinklers spotted around the lush grass twirled and sputtered. We passed through an elaborate gateway. Tall, carved side posts supported an arched overhead signboard. House of Change followed the curve. A large porch with many round columns spanned the front of the three-story building. Gothic-style windows with pointed tops stared sightlessly into the emptiness. As we circled to the rear, an aura of mystery emanated from the dark shingles wrapping the silent edifice. It seemed the embodiment of *The House of Seven Gables* had transplanted into the middle of Texas.

Randy eased the vehicle into the bowels of another forbidding building. It appeared to serve as garage and storage building, housing a Jeep, a pickup truck, and a Mercedes, plus a couple of riding lawnmowers. Sliding out of the front seat, I was confronted by the tidiest collection of garden implements I had ever seen. The whole immaculate property reeked of silence and mystery. I visualized a body swinging from a rope slung over a rafter. Perhaps a stubborn inmate who refused to change.

Out on the driveway again, a gravel walk meandered through the manicured lawn leading to a small enclosure of shrubs. A large cross was barely visible as well as what appeared to be several people kneeling before it.

Randy emerged from the garage with the duffel bag on his shoulder. I came up beside him and rolled it off onto my shoulder and nodded thanks.

"Welcome to House of Change," Randy drawled, touching my elbow and guiding me to the expansive back porch and entryway.

Large double doors opened into a massive hallway that ran the length of the house toward matching doors at the front entrance. Twelve-foot ceilings and walls of dark paneling commanded the attention of anyone passing through. Portraits of religious figures hung in ornate frames suspended on golden cords, their faces set in pious dignity. A crimson runner hugged the floor, silencing our footsteps.

Christ, what have I gotten myself into? Abandonment and anxiety tugged at me again. On sudden impulse, I blurted out, "I'm out of here. Take me back to town, Randy."

Randy stood a few feet away, unmoving, as though rooted to the floor. He pulled off his hat and fanned his face, indecision clouded his face.

"Can't keep ya here against your will, but I gotta check with the boss first."

He disappeared through one of the many doors and was gone several minutes.

I moved back to the porch where we had entered and heard faint voices from an outside altar. It sounded like questions by one person and group answers. A goddamned cult? The door reopened, and Randy and an older person in black clothes emerged.

The gentleman in black moved quickly toward me; he smiled and extended his hand. He was short, fortyish, with rather compelling deep-set eyes. Although dressed in black, he had no white band around the collar. Not being Catholic, I was unsure whether he was a priest or not.

"I apologize for the unpleasant welcome, Mr. Duncan, Damon. My name is David, Father David. Some of the men are out at prayers. I didn't hear Randy drive in. I'm sure you must feel quite alone and in awe." He grasped my hand with both of his and shook it warmly. "Welcome to House of Change. We like to think our men leave here secure in their new self-awareness."

In spite of myself, my eyes welled up, and a tear escaped down my cheek. Sliding the duffel bag down onto the floor, I fished a handkerchief out and blew my nose.

"This dry air and dust bothers my sinuses."

"I understand," Father David replied in a gentle voice. "Perhaps you will agree to spend the night and meet the other men. If you still want to leave, Randy will take you back to the bus in the morning."

"Fair enough, guess my nerves are more on edge than I thought. My judgment isn't the best right now either."

Randy and I reached for the bag at the same time, almost bumping heads. Randy grasped the handle and swung it onto his shoulder again in one effortless movement.

A bird landed on the edge of a twig nest it had constructed under the porch roof. It scratched around, sending dry grass and other debris flittering down. A plop of bird dung ran down the side of the Spartan shingles and splattered on the porch floor just behind Father David's back. We both watched the action but dared not look at each other.

"Randy will guide you to your room. We'll speak again as soon as you are settled." His patronizing smile continued as he turned in dismissal, and we reentered the hall.

Relieved, we made a charge for the staircase through a door off the main hallway.

Randy chortled and whispered, "Father David loves that goddamned bird. He always stands under the nest when he greets someone. Sometime it's going to crap on his head."

I covered my mouth and burst out laughing. Randy made a snorting noise through his nose and doubled over guffawing. This was the first indication of the man having a lighter side.

My attention soon turned to the sharp contrast between the entrance hall and the rest of the house. The stairs were smooth plank with no risers. The upper-hall ceilings were much lower than those below. The walls were painted a bilious shade of green, and a series of flush doors led to rooms with brass number plates.

Randy shifted shoulders with my bag when he opened door number 7. He swung the bag off his shoulder and deposited it on a chair in one easy movement. He hesitated as if to say something but changed his mind and remained silent.

Should he be tipped? I reached for my wallet. Randy's face colored, and he shook his head when he realized what I was contemplating.

"We take turns greeting the new men coming in. I have been here off and on for the past couple of years. Not in therapy," he added quickly, "not all the time, anyway. I like the solitude. It was my turn today, to pick you up, I mean. I was glad to do it."

He seemed to run out of words.

"Thanks, hope you didn't take offense at my wanting to leave down there. You didn't do anything wrong, I want you to know."

I held out my hand, and we shook.

After Randy left, I inspected the room, cell actually. Not exactly the Ritz, just enough room for a single bed, a bureau, a bookcase, and the straight-back chair holding my duffel bag. A naked window looked out onto the desolate landscape. Two white towels and a washcloth were neatly folded on the bureau. A glass and a bar of soap sat beside them. A Bible lay on the foot of the bed.

I took off my shirt, slid out of my sandals, and sat on the edge of the bed, perspiring. I needed to pee and to be hugged, in that order. A full bladder urged me back out into the hall. A door stood open at the end of the passageway, and I was relieved to see it was a bathroom. There were no urinals, only stalls with doors. Four sinks in a row hung on the opposite wall and several shower stalls, doors open in an area beyond. No gang showers or urinal cruising. Life would be different from now on!

⤸

I sat rather stiffly before Father David the next morning. The room was cavernous and swept bare of any extraneous ornamentation. My eyes roamed the room. I sensed Father David inspecting me and perhaps finding my attire wanting. I slid my sockless open sandals as far back under the chair stretchers as they allowed.

"You're wondering about the gracious hall and then the humble rooms." Father David smiled and paused before telling the history of the property, probably for the hundredth or thousandth time. "The house was originally built for a wealthy Texan, now dead, for his bride from back East. Boston, I believe, or was it Providence? No matter. The shell was built and the grand foyer finished when he first brought her here to view it in progress."

"She hated the house, and she hated Texas," I finished for him.

Father David paused a moment, an eyebrow lifted in pique. "Quite so. You know the story then."

"No, just an educated guess. I'm from the East. New Hampshire, north of Boston." I paused, savoring for a moment my next facetious response. "And she shot him on the spot and ran screaming into the night."

Father David stiffened, his face reddened, a forced smile still on his lips. "I see we have a sense of humor. That will help as time goes by if you decide to stay."

"Forgive my rudeness. Go on with your story."

"The gentleman died of natural causes." Father David's forehead creased, and a fake sadness reflected in his eyes. "But the lady did leave the same night and was found walking the next day. Not to drag out the story, they settled in the Boston area, and this building sat vacant for twenty-five years. It became available at a very reasonable price a few years back, and it suited our requirements perfectly. As you can observe, we finished it in a manner befitting our mission.

"Several other clients arrived today as well. We can all meet at dinner. I'm sure you'll have questions as time goes by, and I'll do my best to answer them."

He smiled and concluded by extending his hand. We shook solemnly. A din of voices in the entrance hall seeped through the heavy office door, which Father David threw open, and he stepped back for me to pass.

A dozen or so men stood uncomfortably in a ragged group. They quieted when we appeared. Several of them seemed quite young, one maybe even in his late teens. A thirty-something man with a receding hairline stood a bit apart from the rest. Introductions were made amid handshaking and polite nothings.

We were ushered into a large dining hall setup with several round tables. Room for six at each table. It was quite silent during the meal except for the clinking of glasses and rattle of silver against plates. Occasionally someone would ask a question or make a light remark. Polite, uneasy laughter would follow.

I was aware of a young man seated beside me; his nametag read Paul. The boy's height was exaggerated by his slim, almost emaciated physique. His longish blond hair parted in the middle and fell either side of his face to just below his ears. He brushed it back with a bony hand when it tumbled over his eyes. His face reddened when he was addressed, and he seldom spoke. We touched arms a couple of times while eating, and I smiled encouragement.

After dinner, we carried our dishes to a spacious kitchen, one corner reserved for a large commercial dishwasher. We took turns, I later learned, at loading the dishwasher and stacking the dishes after the cycle was done.

A brief tour of the grounds and then evening devotions followed at the outdoor cross I had spotted on first arrival. The rest of the evening was free time.

Later, after bathing, I lay naked on the bed. A welcome rain shower had blown up, and a slight breeze stirred at the window. I folded a pillow under my head and began reading *Doctor Zhivago*. But the story required more concentration than I wished to use, so I slid it under the bed. The day had been long and draining. As I reached to snap the bed lamp off, a light tap sounded at the door.

"Can I c-come in a minute? It's Paul," a soft-spoken voice inquired.

I scrambled under the sheet and pulled it up to waist height and invited the young fellow in.

Paul's hand shook a little on the knob as he pulled the door together. His face was red to the roots of his hair. He looked even more emaciated than he had at supper. His body in profile resembled a paper doll. He wore chinos cinched in by a belt as though he had recently lost a lot of weight. A tan T-shirt, tucked in, drooped at the neck. A gold chain hung against his hairless chest. His left ear was pierced, but there was no evidence of a ring.

"Sorry to bother you, D-Damon, b-but I had to t-talk with someone. You looked friendly, so I d-decided to speak to you."

I regretted not pulling on my shorts before answering the door. I sat up in bed and leaned forward onto my knees and motioned for Paul to sit on the chair.

"I hate being here, I w-wish I was dead," Paul blurted and glanced at the door as though he might be overheard and reprimanded. His eyes were red, and he had been crying.

"You don't have to stay. You're not a prisoner here. You can get the bus back in the morning." Paul was in great distress and needed to vent. "I have been considering that myself."

"You h-have? Maybe we can l-leave together." He slid a scrawny hand up behind his neck. "I might as well be in p-prison, my folks s-sent me here." He made a snorting noise "They w-want to turn me into a m-man." He snorted again, louder. "I had a l-lover, and when they g-got wind of it, they w-went wild. I tried to explain, but they w-wouldn't listen. My father w-was so mad he even knocked m-me down." He spoke in a whisper, and his voice broke at the mention of his father.

"I know how you feel. My father did much the same to me."

"Honest? Did he k-knock you d-down?" Paul's attention was riveted to my every word.

"No. I'm sure he thought of it, but I faced him down, and he backed off." The ball of bitterness still stuck in my craw after all these months, so I was all the more aware of the neediness of the boy and, hell, of my own.

Paul broke the silence. "C-can I g-get in bed with you?" He was visibly shaking now. "I n-need to have someone s-say I'm okay and h-hug me."

"We all need that sometime." I was startled and glanced at the boy to see if he was serious. He looked so forlorn I nodded. He slipped his slacks and shirt off before I could stop him. Throwing caution to the wind, I lifted the sheet.

"Jesus C-Christ, m-man," Paul uttered.

I straightened my legs, and Paul slid in beside me, shuddering and sobbing. I put my arm out and pulled him close. He snuggled against my shoulder, his heart pumping through the thin layer of flesh. Why in the world would a parent be mean enough to their own, to misuse one as troubled as Paul certainly appeared?

Paul brushed his eyes and studied me a moment.

"I only s-stutter when I'm up-upset."

Paul was hardening against me, and his breathing quickened. He clumsily pulled my hand down to his erection.

"P-please, D-Damon, I'll n-never ask it again."

"I really don't think it's a good idea."

The rest of Paul's body stiffened, and he moaned and then lay quiet against my body.

And then we both slept.

CHAPTER

22

Father David ushered me into his office and indicated where I should sit. He pulled another chair up beside his desk and seated himself a few feet away, facing me. The day was hot, and the constant whir of two paddle fans did little to alleviate the heat.

"I understand you had a visitor in your room last evening."

A patronizing look crossed his ruddy face as he leaned closer, scrutinizing me, my hand caught in the proverbial cookie jar.

"I had a visitor."

Taken off guard, annoyance seeped in; my face felt hot, further irritating me. So we're being watched. He waited, head canted, brow furrowed, expecting me to explain, ask forgiveness, kiss his ring, or some other goddamned thing. We were momentarily startled when his pet bird flew against the window with a thud. I hoped it had killed itself. No such luck, it flew away. I wondered if it was queer.

Father David turned back to me again.

"You must understand how contrary this is to our work here. Do you care to explain the circumstances?" He paused again, twisting the knife with his magnanimous mien.

"Not really." I returned his steady gaze. Thoughts of Paul and his tenuous hold on sanity made me immediately regret my cavalier retort. Paul would be the loser in this situation while my life would go on none the worse for the whole affair. I swallowed my ire and continued.

"Paul was in need of help. I did what I could."

"Ah, it was Paul." He gave a slight nod and settled back in his chair.

Shit, the old bugger didn't even know who it was, and I spilled the beans. I leaned back and placed my elbows on the chair arms, challenging him with my eyes. The room was deadly quiet. I heard his bowels rumble.

He appeared to be weighing the options. His face darkened.

"Your request to leave has been granted." His voice was crisp with rebuke. "Randy will bring the car around in half an hour. I'm sure you'll be ready." He started to rise, reaching for the intercom.

Before he was fully standing, I responded, "I've changed my mind. I'm staying."

Snapping his head back toward me, he dropped back into the chair, skewering me with a look of surprise and disbelief.

"That's not for you to decide, Damon. I want you out of here. You're a troublemaker and a distraction. You think you're so smart. Let me tell you this, young man..."

All civility and piety disappeared. His hand trembled on the chair arm, and the vein on his forehead pulsed. Surprised as he was, I was more so, not sure until that very moment what I wanted to do. He sprang out of his chair, lurched in back of the desk, noisily shuffled and straightened a pile of papers.

He turned back to me, his mind grappling for a decision.

"If I am to agree to your staying, you will have to tell me what happened last night. Our relationship cannot continue unless I can evaluate the seriousness of this, shall we say, indiscretion." His voice was stern as he moved back to the chair, scowling.

Our eyes locked, fighting for the upper hand. But in deference to Paul, I relented.

"Paul is still a very young man, a boy really. I sat beside him at dinner last evening, and we joked about something or other, nothing important. The evening passed without further conversation between us."

The expression on Father David's face seemed to soften, a forthcoming confession his stock in trade. He leaned forward on one elbow, listening intently.

"I had showered and lay on my bed when a knock came on the door. It was Paul. He sounded upset and asked to come in. He was crying and stuttering badly. I was immediately concerned and tried to engage him in conversation, to bring him out. We discussed our backgrounds. As we compared our lives, he relaxed somewhat." I paused, a sly smile on my face, letting the full impact of my next statement sink in. "I was really taken off guard when he asked to get in bed with me."

Father David's head shot forward, and he drew in a noisy breath. He swallowed and waved a hand for me to continue.

"Go on. You told him it would be unwise, of course."

"Of course not. I lifted the sheet, and he slid in. I hugged him while he sobbed and shook. He needed—we both needed kind words and understanding."

Father David recovered his composure, a serious expression crossing his face. He rose and moved back to his desk and picked up a rather ugly-looking ceramic animal of some kind and ran a finger over the head.

"This was given to me by a young man several years ago." His eyes seemed focused far beyond this room. "I wasn't aware of the demons he was dealing with and had no way of knowing." A sigh escaped his lips. "He seemed so happy when he left, changed, he said." He frowned and studied the ornament in his hand. "Later, he met a nice young woman. They married several months later." His eyes lighted up a fraction of a second. "I was delighted and officiated at their wedding. Brian dabbled in ceramics. This is one he sent me shortly after leaving us."

He placed it back on the desk and moved over to a window. He was silent several minutes then sighed again, louder this time, and turned back to me, a world-weary look on his face.

"Several months later"—his voice became so low I had to lean closer to hear it above the rotation of the fans—"he shot his wife and then himself. I think of him when I hear a story like Paul's."

He seemed to crumple into the chair, his mind still absorbed by the tragedy. An emotional pause ensued that neither of us were anxious to break.

"You did the right thing." Father David finally broke the silence, his mind back in the present. "I appreciate your candor. Maybe you've even saved a life. I'll try to help him as much as he will allow." Father David's mood lightened, a half-smile lighted his face. "You were both clothed I presume?"

An eyebrow rose as he looked at me.

Taking my time to answer, my face was intentionally blank of emotion.

"No, neither of us, but nothing happened."

He shook his head in a sardonic manner, but his smile remained.

"I figured. Nothing ever does."

I stood. He came around the desk, and we shook hands.

"Welcome to House of Change." He put a hand on my shoulder as we moved toward the door. "I will pray for you both."

A group meeting was called after lunch. It consisted of our leader, Dr. Kessler, the fifteen new "recruits' and four of the clients who had been there for a month or more, the latter four to observe and interact with us at the end of the meeting.

Dr. Kessler introduced himself and stated his credentials. He had a PhD in human relations and specialized in sexual dysfunction and abnormal child mental development. He had been closely involved with reparative therapy for a considerable number of his twenty-three years in practice.

I was pleased to meet him since I had read several of his writings on the subject. He was a firm believer that change was possible. In fact, he felt it should be mandatory, in most cases, for the good of society. He also claimed a high success rate with those individuals strongly motivated, men as well as women.

"I welcome you gentlemen as you start on the most difficult but important step you will ever take." A serious but somehow understanding glint shone in his eyes as he looked from one to another of us seated in a semicircle.

"The first point I want to emphasize is that we are all men. And as such we should act, look, and dress like men at all times." He paused, letting this sink in. The group, staring intently at him, now gave uneasy sidelong glances toward each other. "Why don't we start with introductions and a little background about yourselves."

Paul looked the most uncomfortable, and Dr. Kessler zeroed in on him.

"What's your name, young man, and what motivated you to change your life?"

"My f-father." Sweat stood out in beads on his forehead. A controlled snicker rippled around the group. Paul's face turned scarlet, and his lip developed a twitch. His head bowed, fingers spread on his lower lip. He slowly raised his head and looked Kessler in the eye. "My name is Paul, Paul G-Gatsas."

"How do you feel about his influence, Paul Gatsas?" Dr. Kessler had a live one, and he knew it. I hated him for putting Paul on the spot.

"I'm m-mad as hell at him." He leaned back and took a strangled breath, wiping his wet cheek with a Kleenex. Eighteen faces with varying degrees of sympathy waited.

I caught his eye and mouthed, "You're okay."

Dr. Kessler spied our interaction and called on me.

"We'll get back to you in a minute, Paul, it seems you have a cheering section." His eyes turned to me.

Anticipating his question, I replied, "I would guess Paul made a very shrewd observation. Aren't we all here, to some degree, because of our fathers?"

Heads nodded slightly as I spoke.

His eyes penetrated me. Dr. Kessler had probably been warned about me by Father David. I had a brief moment of hatred toward them both because of Paul. But I was not in charge and needed to back off. A pause ensued, which he obviously had no intention of breaking.

"My name is Damon, last name Duncan. I'm from New Hampshire and here because my father disowned me." My eyes stung, so I hurried on, words tripping over each other. "Then my lover and I quarreled. He knocked me down and ended our relationship." I paused and took a deep breath. "My sister lives in Fort Worth and invited me out. Ilka was initially supportive of my sexual preference." The emotional moment passed. I felt more in control, so slowed a bit. "I met another fellow on the bus and fell madly in love." A feather hitting the floor would have sounded like gunfire. The space was so quiet, each man devouring my every word.

"You said your sister was initially supportive. Did that change?"

"Drastically. When Carlos and I arrived at her house, she was understandably upset. She had wanted time alone with me after ten years apart." I went on to explain how Carlos had charmed her and she reluctantly appeared to accept him as part of my life. "We stayed with her several days, then one evening Carlos offered to go out exploring so she and I could talk. As soon as he left, my sister delved headlong into my sex life. We soon came to words over a man who had left me money several years ago for sexual favors. Enraged over her attitude, I impulsively rushed out into the night."

Words stuck in my mouth. I was finding it very difficult to relive that time. My hands were sweaty and unsteady; my eyes stung. I swallowed and took a deep breath.

"Something happened that night. Damon, tell us," he encouraged.

"It was around midnight, the streetlights ended, but I kept running." My voice broke, and I started to shake. All eyes were fixed on me, but I couldn't open my mouth. I had never detailed this to anyone else except the police. My breath grew shallow, and spots danced before my eyes, and tears ran unchecked down my cheeks.

"Take your time." Dr. Kessler spoke in a low, gentle voice, handing me the box of tissues.

My heart pounded, and my breath caught as I relived that night. Then, suddenly, I couldn't stop. The dam had broken.

"Every bit of light was eaten up by the blackness. I was moving like a blind man. I thought I heard a noise behind me. It sounded like a sneaker skidding on pavement. I waited. Quiet. I needed to pee."

Knowing smiles broke on several faces.

"Suddenly, someone grabbed me from behind," I rasped. "They were everywhere. Someone grabbed my penis. He said he had a knife."

I stopped for breath. Horror showed on many of the faces around me. My body was awash with sweat, my shirt soaked, my words slurred. I couldn't seem to take enough air into my lungs. "Someone else said cut if off." I saw Paul wince. "They slashed my clothes off and threw me onto the rough pavement. Another one yanked me up, threw me against a fence, and raped me dry. I screamed. He told me to shut up or he'd kill me." My voice was now hoarse from emotion. "And he rammed me again and again." I was now doubled over in pain.

"For God's sake, stop it!" Paul shouted at Dr. Kessler. Kessler seemed quite nonplused. "Can't you see the man's in pain? I hate this. I d-don't want to s-stay here any longer."

Sprinting from his seat, he lunged for the door. He clutched the knob in one hand, beating the face of the door with his fist, howling. He rattled the knob and kicked at the door. Tears streaked down his cheeks. Twisting his torso, he glowered back at Dr. Kessler, a haunted look in his eyes. "I'm a p-prisoner, a f-fucking p-prisoner. We're all p-prisoners."

Suddenly the door yielded, and he raced through.

The group sat openmouthed. My body was in a catatonic state, unable to move. The room pitched and twirled around me, my breath and body someone else's. Dr. Kessler's face moved in and out of my consciousness.

The room came slowly back into focus; the floor felt hard. A circle of faces stared down at me then disappeared. I wanted to close my eyes again and sleep. Hands under my shoulders and knees and I was on a soft surface. I felt hot, so hot. A fan gently moved forth and back. Someone I had not seen before, the tightness above my right elbow, the needle in my arm. I smiled. Soon my life would end.

I love you, Carlos, was my last thought before unconsciousness overtook me.

CHAPTER

⫷ 23 ⫸

I was awake at seven the next morning and read a bit of *Zhivago* but soon laid the book aside again. While I showered and shaved, my mind flashed back to yesterday. Recounting the details of my rape to the group remained. The rest of the afternoon eluded me. Most details were augmented by what others told me. But my desire to escape homosexuality had crystallized.

Later that morning, we sat before Dr. Kessler again, his elbows resting on the chair arms, fingers entwined. He nodded at each of us in turn and cleared his throat. We all tensed, waiting for words that would encourage and make us feel the mission was worthwhile. We were not disappointed.

"I bring good news for all of you men here today. Some of you will be startled, others may initially disbelieve." He paused dramatically so that each of us would be alert to his next words.

"None of you were born homosexual."

We lurched forward in our chairs and looked at each other, amazed. His timing was perfect, giving us a chance to explore briefly in our minds the impact of his words, perhaps the attendant joy if we could believe him.

"Homosexuality is an acquired persona or habit, if you will."

There was uneasy stirring among us. We twisted in our chairs, casting furtive glances at each other. Kessler had hit a nerve.

"It happens in the home, in your early personality development. There are several reasons, the principal one being rejection by the father figure as Paul and Damon have so graphically recounted."

The last sentence was spoken slowly and deliberately, emphasizing "Rejection by the father figure."

"The young boy is ignored by his father, or the father figure is missing. The mother or woman in the house is turned to. As he matures, he feels neglected and ineffectual. His confidence suffers, and he rejects the standard masculine pursuits. He cannot catch a ball and is awkward at sports. He searches for other males to replace his father. That need may become short-circuited and turns into sexual attraction in the mind of the developing boy."

Visions of growing up ricocheted through my mind. I always looked forward to the time Dad left for work in the morning and the nights he had to work late. Weekends were the worst. He bought me a baseball mitt; I hated that damned thing. He taunted me every time I missed catching the ball. The more he excoriated me the oftener I missed. He excelled at everything sports related. I felt guilty, as though I had failed him as a son.

My thoughts were brought back to the present as Dr. Kessler continued. "The first thing I want you men to do is to dress like men. No designer jeans, no sandals, no jewelry, earrings, neck chains, bracelets, or any of the other female adornments." Each article was enunciated slowly and clearly, exclamation points in speech. "Forget Ralph Lauren, Gucci, Banana Republic, Guess, and the other designers for the gay market. Shirts should be buttoned, slacks loose fitting, socks worn with regular shoes." Dr. Kessler surveyed us, eyes sharp, watching for dissent.

I thought of Randy picking me up at the bus. He must not run into Dr. Kessler too often. I wondered why he had buttoned his shirt before getting out of the Blazer when we arrived yesterday.

"Do you have any questions before we go on?" Dr. Kessler asked.

One young man put up his hand rather hesitantly. "All the guys wear these things. They can't all be gay."

There were nervous chuckles, and heads nodded.

Dr. Kessler's eyes sparkled while an aha moment spread across his face.

"That's the devil's work. He's gotten into all your heads. More and more, society is being ruled by the devil. He's taking you under his wing at a younger age each year. Push him out of your life. Look to the Lord."

His eyes glazed, and he appeared to be momentarily on another plain. He coughed and brought his attention back to us.

"We have something special planned for this afternoon when we meet again. A young man who went through training here a short time ago is going to speak. I think you will be uplifted by what he has to say.

"There are a variety of methods to meet our goals, some unpleasant, I must say, but all have proved to be effective. As I interview each one of you separately, we will fashion a program to best meet your needs. Are there further questions so far?"

Somehow, I knew the program was going to work for me. What Dr. Kessler was saying made perfect sense. Why would the Lord make a man who acted like a woman? In the scattered discussions I had with some of the other guys last evening, we all questioned why.

Maybe Dad was right. Did he abandon me first, or was it the other way around?

One thing was sure—Mike had my number. He could see what was happening, and he had the brains to end it. Someday I'm going to thank him. But what about Carlos? He's big, strong, masculine, like Mike. I'm going to lick this. And if I ever see him again, we can shake hands, "Nice knowing ya, see ya around." And we walk away.

"Damon"—Dr. Kessler shook my arm gently—"we're breaking for lunch. You seem to be in another world. Why don't we chat after we listen to the inspiring story Cliff Taylor tells us this afternoon?"

I nodded and felt embarrassed that my mind had wandered, even more embarrassed that I had a slight erection. I hadn't masturbated for some time now since it brought thoughts of Carlos. I lied and said I was working something out in my mind. He patted me on the shoulder and headed for the door.

The air outside was oppressive; I broke into a sweat just walking across the parking lot.

The crushed stone on the path to the cross felt sharp on my feet through my thin-soled shoes. No one was around as I slid onto one of the rustic plank benches. I peered up at the cross and pondered how to pray. I had never been much for church. I didn't want God to think I was a hypocrite and only went to him when I wanted something.

"I'm here, God," I whispered, tears weaving down my cheeks, hoping no one around could hear. "I need your help. Bad. I'm afraid we've never talked much before, but that's my fault. This thing going with me, it's bad, I know, and I'm trying to beat it. Tell me what to do, Lord. It's killing me."

⌒

Cliff Taylor was of slim build and carried himself well. His stride was confident as he moved before us that afternoon. He stood feet slightly apart, hands at his sides. He looked at each of us in turn, a slight smile on his face. There was charisma about him, hard to put my finger on, but I liked it.

"Hi, I'm Cliff Taylor." His voice was modulated but firm. "I sat where you gentlemen are now sitting less than two years ago, so I have a pretty good idea of what most of you are going through.

"Let me share a little of my background. I grew up in a small town here in central Texas in what seemed a normal family—one brother, older, two sisters, younger. My dad was a lot older than my mum and was away much of the time, a farm-equipment salesman. Mum was an outgoing, take-charge kind of woman. She had to be with Dad away so much."

Head tilted slightly, he looked up. How many times he must have recounted this part of his life. Paul hitched around in his chair, and Sam continued looking at the floor, a sad expression on his face.

"Not much for sports, I was kind of a loner, very shy, never one of the guys. I felt different but couldn't quite pin it down. I hung around with the girls until they showed romantic interest in me. Then I was out the door."

We all nodded our heads at that.

He continued with his story of isolation, anxiety, and alienation, and then his first experience with another boy when he was fifteen. My experience with Seth Porter hit me between the eyes; I started to sweat. Many eyes were moist, including his, when he recounted the terrible day when his older brother caught him naked, kissing and fondling another boy.

"He couldn't wait to tell our mother. She called Dad, sobbing hysterically. He rushed home from an important deal he was working on. He was furious. I was beaten and locked in my room. I was crushed, my life destroyed. I snuck out a few nights later and never went home again. I wanted to die. And the worst part of all"—he struck his right fist into his left hand with a loud snap—"they never tried to find me." His voice broke, and he cleared his throat before continuing. "I lived with a guy in his twenties for a number of years, always feeling guilty because I enjoyed the sex."

A pall fell over the room. Hands folded, we avoided eye contact with him.

He paced forth and back in front of us, hands behind him and the fingers of his right hand holding his left index finger. He paused and faced us again.

"But it was wrong, gentlemen, it was wrong. I knew it, but I was unable to break away from it. In the depth of my despair, contemplating suicide, I was surfing the Internet late one night, looking for vicarious sex, when House of Change appeared on the screen. How did it appear amid all the smut?"

He fell silent, looking at each of us again. Then he continued in a soft, reverent voice.

"I know now, God was looking out for me. Open your heart to God and he'll look out for you too."

A smile spread across his face again.

"My daughter will be a year old next week, and my wife and I expect another child in a few months."

We all applauded, some with more enthusiasm than others. I noticed Paul was wiping his eyes and left the room quietly. The rest of us gathered around Cliff. I looked for any telltale body language and felt he was being up-front with us.

Later that afternoon, I sat in Kessler's office. It felt a bit like being back in high school, but I was okay with it. Kessler came out from behind his desk when I entered and moved to a chair a few feet away, facing me. A box of tissues sat on the edge of his desk.

He seemed much more relaxed than he had with the group. He kept smiling at me, giving me the complete once-over, but made no conversation. It began to feel creepy. He reached for a clipboard and pencil and then contemplated me again. Something was going on I couldn't explain or understand.

I finally broke the silence. "I have a feeling you're cruising me," I blurted out, barely believing what I had just said.

"How does that make you feel, Damon?"

"It makes me mad as hell," I shot back.

"Don't ever forget that because that is what gay men do to other men, whether they realize it or not."

My first reaction was to argue. Then I thought about it and took it to heart. He couldn't have made the point more succinctly. My early experience with Seth Porter, was I telegraphing a message to him? And what of Mike? And then there was Carlos on the bus. A touch of nausea rose from my midsection. Was I as obvious as some punk hanging out in an alley on Castro Street or Greenwich Village?

"What really brought you to House of Change, Damon? Father David and I both feel an ambivalence on your part."

Assholes, I thought, *so they have been discussing me.* No need to cross swords with him yet though. "I will admit to being conflicted. My parents and sister don't even know I'm here."

I had the feeling he didn't believe me. He had the irritating habit of twisting slightly in the swivel chair. It had a squeak, which bugged the hell out of me. He continued to sit wordlessly, the chair whining under his weight. I felt like blurting out, "Cat got your tongue?"

"Damon," he urged finally, "there is a real reason why you came here, and you and I need to get at it before I can help you." He eased up out of the chair and sat on the edge of the desk. "Doesn't your family want you to change?"

"Sure, they'll be happy as hell. Dad can hold his head up again amongst his friends. But they can go fuck themselves as far as any support they're giving me. The rape was a very degrading thing to me. I'm still afraid of dark streets. Is that what you guys call my feminine side?"

The gall was rising in me; it was hard to sit still. I slumped back in my chair, feet sticking out.

"What do you think of your so-called feminine side?"

"Call it what you want, I don't feel feminine. I don't knit or sew or want to wear a skirt."

The air in the room seemed to close in on me. I hitched my chair over under the ceiling fan.

Kessler paced across the room several times then turned back to me.

"What can you tell me about Carlos?"

"Nothing."

"So he's out of your life then?"

"Yes."

"That's good."

"Why is it good?"

"Because he's gone, you don't have to think about him anymore. You have agonized too long."

Kessler seated himself in front of me again; his stare, this time, had a kindness. He had touched on the truth with his questions.

"We both know better." Hurt and resignation gored at me like a fish under a filet knife. "Every man I've ever been involved with has either died or dumped me. But I can't get over Carlos. His image haunts me. If I can get him out of my system, maybe I can move forward with my life."

CHAPTER

ᘓ 24 ᘗ

Am I making progress? Hard to say. Weird, being "locked up" in a world of men yet not supposed to think about men—sexually.

The three men most influential in my life so far, Dad, Mike, and Carlos, somehow fit into the puzzle, yet the pieces wouldn't quite interlock. Then there are the three most influential women in my life, Mom, Ilka, Shirl. More pieces, but the puzzle makes even less sense. Most days I write in my diary. It helps.

> Nov. 5—The most difficult obstacle remaining is Carlos. Almost every man here has a Carlos in their past. Or so they say. At each one-on-one or group session, it seems at the time like Carlos is receding more into the background. Wishful thinking? I hope not.

> At least I had commandeered Ilka into revoking the restraining order. That allowed Carlos to spend just one night in jail, one night too many. If he had only come back to the house the next day. Is being here at House of Change the right thing to do? If it works, Carlos will be forgotten. If it doesn't?

Nov. 6—Played baseball today. Dr. Kessler says we can learn masc. pursuits in a peer-protected atmosphere. Fuck you, Kessler. I hate you more every day. But you're right, dammit! Some different from elementary school, where every little shit taunted me about not catching the ball. I caught one today, and it felt good!

Nov. 7—Spivick remains a thorn in my side. He never misses a chance to needle me. His day will come!

❧

Paul tapped on my door around 9:00 p.m.

"Damon," he said, stuttering badly, "I've got to get away from here. The pressure is too much. I can't catch a fucking ball or hit it with the bat. I hate this place. I wake up some nights and can't breathe. You're the only one I can talk with. The others are developing this macho crap."

"I know how it is, Paul. A lot of the time I feel the same way. But I did better the past couple of days." He always seems to bring out the paternal in me. "Why don't you pick one of the guys with about your same ability and play one-on-one with him? That's what I did." I saw doubt in his face. "It's not exactly the end of the world if you don't want to play baseball, ya know. Maybe we can play catch."

He shrugged his shoulders and shuffled around in the small space, hands stuffed in his pockets.

"I shouldn't bother you with my problems," he stuttered. "I've got to work them out myself."

"Since when have you been a problem? We're all here for each other. You can do it."

I patted him on the arm.

211

"I've written a letter to my father." He looked at me for some kind of reaction. I was startled. "Do you think that was wise?"

"Probably not."

He sat on the edge of the bed, careful not to touch my leg. "I've tried like hell to do something here—feel something. I don't hate women, honest. I just love men. I hope he'll understand this time."

"I know you've tried, Paul. I'm struggling myself. Buck up, matey," I said in my best English accent. "The ship may be leaking, but shore is in sight."

"And what shore is that, matey?" he parroted back, irony in his tone.

"The one you can see if you shin up the mainmast with a high-powered telescope and use your imagination a little, old thing, and all that sort of rot." At least I got a grin out of him at last.

"Do you suppose it would be okay if we keep in touch after our 'sentence' is up here?"

"I'd be pretty pissed if you didn't."

"Promise?"

"Promise."

He gave me a very chaste hug. I know he ached for more. We said good night. I stood at the door and watched him go down the hall. I could only imagine the hell he was going through. I went back into my room and got out my diary.

> Nov. 11—I gave Paul encouragement. It seemed to help. He's not going to make the cut, I'm afraid. He's fighting change. He can't just lay back, go with the flow. He's a nice guy, but his father has torn him apart. P needs to stand up to him!

> Nov. 12—Today is day 35. Better than a third of the way thru. Have been counseling with

Dr. Polanski. He's a nice guy. He gets right to the heart of things.

༄

Today was the day from hell!

> Nov. 17—Carlos's birthday. He's twenty-six. I was doing great until I remembered. We never even spent one holiday or special day together. No, can't say that, every day was a special day with him.

I looked at my red-rimmed eyes in the mirror. Can't let the others see them, especially Spivick.

Shaving and dressing occupied more time than necessary. Perhaps my mood would lighten. Maybe I'll see Paul this morning. We can commiserate, debate over who's the most depressed. I shuffled through my belongings and found a pair of Foster Grants, not caring whether they would be approved or not. I dawdled down the stairs a step at a time. Even the smell of fresh coffee repelled me.

I walked through the breakfast line, scooping out scrambled eggs, a slice of bacon, and a muffin. No coffee for me, just a glass of juice.

"Hey, Duncan," Spivick called out as I set my tray down. "Why the shades? The egg yolks too bright?"

The guys at his table snickered as they turned and gawked at me—the last thing I needed. The bastard had bothered me from day 1. Little digs, snide remarks.

"Certainly not like some of the present company," I shot back, giving him the finger. "If you know what I mean."

"Good one, Duncan. Just wait, I'll get back at ya at baseball today."

"Sure, an underhand pitch, I suppose."

We kidded with each other about throwing underhand like girls are supposed to do.

His face turned red, and he leaned in toward his buddies, and they shared a coarse joke. I caught a word or two—*asshole, comeuppance*—all hateful.

No longer hungry after a few mouthfuls, I rose to carry the rest of my breakfast out to the garbage. The space past Spivick's table was the shortest route to the kitchen. I usually took the long way around. Not today. *Try something, Spivick, you prick*, I said to myself. He didn't look up as I approached. Good, he's finally ignoring me. Suddenly, he twisted and stuck his foot out. I stubbed and almost fell flat. The contents of my tray flew against the backs of a couple of guys at the next table. Spivick's confederates chuckled.

I grabbed some napkins, trying to wipe food off the guys' backs. They were none too happy.

Shaking with fury and using poor judgment, I shouted, "If your cock is half as big as your foot, you'll make some guy a nice wife."

He vaulted out of his chair and gave me a shove. I crashed backwards onto another table. Food, dishes, and silverware flew in all directions.

Enraged, I gathered myself and shoved my foot into Spivick's gut. He shot backward, landing half onto his chair, grasping at anything to right himself, in this case the tablecloth. His buddies grabbed plates and coffee cups before everything crashed onto the floor.

I corralled a tray.

"You son of a bitch," I snarled and clubbed at him.

His hands flew up, deflecting the blow.

I bent over six inches from his face.

"You've pestered me every day since we've been here. No more!" I was so goddamned mad I wanted to kill him. The isolation, the interviews, the counseling sessions, the tension of searching my most intimate feelings—all the frustration of the past month came to a head.

Spivick jumped up and nailed me beside the head with his fist. I dropped the tray and belted him across the mouth with the back of my hand. It drew blood. He snatched me by the collar, half-tearing it off my shirt, and rammed me against another table.

As he bent over to strangle me, hands on my neck, I kneed him in the balls. He doubled over, pitched backward, and crashed onto the floor. The surrounding tables looked like a war zone. Everyone was standing, mouths open, watching the bizarre scene in various degrees of fascination.

"Break it up, guys," Johnson, a senior fellow at the retreat, shouted. "Duncan"—he took me by the shoulder—"you've overreacted."

It felt like ice water had been thrown into my face, bringing me back to reality.

Then he spun around.

"But you," indicating Spivick, "got what you deserved."

Johnson was six four or so, and Spivick was about five eight. Towering over Spivick, he spoke in a cold voice. "We need some cleanup here." He grabbed Spivick by the forearm and stood him on his feet. Spivick, bully/coward that he was, didn't argue back. He set to work, hunched over, still favoring his testicles. With dirty looks in my direction, his cohorts scrambled to help.

Feeling mortified, I conceded to Johnson as he turned back to me. He brushed a piece of egg off my shoulder, stepped past destroyed food and coffee still drizzling onto the tile floor. He walked me out to the back entry, arm around my shoulder.

"You're having a bad day," he spoke in a kind voice.

Eyes searched mine. My sunglasses lay mangled somewhere on the floor back in the dining hall.

I nodded, looking down.

"Memories?"

"Yeah." I turned away, teetering on the edge of losing it.

"We all do, Duncan. After all, we're only human. This friend of yours, a nice guy, I'll bet." I noticed he didn't say *lover*. That word was absolutely verboten in this facility.

"Yeah, the best. Today's his birthday." I spoke in a half-sob. I had cramps in my stomach, and my nose was running. "I'm a fucking mess." I half-laughed amongst the tears.

"You'll be okay, you're making progress. In fact, you are probably over the hump. You've been holding it in, just coming to realize all the brave words we say each day to hide our true feelings. Go with it. It will pass." He put both hands on my shoulders, looking me in the eyes. "The 'cure' here is seldom 100 percent—you'll learn to pack those old memories in the back of your mind. They're too precious to throw away. But we move on. We have to."

Words failed me as he squeezed my shoulders, turned, and returned to the fray. As he walked away, I had to blink several times; he was the spitting image of Carlos. The comparison was like an arrow through my temple.

I checked for mail in my cubicle, stumbled up to my room, and threw myself onto the bed. Gotta see Polanski. Later. Go for a run? No, stay and tough it out. A tear dropped onto a Kleenex wadded in my hand. The moisture slowly oozed to a circle four times the size of the drop. Then it dissipated.

All things come to an end.

∽

I must have fallen into a sodden half-sleep. Voices shouting and people running echoed up to my open window. Pulling myself up, I groggily moved to the window and peered out. A blanket was spread on the lawn, and a motionless body lay in the center. Several people on their knees surrounded him, one performing CPR.

Paul was the first thought that came to my mind. Jesus, help us. What desperate thing has he done? I slipped into my shoes and clattered down the stairs, as though speed could save a life. I hoped!

It was Paul. Inching in by the onlookers, unsure what to do, I was horrified at the sight. His tongue was being held so that he wouldn't swallow it as they blew air in mouth-to-mouth. As they released, a horrible red mark and scratches showed around his neck. It sickened my heart.

Thirty-five days ago rushed into my mind like a blow to the head. I remembered arriving here with Randy when he drove the Blazer into the dark and forbidding barn. My eyes had strayed upward to the lofty beams and visualized somebody swinging from one of them. Was it a premonition of today's horror? No, it couldn't be. My gut wrenched like a belt cinched around my midsection and breath caught in my throat.

Dropping on one knee at his side, I clutched his hand and whispered, "Don't give up, Paul. Live. It can be worked out. Come, Paul, open your eyes, give me a sign."

I was sure there was just the faintest flutter of an eyelash. He had something clutched in his hand—a letter.

"Sorry, Duncan," one of the senior fellows spoke, "you will have to move back out of the way."

I shook my head. I was his friend and closest confidant. No way would I leave him now. Then Paul's lips moved. Just a very faint, gossamer whisper. I had to put my ear close to his mouth.

"Damon, take the letter."

"I'm with ya, buddy," I choked out. "Squeeze my hand."

I tightened my grip slightly and felt a twitch in his. He loosened his fingers, and I took the letter. Tears started down my cheeks. Could I have done more to prevent this?

"Hang in there, I love ya. Don't leave me."

Father David knelt by me. As I was speaking to Paul, I caught the slightest tinge of disapproval form on his lips.

"Damon," he said, his voice tight and under control, "you must move away. You are impeding the actions of the men with medical training. An ambulance is on the way."

He reached for the letter.

"No," I snatched it back out of his hand, "don't you see what is happening? He's responding to my presence. I've gotta stay with him."

Father David reached for my arm to pull me up. I shook out of his grip. He reached again, his grasp firm on my arm this time. A quick snap of my elbow repelled his arm once more. Strong arms clutched under my shoulders, jerked me off the ground, and dragged me several feet away, my body limp as I had seen in protest marches. The man looked familiar, but I didn't know his name. He stood over my body as I lay on the ground. I remained impassive, waiting. After a few seconds he moved over to speak with Father David. They conferred several seconds while glancing at me. Their intent was obvious; they wanted the goddamned letter.

The strong man started back toward me, mouth set. I lay in wait. Leaping into the air, I caught his leg behind the knee with my toe, and he pitched forward, flat onto the grass. The barn was nearby, and I made a dash for it. I knelt in a dark corner while my respiration slowed.

A rope looped around the rafter twisted idly in the breeze; a knotted loop with frayed ends lay on the floor below. I leaned my head against a rough partition and puked. It took several minutes to regain my equilibrium. If Paul didn't make it, I vowed in my mind to confront his parents with what they had caused.

A hand lightly touched me on the shoulder. Startled, I snapped my attention to the intruder. It was Dr. Polanski.

CHAPTER

⊰ 25 ⊱

Paul's death sent me rocketing back into despair. I couldn't eat, and falling asleep was impossible. The horror hit anew upon waking from any exhausted napping. What could I have done to help Paul? Why did I have that terrible premonition when I first entered the barn with Randy those many weeks ago?

Paul spoke of leaning on me. Now I knew how I needed him as a friend and confidant. My sessions with Dr. Polanski were the only thing that kept me from going mad. He was so different from Father David, who now treated me as a pariah. At our next session, I spilled my guts to Dr. Polanski about my relationship with Carlos, which I couldn't seem to shake, and my innocent friendship with Paul.

"Do you feel guilt about not being able to help Paul, Damon?" he pressed.

"Yes, he came to me for help the night before."

"Do you care to discuss what happened?"

I related our conversation and Paul's feeling of desperation. I choked up as I recounted observing Paul travel down the hall, head down, shuffling like an old man. Dr. Polanski observed me as I spoke. Not an attractive man physically but charismatic, a gentle man as well as a gentleman, he inspired my absolute trust in his words and more importantly in our interactions. He paused, waiting for me to go on.

"I haven't read the letter Paul was holding. It had his father's return address. I've kept it as kind of a sacred trust, you might say. The last thing he entrusted anyone with."

Was I afraid of what it might say? That didn't make any sense. So why hadn't I read it?

"Do you have it with you?"

"Yes, I keep it in my shirt pocket." My hands shook as I slipped it out of the envelope. "Should I read it to you?" My voice was at once weak and unsure.

"If that's what you wish."

I spread the crumpled page out on the desk and smoothed it with the palm of my hand. With faltering fingers I picked it up and began to read aloud.

Dear Son,

Having not heard from you this past month, your mother and I have become anxious to know how you are coming along. A third of your time has passed already, and we have every confidence that you will have seen God's will by now and will return to us the man we know you can be.

I had to stop reading to control my anger at this uncaring, bullying bastard. I struggled to read on, my voice shaking with emotion.

Your friend has called several times and stopped by the house a few days ago. I tried to reason with him and said you would no longer have interest in him. He became insolent, and we asked him to leave or we would have to call the police if he persisted further. A regular ruffian!

On a more positive note, we have a little surprise planned for when you come home.

We rejoice in your new life and can now
look forward to grandchildren someday.
Your mother sends her love!

Sincerely,

Dad

We both remained quiet several moments after I stopped reading. I felt a strong presence of Paul in the room in a way I could not explain. I raised my eyes from the letter to Dr. Polanski. His jaw was set firm, and he seemed ready to comment but remained silent.

The room was quiet except for the monotonous whir of the overhead fan. The western sun slanted askew onto the uncarpeted floor. The view from the window, as in all the windows in the building, looked out onto flat, sandy terrain to infinity.

I refolded the letter and slid it back into my shirt pocket.

"Paul had written a letter to his father," I said, breaking the silence.

"Had he sent it?" Dr. Polanski glanced up.

"I thought so, but apparently not. This letter doesn't indicate it."

"Nothing of that sort was found in his room. There's been a thorough search done by the police looking for a suicide note or any other indication of what might have caused Paul to take his life."

"The police will most likely want this letter." I pressed my hand protectively against my pocket.

A sharp knock sounded on the door. Startled, we looked at each other; I moved over by the window.

"Come," Dr. Polanski spoke, raising his voice to be heard through the heavy door.

A police officer stepped in and held up his badge as Dr. Polanski advanced briskly toward him.

"What can we do for you, Officer?"

"I am looking for Duncan, first name Damon." He looked over Dr. Polanski's shoulder in my direction. "Your Father David said he'd be in here."

Dr. Polanski turned back to me.

"This is Damon Duncan. What is this about? We're in the middle of a session."

"We're investigating the events leading up to Paul Gatsas's death." The officer loomed in front of me and flipped his badge again. "Father David out there"—he motioned with his thumb over his shoulder—"says you took a letter or piece of paper from Gatsas's hand before he died. Do you have it?"

"I did, but I misplaced it. It was just a page of notes he had taken in one of our class sessions."

I hoped the edge of it wasn't showing in my pocket.

The officer looked doubtful.

"It may help us determine why Gatsas allegedly took his life. If you know where it is, you will be withholding an important piece of evidence."

"It's gone. I threw it in the trash."

"A minute ago you said you'd misplaced it."

Dr. Polanski, in back of the officer, motioned me to give him the letter.

"Okay, I do have it here in my pocket. I didn't want to give it up as Paul entrusted me with it."

I pulled it out and handed it to him.

"It's just a letter for Chr—for God's sake. You guys are a puzzle to me."

"Why, because we're queer?" I snapped out before thinking better of it.

"Watch your temper, young man, that's not what I meant."

"Thank you, Officer." Dr. Polanski put his hand out. "Let us know if we can be of further help."

The officer stopped at the door and turned back.

"Mr. Duncan, where were you at the time the young man was found in the barn?"

CHAPTER

❧ 26 ❧

A pall hung over us all like a blanket of snow covering a tropical island. I took no satisfaction in seeing Father David and Dr. Kessler under close police scrutiny and interrogation. By contrast, Dr. Polanski rose above the fray. His air of benevolent authority and concise answers to difficult questions pushed the police in other directions.

Lingering doubts tickled my conscience from time to time as to the ethical bounds of the whole reorientation program. By the same token, we were all free agents and could leave whenever we wished. Paul was the youngest client House of Change ever admitted. The bulk of us were mid to late twenties, a few early thirties. Above that age, men were considered too set in their orientation to be reachable. I later found out that House of Change had been enticed into admitting Paul after a large financial contribution from his father. It was the perfect setup for the tragedy that resulted.

No meetings or sessions were held for several days after the catastrophe. The population soon shrank to half its normal numbers. Spivick remained, much to my annoyance, but he was a changed person. Was is it because of our altercation in the dining hall, or was it something more sinister? I never quite understand how Paul could have arranged hanging himself unaided. From that day forward to my last day there, I put a chair under my doorknob at night and attempted to never be alone with Spivick.

Having no particular place to return to, namely my apartment under Shirl's, and an almost nonexistent family, I stayed on. For whatever reason, Dr. Polanski stayed on as well; although he left shortly after I did. It grew into a deep friendship, which, ironically, through the calamity, was what the school was supposed to stand for. In other words, the younger man is to be mentored by the older man in a non-sexual, non-threatening environment. We took long walks together and discussed our philosophies. I still had hopes of the program working for me.

He suggested books for me to read, and we discussed them at length afterward. The slow realization spread through me that this was the first person—man—I had ever had a rewarding friendship without any physical overtones. I never used his first name, and he never used my last.

"Damon," he said to me one day in a one-on-one session, "why did you feel the need to change your orientation?"

I was caught completely off guard and had to think a moment. It was the most obvious question that had never been tendered to me. How cogent yet how obtuse. I turned my answer into another question.

"Can a gay person ever find happiness in this world?"

His answer rattled me. "Of course, many homosexual men and women are in very rewarding and accepting relationships."

"How can that be? All I ever hear us referred to is fags and dykes." I could feel my face growing hot, and I wondered where he was headed.

"It's the simplest yet the most difficult thing. You must know yourself, Damon. What do you really want? When you understand that about yourself, there will be no stopping you."

"I have never felt good about myself, I mean really good. The wall is always up, always on guard. Am I going to give myself away? What are people saying about me?"

"Stop right there. You're talking about people around you. What about you, your inner self?"

"I want to feel good about myself. I don't want any more rejection."

"You're talking about Carlos now."

"Yeah, I guess. I need to end this conversation. Can we pick it up later?"

"Of course, we've done enough for today."

We shook hands, and Dr. Polanski looked into my eyes.

"Give it some thought, Damon, you're a bright young man with potential for a brilliant future. Stop whipping yourself."

He patted me on the shoulder and was gone.

I stepped outside; it was a beautiful late fall day. The temperature was in the sixties, but we had had a frost just the night before. Some of the guys were playing baseball. It was a ragged crew, but they seemed to be having fun.

"Hey, Duncan," one of them called, "wanta join us? Third base is free."

"Nah, not today. Thanks."

My mind turned back to Paul. How did he manage to hang himself? I wandered over to the barn and peered up in the dim light. The rafter was very high, at least twenty feet, and the rope would have had to been tossed over it from the floor. The rope was gone. Evidence probably, or was my mind working overtime? I opened a side door and rummaged through a rough wooden sided space that adjoined the garage area. It was as tidily kept as the rest of the building. Several coils of rope were neatly hung on pegs. One peg was empty.

I lifted a coil off its holder and hefted it, ten pounds at least. A voice from behind startled me.

"What're doing?"

I spun around; it was Spivick. He was smiling, but an uneasiness invaded me. He'd followed me here. I didn't reply but slowly revolved the coil in my hand.

"I'm sorry about Paul. I know he was your friend."

"Thanks."

Spivick nodded and departed from the barn. I placed the coil back on the peg.

As the weeks slid by, an inner peace crept into my being. The wise counsel given by Dr. Polanski washed away much of the clutter from the past and lay my soul out into the warming sun. Thoughts of Carlos wafted in and out of my mind, but in a new, healthier way.

The initial shock of losing Paul faded, and I hoped he was in a better world. Two things still troubled me about his suicide, however. Why did he make a point of wanting to stay in touch after we left here if he was planning suicide? And more puzzling, how did he get the rope over the beam?

A service was held for him at the outdoor chapel many weeks later, which turned out to be quite emotional.

His last act—if it was his doing alone—touched each one of us in a most personal and sobering manner. Hadn't we all contemplated similar acts of desperation but somehow pulled ourselves back from the brink?

⁂

Time was fast approaching when we would return back to our own worlds, in varying degrees of success, to again face our challenges.

On the last day, we held a small graduation exercise. Each of us made a short speech about the progress we had made and plans for a new future. We all professed to have been helped, but there wasn't a great deal of enthusiasm. Only eight of us were left, and the event moved swiftly and was over. Spivick was one who left at the height of the investigation of Paul's death. Several of us mentioned forming a support group back in Fort Worth. It was worth noting that no new "clients" had arrived, and the place was nearly deserted when we left.

The sun was shining, and a slight breeze ruffled our hair as we marched back to the main building. I collected my few belongings and shouldered my duffel bag as I had done several months ago. The building seemed smaller as time had gone by and no longer as sinister. I plied my way back down the staircase for the last time. I said my good-byes to Dr. Kessler and Father David. Their handshakes were weak and perfunctory.

Dr. Polanski would be leaving in another week or so, returning to private practice in Dallas. He stood and approached me as I walked into his office.

"Well, Damon, you've made it through. I expect great things from you. Any plans?" I dropped my burden on a chair as we met. His handshake was firm, and he gave me a hug.

"Some heavy-duty affairs lay ahead of me." His brow wrinkled as he slipped his glasses off and wiped them with a tissue. "I told you about the rupture with my family." He nodded. "That will be the first thing to repair. And then a job."

"Don't try to do everything at once, take your time. Do it well."

I was dreading the good-byes after spending so much time with him. I sensed he felt the same. He walked me out to the Blazer, now holding three other men. Randy was at the wheel once more. Full circle. Dr. Polanski shook hands all around then touched my shoulder. I looked up, and he mouthed, "God bless and good luck." I nodded, feeling very emotional. And we were off.

As we pulled out onto the dirt road, I glanced back at the Victorian monstrosity a foolish old man built twenty-five years ago for his trophy wife. Its architectural hulk no longer as forbidding, its mass no less ugly.

✍

On the seemingly endless bus ride back to Fort Worth, we spread ourselves throughout the cabin. Our minds numbed from so much isolation, our tongues were silenced. Perhaps fear of comparing notes as to our success, or lack thereof, bedeviled us more than we cared to admit. We finally arrived in Fort Worth, and I shook hands with the guys and hailed a cab.

After a brief ride, the taxi braked in front of my apartment building. I handed the driver a twenty and assured him I could handle my bag. I threw the door open and struggled out of the backseat, yanking on the unruly duffel bag. The cab rolled away from the curb, and I stood motionless for several minutes, drinking in the vibes of the city around me. The bright sun beat down onto the sidewalk, but a chill wind swept around the building.

I tightened my jacket collar and shaded my eyes to look up at Shirl's apartment windows. Surely, after the card I had sent, she would spot me and run down. She had probably forgotten what time I would arrive. I shouldered my bag and headed for the front entrance. The same tacky, artificial fichus greeted me in the hallway as I ascended the stairs. A dank, musty odor permeated the space, now winter-chilled. Neither heat nor air-conditioning was wasted in the public areas.

It always puzzled me why such a classy lady as Shirl would rent in such an ungracious building. My mind, a swirl with amorous fantasies, pictured her waiting inside my apartment, dressed impeccably, with champagne and a feast. I would even buy a decent bed for our occasional dalliances. It was pleasing to feel somewhat aroused!

The key turned easily in the lock, and I pushed the door open. Emptiness! The only sound was steam hissing in the radiator. The rooms looked abandoned just as they had been left. Time and perspective had changed my opinion of the place. Surveying the scene, it became obvious how stark and severe it really was. After relieving my bladder, I noticed the crack in the bathroom mirror had run farther down the side and sprangled at the bottom corner.

So much for welcome home. At least it was warm.

It was late afternoon, and dusk would soon be closing in. Had I gotten beyond the fear of a dark street? Grabbing a green corduroy jacket hanging on the bedroom rack, I departed to get essentials. Shadows deepened as I turned the corner toward a convenience store. My throat tightened and my step picked up as two young men appeared at the next intersection. I stifled the urge to run. I arrived, a bit breathless, and welcomed the brightly lit store. Basic necessities half-filled my basket when I stopped at the magazine counter to pick up a copy of the *Wall Street Journal* and a local advertising rag.

After a quick perusal, I tossed it in the cart when my eye was caught by an intriguing headline on the cover of *People Magazine*, New Rock Star to Appear at American Airlines Arena.

Why I bought the magazine, I'll never know. At any rate, I tossed it into my cart and went to check out. A handsome young man cashed me through. I furtively studied his features, but there was no attraction! Unfortunately, the pretty young woman just entering the store didn't do anything for me either.

I left the store; darkness had deepened. The streets were well lighted, so I felt no impending danger. Fortunately, the hall and stairway had twenty-four-hour lighting. I locked the apartment door behind me, rested the two bags on the sink counter, and put perishables and milk into the fridge. The kettle soon whistled, and I poured boiling water over a tea bag in a new ceramic mug.

I carried it to the table, the local rag and magazine under my arm, and sat down. Nothing particular going on in town. The usual muggings, DUIs, and traffic violations. I took a couple of sips of tea and leafed through *People*.

My heart leaped when I saw a picture and story on Carlos. It was taken at a nightspot in Miami. He was wearing the white Stetson. My heart pounded, and my eyes filled with tears. I closed the magazine and slid it into a box in the bedroom.

Brushing my eyes, I was startled by a knock on the door. I hurried over.

"Is that you, Shirl?" I asked through the door.

"Fort Worth Police Department. Open the door, Mr. Duncan."

CHAPTER

27

I opened the door to a police officer and several reporters, notebooks and pens poised. What was going on? The police officer soon explained the situation. For the first several weeks, my family thought I was avoiding them. As time dragged on, they swallowed their pride and started investigating. No one had seen me, so the suspicion of foul play or accident surfaced.

"I left word with the lady upstairs in 428 where I could be reached in an emergency."

"There isn't anyone in 428. The entire building has been searched. There were only two vacancies, 428 being one of them. Do you care to explain where you have been?"

I didn't care to explain in any detail.

"I attended a retreat for the past ninety days in Ratison. The blonde upstairs was to be able to inform of my whereabouts."

"There is no blonde or anyone else in 428. We need you to come downtown to sign papers and answer some questions. What you did was no joke. A lot of people have put in countless hours searching for you." Annoyance twisted his face. "Surely you must have seen or heard reports of the search for you."

It finally sank in. What a childish, self-centered fool I had been. But where was Shirl?

"Unfortunately, one of the requirements of the retreat was no contact with the outside world. No radio, TV, or newspaper."

The officer's face reflected doubt. As we started down the stairs, flashbulbs popped, and cameras whirred. Probably this would be big news for the next several days.

Down at the precinct, I recited my desire to rectify some of the problems in my life and didn't want family involved. When I told them about my attendance at House of Change, a sergeant at the next desk glanced up sharply and motioned for several other officers to come over and listen to my story.

"Tell us what you know about any activities out there in the past several months," one of the officers inquired.

Another one held up a two-month-old newspaper. The headline screamed in huge black letter, Tragic Death at House of Change in Ratison. Prickles ran up my spine when my eyes lighted on a picture of Spivick and his two comrades. The story went on to say,

> A young man was found yesterday hanging from a beam in an adjoining barn at House of Change in Ratison. Foul play is being investigated due to circumstances surrounding the manner of death. The victim's neck was alleged to have been snapped. Three young men enrolled at the facility are being questioned. Investigations are ongoing, and the facility has been shut down. Many clients have left, pending a full investigation.

The news story continued, but I had seen enough. I blew my nose and recited the events as best I could remember them.

I knew in my heart Spivick and his buddies murdered Paul. I was charitable enough to ponder if it had been a prank that went bad.

❧

It was a difficult and demanding session going back to Ilka's to face the family. As much as I would have preferred to keep my whereabouts for the past three months to myself, in fairness, I briefly outlined my activities. Dad seemed to be recovering quite well from the stroke and gave me an awkward hug. Mom was tearful, as was I. Ilka was a mixture of relief and annoyance—light on the former, heavy on the latter.

"You might have told us," she snapped, glaring at Mom because she still had her arms around me. "We've all been out of our minds with worry, not knowing if you were dead or alive."

Mom stepped back. In a glance, I could imagine her thoughts.

"Feeling a little guilty?"

I raised an eyebrow and gave Ilka a steely stare. I felt swamped with the same old family-induced angst bedeviling me from the day Carlos and I first arrived.

"Guilty? Why would I feel guilty?"

"You should have guessed where I was after all the damned brochures you left in my room. Besides, Shirl knew. I was just one floor below."

"We finally called her, several times. No answer."

Then Ilka did something that amazed me. Her face softened, and she gave me a hug and a peck on the cheek.

"I've never been able to deal with emotion. I say things I regret afterwards." It was obvious these words had come with great difficulty. "I'm glad you're home and we can be a family again."

As her words sank in, I immediately felt on guard. Being her father's daughter, she would be hell-bent on running the family's life again, my life. I nodded, and the moment passed.

For the first fifteen or twenty minutes, the eight-hundred-pound gorilla in the room was not mentioned. I appreciated the respite but decided it best to face it head on.

"You're all wondering what results I come home with. The news is good." Everyone seemed to let out a sigh of relief. "I have a ways to go and will be joining a men's group here in Fort Worth." I don't know for sure what was going with Dad, but he looked horrified. "It's a group of former homosexual men who are dealing with a change in orientation." Relief spread across his face.

"Carlos is out of the picture for good then?" Ilka inquired, her expression indicating it was too good to be true.

I made no comment, and an uncomfortable silence ensued. Mom started to say something, but Ilka grabbed her arm and rushed her into the kitchen under the pretext of needing to get a meal onto the table. A muffled discussion ensued with protests from Mom, which I finally understood ten years later in San Diego. Had I known then, life could have been very different.

We had a relatively pleasant meal. Ilka insisted that she and Mom clear up after and Dad and I could "retire" to the porch. It was a pleasantly warm early winter day. Dad made a production of lighting a cigar and belatedly asked me if I would like to join him. I shook my head. It turned out we had little to talk about.

From the few comments he made, it became apparent that now I was "cured" I would probably be playing baseball, watching football on the tube, and pursuing other manly pleasures.

As the afternoon dragged on, I knew the further I stayed away from the family the better for everyone. Already the strain of remaining civil was wearing thin. I needed to get out and away. Over protests from Ilka, I announced my intention of returning to my apartment. I caught Mom's eye, and she nodded in understanding. That was all I needed.

Ilka insisted on driving me and, before leaving, reminded me of my duties to the family. In other words, be on hand when summoned. With great difficulty, I held my tongue and nodded. Our brief truce was over.

CHAPTER

28

For the next several days, I wandered the streets, trying to decide what to do with my life. The shadowy sidewalks in the evening posed definite problems. The edge of night in well-lighted areas offered a slow process of building back my courage. Any quick movement or unexplained steps behind me remained unnerving.

Quite by chance I passed by the place where Carlos had played piano. What a name, Warm Beer, Lousy Food, and All That Jazz. I toyed with going in for a drink but discarded the idea as soon as I considered it.

The stupidest thing I did, however, while attempting to clear the past was to revisit the motel where Carlos and I had stayed before we met up with Ilka. I rented the same room for the night with no intention of actually staying. The bad choice was immediately apparent as I slipped the key into the lock, but I pressed on anyway. My hand shook, and I felt moisture under my arms. The room looked the same, nothing out of place. But now it brought back the nightmare coming to Fort Worth had created. I sat on the edge of the bed and bawled like a baby. Had it all been a fantasy? Had I elevated the whole short affair into something it never really was?

Was I now bisexual? If Carlos were suddenly to materialize, would the same feelings still be there? Or would they slowly diminish and finally depart? Funny thing, I had no sexual longings for either men or women. Was I in the twilight zone, between two worlds that might never quite come together? Evening was settling in. If I stayed much longer, it would be dark.

Passing the window on the way out, an apparition appeared. I was standing naked with Carlos's body pressed against mine. My head spun; my breath came in gasps. I felt for the door and stumbled out. Little memory remains of my escape. I dimly recall hauling the office door open and tossing the keys onto the counter. The attendant had a stricken look as I bolted for the street. I raced several blocks before hailing a cab.

Sleep would not come that night, only a false sense of half-sleep punctuated by a blur of images and events. Nothing tied together in this Alzheimer's tangle of unrelated visions. Mike snapped into focus, and we were dancing at a gay disco. Shirl swooped in from somewhere else and tried to grab my arm. Dad had my favorite cat in his hands, threatening to strangle it unless I would play baseball. I jerked up with a start, my head pounding as I rolled off onto the floor. My knees protested against my weight as I lurched into the living room and scrambled around in my still unpacked duffel bag to retrieve my Bible. By the dim light from the single socket I sought out passages that had helped me at House of Change.

"Surely goodness and mercy shall follow you for the rest of your days, and I shall dwell in the house of the Lord forever," I read, wondering what the Lord would think when he looked into my heart.

No friends, no job, no future. Something had to give.

❧

Job hunting went much slower than I had hoped. Fort Worth is full of banks, mortgage companies, and insurance companies. Shank's mare became fruitless, so I picked up a paper at a newsstand and perused any worthwhile leads. As luck would have it, I scored an appointment with Texas Trust Company for ten the next morning.

Bathed, shaved, dressed, and coffeed, I studied myself in the cracked bathroom mirror the next morning. Today was the beginning of the rest of my life.

I arrived at the appointed hour, keyed up for the big interview. This was not to be my day, however. As I slicked my hair back one more time before entering, momentarily unaware of an obstruction on the sidewalk, I stubbed on a large carton, pitched awkwardly forward, groping for my balance, and struck my forehead on the sharp edge of a cut marble windowsill. I grabbed my handkerchief to stave off the blood from ruining my clothes, but pain jangled through my scalp. Fortunately no one inside saw my embarrassing predicament.

An attractive young woman witnessed the mishap and rushed to my aid. I soon learned she was a nurse on her way to the hospital. She checked my pulse and felt for broken bones. My left arm, still tender from the debacle now half a year ago, was unharmed. Over my protests she insisted that I go to the emergency room. I called the bank from my cell phone as we headed to the hospital, explained the situation, and rescheduled for the next day.

Dappled sunlight shining through the trees highlighted wisps of her auburn hair. Her arms and body looked frail yet somehow exhibited a strength that superseded her lack of dimension. She had a wonderful sense of humor and soon had me laughing.

We pulled into the hospital entrance, and she parked her white Maxima near the emergency entrance and tossed the keys to the parking lot attendant.

"Top of the mornin' to ya, Joan," he cried, approaching her car.

"Same to you, Les. How's the wife doing?" Sympathy sounded in her voice.

"It's a long, hard road for her, slower than we hoped." His face clouded.

"I'll stop by and see her this evening. Hang in there."

"She'd like that. Bless you."

"Take care of yourself too." He nodded, forcing a smile.

As we moved toward the entrance, she whispered to me, "Poor man, wife's got breast cancer. They hope they got it all." A far-off look was replaced by a smile. "Let's get you in there and cleaned up. By the way, my name's Joan, nice to meet you." She stuck her hand out.

"So I gathered. Nice to meet you, Joan. My name's Damon."

Her hand felt warm and firm in mine.

Passing through the waiting area, she was somewhat surprised when the staff recognized me and treated me like an old friend. The aha moment came for her when she saw my last name on the clipboard.

"I was in ER when you were brought in. You looked like someone tried to make hamburger out of you." I winced. "Now that wasn't very nice of me, you'd been through hell. Sorry."

"Don't be. It's in the past, at least most of the time." She nodded, and I felt she would like to hear more. "While we're on the subject, I might as well mention the OD."

"Not unless you want to."

She smiled, taking my left arm for testing blood pressure. She slipped the stethoscope under the cuff on my forearm, pumped it up, and slowly released it. Then she pumped it up again. A slight frown crossed her features.

"Your BP is 147 over 89. That's a bit high. Have you had problems in the past?"

"It's apt to go up when I have an injury."

"What is it normally?" She released the cuff and slid it off my arm.

"Around 110 over 70. Maybe it's your charm," I said with a roguish smile.

"Now, Damon," she admonished, a twinkle in her eye, "I may be a sucker for flattery, but we need to get you patched up now."

I groaned when the gurney arrived, and she held my hand as I loaded on.

"Is this necessary?" I complained weakly.

"We need to CT that head. We don't want you walking around with a concussion."

Everything about her made me feel warm and protected.

"Can we go for coffee after?" I wrinkled my brow as they rolled me along.

"Sure, I'll look in on you a bit later."

Finding no problem with the CT scan, Joan was still concerned because of a sluggishness in my left eye. She did a neurological exam and pronounced me okay. The emergency-room doctor applied an antibiotic ointment dressing and sutured the cut. I was to return in four days for their removal.

I idled around in the waiting area, hoping to see Joan again. I looked through most of the magazines and finally decided it was foolish to think she would bother to come back.

Just as I was stepping through the automatic door, someone tapped me on the shoulder.

"Trying to run away without buying me the coffee, huh?"

I spun around and grabbed Joan's hand, delighted to see her again.

PART 2

CHAPTER

⪧ 1 ⪦

Carlos slept little that last night. The steady strum, strum, strum of the building's mechanicals suddenly sounded louder now that he would be leaving soon. Five months of his life gone, and for what? He rolled over for the fiftieth time and raised himself up on one elbow, staring at the bars, pondering. Funny how things you must bear become almost unbearable when the end is in sight. He flopped back down, cradling a hand under his head, thinking of the future. In the morning, he was being sprung a month early on good behavior. Good behavior, what a laugh. He'd practically killed a guy his second night in prison. The bastard had earned it though. And he'd never been bothered by any of those losers since. The real reason he was being released early, he figured, was because they needed the space.

He'd let his hair grow back and shaved his beard the last couple of weeks; just a V remained below his lower lip. He'd had two thousand dollars when he was arrested. And then there was the white Stetson. As for the bottle of steroids, which Haines had probably planted on him, one of the arresting officers would be strutting around with broader shoulders by now, he surmised.

The key rattled in his cell door at 6:00 a.m. The last time he'd hear that. He shook hands with his cellmate, and they did a peremptory hug, wishing each other well. Carlos had earned the respect of many other prisoners, and they gave him the high five as he passed by. The smell of urine and industrial cleaner trailed him as he followed the guard out to an anteroom.

He was offered his belongings. Easing the hat back onto his head was the first taste of freedom. Everything seemed to be in order until he opened his wallet. Both credit cards and the cash were missing. A rage swelled in him as he slammed his fist on the desk.

"Where the fuck's the money?" He shoved his face six inches away from the guard's.

"Does it say anything about that on the list you're holding?" Insolence oozed in his response.

Carlos perused the paper more carefully. "Right there under the Wite-Out," he stammered, his finger shaking as he pointed it out.

"What seems to be the trouble here, Bravara?" The desk sergeant shuffled into the room, hitching his britches up under the weight of his revolver.

"This here asshole has accused us of stealing his money." The guard wiped his hand across his mouth where dark brown goo streaked out. "Fuckin' rules," he snarled under his breath. "No smoking allowed in public buildings."

The sergeant patted Carlos on the shoulder. "Get back into your street clothes, and we'll see about the money and cards." He winked and moved back out to the front desk.

Carlos was not mollified. Rage continued to build, but he tried his best to stem it. Not now, the first thing is to leave this place far behind. The money would come again. He had developed plans and made contacts during the long days of confinement. A guy in Hollywood with the right connections that he had been in touch with months before jail had been able to assure Carlos that a job would be waiting. He took a quick shower and shaved. His image in the mirror looked a trifle gaunt as he ran a brush over his short hair. Shit, at least he'd leave with his head held high.

The sergeant nodded as Carlos appeared before him. He glanced either way to see that no one was watching, reached down to a desk drawer, fumbled with a collection of keys on his belt, pulled out a bulky envelope, and handed it to Carlos. He lowered his voice.

"Some of the slimy cocksuckers around here couldn't wait to get their hands on this money. It's been in, shall we say, protective custody these past five months."

Carlos tore it open and flipped through the edges of the bills, a smile developing.

"I owe ya."

He stashed it in his inner jacket pocket.

"What's yours is yours, brother," the sergeant replied, spreading his hands.

Carlos reached up, and they shook, a strong connection holding a bit longer than necessary. The emotional impact of this day staggered him.

"I'll deny I ever said this, but I know you got railroaded in this deal. Somebody had it in for you and forced us to confront you that night."

"A woman?" Carlos asked, regaining his equilibrium a bit.

"Yeah, a woman."

They eyed each other.

"And the note?"

"Couldn't say, buddy." Apprehension clouded his face. "Watch yourself. Good luck, brother."

Their eyes met again. First the policewoman at the front desk, and now the sergeant. No matter the everyday shit they dealt with, trust was not always lacking.

Carlos slid the Stetson forward then tipped his head back.

"What about the restraining order?"

"For six months, couldn't be cancelled. They gave you a month off for good behavior. The pills"—he spread his hands—"bottom of Trinity River for all I know."

"Got a phone I can use?"

"Local?"

"LA."

"Pay phone down the hall." He hesitated." You never used your one call. Use the phone in there." He jabbed a thumb toward a small office. "Don't overdo it."

A lot rested on this call; this could just be the big step. He punched in the numbers from a slip of paper he held braced against the wall.

"Hudson? I just got sprung," Carlos crowed, his eyes running around the smoky walls. "Have we got a deal?"

"All right!" Hudson, the owner, manager of JAH Talent Agency exclaimed. "Get your ass out here by tomorrow. I'm putting a male dance team together, taking it to Vegas."

"Hot shit, I'll be there. Got one more thing to take care of here first."

"Tomorrow, cowboy, ya hear?"

Carlos gave the sergeant a thumbs-up and pushed the heavy door open, meeting the Texas sun. A free man again.

It was late evening when the rented Chevy Impala slowed across the street from Ilka's, then pulled around the corner out of sight and came to a halt. Darkness enveloped the vehicle save for the intermittent glow of a cigarette butt as Carlos inhaled. He'd picked the habit up again in jail. He finally stubbed it out in the ashtray and stepped cautiously out. Anticipation sparked as he crossed the street, paused, and then strode up to the door. What terrible memories this place held. He put his hand up to knock then withdrew it.

"Hell, what am I doing here?"

He turned, indecision trailing him back down the walk.

Reaching the street, he stopped and twisted the Stetson around in his hand. Punching his forefinger into the crown, he placed it back on his head at an angle much as Damon had done.

"I need to give it one more try before I leave," he said under his breath.

He turned and rambled toward the door. The curtains were pulled back in the front window, revealing a man seated where he had last seen Damon and a woman, probably both in their fifties. He tapped on the door.

"I'll get it," a woman's voice called.

There ensued a rattling of the lock as the middle-aged woman opened the door, leaving the chain in place. Lack of recognition blanketed her face as she peered through the screen door.

"Sorry to bother you, ma'am, but I'm looking for Damon. Is he in?"

Before she could answer, Ilka appeared. She made a guttural sound in her throat.

"What do you want?" she asked, leaving the door on the chain.

"Damon, of course," he replied between clenched teeth. His hands were thrust deep into his pockets, fingers flexing. He hated this woman, but he attempted to control himself. The need to see Damon, talk with him, maybe hold him in his arms, twisted his gut into a knot.

"You know as much about where he is as I do."

Her face was set in anger and distrust.

Carlos was startled, a chill clutched at his heart.

"Come on, Ilka, that's bullshit." He held her eye, but she didn't flinch. He half-believed she might be telling the truth. "Tell him I stopped by."

"He wanted to be far away when you got out is all I know."

She slammed the door.

The main hope sustaining him in prison was the possibility that the relationship might be rekindled. The letter in prison from Damon rustling in his pocket stank of Ilka's hand. Why had he hung on to that evil document? Should he have engaged Ilka in more conversation? Smoked her out?

He plodded toward the car, head down, slid in, hands clutching the wheel, head tipped back, Stetson covering his eyes.

The early evening sounds of Fort Worth quieted for the balance of the night.

∽

Carlos awoke with a start as the sun peeped up over the city.

"Shit, I've got a plane to catch."

With barely minutes to spare, he raced into the terminal and picked up the ticket he had reserved yesterday morning when he left jail. The walkway was about to be wheeled away when he rushed through and met the stewardess. A pretty blonde, she eyed him with interest, checked his boarding pass and indicated his spot by a window. Sprawled in his seat, he studied an entertainment magazine he'd found in prison.

"California, here I come!"

CHAPTER

2

Carlos was hired on the spot by the JAH Talent Agency office. Their subsequent relationship involved much more than the usual bargaining and contracts. Yes, indeed.

After a week of strenuous rehearsals, Carlos appeared in John Hudson's office for edification of his contract. Carlos had been aware of Hudson's interest in him far beyond the exercise floor.

"So you never fucked a woman till you were twenty-five, huh? What were ya doing, saving yourself for marriage?" Hudson snorted, lifted an eyebrow, and smirked at Carlos. He propped his cigarette on an ashtray and removed a bit of tobacco from his tongue.

"Something like that." Carlos was clad in loose-fitting white cargo shorts that rested low on his hip bones. A shiny neck chain dangled to his navel, and the gold stud glinted in his left earlobe. His buffed shoulders and ruddy complexion appeared even darker against the white fabric.

"So been married, I presume."

Hudson glanced again at Carlos's crotch. His hand shook slightly when he lifted the butt back to his lips and took another drag. Smoke encircled his face for a moment, and he coughed. He looked back at Carlos, one eyebrow cocked.

"Nah, decided against it,"

"I thought you said…" Hudson hesitated.

Carlos shrugged. "Go figure."

"With your looks the girls must be all over you."

"Or the boys," Carlos replied with a flick of his wrist, eyes boring into Hudson.

The blush started at Hudson's shirt collar and spread up over his face. Carlos enjoyed tormenting him over making such a big deal of being married while at the same time eyeing all the male dancers.

"So am I making the grade for your Vegas show?" he asked, legs spread, hands on hips, rocking forth and back on the balls of his feet.

"Shit, yes. You have to ask?" He took a pile of papers, shuffled them, and dumped them into a file folder. "You can dance circles around the other guys, and you haven't got a freaking nerve in your whole freaking body." He looked Carlos up and down, his eyes gleaming, beads of sweat forming on his brow. "You're going places, young man. Ever thought of getting an agent?"

"It's crossed my mind. Why? You interested?"

"I could make you a star. The talent you have, shit, you're one in a million. Most of the young guys who come along"—he pointed at the practice hall next door—"want to hit the big time with a pretty face and no talent."

"I'm not so young anymore, turned twenty-six a coupla months ago."

"Come off it, boy. You've got a good fifteen, twenty years ahead of you. By then you won't need to get it up anymore."

"I'm not planning to make my career 'getting it up,' not after a while anyway. I've got other plans, big plans."

"That's why I want to help. I believe in your talent."

"And the 10 percent off the top."

"Twenty."

"Like hell! Dig up some other chump." He turned as if leaving.

"Hold on, Bravara. Seventeen and I'll make some calls right now." He reached for the phone, holding his other hand out to Carlos, motioning him back and pointing to a chair.

Carlos hesitated, turned, but didn't sit. He leaned a hand on Hudson's desk, picked up the ashtray, and flipped it into the wastebasket.

"Get rid of the butts, they give me a headache."

Hudson placed the phone back into the cradle, annoyance distorting his face.

"Fifteen percent, one-year deal, that's it." Carlos locked eyes with Hudson.

"You're one arrogant son of a bitch." Hudson reached into the basket, retrieved the ashtray, and placed it back on his desk with a thump. "I usually get 20 percent. You're not exactly Elvis Presley, ya know."

Carlos eyed the ashtray. "And you're not exactly Colonel Parker."

Hudson covered the ashtray with his hand and pulled it toward him. "That was a gift from someone."

"Was he cute?" Carlos settled into the chair, feet outstretched, hands behind his head.

"Bravara"—Hudson stood up and came around the desk and tapped Carlos on the chest with his index finger—"you wanta get somewhere in this business, you gotta kiss a little ass. Ya know what I mean?"

Carlos stood up, a good eight inches taller than Hudson, stuck his thumbs in the waistband of his shorts, and hitched them down a notch lower. "Fifteen percent and these'll be around my ankles."

"Good Christ, Bravara." He grazed the corner of his mouth with the back of his hand. His upper lip twitched, and sweat soaked the underarms of his silk shirt. "Let's see what I'm buying." He reached for Carlos's zipper.

"Whoa, not so fast. Let's see you make out one of those contracts you've got there on your desk." Carlos took Hudson's wrist, grabbed his shoulder, and spun him back to the desk.

"You drive a hard bargain, Bravara," Hudson replied, voice unsteady, tongue licking sweat off his upper lip.

"We get that contract signed and you'll know what hard really is."

Hudson's eyes kept flicking toward Carlos's crotch. He had trouble separating out papers, and his hand shook as he scratched some figures onto a page.

Carlos released the top button and let the shorts start to slide. They halted as thicker pubic hair appeared, stopping just above the shaft of his penis.

"Let's have a look at those papers."

"Check 'em out all you want, you cocky son of bitch."

His face was scarlet now, and his hands shook as he turned the papers toward Carlos, pen in hand.

Carlos collected the papers, scanning from one page to the next. He nodded slowly, leaned forward, signed his name, and eased his zipper down, and his shorts slid to the floor.

"Holy shit, man," Hudson managed to spit out, "you could make a living off that monster alone."

He stood up, the front of his pants bulging, and knelt in front of Carlos.

Carlos pushed him away.

"Got a condom?"

"Hey, wait a minute, I'm not into that scene."

A touch of alarm spread across his face. The ticktick of his rapid pulse was visible in his neck.

Carlos grabbed Hudson's belt buckle, pulled the tab back, whisked it out of the loops, and tossed it across the room. He kicked his own shorts out of the way, yanking Hudson's pants down at the same time.

"Wait, now hold it right there, Bravara. This is all out of hand. You're getting the wrong idea here. I just wanted a little fun, no rough stuff."

He backed away, weakly holding his hands out in defense.

"Cut the shit, Hudson, you've had it up the ass more times than I can count on ten hands."

He reached for the contract papers then bent over to retrieve his shorts and started to slip them on.

Hudson grabbed Carlos's hand.

"Let's not be hasty here."

He began unbuttoning his shirt. He wore no undershirt and had the image of a serpent tattooed on his hairy chest, head and tail wrapped around his nipples. The shirt slid to the floor, and he stood naked.

Carlos stepped back, left elbow in his right palm, chin resting in hand. He walked around Hudson, appraising his body and saying "Hmm" several times, nodding in grudging approval. "Maybe ten pounds off the midsection and a little gym time, hmm." He poked and prodded Hudson's body as he continued the inspection.

"For Christ's sake, man, have I gotta beg?"

Hudson's body trembled. It appeared as though his knees might buckle.

"Why not?"

Carlos paused then knelt in front of Hudson and grasped his pulsing erection in his mouth. After a few deep strokes, Hudson climaxed into Carlos's mouth. Carlos gagged and spit. Hudson's whole body crumpled. Carlos caught him around the waist while Hudson gave him a sloppy kiss on the mouth. Carlos half-dragged him to the couch, where he deposited Hudson's sweaty body into a heap. Carlos slid on his shorts, preparing to leave.

"Wait, wait. One more thing, I want some pictures. I'll need them for advertising."

Regaining some composure, he slipped into a robe.

Carlos turned back.

"Sure, I'll need some professional photos, head shots. Who does your work?"

"No, I mean right here. I've got a digital camera, and we can look at them. I'll bring 'em up on the computer."

Carlos turned and grabbed Hudson by the shoulders.

"Sure, pictures of me jerking off, close-ups of my cock. You lousy little weasel." He gave Hudson a push with both hands onto his desk and clutched him by the lapels. "Yeah, they'll look great on the front cover of *Advocate Men*."

Hudson pushed his body forward, circled the desk, and sat down with a thump. He played with the ashtray with one finger, swirling it on its edge while eyeing Carlos. He spun around in his leather chair and looked out the window. He gestured toward the street with a flourish of his arm.

"The streets are full of talented people out there who'd give their right arm to have the opportunity I'm offering a cocksucker like you. You've got me by the balls with that contract I signed, under duress, I might add. Don't try to mess around anymore with me or shoot your mouth off about what happened here. Cross me up and you'll never get work again in this town. Do we understand each other?"

"I think we understand each other perfectly. I'll live up to my end of the bargain, and we'll both be rich. You live up to yours, and we'll both be richer. Now that's what we both want, isn't it?"

Carlos approached the desk with his hand out.

"One more thing."

Carlos gripped Hudson's hand.

"Oh Jesus, don't kill it now." He wrinkled his forehead. "What is it?"

A broad grin spread over Carlos's face. "You're getting it up the ass next time."

"Get out of here," Hudson said, a gleam in his eye, releasing his hand. "Promises, promises."

∽

It had all started as a fluke for Carlos. First step, a rigorous schedule of voice training, dance movements, rehearsals, and more rehearsals. Then on to Vegas. Carlos and ten other male singers/

dancers cavorted their scantily clad bodies in front of a mostly female audience at the Sands.

After a few performances, Carlos flew back to Hudson's office in LA. Hudson was ecstatic.

"Let the other swinging dicks entertain those Vegas bitches. You're wasting your time there."

Carlos, dressed in white slacks, white golf shirt, three buttons open, rested his green-and-white Skechers on the edge of Hunter's desk.

"Whatcha got in mind?"

"I've got plans for ya, babe, big plans. You've got the voice, you've got the movements, and God knows you've got the looks!" He twirled around in his desk chair. "You're a solo act, a headliner. But you'll need a few good musicians for backing. Know anyone from your Boston days that need sunshine and warm weather?"

"Yeah, as a matter of fact, I do. Remember Jerry Haines? He's working a hole-in-the-wall nightclub in Miami. He's a real prick and owes me a bundle. He's been after me to join him."

"Is he any good? We don't want just any motherfucker. The act has got to have class."

Carlos dropped his feet off the desk and leaned forward.

"You bank roll us on a flight to Miami, judge for yourself. We can catch his act and see what you think. No need for him to know who you are or what we're up to. Trust me, he'll go for it."

∽

Carlos and Hudson found Haines playing in a small Miami club, struggling to meet payroll. He had a band called Night Paving Now. The men were all seasoned musicians who couldn't get work due to drug charges and prior arrests, among other liabilities. No other promoter wanted to take the risk. Grease the wheels a little and Haines could pull it off, Carlos assured Hudson.

Carlos joined the group for the next several nights to thunderous applause. Live performing thrilled him. He could have sung all night.

"He's our boy," Hudson said, slapping Carlos on the back, enthused after the place closed down for the night. "Think we can make a deal with him?"

"We're filling the joint here every night now. He's got everything to lose if I leave."

"Listen to this, babe. Bon Jovi's sick. Gotta take a month off."

"So what's that got to do with us?" His ego was instantly excited, however.

"Word's out the American Airlines Arena's in a fuckin' bind. They've got Margaret Cho to open, but they need a musical act. A two-week opening."

"Right, Haines and I can replace Bon Jovi. In your dreams."

"Where's your confidence, babe? You can do it."

Carlos paced around, his head spinning with possibilities.

"Maybe we could dress the guys up, put on plenty of makeup, keep 'em away from booze and broads for the run, and change their names. No leaks to the press. Hold back on the money till the gig's over."

"One thing more, you okay with dropping your last name, babe?" Hudson encouraged. "Carlos Santos has a better ring."

"To start with anyway. You're the boss."

Early buzz had gotten out about Carlos, so the booking agent for the hotel, desperate to fill the void, agreed to listen to an audition. Carlos took a chance and dressed in cutoff jeans, a sweatshirt with chopped-off sleeves, and scuffed sneakers.

"Want me for my talent, not my looks," he said to the mirror, ripping a bit more on one pant leg.

At the club, he made an exaggerated bow to the talent agent, who peered down at his clipboard, looking sour.

Carlos sprang into action. He belted out a Beatles's song, joked with the piano player, broke into an impromptu dance number, and finished by leaping off the stage and playing harmony on the piano with his elbows. The booking agent knew talent when he saw it, and he would be the dude that introduced Carlos to the jaded Miami scene.

Carlos was signed on the spot. His hand shook scribbling his name.

Haines was included in the deal but feigned unhappiness since his billing would be smaller and placed under Carlos's name. But Carlos knew Haines wouldn't miss out on this for a million bucks.

Hudson had a batch of posters made up and spread throughout the city. Fans tore them down as fast as they were put up, Carlos's face landed on every young girl's (and gay guy's) bedroom wall in South Beach and beyond. *Good Morning America*, filming a story in Miami, caught the hype, and Katie Couric agreed to interview "the new Elvis."

Carlos was all over the set. He played on the Baldwin while the grips pushed it around as he danced in sync with the music he was playing. He reclined on the piano cover and serenaded Katie while reaching down to finger a couple of notes. He jumped off and pulled her into a dance and finished by whirling around as she tipped backwards in his arms. After the interview part of his appearance, he gave Katie a big buss on the cheek and pulled a dozen roses from out of his Stetson. The act was carefully set up by a magician, also appearing later.

Through the two-hour show, shots of him working the curtain, taking over one of the cameras, putting on headphones, and directing were interspersed. A final shot of him, shirt unbuttoned, gesturing at a poster advertising his two-week gig at the American Airlines Arena.

The Internet and NBC were abuzz after the segment aired.

CHAPTER

3

The humid early evening air pulsated with excitement as a rowdy crowd of young people waited impatiently for the American Airlines Arena doors to be thrown open.

Introducing new singing sensation Carlos Santos with Jerry Haines's and Night Paving Now.

The doors unlocked at seven; the show started at eight thirty. Margaret Cho, the first act, appeared on stage, wearing a white Stetson and a tie-dyed muumuu. She was in rare form, and her raunchy humor stirred the rambunctious crowd into hooting and clapping in unison.

Sweat stood out on Carlos's brow as he fidgeted and paced around backstage. A lot was riding on him tonight, and he was feeling the tension. This was a rare break few new entertainers were lucky enough to receive.

Adrenalin pumping, he clambered down the back stairs, stage left, trotted across the lower level, and bounded back up a stairway near the front entrance, where he waited in the shadows. Life-sized posters of Carlos wearing an open vest, jeans, and cowboy boots were splashed on the walls. His heart beat faster, more from excitement than exertion, but he had confidence in his own talent, and he was ready. This vantage point allowed him to see the theater but not be seen. After scoping out the packed-to-the-rafters crowd, he rapidly retraced his steps. Jerry Haines's group was in full sway; the seven members regaled in jeans and shiny red shirts. Cho gave a parting monologue and swept off stage.

Pandemonium broke out as the PA system blared forth, "Ladies and gentlemen, guys and dolls, and all of the rest of ya, Miami's South Beach is proud to present the new singing sensation, Carlos Santos! Give him a big hand."

The audience went wild, screaming, clapping, and chanting, "We want Carlos, we want Carlos!" Eager spectators fanned themselves with program folders and climbed onto the seats, jostling each other in an attempt to catch a first glimpse. A spectacular light show ricocheted on the stage backdrop. A rapidly modulating kaleidoscope of colors swirled from red to green to blue to white; sparklers flashed and twirled. Glittery streamers projected out over the jubilant crowd; the whole building seemed to sway. Night Paving Now was barely audible above the racket. The house lights dimmed as a blue spotlight exploded onto Carlos, stage left, mike in hand.

Haines's group broke into a rousing "Hard to Handle" as Carlos swaggered forward, belting out the words in his full, husky baritone. He wore tight, faded black jeans, a black leather vest, unbuttoned, and neck chains dangling to his waist. He used a black Stetson as a prop, dropping it on his tipped back head, peering out from under the brim, shoving it back with finger on crown, scooping it off, and twirling it.

Fans jammed the edge of the platform, reaching toward him as he moved forward, touching as many fans as possible. For the next fifty minutes, he commandeered the place, singing, dancing intricate steps, prancing down into the audience, touching, shaking hands, then going back onto the stage, never missing a beat.

ℝ

The intermission over, the crowd chanted, "We want Carlos, we want Carlos!" He sprinted onto the stage clad in ragged blue jeans, red torso shirt with slits across the chest, a plaid bandana tied around his head, fringed leather wrist straps, and black cowboy boots. He waved his arms for the crowd to quiet so he could field some questions.

"Got a wife?" a young woman shouted.

"Not yet. Ya offering?"

The girl nodded, blushed, and fanned herself. He blew her a kiss. Catcalls and shrieks rippled through the ecstatic crowd.

"Where ya from?" a young man shouted over the din.

"Miami's my hometown."

The crowd roared and cheered; items of clothing and papers were thrown into the air.

"What comes after your stint here?" a middle-aged woman called out.

"Probably a coronary."

A unanimous groan built up. "No way," they chanted.

"Back to the music, guys," he shouted as the jubilant audience whistled and cheered. A stool sat in the middle of the stage. He grabbed it and swung it around like a dance partner, fast-stepping and whirling. The stage was alive with drumming and guitars twanging; lights swirled from all directions. Carlos went to the keyboard, whipping the stool under him and pounding out "Help" while the band members joined him in riotous gyrations. Mike in hand, he belted out song after song one into another, singing and clowning, then rocketed around the stage amid cacophonous yelling and applauding.

Later, he ceremoniously wiped his brow with a huge handkerchief from his rear pocket and settled himself onto the stool. The audience cheered their approval. He had the crowd in the palm of his hand, and he knew it. The last song of the night was his own composition. He leaned back, one heel on a stool rung, the other pressed onto the stage. His voice, huskier than ever, caressed the mic. He gazed over the audience, wishing Damon was among them. He paused between each stanza. The fractious crowd quieted to savor each word.

After you left, my love
After our last good-bye
You left me bereft, my love
I wanted to cry
After you left, my love
After our last good-bye
Gray clouds in the sky above
I wanted to die

But I will go on with life
There'll be others I know
I will hold to my heart a wife
And children to grow

They say time will heal each wound
The past will recede with time
My life is again resumed
And you stray from my mind

But you're still here in my heart.

He sang several choruses as the audience remained breathlessly quiet, many dabbing at their eyes, absorbing the words, so personal and heartfelt. For several seconds after the last chorus, a hush pervaded the hall. Then there was a standing ovation, and cheers resounded.

The spell was finally broken by Night Paving Now tearing into a raucous, upbeat Matchbox Twenty song, drums and cymbals pounding and crashing, bass twirling as band members gyrated across the stage. In the commotion, Carlos was able to slip out. He stopped in a narrow passageway and leaned his arm against a post. He had gotten what he wanted—to entertain, to work a crowd, to let loose with all that was inside himself. Yet there was this emptiness.

The cheering and chanting continued until he exploded back on stage and crooned a couple more love songs, the band once more sounding off so he could exit.

His reverie was short-lived as a swarm of fans, autograph books in hand, converged onto the backstage, spotted Carlos, and surged forward. The police assigned to the hotel did their best to allay the crowd but could only do so much. Carlos was squeezed into a corner, scribbling his name onto slips of paper, programs, and anything else that could be found. One girl wanted to buy his "sweaty" underpants. Another even wanted him to autograph her boob. He felt a moment of panic as the crowd pressed against him.

"Back off, guys, give me room to breathe. I'll sign your programs if you'll give me some space."

The crowd thinned very little over the next hour. Carlos noted a young man of giant proportions edging around in the background. Carlos tried to catch the young man's eye, but he appeared to be shy. Carlos wanted to encourage him forward, but the boy suddenly disappeared. His demeanor indicated though an autograph would be a great thrill.

"Thanks a million, guys," he finally shouted over the din. "I'm bushed and need to crash."

The police commenced pushing the crowd back amid groans and protests.

The usual collection of bras and panties cluttered the auditorium after the noisy, high-spirited crowd filtered out. Carlos's dressing room was a quagmire of gifts, flowers, candy, even a gift-wrapped box of condoms with a perfumed note. Haines and his guys crowded into Carlos's dressing room, high-fiving and slapping each other on the back. Everyone was revved up, and jokes and insults flew like moths jabbing a luminous post lantern.

Many fans waited outside by the rear entrance till after midnight, cameras ready, hoping to get a shot with him. Anticipating this eventuality, Hudson told Carlos not to worry; he had a comfortable oversized couch installed in the dressing room. A toilet and shower made the accommodations complete. Hudson checked with Carlos and also ordered steaks and salads plus champagne. Carlos could hear Hudson fussing around the room, arranging and rearranging after the rowdy band left.

He emerged from the shower with a towel around his waist just as Hudson opened the bottle of champagne.

"Here's to the star." He handed a foaming glass to Carlos, and they clinked.

Carlos took a sip and flopped onto a comfortable chair and scratched his head, deep in contemplation. Hudson dragged a chair up and straddled it, facing Carlos.

"A penny for your thoughts."

"I'm thinking of the old Peggy Lee song, "Is That All There Is?" He set his drink down and rubbed his thigh, a hint of sadness in his voice. He rose, crossed the room, and offhandedly fingered his white Stetson lying on the table.

"Is that all there is? Christ, man, what more could you want? You've got the music world at your feet. We're going to have so many offers there won't be time enough to fill 'em in twenty years."

"When I'm on stage, I'm top of the world. It's the most wonderful feeling when I'm connecting with the audience."

"Hey, what's eatin' ya, babe?"

Carlos stepped over to the piano and fingered a couple of bars from several recent hit records then a couple of lines from "After You Left, My Love." He stopped, whirled on the stool toward Hudson.

"How do you go about finding somebody who's missing, someone who may be in danger?"

Hudson looked startled. "In danger? Who?"

Carlos made no reply.

"Hire a private dick, I guess."

"Know any good ones in the Dallas-Fort Worth area?"

"The phone book's full of names." He lifted the metal dome off a plate. "Have some food, you'll feel better." Hudson slashed off a piece of steak, stabbed it with his fork, stuffed it into his mouth, and chewed. "Good, have some."

"Not just anyone, someone discreet. I don't want this person to know he's being traced."

He lifted the other lid, took a bowl of Caesar salad, and paced around, hardly noticing what he was eating.

"Okay, so who's this wonder boy you've been mooning over?" He looked annoyed but didn't meet Carlos's glare.

"It's a long story, something you wouldn't understand." He slid into a chair and hacked off a piece of steak. "He's a small-town guy, naïve as hell, the best friend a guy could ever have," he replied between mouthfuls.

"And a great fuck?"

"I won't argue that."

"Anything to do with your being in jail?"

Carlos looked disgruntled. "Yeah, in a way. But you keep your nose out of this, ya hear?"

Hudson's face reddened; he started to argue back then thought better of it.

"I'm bushed, gotta get some shut-eye." Carlos jumped up and pumped Hudson's hand with a firm grip. "Thanks, man, for everything. You've been great to me, especially the accommodations. Couldn't face the crazies out there tonight."

"Lock your door."

"Yes, Mother, I'm a big boy now."

"You can say that again." Hudson patted his butt and smirked.

CHAPTER

4

Carlos awoke with a start. Was that a car backfiring? A pistol shot?

Silence.

He settled down again onto the pillow, punching it into a more comfortable position, sighed, and closed his eyes again. A loud knock sounded on the door.

Shit! Should have told Hudson he'd rather return to the hotel. What time is it?

He groped around for the light switch and squinted at his watch, 3:00 a.m.

Who the hell could this be?

He threw off the sheet and slipped into his robe.

"Yeah, who's there?"

"Police, Mr. Bravara, there's been an accident. You need to come with me."

Carlos was immediately alarmed. Who could it be? Accidents in Boston raced through his mind. But this was Miami. An officer stood at the open door and flashed his badge, Kirk McVey, in a gloved hand. He looked familiar, about Carlos's size, well built, probably midthirties, but the name and face didn't quite register. Carlos motioned him in. Something about his eyes gave Carlos a queasy feeling. Trouble?

"It's been a long evening. Afraid I'm a little groggy. What's this about, Officer?"

"Your agent has been in an automobile accident. He's calling for you."

"Oh Christ. Bad?"

Carlos stomach did flip-flops. Hudson could be a pain, but they were starting to get their act together.

"I'm afraid so."

"Let me get some clothes on. I'll be right with you." He slipped into jeans and a T-shirt and wiggled his feet into sneakers, fingers clumsy tying the lacings. Nerves.

The officer watched every movement; it felt like being cruised. As they were ready to leave, Carlos's back partly turned, he saw McVey pick up a couple of pieces of fruit and some chocolates and slide them into his pocket.

"Oh yeah, help yourself."

McVey didn't seem embarrassed and took some more. Carlos's radar was working overtime now, and he didn't like the reception. What was it about McVey that was so spooky? Should I know him? Why?

They moved to the door.

"After you, Mr. Bravara." They stepped into the passage, and McVey flipped the lock on the door and motioned Carlos toward the back entrance.

A chill ran up his spine. "How did you know where to find me?" They were out on the pavement now with just the light over the exit door for illumination. Carlos cast his gaze around, no security vehicle.

McVey ignored the question and pointed to a vehicle barely visible in the darkness.

"Over there."

Carlos searched for company markings and lights on the roof, being pretty familiar with police in the past. It was a big car, probably a Lincoln, ten years old anyway, not a typical cruiser. His scalp tightened, and his lungs squeezed. This was a setup; he probably had a gun. Nothing to do but play along. He opened the passenger door and slid in. Okay, he could overpower McVey while he drove and grab the wheel.

McVey stood by the door.

"Move over behind the wheel."

This was Carlos's chance. He started to slide over then made a quick lunge for McVey, his head ramming McVey square in the gut. McVey grunted and staggered backward, catching his heel on the pavement. Carlos felt himself yanked violently forward when McVey grabbed his shirt as he fell. Carlos crashed atop McVey, his knees connecting painfully with the pavement. Fingernails scratched angrily across Carlos's face. The rough hardtop dug into his body as they wrestled back and forth, neither gaining the advantage.

Carlos ended up astride him again. He felt the warm pulse in McVey's throat while pressing his thumbs into the soft flesh of his neck. McVey played dead. Suddenly, he arched his midsection up with a jerk and bounced up onto his knees. Carlos was dislodged, his arm grinding onto the blacktop. McVey pounced, and Carlos felt his breath strangled with the pressure of an arm around his neck from behind. He clawed and bit at flesh. He sank his elbows back into McVey's ribcage and felt the stranglehold loosen. He twisted sidewise and ducked out of McVey's grasp. He drove a heel into his assailant's groin and made a dash across the parking lot.

He glanced back over his shoulder. McVey was nowhere in sight. He grabbed the backstage door handle where they had just exited; the latch was immobile. He shook the door and kicked it. No dice. The bastard must have flipped the lock. Carlos hauled air in and out, throat dry, knees starting to shake. Where the hell was McVey?

He broke into a run, hugging the building, then cautiously broke out into the open and crossed a couple of streets, eyes constantly checking over his shoulders. One more glance back before ducking into an alley. He stood absolutely quiet, leaning against a brick wall, catching his breath. The muggy night air seemed to stick to his body.

A couple of minutes passed. No sound. Then a car started up and screeched out onto the street. Unsure what to do next, he hauled ass up the narrow alley, hoping it came out onto the street. He trolled his hands along the crumbling brick walls, hoping to feel a door. His head painfully connected with a grillwork barrier. He was staggered by the impact for a moment before regaining his balance. He groped for a handle, but a heavy padlock held it firmly in place. Razor wire bit into his fingers along the top of the gate.

Nothing to do but go back. He ran his bruised fingers along the uneven walls again, might have missed a door. The eerie glow from a light over the back of a building reflected faintly into the opening about ten feet from the exit. The only sound was a faint rumble of the city in the distance. A touch of vertigo set in; he wished now he'd gone a little easier on the champagne.

The guy's got to want something real bad. He's had plenty of time to circle around and come back. What to do?

The bastard would nail him the instant he stepped back out into the street. He slid his back down the rough and uneven brick wall to a sitting position and tipped his head forward as though resting and waited.

He soon sensed McVey creeping in. His heart pounded so loud McVey must have been able to hear it. Using the same ploy again, he lunged. McVey was ready this time and sidestepped. Carlos landed flat on his belly; pain radiating through his nose and chin. McVey landed on top, and they wrestled again. Struggling for an advantage, Carlos pinned one arm down, but McVey swung at him with the butt of his pistol. It connected with Carlos's head, and he saw stars.

The advantage now McVey's, he rolled Carlos onto his belly and put his knee in the small of Carlos's back and bore down hard. McVey knew what he was doing; pain shot down both legs and up into Carlos's shoulders. McVey cranked first one arm and then the other around and snapped on handcuffs. Blood oozed from the scratches on his face, and his nose felt broken. The cold steel of the muzzle bore into his neck.

"Up on your feet, cocksucker. One false move and you'll never stick it up anybody's ass again."

Carlos struggled onto his knees, got one foot flat on the ground, and pushed up awkwardly to a more or less standing position. McVey walked him, gun at his neck, back to the car through the empty streets. He opened the rear door and shoved Carlos in with his knee. He landed on the floor, head driven against the farther door with his legs sticking out. McVey doubled them up and slammed the door. It was hard to breathe, and pain racked his body. With handcuffs and his body wedged, he had no way out of that position, try as he might. His head pounded, and warm liquid, his own blood, pumped out with each heartbeat.

"What d'ya want?" Carlos twisted his head and managed to croak, trying not to choke on his own blood. "I haven't got much money, but I could get some."

"Revenge, Mr. Bravara, revenge." He spit out the last word, circled the car, and opened the door by Carlos's head. "See this hand? Take a good look, take a real good look."

He yanked his glove off and held his hand up; the dome light dimly revealed most of his right thumb was missing.

"I don't understand. What's that got to do with me?"

McVey pulled his hand back and slammed the door, the impact like a hammer against Carlos's head. A foggy vertigo swam in his brain, and he almost puked. McVey gunned the engine, and the car shot forward. Carlos was vaguely aware of the steady staccato of road bumps against the suspension.

He had no judgment as to the distance they traveled, but it seemed like forever. He wiggled and churned his body. He was stuck tight. His body was wedged on the floor between the front and rear seats, completely ensnared and under McVey's control. A wave of panic surged through him as he struggled to turn his head enough to get air. He forced himself to keep a clear mind.

Avoid thinking the worse. McVey must be someone from the past. But who? He's crazy, and I could end up dead! And goddammit, why?

Damon ran through his mind. Was this what he had to endure? Tears trickled down his cheeks and mixed with the blood.

At last, they slowed and made a sharp turn. The car bounced around and over obstacles in its path. It seemed like every bone in Carlos's body was on fire. McVey braked suddenly and came to a jolting halt. What was going to happen now? *Please, God, don't let it end like this.* He formed the words as though God could lip read.

The emergency brake made a chirring sound, then his tormentor stepped out. He could hear McVey piss then zip his fly. McVey wrenched the rear door open, grabbed under Carlos's shoulders, and yanked. His body had become further wedged between the seats with the movement of the car. McVey grunted and cursed as Carlos's body was essentially dead weight.

"Take off these fucking handcuffs. You're going to shoot me if I run anyway." McVey reluctantly complied. "And move the goddamned seat forward to give me a little room here."

"A real smart-ass, ain't ya?"

He paused long enough for Carlos to wonder what he planned to do. Then the whirr of the power seat and the pressure on his shoulders eased.

Although Carlos was in no condition to be of any physical danger to McVey, he kept Carlos covered with the pistol. Carlos worked his way out onto hands and knees and breathed in fresh air. McVey's toe connected with his ribs. The pain was intense, and Carlos twisted enough to bite McVey's leg, hoping to divert him a few seconds. He clobbered Carlos by one ear with the butt of his revolver, flattened him out on the ground again. Carlos feigned unconsciousness to give himself time to think.

Did he have strength enough to grab McVey's leg and push him backward? Not wise; he had nothing left to fight with and would probably get shot. He groaned and rubbed his head as though just regaining consciousness. Managing to struggle up, his legs felt like rubber. Was opening night also going to be his swan song?

McVey grabbed Carlos's right arm, twisted him around, the barrel of the pistol rammed just above the kidney. The outline of a pitch-black building loomed ahead. His toe hit a step, and he barely kept his balance. A board creaked then snapped under his weight. He pitched forward, grabbing for support, and sprawled headlong onto a porch floor. McVey was on him in a second, pressing the pistol against the small of Carlos's back.

"Get up on your dancing feet, asshole. Your little act ain't foolin' me none."

"Turn on a light then, asshole, so I can see where I'm going."

The pressure of the pistol increased, but McVey didn't say anything. Carlos struggled to his feet, strength nearly gone.

"Straight ahead, the door's just in front of you."

Carlos ran his hands around on a wall, found a door, and groped some more for the knob. It felt like some kind of a wooden contraption. He pushed, and the door swung in, hinges protesting. The stench was nauseating. He moved blindly forward groping for something for balance. McVey kept the gun on Carlos as he struck a match and lighted a kerosene lamp, placing the glass globe on with his free hand. Dirty clothes hung on every projection, papers strewed everywhere. There was a sink full of dirty dishes and maggots crawling in garbage on the floor. Carlos clapped a hand over his mouth to keep from puking.

"Not quite the fancy digs you're used to, huh?"

"No one but a pig would stay in a place like this."

"You're pretty fucking mouthy for someone in your predicament, I'd say."

"And just why the fuck am I in this predicament? I'd like to know."

"So you don't remember me? Well, hot shit, I remember you. That young faggot turning tricks on L Street in Boston. That old boxer you and the other bunch of losers knocked the shit out of, almost killed." He was snarling like a mad dog, spit running down his chin and waving the gun around as he ranted.

In spite of the peril he was in, gall was rising, and the past was returning.

"Sure, a bunch of gun-happy rookie cops rousted us and killed a sixteen-year-old boy. Sure, I remember."

He longed for the strength to deck this monster and drive his filthy, perverted body into the ground. Struck with nausea again, Carlos swayed toward McVey, more from weakness than threat. A loud bang erupted, and Carlos was thrown backwards, crashing onto the floor. A searing pain erupted in his left shoulder. Blood soaked the sleeve of his T-shirt and ran down his arm. He grabbed the wound; the torn skin felt hot on his hand. He applied pressure, attempting to stop the bleeding. The bastard was going to finish him off, but not before he got told off.

"So you and your queer partner took me for a ride, going to get your kicks by raping a seventeen-year-old boy. At least I had the guts to say I was queer. You two hid behind macho badges."

"You shut your fucking dirty mouth. You were givin' it to everyone else, what was the big deal with me?" He waved the gun around and shot a hole in the wall just above Carlos's head. Plaster dust and dirt showered down onto him.

"You're too stupid to understand, you filthy piece of crap."

The room pitched and swayed. It was hard to swallow. McVey kept going in and out of focus. He was lying on a bunch of garbage and could feel vermin scuttling under his elbow.

"You ratted on me, made me lose my job, couldn't get another one. Made me blow my thumb off wrestling with the gun. Your fucking name came up on every job application I made. You ruined my life. Now I'm going to get my revenge." He pulled out a straight razor and slapped the side of it against his hand.

All fight left Carlos's body. He felt himself shaking in spite of the heat. He threw his right arm up; the razor made a clean slash across the back of his wrist. McVey backed off by reflex when Carlos started to heave everything he'd eaten that day. It splattered on his leg and mixed with the other foul trash on the floor. McVey was momentarily sidetracked.

Carlos wiped his mouth with a bloody hand. He was desperately trying to think of something to stave off this crazy man.

"I'll get you money, maybe even a job, hold me here, whatever you say."

His teeth chattered, and he was close to passing out. His insides were starting to atrophy from lack of blood; his legs felt numb.

"Liar, liar, liar," McVey said in a singsong voice. "That's what they all say just to get rid of me." He knelt over Carlos again, brandishing the razor. He stabbed at a cockroach, cutting it open. "Think I'll start by carving up that pretty face of yours. Those innocent eyes as you ratted to the judge. First, I'd like that gold earring of yours."

"Take it," Carlos babbled. "It's yours."

He was exhausted, unable to think of anything but the disfigurement. His bladder let go. All the choices he had made in his life had been wrong. Now he lay in piss and squalor. Even if he lived through this horror, he would bleed to death before anyone found him.

"I think I'll take the ear too, just a souvenir from the great big rock star."

Carlos mustered every particle of strength he had and grabbed for McVey's arm. Another explosion rocked the room, and a bullet ripped into Carlos's gut. Time, events, and place stood still. So this is how death feels. He felt no pain as the razor slashed the top of his ear.

A grotesque shadow flitted across his vision.

Then blackness.

CHAPTER

5

Simon and Leenora Gideon shuffled past the front entrance of the American Airlines Arena for what seemed like the hundredth time to Leenora's weary legs. She stopped and sat down on the curbing and massaged her legs and ankles. Simon was so wound up by the concert, he was unable to think of anything except meeting Carlos.

"Let's go home, Simon, it's nearly 3:00 a.m. He probably went out the back way hours ago."

She pushed herself up from the granite surface, groaned, and caught hold of his arm.

"I dunno, Lee Lee. Let's take one more look in the parking lot. Maybe his car is still there," he said in a hopeful voice.

"We don't even know what kind of a car he drives." Resignation sounded in her voice.

Simon was near seven feet tall and weighed close to four hundred pounds. The umbilical cord had wound around his neck when he was born, and the lack of oxygen severely damaged his brain. He was a good-natured boy, unless taunted, but had no capacity for learning. As he matured, other students would tease him to great feats of strength. He could lift one side of a car or carry two men at a time, one on each shoulder. Tenderhearted, he would weep if a squirrel was run over on the street. Country and Western music was his passion, and he was inconsolable for weeks after Johnny Cash died.

When their parents were killed in an automobile accident, the mother's last words to Leenora were, "Promise to take care of Simon." Leenora, a rather plain, masculine-appearing woman, assented and for the past ten years had honored her mamma's wishes. A large insurance settlement allowed them to live comfortably although conservatively.

∽

When Simon saw posters of Carlos in his Stetson, he had to go to the concert. They sat six rows back, and Simon was sure that Carlos would sign his program after the show. Being shy, try as he might, he couldn't get anywhere near Carlos while he signed autographs.

Leenora unwisely suggested they wait out on the street, maybe catch him there. Simon took it to heart, and they waited and paced.

Realizing they had several more days to catch another show, Simon reluctantly agreed to leave. As they neared the parking lot, their attention was riveted by two men involved in a vicious brawl. Simon was aghast and ready to wade into the fray. The area was still in semidarkness, and the combatants were far enough away to be indistinguishable. Leenora grabbed his belt and set her feet. Simon never openly defied her, he just grunted and pulled her slowly along. They moved nearer and continued to watch in horrified fascination.

"It's him, Lee Lee, it's Carlos, he's going to be killed. I gotta stop it."

Leenora peered closer. "He's a cop, Simon, see his uniform."

The cop had his knee in the other man's back, putting on handcuffs.

"He's got a gun. You show your face and you'll get shot. Besides, there's nothing we can do. It's probably just a drug bust."

"No, Lee Lee, it's Carlos, he's going to get hurt." He burst into tears.

The cop grabbed the man, pulled him to his feet, and shoved him into the backseat and slammed the door. Then he went around, spoke to the victim, got into the car, and raced out of the parking lot.

"Follow them, Lee Lee, it's Carlos, I know it is."

"Okay, we'll follow them to the police station. You'll see it's not Carlos." Leenora sighed as they climbed into the car, started the engine, shifted into drive, and took pursuit at a distance, as she had seen on television. The streets were nearly empty this time of night, so she had to be careful not to be spotted. Under the streetlights she could see it wasn't a cruiser. Curious, she thought. They've gone by the police station and headed out of town.

As the miles started to pile up, so did Leenora's feelings of impatience.

"We've been on the road half an hour now and getting farther from home. Besides, we're going to run out of gas soon. I'm going to turn around and go back."

"No," Simon pleaded, "it's him, and I'm going to save his life. Just a little while longer. Please."

Leenora leaned her elbow against the window and ran her fingers through her short black hair. Simon always had good instincts, even as a child. Maybe he was right. Nothing seemed to add up. Why would a cop go this far away with a captive?

They rounded a corner, and the car was no longer in sight. She speeded up. The road was paved but narrow. No other car had passed in the last fifteen minutes—still no sign of the other vehicle.

"We've lost 'em, Simon, I'm turning around."

She swung the car around in a picnic area and headed back. Simon sulked in the seat beside her. They had gone only a short distance when he grabbed her arm.

"Stop," he shouted.

Leenora slammed on the brakes.

"What is it? What's the matter?"

"I know where they went. There's a dirt road off to the left." His hand clutched the door handle. "I'm going after 'em." He grabbed a flashlight from the glove box, threw the door open, raced across the street and up the rock-strewn rise.

"Simon, wait," Leenora shouted.

❧

The graveyard shift at Hollywood General ER was in various degrees of alertness after an unusually quiet night. Their ennui was shattered by an emergency call breaking the spell. The eerie wail of a siren approaching in the distance exploded in the still night air.

"A gunshot victim, massive blood loss!" was the terse mobile message.

The big white ambulance swung up to the emergency entrance, and the doors were thrown open. An EMT hovered over the stretcher, administering pressure to an apparent shoulder wound. Another was working on what might have been additional lower abdominal wounds. A large blood-soaked bandage covered the left side of his face. An IV bottle swung freely while the stretcher was whisked into the emergency room.

"My god," one of the admitting personnel gasped, coming from behind her cubicle. "That looks like the new singer over at the arena. I went to his concert just a few hours ago."

At that moment, an older, dark-colored Buick Park Avenue pulled up near the emergency entrance. A huge man, bare chested and covered with blood, threw the door open and stepped out before he could be allayed. The guard was immediately on the alert, gun drawn. Simon put up no protest.

"Looks like you've been in a fight, buddy." He performed a quick frisking and, finding no weapon, motioned to a white coat nearby. "He's clean, get him inside." He turned and approached the car. "What seems to be the matter, lady?" Hand on his gun, he saw she was covered with blood as well. "Are you injured?"

Leenora stepped out, hands shaking, on the edge of tears.

"I'm all right. The big guy is my brother, Simon. He…we found Carlos, the guy in the ambulance, in a shack. Some guy shot him two or three times. Simon hit the man with a rock. He carried Carlos down to our car. We tried to stop the blood with rags. Simon tore up his shirt." Tears cascaded down her cheeks. "Is he still alive?"

"Calm down, lady, he's in good hands," the guard said, helping her into the waiting room. "I'll call the police, and you can tell them all about it."

A candy striper ushered her into admittance room, and a nurse sat down with her, taking notes.

Leenora glanced suspiciously around. Simon was nowhere in sight.

"What have they done with my brother?" Leenora asked with a tremor in her voice.

CHAPTER

6

"How ya doing, partner?" Jerry Haines asked, standing awkwardly beside Carlos's hospital bed a few days later. He flopped several magazines on the nightstand and crammed an arrangement of carnations onto the crowded bureau. Carlos's bed was cranked up to a half-sitting position, and Jerry took his left hand in a wan handshake.

"Thanks for coming, Jerry. Guess I'm doing as well as can be expected. They say I'm lucky to be alive. Can't prove it by me though." He winced, turning toward Jerry, grunted, and squeezed out a weak smile.

Jerry sidled around the bed to better observe the large bandage. "Christ, kid, what happened to your face?"

"Thanks, Jerry, that sure boosted my morale." He manipulated his legs restlessly and moaned, trying to get comfortable. "The bastard slashed off my ear. They've sewed it back, but I may be scarred for life. My nose is broken too. At least that can be set.

"Jerry, I'm not ashamed to say I'm scared shitless." His voice broke. "I've always taken my looks for granted. It was the one thing I had going for me." He balled up his left fist and punched the pillow beside him, grimacing at the pain the movement caused to his wounds. "Just a few days ago I was knocking myself out at the arena. I loved it." He twisted his head toward the window, exhaustion clouding his voice. "They can't tell me how much I'll recover from this. I may be partially crippled."

"Oh shit, no. You're going to be okay, kid. Where's the old fight?" Jerry reached tentatively toward Carlos's good shoulder then yanked it back as if he had been stung.

Jerry leaned against the foot of the bed, fingers nervously running along the shiny rail. "Have they found the bastard?" he asked, his voice was growing stronger.

"Naw, it's possible he made a clean break, or he may have crawled into the underbrush and died. The police are still looking." He eased his head back toward Jerry, lifting it slightly. "Maybe he'll find me and finish the job."

Jerry winced. "Anything I can do to help?" he inquired in a facile voice, brushing aside the pessimistic remark.

"Money, Jerry. This is going to be damned expensive. I've only got a couple of thou to my name. No insurance. Christ knows when I'll work again—if ever." He gingerly laid his head back down and stared at the ceiling. "I could use the twenty-seven Gs you owe me."

The room became ominously quiet. Jerry coughed and cleared his throat. His face turned red, and sweat speckled his brow.

"Jerry?" Carlos immediately felt apprehensive. He lifted his head, groaning. "Jerry?" he repeated louder.

"Ya see, kid," Jerry replied, not looking Carlos in the eyes, "I had to have money to keep the band together. They have problems with work ethics. When they heard you, when they heard we were shut down, ya know, they wanted to split. No more work, ya know, and they have expensive habits." He slouched over to the window and fiddled with the blind cord.

"Any of it left?"

"Not much."

"How much?"

Jerry didn't answer, twisting the knob on the crank handle and peering out the window.

"None, right?" Carlos's voice was heavy with anger and frustration.

"I had to use it. Things were not going well at the club, until you got there, anyway. People started flocking in, money was loosening up. Then this gig, I thought we had it made. I gave all the guys advances."

"I'll get bullshit from opening night. Hudson told me it would be several days before our overhead was cleared. It was never going to be big bucks anyway. This was a test to see if I had the goods. He could negotiate a higher take next time if the act was a success," Carlos said, reaching for a glass of water and wincing.

"Christ, kid, I don't know what to say," Jerry mumbled beseechingly, his voice little louder than a whisper.

"I do, you stole my fuckin' money. You didn't even pay me for the performances at that fleabag club you were running. I trusted you again, Jerry, and you fucked me over. Get out and don't come back, ya hear." His hand shook as he reached for the emergency button for the nurse.

"I'll make it up to ya somehow," Jerry blathered in a whining voice. "Not right away, the IRS is after me. I had to sell my place in Boston. Somethin' will turn up. We're a team, kid."

Carlos jabbed a finger at him, his voice stern as hardened steel. "Don't call me kid again. Ever. I'm not that seventeen-year-old sucker you used once before. Get out."

A young nurse hurried in around the foot of the bed. "What can we do for you, Mr. Bravara?" Concern etched her face.

"We can throw this bastard out." He jabbed at Haines.

"Why, Mr. Bravara," she mock scolded him. "You should be leaving now," she admonished Jerry. "He needs rest." She straightened Carlos's pillow and took his wrist. Her face was stern as she checked his pulse.

Jerry vacillated at the doorway, sweat stains spreading under his arms. The nurse motioned again for him to leave. Jerry lifted his right hand in a half-wave, turned, and ducked out of view.

"When am I going to know more about my prospects?"

"You're scheduled for more tests, first thing tomorrow morning. Your doctor should be in later today."

⚏

Hudson appeared toward evening. He had several packages. He pulled out Carlos's Stetson from one and laid it within Carlos's reach. He piled the others on the floor, came over to the bed, took Carlos's hand, and gave him a peck on the check.

"Thanks for letting me come in. They say I can only stay fifteen minutes."

"I'm glad to see ya, man. I need someone to count on." He fingered the Stetson, punching the crown with his index finger. "Jerry was in earlier, and I finally threw him out."

"Jesus"—Hudson looked alarmed—"what did he say, babe?" His face grew serious, and he tightened his grip on Carlos's hand.

"You remember the twenty-seven K he owed me?"

A rueful look crossed Hudson's face. "The bastard's spent it."

Carlos nodded.

"Yeah, it's gone. I got no insurance, and it's going to be damned expensive for the hospital and plastic surgery." Carlos turned his head away, tears smarting in his eyes. "Dammit, John, I've been an optimist all my life, but this one has really got me down big time."

"What are the doctors saying? Have they given any prognosis?"

"They are still marveling that I'm alive. Three bullets went through me, so I didn't need surgery, at least at this point. One shot grazed my hip bone." He paused, and his voice quavered. "I may have a limp."

Hudson tightened his grip again and gently pulled Carlos's hand up to his cheek as he bent toward him. Carlos cleared his throat and went on.

"My shoulder is going to be okay. I asked the doctor if I could play the piano after my arm healed, and he got a kick out of that." He chuckled in spite of his mood.

"What about the bandage on your cheek? Nothing that's going to spoil that gorgeous face. I won't stand for it." Hudson plied, smacking one fist into the other.

"Lying in bed here, what a vain fool I am. My face has always been my meal ticket. It allowed me to get what I wanted without working for it. I've just turned twenty-six, and I haven't a dime to my name. My ear was only cut about a third off, more down toward the back. Just a small laceration on the cheek. Plastic surgery will take care of it." He sighed again, staring at the ceiling. "My nose is broken, but they have been able to set it."

Hudson took Carlos's hand again. "There's some good news, babe."

"What kind?"

I've been negotiating with the arena. They're insured for this kind of accident. I've been talking with an attorney. He says they are liable for the doors being unlocked so this creep was able to get in. There's supposed to be a night guard. Found out he was out at a bar, drinking. You were forcibly abducted on their property. You with me so far?"

"I hardly dare to breathe."

"Let out your breath. We're sure this won't go to court. It will be more expensive for them to fight the case than to settle. Your hospitalization should be fully covered, plus."

Carlos looked at Hudson then at the Stetson, fingering the brim with his left hand. Hudson watched as Carlos dozed, bent, kissed him softly on the cheek, then left.

CHAPTER

7

Several arduous days passed. Carlos sat up in bed. The pain was intense, but he clenched his teeth, twisted his body gingerly, and swung his feet onto the floor. This would be the first test of the damage done to his hip. One arm under his left shoulder, the nurse helped ease him up to a standing position and guided his hands to a walker.

"See if you can bear weight onto your right foot, Mr. Bravara."

"Call me Carlos. You've seen every inch of me and know all my weaknesses, physical at least."

He shifted his weight and sucked in his breath.

The nurse looked up at him, color spreading up into her cheeks. "All in a day's work. How does the hip feel?"

"I don't feel like dancing."

"Can you take a step?"

Sweat broke out on his brow, and he felt light-headed. But he gritted his teeth and pushed his body to move slowly forward. There was much weakness in his right hip and down the leg. The pain was only just bearable as he hobbled to the door and back. Easing back onto the bed again, the nurse lifted his legs up. She plumped his pillow, helped him to recline, and pulled the sheet up over his knees. He leaned back and closed his eyes.

The horror of the attack reappeared once more. Tiny fragments of the rescue nibbled at his brain. Who was his savior? A face. He was big, huge, a giant, and strong. And a woman talking on a cell phone—she was driving. Everything was red. Blood was everywhere.

Evening settled in. Sleep overtook him after the most challenging but most promising day since the attack.

Suddenly he was seventeen again. He was shackled to an automobile, being forcibly raped.

Can't get away. A gun. Help! They're gonna kill me. McVey! Gotta get away. The pain, oh god, make him stop. McVey, the cop in Boston. Oh god.

"Hey, wake up, babe, you're having a nightmare," Hudson spoke, gently touching Carlos's arm.

Carlos awoke with a start, confused for a moment, and rubbed his eyes. He stared at Hudson as his mind cleared.

"Any word about what happened to the bastard who put me here?"

"Afraid not, they're still looking."

At the end of twenty days, Carlos was able to walk several steps at a time without the walker. He was pushing himself in rehab. Already, strength was developing in his right arm, and he started lifting weights. The right hip was still weak but strengthening.

Hudson appeared in his room late one afternoon several days later.

"Good news, babe, they're gonna release you tomorrow."

Carlos looked up from the magazine he was reading, a smile spreading across his face. "Hot shit. Great." His excitement was broken with a disheartening thought. "But where am I gonna stay? I still need a lot of therapy."

"With me. I've got an efficiency nearby. There's an extra bed, and I've rented a car. Thanks to the American Airlines Arena. They're treating you like a king." A flush spread over his face. "There's also a king-size bed. I could keep good watch over you, anything you need in the night." A sly grin pressed his cheeks. "Anything."

"Hell, man, I don't know what to say."

"There's nothing to say. I've arranged it with your doctors. They agree you need to get out of here." He came over and sat on the edge of the bed and laid his hand on Carlos's stomach. "I'm gonna take good care of you, and some day you're gonna take good care of me."

"Watch where you put that hand. It's still pretty tender in that region."

They clasped hands. Hudson moved over beside Carlos and gave him an awkward hug then kissed him on the forehead.

"You're my Greek god." He stood up and looked down onto Carlos. "I've been in this business for eighteen years and never seen any one person come near havin' what you've got."

CHAPTER

8

On advice from the doctor and Joan, I spent the next couple of days resting and recovering. Still couldn't understand how I had been so clumsy outside the bank entrance. I smiled to myself. Fate must have stepped in; otherwise, what were the chances I would have met Joan?

To my great surprise, the president of the bank where I was to interview called. In going over my references, he had contacted the bank where I last worked in New Hampshire and got rather impressive background information. It even surprised me. Investments were my main interest, and I had steered several people (including myself) into excellent stock market portfolios. My former employer said I should wind up on Wall Street. A job awaited me. Wow!

I needed to share my good news with someone special. I could imagine the cross examination from Dad and Ilka, always looking on the downside of anything I did. Mom was not really available without them, and her enthusiasm would be stunted by years of subjugation. I'd tell her later when she was alone.

Joan's voice on the phone was like an aphrodisiac. I so needed a friend, someone to confide in. She seemed genuinely pleased and delighted with my good news.

"Would you like to have dinner with me this evening?" I asked rather hesitantly. "Kind of a celebration."

"Should I bring my first aid kit?" Then her wonderful laugh. "I'd love to have dinner with you." There was a smile in her voice.

I found myself rather excited for the first time in a long while. It felt good and so right. It was around four when we spoke. I rushed down to a florist shop and bought a single red rose and an expensive box of chocolates. Not very original, but it was my first date with a woman! I slipped a note in with the chocolates, which I carefully wrapped promising eleven more roses "next time."

The time dragged until seven thirty, when she would stop by and drive us to the restaurant. By Joan picking me up, it again switched the usual male-female role. I kicked myself for not hiring a taxi, which would allow me to be in the dominant masculine role. Joan wouldn't hear of it. She lived a ways out and felt it logical to pick me up.

The tenth time I checked, it seemed like, she had finally arrived, and I hurried down to meet her with the candy tucked under my arm and the rose in my teeth. She chuckled and slid over and ran the passenger-side window down, the fragrance of her perfume wafting out. She smiled.

"I'd like you to drive if you don't mind."

"I'd be delighted." I presented her with the rose and the chocolates. I had attached a tiny plastic vial of water to the bottom of the rose. I leaned in and brushed her cheek with my lips. I went around and slipped in behind the wheel.

Her clothes were stunning: a burgundy sheath, off one shoulder, low-cut back with matching fabric lacings, a single strand of pearls and matching earrings. She was a natural beauty with silky smooth skin with little need for makeup. Her hair was piled into a chignon, also wound with pearls. Evenings could still be chilly, so she had wrapped a paisley scarf loosely around her shoulders.

Traffic lightened somewhat from rush hour, and we headed out on Route 30. I had spotted an exotic restaurant just off the highway. It was even more posh than I had imagined. A huge glass atrium protected tropical plants of all sorts. Parrots perched on full-sized tree limbs, and a bougainvillea-entwined trellised walkway led to the main dining rooms. Potted hibiscus surrounded the entrance. The floor was paved with polished granite squares, and paths led to tables spotted in intimate settings. We chose to dine inside, however, in one of the several themed dining rooms. Joan picked a New England theme in my honor.

We started our evening in the lounge, seated in celadon velvet wing chairs. Our very attentive waiter took our liquor orders and soon returned with a Manhattan for Joan and a vodka and tonic for me.

"We know so little about each other," I said, sipping my drink. "I have never been with a woman who made me feel so at ease." She had no idea how true this statement really was.

"I take that as a high compliment, I guess." She flashed her cute little smile.

I reached for her hand and smiled back. "Why is it sometimes you feel like you have known someone forever, at first meeting, and other people you never really know after many years?"

"I know what you mean. We must have met in another life."

"I think I was a baboon."

"Funny, I was about to say the same thing." She clutched my hand, laughing, then touched my cheek. "Why is a man as nice as you still unattached?"

"Maybe waiting for someone as nice as you to also be unattached."

She blushed as I drew her hand up and kissed it. I felt ready for whatever this might develop into. She allowed me to stay in my comfort zone without feeling emasculated.

The spell was broken by the waiter announcing he had a table for us if we were ready to dine.

Our Queen Ann table was replete with a damask cloth and napkins. The waiter slid out the flame-stitch upholstered Chippendale chair for Joan, and I seated myself across from her. The furnishings reminded me of New Castle and our beautiful Federal house, no longer home to me.

The many themed dining rooms fanned out like a wagon wheel from a central stage where show tunes issued from the live orchestra. A dance floor surrounded them, and several couples swayed to the music. We both ordered another drink while perusing the menu.

We chatted and giggled like kids while we made our entrée selections and consumed our salads. Joan settled on pan-roasted squab breasts with black trumpet mushrooms, and I ordered chicken breast with escarole, temple apples, and mini potatoes. I felt a warm glow enjoying Joan's company as we dallied over our meals.

Later, after dessert, we headed for the dance floor. The dim lighting, strains of the stringed instruments, and holding Joan in my arms made me wish the night would last forever. Back at our table, we finished the evening with liquor-laced latte served in Limoges demitasse cups.

On our way home, Joan said, "I have a confession to make," looking very serious.

"Let me guess," I said, "you have five boyfriends. They will all be waiting for you at home, and they're all weightlifters."

Joan looked sly as passing headlights flashed on her face. "Actually, only three, but I'll sneak you by them." She adjusted her skirt and moved a little closer. "No, what I was going to say, I know your sister. I never knew Ilka's last name until this afternoon quite by chance. She volunteers at the hospital, and we chat quite often at break."

"And she told you about me." A touch of anger had entered in my voice.

Joan turned to me, a bit startled. "Yes, but you have nothing to worry about. She was just trying to matchmake you and me, not knowing we had already met." A question showed on her face.

My heart sank. Did she tell Joan about my change in orientation? I smoothed my voice and inquired as calmly as possible. "What terrible secrets did she reveal?" My heart pounded. Ilka had a loose tongue and enjoyed troublemaking.

Joan snickered. "Oh, nothing important. She just said you were sweet, handsome, and available."

I eased my grip on the wheel.

"All true," I avowed and relaxed, but I needed to keep my guard up with this little revelation. "Is there something else you're not telling me?"

Her brow wrinkled.

"I guess we all have our secrets."

She nodded, and we rode in silence several minutes.

It was after eleven when we pulled in by the curb across from my building. I expressed concern about her going on alone.

"Don't worry, it's a gated community, and we each have our private, locked garage spaces with an elevator to our floors. And I have a hell of a karate chop." Her face broke into a smile as she slid over nearer me.

"I can't remember an evening I have enjoyed more than this one." I reached over, put my arm gently around her, and drew her close. I kissed her on the cheek as she turned, and we kissed on the lips. I had never quite realized before how wonderful a woman could feel in your arms.

I reluctantly released her.

"Call me when you get home."

I slid out and hurried around to the passenger window. She smiled and reached up for my hand, and we clasped a few seconds through the window. She slipped over behind the wheel and started the engine. I opened the door and reached for her. We kissed again. I would have asked her up, but not to my dingy apartment.

"I'd ask you up, but—"

"It's late, and you have a big day tomorrow." And then she was off.

I took my time climbing the two flights. I needed to take it one step at a time. Get over feeling awkward and clumsy. Twenty-four and only one fleeting sexual experience with a woman. Carlos flashed into my mind, staggering me for a moment, as I unlocked my door. What was he doing tonight, and who was he with? Six months, six years, would it never end?

The table was piled with business magazines and newspapers. I removed my shoes and hung up my clothes. Seated at the table in my undershorts, I leafed through the *New York Times,* my new bible.

Shortly, the phone rang.

"Hi, I'm home, Damon." She paused then continued. "There is a gentleness about you I have never experienced with a man before. Thank you for a wonderful and unusual time."

"Lunch at the cafeteria tomorrow?"

"Let's, my treat. Around twelve?"

☙

My first week at the new job included meeting all the department heads and getting a feeling for the bank procedures. I took a great liking to the president, and the feeling seemed to be mutual. Investments at the bank had been a problem. The head of that department was an affable fellow but basically inept. I gathered he was a relative of the president but had not worked out. I came along in time to replace him. It was a heavy load, but they eased me into the position over the next six months.

By the end of the year I had my own office, albeit small, and worked overtime many days. It was demanding and time-consuming but was just what I needed. It didn't hurt that my two hundred thousand plus a handy interest accrual traveled with me.

One of the early stories that reached my ears was about an unfortunate young man who had been wiped out of his savings and credit cards by a person or persons unknown from back East. The records available at the time indicated it was a true story.

Unfortunately, he had left without giving further info that could help track down the culprit. For some reason, it struck me about Carlos, but I dismissed it as improbable.

During this period I purchased a secondhand BMW, red with black leather interior. My relationship with Joan blossomed, and we were in touch most days. I felt much easier taking her home now so I knew she was safe. We decided to take it easy as she had been involved in an earlier marriage that had turned out badly, and of course, I also had a bad track record, although unknown to her, I hoped.

After the first several months I knew I wanted to be with her more and more. *Forever* was not a word I used much after the times I had been burned. About six months after our first date, we decided we should move in together. She had a nice apartment with plenty of space, so it was a no-brainer. I even set up a mini office in one corner of her den.

She had two bedrooms, and most nights we slept together. I still had flashbacks and was restless at times, so we reserved those nights for me to be alone. At first, I hesitated telling her the nature of my support group and agonized about it endlessly.

Finally one night I faced up to it. We were sitting by the gas log in the den and were sharing a bottle of Chardonnay. I was feeling unusually mellow and loquacious. The wine helped.

I put my arm around her and drew her close.

"Darling, there is something I need to tell you."

My hands suddenly felt sweaty, and my stomach churned. There was so much I needed to say yet hardly knew where to begin. She turned to me, a quizzical look on her face. I didn't want to screw this up, she meant too much to me.

"You've probably wondered what my support group is all about." I took another sip of wine.

She didn't answer, just smiled encouragingly. I slid out of her arms and moved to the fireplace, leaning my elbow on the mantel. I cleared my throat and looked down at the hearth, swirling my wineglass.

"It's a men's support group for reoriented gay men." I studied the flames, afraid to see the look of disgust and revulsion I expected on her face.

I felt her hand on my arm, and I turned to her, a tear forming in my eyes.

"Thank you for telling me." Her voice was full of emotion. "You see"—her eyes brimmed—"don't be mad, Ilka told me soon after we met. She said she and her family had encouraged you to go for help last year."

I tried not to let my annoyance with Ilka color Joan's acceptance of my revelation. At that moment, I knew how much I loved Joan. A millstone had been lifted from my shoulders. I hugged her, and our kiss was long and passionate. But damn Ilka for being the snitch.

"I know—have known of the risk." She cleared her throat and moved back to the sofa, patting a spot for me. "But I knew from the beginning you were worth the risk."

We slept together that night, and for once our sex was passionate and unrestrained. We awoke the next morning, my arm still around her.

The next few months passed by in quiet and comfortable tranquility. My work went well, and we were both exhilarated. I ate lunch with her at the hospital most days, and she joined me occasionally at a restaurant near my work.

Then something happened that turned my happy new life upside down. It started so innocently. Trite but true. We have endless board meetings, which seem to be the norm in the banking business. One of these meetings, every other week, included new employees.

My first awareness of Kent was at one of these meetings. He bore a vague resemblance to Carlos, not as tall but ruddy complexioned with a certain confident manner not unlike Carlos. My sublimation had become so complete that none of this occurred in my conscious mind, until later. I am a private person by nature and don't look for friendships. In fact, many of my coworkers find me aloof.

Kent and I, however, struck up a friendly interaction. He was very personable and fun to chat with. He avowed a great interest in investments, and we brainstormed on many occasions. If my office door was open, he would stop in to chat.

"Damon," he said one day, parking his rump on the corner of my desk, "I'm living with a girl I have known for some time. We get along most of the time, but she thinks I'm clumsy in bed. Not good for my ego."

"I'm afraid that's pretty much out of my line." A shiver ran up my spine for no particular reason. The phone rang, and he edged off my desk, excused himself, and went about his work. He was the first man I had found attractive since the retreat, but only in a platonic manner. Several weeks passed, and it was never mentioned again. He even went to lunch with Joan and me one day. She found him interesting, and they bantered back and forth.

Several days later, I went to the men's room. It appeared to be empty. I was standing at the urinal when someone tapped me on the shoulder. I was startled and leaned forward in reaction. It was Kent. He took the urinal beside me, gazing at my penis out of the corner of his eye. I finished and zipped, my heart pounding.

I started to leave. He moved to a stall. My hand was on the exit door handle when he spoke. I turned. His back was toward me.

"I want to show you something,"

"Not a good idea," I choked out.

"Please, it will only take a minute."

Against my better judgment, I approached him. He pulled me into the stall. He had an erection. I was horrified yet fascinated. His tongue was in my mouth before he fell to his knees, had me unzipped and in his mouth while massaging himself.

"This is not happening" was the only stupid thing coming out of my mouth. I couldn't move or say anything else. I was ashamed, embarrassed, and scared. Semen dripped out of the corner of his mouth and down onto his tie.

"This will never happen again, Kent. Do you understand?" He remained kneeling and climaxed onto the floor. My face in the mirror as I washed my hands looked ashen. What had I done? It would never happen again.

That night I proposed to Joan.

CHAPTER

9

The house was small but served our needs. The monthly payments were reasonable, and with both of us working, we managed quite well. It was a single-story, two-bedroom house in what was called prairie style. Similar to Ilka's but smaller. I took twenty thousand out of my inheritance from Seth Porter as down payment. I mentioned to Joan I had some money in savings but never told her how much or where it came from.

We lived about five miles from Ilka, and she stopped by often. We three had supper together several times a week. It was heavy-duty. She and Joan seemed to get along well, so that helped. Joan had the wonderful ability to bring out the best in people. They could chat while I slipped off to the den.

In bad days, my assault two years ago seemed like yesterday. During good days, it was like years ago. I was able to sleep most of the night now, and the nightmares were less frequent. Group therapy was progressing quite well; the group was supportive, and many of us had or planned to get married and live "normal" lives. I seldom thought of men in a sexual manner anymore. Kent left the bank a few weeks after the men's room debacle. Joan and my marital relations were infrequent but satisfying. Joan was very understanding and allowed me the space I needed for recovery. We never discussed homosexuality or my therapy.

Ilka was so proud she had had a major hand in my "cure" that she had to brag.

How did I feel about Ilka now? I chose to close my mind to her involvement after the rape and the subsequent harm done to Carlos. When she was around, my guard always had to be up.

Carlos was the last part of my therapy and what I had the most trouble overcoming. I received major support from the group on this issue since many of us had parted from long-term gay relationships. We never discussed this outside of group because it was too painful without our therapist.

Several weeks later, I slid the key into the new lock on our front door. All of them had been changed, and we were particular about always keeping doors and windows locked. By instinct, I glanced around each time I came home as though someone might spring out from behind a tree. My rapist might still linger somewhere in the area.

I gave Joan a hug, and we kissed then chatted about our day for a few minutes and went into the kitchen. We usually had a couple of glasses of wine on the back patio before dinner. Joan had the glasses chilled and the ice bucket and wine in a cloth in a wooden container ready to take out. We cooked most of our meals on the weekend and froze them so they were easy to pull out and micro.

I sensed something was troubling Joan tonight. She was unusually quiet. She was anxious to have a child, but we had had no luck so far. She was worried about her biological clock after seeing so many older women having major problems with childbirth. Joan was twenty-nine, and I was now twenty-five. She had been to the doctor today, and I waited for her to tell me the news. She remained quiet, and I didn't want to push her.

I went to check the front door to be sure the bolt had been thrown and to pick up the mail on the hall table. Joan collected it and placed it on the table each evening. I rifled through it, mostly bills and charitable requests. Most landed in the basket. The letter was mixed among the rest of the mail. I felt tightness in my throat.

The return address was from Michael Washington, Portsmouth, New Hampshire.

We had discussed Mike in depth in the group. I felt I would never hear from him again. He had been involved several years of my earlier life, however, and I couldn't deny many of them had been pleasant.

He was invading my mind once again, more than I wanted to deal with. I heard of other men meeting up with ex-wives and had felt they were right to dissolve the marriage. My concern dealt with the feelings I so much wanted to forget. I fervently wished to have been the one to break off the relationship. In our five years together I never had near the depth of feelings for Mike as I'd had for Carlos in just ten days.

Carlos! Tears sprang into my eyes, unwanted as rain during a flood. The pain of our last meeting, ending in his arrest, stabbed at my heart like a fresh flesh wound. I doubled over with stomach cramps, grabbed for the table to keep my balance. Psychological, my doctor said, anxiety reaction. Was two years of therapy negated by a single letter in the mail? I couldn't let it happen.

I was brought back to reality by the doorbell. It must be Ilka. Terrible things passed through my mind. I wanted to open the door and strangle her. I had to get hold of myself, start thinking straight, finally accept blame, and move on.

"Was that the doorbell?" Joan came into the hallway. "Damon, what's the matter?" she asked in alarm. "All the blood has drained out of your face."

"It's a touch of indigestion," I lied. "The chili we had for lunch was pretty hot." She nodded. "See who's at the door, would you, I'm going to lie down a few minutes."

"Of course, darling, I'll get you something to take." Worry creased her forehead. Had she figured out the truth about the letter? I knew that was stupid; she had no frame of reference.

It was Ilka, and she immediately had a hundred cures when she stepped inside and saw me. I needed desperately to be alone. I was in crisis and dangerously close to another breakdown. I headed for the bedroom and said through gritted teeth, "Out, I can't deal with her," as I collapsed onto the bed.

Joan reappeared with an antacid pill and water. "Are you sure it's only indigestion, darling?" She sat on the bed beside me.

Ilka appeared at the door, and Joan motioned her out and held her finger over her mouth. Ilka backed out, her heels clicking on the hardwood floor as she returned to the kitchen.

"Don't worry, it will pass," I assured her and reached for her.

We remained silent; the warmth of her hand and the nearness of her body comforted me. I still had the letter clutched in my fist. Joan reached for it and looked at the return address and then quizzically at me.

"Do we know a Mike Washington? Oh, of course I wouldn't. He's from New Hampshire."

She said no more, the question of what had upset me, if it was the letter, was left unspoken between us. She bent and kissed me. Our eyes met; her love showed so softly. She rose and eased a pillow under my head and laid a shawl over me. I closed my eyes and tried to empty my mind of all thoughts.

She stood at the door for a minute, brushed at her eyes, turned toward the hall, and was gone. I heard her and Ilka speaking in soft tones from another room.

The cramps eased, and I must have slept for several hours as the room was dark when I awoke. I wasn't sure at first if it was late evening or early morning. I hadn't dreamed, which seemed like an encouraging sign. My mind slowly cleared. Then I saw the letter lying on the bureau. The first shock had worn off, and I knew I must read it although I wanted to through it away.

I arose, went to the bureau, picked up the letter, and ran my index finger along under the flap. The letter was handwritten. Mike hated computers. At least he hadn't enclosed any pictures. I unfolded the page and read.

Hi, Buddy,

> I finally got up the courage to call your folks. Your mother answered, thank God, to find out how to get in touch with you. Have hesitated about writing, didn't know what to say after the way we parted.
> Are we still friends? I hope so 'cause we had some good times together and a lot of laughs.

A thrill of relief ran through me. I wasn't feeling any longing or desire for him. What had triggered the awful reaction earlier? Another positive step. I had reacted violently but then been able to come to terms with it.

> I've never quite been able to let go of the damned way I left you that last time. It was a shitty thing to do. Can you forgive me?
> I understand congratulations are in order. You devil you. Who would have thought the two of us would end up married, to women that is? Ha ha.
> My wife's name is Kelly. We have been married for over a year. She works for a florist shop here in Portsmouth. She's full of life and has lots of energy. We both love to cook, but I have to watch my weight.
> We rent an old house by the ocean and have an option to buy when we have some money saved. I've got the restoration bug. I would love to buy up houses and restore and resell them. It's big business here in Ports.
> Now let me get to the real reason I'm writing. We're planning to come to Fort Worth!

Oh shit, he's got to be kidding. I don't want to see him. I don't hate him, but it's over and in the past. Why does he want to see me again now? Damn, I can't tell him he's not welcome.

> Kelly has been on the Internet (ugh) and found us a nice hotel near where you guys live. We'll be arriving the twenty-third. We have so many things to talk about. Kelly sends her love as I do to you both.

> Your Buddy,

> Mike

I sat on the edge of the bed. A distress developed between my shoulder blades, and pain started at the base of my skull and ended behind my eyes. I leaned forward, resting head in hands, then finally stood up and walked into the bathroom, opened the medicine cupboard door, and peered blankly into the shelves. My gaze finally landed on the aspirin bottle, and I shook out two tablets. A tremor developed in my hands as I remembered two years ago swallowing a handful of painkillers. The glass suddenly slipped out of my hand and smashed on the tile floor.

I've got to get a grip on myself. I could hear Joan and Ilka talking in the hall. Ilka hated to leave without seeing me, but Joan assured her I needed rest when I had these spells. The front door closed, and Joan came to the bedroom door. She was alarmed to see the broken glass. It was never far from her mind that people with my background were prone to suicide. She visibly relaxed when I laughed and called myself clumsy; although I felt anything but jolly.

I scraped the glass together and used an old envelope as a dustpan. The glass rattled in the aluminum basket. We returned to the bedroom; Joan had made a sandwich and brought a glass of milk. She sat rather tentatively, I thought, on my desk chair, and I sat on the bed and took a bite of sandwich. The room was silent except for the soft whir of the air conditioner. I finished eating and sat the plate and glass on the nightstand.

"I need to tell you about Mike Washington," I said finally.

I could see a haunted look in her eyes. Something like "What in hell am I going to find out next?"

"I guessed it might be something we needed to discuss," she replied.

Joan leaned forward and seemed to relax as I talked. I rambled on about all the things we did together. Dad wasn't happy about Mike, but at least I was into sports.

I knew I had to spring the rest of the story on her. I watched closely for her reaction as I continued.

"The first time Mike came to the house, he stayed for dinner. Dad was cold and distant through the meal. Mom made little jokes to lighten the mood. After dessert, Dad got up abruptly and left the table. Mom and I looked at each other, and an awkward pause ensued. Mike was plainly embarrassed, and once more, I felt Dad undermining my life. Mike and I went up to my room and horsed around for a while." I paused, my heart pumping a little faster, trying to choose the right words to go on with.

"It's all right, Damon," Joan said. "I know this is difficult for you after all you've been through, but talking about it may help."

Our eyes met. I could see so such love in them. I wished I deserved her. Yet I knew she wanted to help me, and maybe it would.

"Around ten, Mike thanked Mom for having him over, and I followed him out to his car. I slid into the passenger side, and he got behind the wheel. He put the key in the ignition but didn't start the engine. He turned toward me, and we looked at each other. We didn't say anything for several seconds. He suddenly took hold of my hand, leaned over, and pecked me on the cheek. I was speechless. He apologized and assured me he had a nice time and hoped I wasn't mad. Then he tried to start the car, but the battery was dead. He had left the radio on."

I could see tears glistening in Joan's eyes, and my voice was a little shaky. I stood up and took her hand, and we looked at each other. I leaned down and gave her a hug and kissed her on the cheek. I knew this was difficult for her.

"I want to hear the rest of the story. It may help both of us." She took out a tissue and blotted her eyes. "We have never discussed your past, and I have started a hundred times to ask you things."

"You know about Carlos."

She looked startled, and her guard went up. "Yes, a little. But tell me more about Mike, we'll get to Carlos later." She settled herself in the chair and nodded for me to go on. "Mike stayed the night?"

"It was too late to call the garage, and Dad would have had a fit jump-starting Mike's jalopy with his Mercedes. I asked him to stay overnight. No big deal. He insisted he could walk home or crash in the backseat of his car. He lived better than ten miles away, and his father worked nights."

"I insisted he stay overnight. He argued with me, and I thought he was mad at me. Suddenly, tears ran down his cheeks, and he mumbled something I couldn't understand. I asked him over again. 'I love ya, man,' he said and I said, 'I love you too.' And he said, 'No, I mean I love you.'"

"I was flabbergasted, and words failed me again. Then I started to cry. Then we hugged. We slept together that night, but that was the last night he ever spent in our house." I paused again, remembering that night. It was the first real sex I had ever had with another man. It seemed so natural to me at the time; it fulfilled the rather chaste interactions between Seth Porter and me.

"After we graduated from high school, I went to college, and Mike went to work for a telephone company. We got together weekends. When I got out of college we rented an apartment together, but it was never the same between us."

We fell silent again. Flashes of lightning lit up the sky, and thunder rumbled in the distance. Joan got up to leave the room, and I touched her arm. She turned to me.

"Mike's married now," I said. "They're coming to visit. That's what the letter was about."

"I wondered what he might say."

I didn't reply.

"How do you feel about him now?" she asked. Her face was serious, but her eyes were strong and unblinking.

I hesitated. How did I feel about him now? I felt emptiness; something had been stripped from me when he knocked me down, and I was somehow glad to be rid of him. It was over by the time I left for Texas.

I started to smile then threw my arms heavenward. "I don't feel anything for him now. Thank God, I don't have any feelings for him at all. I wonder if he wasn't more of a crutch than a...than a..." I hesitated.

"A lover," she finished.

"Yeah." I paused again. "Now that I look at it, we weren't really lovers, we used each other. But I don't have any regrets."

"And now he's coming to visit?" Joan continued.

"Yeah."

CHAPTER

❧ 10 ❧

Mike and Kelly were due to arrive at the Dallas-Fort Worth Airport at 2:00 p.m. Sleep last night was brief and intermittent. How did I really feel about Mike after the way we parted two years ago? Some say you never quite get over your first love. Forgetting Mike wouldn't be expected, but on the other hand, seeing him again at this point might pose some serious problems. We had foolishly invited Mike and Kelly to stay with us. It seemed the decent thing to do after our high school friendship. Mike was probably a happily married man now anyway.

The September sun rose hot and steamy. I rushed around the house in shorts and was barefoot, doing last-minute straightening up despite Joan's cleaning the day before. The AC was running at full speed, but I still perspired. Joan and I finally sat down for a cold drink. Her face was serious, and I noted the slightest tremor in her hand as she lifted the glass. There was a lot at stake for both of us.

"Are you nervous about seeing Mike again?" Joan asked, holding my gaze.

"I'd be lying if I said no. It's probably just as well though to get it over with." I glanced at the clock and frowned. Eleven already.

Joan reached for my hand, her face softening. "I know it will turn out okay. I love you."

Her eyes grew misty, and I squeezed her hand. "I know you do, and that makes everything worthwhile," I replied, but a shard of apprehension descended as I wasn't able to say "I love you too." She meant the world to me, yet something was missing in my life.

Around twelve thirty, I took a quick shower, shaved, and inspected the clothes I would wear. My reflection in the mirror revealed a few extra pounds around the waist. That would be something to watch as I had been overweight in my early teens. Running would be good for me again but only serve to remind me in a subliminal way of that horrible night two years ago.

Stepping into my shorts, I paused. Mike had always liked my legs. Paranoia pushed me in ways I hated to admit. A pair of lightweight slacks would serve just as well. If only Kelly has taken care of his needs and we could just be friends again. I ran a comb through my hair one more time and headed for the kitchen.

Joan looked stunning in a sheer lime green flowered sheath scooping halfway down her suntanned back. Fringed ends of a matching scarf draped over her shoulders and down over her breasts. A large straw hat framed her delicate face; ringlets of auburn hair peeked out around the band. Pale pink lipstick completed her carefully applied makeup, and sunglasses hid any emotions she might need to suppress. She slinked toward me and ran a finger down my cheek and reached up with a kiss.

"Wow," I stammered.

"I'm ready for my close-up, Mr. De Mille." She smiled.

"Thank you," I whispered, a tear teetered on my eyelid as we pulled out of an embrace.

"For what?" she asked, cocking her head.

"For making me realize once more what a wonderful choice I have made for my life." God bless her; she wanted Mike to know I was hers and willing to fight for me.

✍

The trip to the airport was an ordeal. We drove in silence; Joan slid her hand on my knee, and we glanced at each other. I was hanging on with every fiber of my being to my new orientation. Mike's arrival, now so imminent, tested my courage and resolve to the ultimate. Why hadn't I told Mike it wasn't a good time to visit? Maybe wait another year. Was Mike testing his relationship with Kelly as well? Would our old relationship rear its ugly head and take us crashing to the ground?

Joan bought a magazine at the airport and glanced at it occasionally. I sensed her eyes following me ambling forth and back, scanning the sky through the enormous tinted windows. The plane didn't land until nearly four—something about bad weather in the East. Finally, the silver monster skimmed the runway and taxied to the arrival gate. I moved over to the baggage pickup area where the rotating belt disgorged luggage from the flight.

Mike spotted me first and came up from behind. The familiar sound of his deep voice and the aroma of aftershave like I had given him for Christmas three years ago signaled his presence. I swiveled around, and he gave me a bear hug and a peck on the cheek. I felt suffocated in his huge presence.

"Christ, I've missed you man," Mike enthused. "We've got a lot to catch up on."

"It's been a while, a lot has changed in the past couple of years," I replied.

He peered into my eyes as we spoke. Was he trying to give me some kind of signal? My knees all at once felt weak, and I needed to sit down.

"Are we being super serious today?" Mike asked, a bit of a taunt in his voice.

"The pressures, Mike, the pressures." I glanced at him, and he glanced away too quickly. He shuffled change in his pocket and cleared his throat as if to speak but didn't. I was half-relieved, in a perverse sort of way, it was difficult for him too.

Mike, at the age of twenty-five, was a specimen of manhood. His shoulders had bulked up, and he had thickened some in the middle too. He wore a blue striped jersey, tan shorts, and loafers. His handsome features were entirely Western, but his skin was dark. There was an air of silent authority about him that conveyed the message "I'm not to be fucked with."

Two years ago flashed before me, lying on the kitchen floor where he had decked me. I had long since gotten over it and was the better for it. We were both at a loss for words for a moment. I detected a hunger in his eyes. An ominous stirring in the pit of my stomach set my nerves on edge. I was all too aware of the time we had spent together during very formative years and even after. Such memories are far better left in a discarded diary in the attic.

"Where's that lovely wife of yours?" Mike asked, launching back into his easy manner.

"She went to a concession stand. Here she comes." I turned toward her approaching figure, glad to have the spell of the moment broken. "She's anxious to meet you."

"I'll bet," he said, rolling his eyes. But a broad smile crossed his face, and I could see he was impressed with what he saw.

After introductions, Mike hesitated, started to shake hands, but Joan stretched out her arms for a hug. Mike looked at me over her shoulder with a quizzical look on his face.

"It's wonderful to meet you, Mike. Damon said you were best friends back in high school and college," she said without a hint of underlying connections.

Mike shrugged uneasily and glanced my way. "College for Damon, high school for me." I knew that regret over the latter never quite left him.

"Where's Kelly?" she asked, looking around.

"The flight was bumpy, and she got a little airsick. She headed for the ladies' room the minute we got into the terminal. Here she comes now," he replied, turning toward her approaching figure and beckoning. "Hey, Kell," he called as she trotted up to us, slightly out of breath. "Feelin' better?"

"Fine! I feel so silly. I never get airsick. Wow"—she cast her gaze around—"everything's so big here in Texas. Manchester Airport looks pretty small compared to this."

Kelly was clad in knee-length blue denim capris, a multicolored boatneck jersey, and open-toed sandals. Her curly black hair was done in an afro, and she wore no makeup. Her figure was slim with a physique more like a boy's than a young woman. She had an easy smile, and the two women hugged after being introduced.

Kelly turned to me, put her hand out, but it morphed into a hug. "You look familiar somehow, Damon. I'm sure I've seen you before." Her face clouded in attempted recollection.

"Can't remember," I lied. "I'm just the ordinary brown-haired, blue-eyed everyman." A flash of anger ran through me. *Yeah, you and Mike were messing around while he and I were still supposed to be an item. But why should it bother me now?*

I turned a little too abruptly and suggested we needed to get on the road before the rush hour. I took one of the suitcases, and Mike rolled the other out to the car. It was decided Mike would ride in the front seat with me, and the two women would ride in back. Kelly and Joan hit it off right away. They had no shared past. Kelly laughed and joked, and Joan was a good audience.

"Remember the first time I stayed overnight at your folks house, Damon?" Mike asked, chuckling.

"Yeah." I kept my eyes on the road. Was he trying to make me uncomfortable, or was he just being stupid? Traffic was heavy, thank God, so I needed to concentrate on driving.

"Your father had a pretty low opinion of me, didn't he?" Mike continued.

"He got over it though, after I…after we got active into sports. He wanted me to be the jock he was in high school. Track, baseball, football."

"No shit. Little did he know. Hah!"

"So," I broke in, "you and Kelly have an old house in Portsmouth. How's the redo going?" My hands felt sweaty on the wheel.

"Oh, great, I'm really into the restoration jazz. Kell and I have been eating plaster dust for the past six months."

I nodded and attempted a smile. He glanced at me and then away. We fell silent. Joan had taken off her hat, and Kelly was inspecting it. "Man, is this what you have to wear against the sun out here?"

"It helps," Joan replied. "Try it on."

Kelly perched it on her massive hairdo, and they both burst out laughing.

Mike twisted around in his seat and folded his hands in his lap and then shifted them onto his knees. I turned to speak to him, and he made a slight motion with his head toward his midsection. My eyes darted down as he swung his body a little more toward me. There was the outline of an erection in his shorts. A shiver ran through me, and my heart sank. I mouthed "No, Mike" and ran my hand across my throat, forefinger sliding by the scar on my Adam's apple.

My head felt like someone was chopping wood inside it. I slipped on my sunglasses and concentrated on driving. Were it not for Joan, I would have gladly crashed into a utility pole and ended all this horror. It was now clear in my mind that spending any time alone with him was out of the question. I wondered if Kelly had a clue as to Mike's and my past relationship. She seemed very much at ease. I liked her. But there was no way this visit wouldn't end in disaster.

We had decided ahead of time to take them out for dinner. The original plan was to stop at the house, let them freshen up, and then go out for the evening. Change of plan flashed in my head. I pulled into an elegant restaurant, the Sirloin Tip, and eased into the parking lot.

"Hope you guys are hungry."

Joan tapped me on the shoulder and whispered, "Maybe they'd like to unwind back at the house before we eat."

"Hell no, guys," Kelly overheard and responded. "We're fine and ready for some Western hospitality, right, hon?" she spouted, leaning over and squeezing Mike's shoulder.

The ladies got out before I could get their doors. Mike didn't budge. He had a problem that gave me wry pleasure. He grabbed my right arm before I was able to escape.

"We'll be right with you ladies," he called. "Goddammit, Damon," he hissed. "You know I've got a woody. Sure, we've had issues in the past, but I knew the minute you invited us out we'd be bedding down again, just like we used to. Look me in the eye and tell me you don't want to get fucked!"

His grip could have snapped my arm.

My scalp prickled, and sweat ran down my face. I no longer knew this man and was alarmed by his intentions. I gathered my courage and snapped back, "Two years ago I was raped on one of these streets. I swore then another man was never going to touch me again. Let go of my arm, or I'll lay on the horn until the police arrive."

A smile spread over his face, and he loosed his grip. "Hey, buddy, I was just testing you out. No harm in trying. No hard feelings, huh?"

I forced myself to smile as well. "What did you plan, to fuck me here in the parking lot? Have you forgotten I have a wife? And so do you, remember?"

An evil thought struck me. I reached under the seat and took the thermos with ice cubes we carry on hot days, unscrewed the cap, and before he knew what was happening, dumped the contents into his lap. He let out a squawk and jumped out, brushing himself off.

"Maybe this will cool ya off and help your problem."

I gave him a drop-dead smile and jumped out, slamming the door.

To my relief, Mike took it as a joke and shouted, "Good one, Duncan, your turn next time."

He sat, composing himself as I entered the restaurant.

My reprieve was only temporary. Mike was a persistent bastard and would try every method to get his way. Joan called to me from a table and motioned me over. Kelly was already seated and looking at the menu.

"Where's Mike?" Joan asked, an eyebrow raised. She came toward me and spoke in sotto voce, "What was that all about. What did he want?" She searched my face, her eyes darting from me to the door and back. "Are you okay?"

"Slow down, slow down." I took a breath to clear my head. "He had a little accident, but he'll be right along." I hugged her then rocked her back and forth a couple of times. "I'm fine, and I love you."

"Damon," she said, eyebrows arched, "what's going on. What's really going on?"

"Everything's under control. Tell you about it later. Let's have some wine."

We moved back to the table. I pulled out the chair for Joan, gave her a peck on the cheek, and sat down. Kelly seemed unconcerned about Mike's whereabouts and continued to study the menu.

Keeping my mind on the menu and the wine list while acting like everything was normal took great effort. The apparent challenges ahead were taking their toll. This would be the first real test of Damon Duncan, heterosexual, married man. Joan sensed my dilemma and tried to keep the atmosphere light. She surprised us by telling a slightly off-color joke, which sent Kelly into gales of laughter.

Mike finally appeared at the entrance and spotted our table. He had changed pants, somehow, out in the car. It was still early, so the dining room was less crowded than it would be with the dinner crowd. Mike joined us and acted as though nothing untoward had occurred. We ordered drinks and discussed what to choose for an entrée.

Me not being a drinker, a gin and tonic did wonders for my nerves. If I was to make it through the evening, liquor was going to be my friend. The second glass made me light-headed and a trace dizzy. I was feeling considerably better about Mike and Kelly all the time. Joan declined a third hit and nudged me with her knee. Mike was always able to drink me under the table and had not lost his touch.

He ordered steak, the usual. He used to claim it made him a sex bomb. Oh god! Kelly ordered chicken creole, and Joan and I ordered seafood. After another round of drinks, the waitress served the food. I requested a bottle of Pinot Grigio and a bottle of Merlot, at Mike's request, for Kelly and him. Both the fork and the plate appeared oddly distant, and my hand felt heavy reaching for them. The shrimp seemed to be swimming around, and I had to blink to make them stop. The wine steward poured as my hands were playing tricks on me. The glass was entirely too small and far away.

"Whas the matter, Joan, honey, you don't look like you're havin' fun? Come on, guys, drink up, we're havin' a party, me and my old friend Mike. How the hell's everthin' back in old New Hampshire?"

"Damon," Joan whispered, stabbing her finger at my plate, "eat, you need food in your stomach."

Nonplussed, Mike replied, "I'm still working for the telephone company. It recently sold out to TDS. And I pick up a few remodeling jobs from neighbors." Mike's eyes never left my face.

"Still getting a little nooky on the side?" A hiccup ended my sentence.

Joan looked shocked, Kelly's head shot up, and Mike tensed noticeably, a piece of steak halfway to his mouth. He stared at me and glanced at Kelly, who had stopped eating as well. She dabbed the napkin on her mouth and glared at me.

Mike was the first to recover. He put his fork down, eyeing me with a smirk on his face. "Good old Damon, always the smart mouth and the put-down."

We glared at each other. It was a foolish remark, and my addled brain soon realized it. Mike had a mean temper when aroused. Joan motioned to the waiter and asked for coffee.

We pushed the remains of our dinners slightly forward so the busboy could clear. The coffee arrived and the hot black liquid cleared my senses somewhat. Once again, I realized the favor Mike had done me when he instigated the breakup two years ago. Kelly was going to know the truth about the relationship we had back in New Hampshire. Mike owed me that.

Kelly must have sensed the extreme tension between us to be more than guy-stuff banter. Mike's jaw was set, and he slammed his cup down. The waiter offered refills, and Mike slapped his hand over the cup and shook his head.

The bill came, and Joan took it over a mild protest from Mike. Joan stated firmly that Mike and Kelly were our guests and would be treated as such. The waiter took the credit card and disappeared.

Joan caught Kelly's eye. "We're going to freshen up, back in no time."

✑

Fortunately, the ladies' room was empty. Joan went to the mirror and made the motions of checking her makeup. Kelly paced by the bank of lavatories and then back to Joan. She put her hand on Joan's arm.

"What the hell is going on out there anyway?" Kelly inquired.

"Damon has had a little too much to drink."

"Does he do this often?" Kelly asked, alarmed.

"I've never seen him like this before. We usually have a glass of wine with dinner, but that's it. I don't know what got into him." She half-turned back to the mirror, but Kelly spoke again.

"What in the hell is really going on out there, Joan? It's something about their relationship back in New Hampshire, isn't it?" Her expression grew serious, and she turned abruptly toward Joan, waiting for an answer.

"Damon has been under a lot of tension at work recently, and Mike is probably tired from the trip. A good night's sleep and we'll all feel better."

"That's crap, Joan. They're bickering like two lovers, for Christ's sake," she said, looking annoyed.

Joan's face froze for a second, but she recovered quickly and said, "Yeah." And she laughed.

Kelly didn't miss the body language or the momentary cast on Joan's face. "Oh my god, Jesus Christ!" She paused and clutched the side of the lavatory. "It's been there all the time, I just didn't want to believe it. Mike has always been wary when Damon was mentioned, uncomfortable, evasive. Tears started, and she struck the cold china several times with the side of her hand. "And he's still in love with Damon. Oh, Joan, what am I going to do?"

CHAPTER

11

Silence enveloped the table as Joan's and Kelly's presence faded from view. I avoided Mike's gaze, instead fiddled with my coffee cup before raising it two-handed for a last sip. In spite of the effect of booze, I was now alone with Mike, and an aura of alarm blanketed me. My inebriated brain began snapping back into reality, one tiny cog at a time, like damaged gears in a transmission climbing a steep hill.

Mike's hand was steady bringing the coffee cup to his lips, eyes clear and expression relaxed. No longer the vulnerable teenager I thought I loved so many years ago, now a man with a quick temper who knows what he wants and will get it one way or another.

He finally broke the silence.

"Well, here we are."

"Yeah," I said after another pause.

"Guess I came on kinda strong out there."

"You could say that."

Mike's mouth curled into a sneer. "Goddammit, Damon." He banged the table with his fist, lowering his voice when heads turned at a nearby table. "The last time I saw you, you were begging me to stay." He reached for my hand, but I snatched it away.

"As I recall, you made it damned clear it was over." Gall rose in my throat, but I choked out, "Did you think I was such a pussy

I'd pine over you the rest of my life?" I pushed the saucer back, concentrating on keeping my hand steady.

Mike picked up a napkin and inspected it. "As a matter of fact, I did. If you could admit it to yourself, you'd like me inside you right now. Why the fuck else did you invite us—me—out here for?" He tipped his head and squinted one eye.

"I believe it was you that did the inviting," Damon replied.

"We were going to stay in a hotel till you asked us to stay with you. Whatdaya expect I thought. And what's this shit about you being raped? You probably asked for it, knowing you." His fist wrapped around the napkin, crushing it, opening and closing his work-toughened fingers around the linen, his eyes boring into me. A hot flash of anger emblazoned me, and I spoke slowly through clenched teeth.

"You son of a bitch. If there was ever any chance of continued friendship between us, you just blew it. I was raped, all right, then beaten, and would have been murdered if the cops hadn't come along."

Mike wrinkled his brow, tipped his head back, and stroked his chin. "Gay men don't get raped, Damon, they get fucked. What were you doing? Out cruising, lookin' for some action and it got a little outta hand?"

A deadly anger I struggled to control suffused me. "No! Ilka and I had a quarrel, so I went out for a run."

"And where was Prince Charming while this was all happening, reading a book or cheering from the sidelines?" Mike clenched his fist around the napkin again.

I was taken up short. Did Mike know about Carlos? "What the fuck are you talking about? What Prince Charming?"

The din at surrounding tables abated at the raised voices. Mike leaned in and spoke just above a whisper. The restaurant chatter picked up again, and Mike repeated in a louder voice.

"Carlos, something or other, that rock singer? Understand you had a little fling with him out here." A sneer spread over Mike's face. "What did he do, rape ya and leave ya for dead?"

Emotion exploded inside my head like a bullet between the eyes. Anger then retaliation clashed to be released, but that was what Mike wanted, and I'd be damned if I'd oblige. I gripped the steak knife the steward had missed and stabbed the point into a dessert menu.

"Yes, I met him on the bus coming out. We hit it off right away. He stayed with Ilka and me a couple of nights until, well, he was on his way to California."

"Right, after the motherfucker spent time in jail."

Time in jail, right, one night. "Okay, Mr. Hot Shit, you think you know all about what happened. Go ahead, spill out the rest of the venom churning in that gut of yours." I leaned back in my chair, faking an impassive blankness on my face.

"Sure, it was all over the Boston papers, how that motherfucker tried to screw Jerry Haines out of thirty thousand when he skipped town. He thought he was some kind of a songwriter. I knew well enough he was with you. The *Boston Globe* said he was stalking a guy from New Hampshire he'd met on a bus to Fort Worth."

Every nerve in my body tightened like a violin string before a concert. I fantasized thrusting the steak knife deep into Mike's fat gut or holding a pistol in my hand and exalting over the blood gushing from the round hole between his eyes. Hateful words formed in my mind and coalesced in my brain. Mike will pay, big time, no matter how long it takes. His careless, uninformed accusation stung like a quick knee to the groin. The injustice of that terrible period has never been resolved. Now Mike has kicked open the scab.

"Was he a good fuck?" Mike inquired, a sick grin on his sweaty face as he looked around to see if he had been overheard.

"As a matter of fact he was, damned good. Sounds to me like you're jealous."

It was Mike's turn to be caught off guard. He shifted in his chair, doubled up both fists, planted them on the table, and gave a menacing snarl. "Like hell I am. I can have better than you anytime I want it."

"Then go for it, I'm not your fuck buddy anymore. Sure, we were good friends in high school, but a lot has happened since then. We're not the same people we were five years ago."

Joan's hand on my shoulder startled me. Her face was somber, and Kelly's eyes were red and puffy. Mike reached his hand out to Kelly, but she drew back like she had been stung. Mike jumped up, upending his chair. He turned, clutched Kelly's arm, and escorted her out. Joan and I looked at each other, and I put my arm around her.

The waiter approached and handed her the credit card on a salver. "I hope everything is under control, ma'am."

"Thank you, I hope so too," she said, signing the receipt and adding a tip then handing it back to him.

Outside, the humid early evening air clutched at our lungs like a dragon's breath. A film of fog had settled, and streetlights were fuzzy glowing orbs. The parking lot bristled with expensive automobiles. Attendants were now on duty, directing patrons to empty spaces. Mike stood in the path of an Audi inching up toward him. The driver tapped his horn. Mike snarled and stepped out of the way, thumping his hand angrily on the rear of the vehicle as it passed by.

Joan punched a number into her cell phone. After a brief conversation, she approached Mike. Kelly sat on the curbing twenty feet or so away, looking down at the pavement. Joan informed him she had called a cab to take him and Kelly back to the house. It was better that way; everyone could cool down. Mike made no comment but nodded assent. Joan beckoned the cab as it drew up smartly beside them. The driver stepped out and opened the rear door. Joan conversed in low tones with him, gave directions, and then slipped him a folded bill. Joan encouraged Kelly to get in the cab. Kelly shook her head no until Joan whispered in her ear. Kelly finally nodded. She and Mike sat on opposite sides of the rear seat as the cab pulled away.

I was waiting in the car. Joan came to the driver's door and told me to slide over.

"Thanks for taking charge, I wasn't up to it."

"You're in no shape to be driving either. What happened between you two anyway?" she asked, adjusting the rearview mirror and nudging the electric seat forward.

She started the engine, and we swung out onto the street. She glanced over at me.

"Mike and I had words out in the car. He wants it to be the same as it was three years ago back in New Hampshire. He tried to strong-arm me."

"The bastard," she snapped.

I was amazed and stifled a smile despite the situation. Joan rarely swore. "I don't look forward to the next few days. Christ, what a mess." I twisted around in the seat to face her. "The good news is he repulses me." It seemed Joan's hand relaxed a little on the wheel.

"I had planned to take Kelly shopping tomorrow then go over to the zoo. Not such a good idea under the circumstances."

"It's okay, I need to deal with Mike once and for all, tell him what's been happening with me, with us."

"Think you're up to it?"

"I don't know, but I'll give it a try. Bad words passed between us tonight. Maybe we can patch it up enough for them to finish their vacation here."

"He scares me a little. Kelly admitted she is afraid of him when he gets into these moods."

"But still she stays with him."

Joan nodded.

We rode in silence for several minutes. We have such a comfortable life with many happy evenings, sharing music, literature, and movies. It's not a passionate relationship. I've had passion, have I ever, but the pain after it was over hurt too much. And it always ended.

Always.

Now Mike has reappeared, but not the Mike I remembered. Maybe I've never knew the real Mike. And to make matters worse, Mike had to throw Carlos into the fray.

Joan broke my thought train.

"Kelly guessed what your relationship with Mike had been. I tried to calm her, but she's fighting mad."

The cab sat at the curb when we pulled up. Kelly stepped out when our car lights swung into the driveway. She tried to pay the driver, but he shook his head. Joan had slipped him a fifty back at the restaurant.

Mike was nowhere in sight. Not a good sign. Joan pulled into the garage and hit the closer.

"I'm sorry, Joan, really sorry." She turned off the engine and pulled out the keys.

"It's not your fault. How could you have known? Something must have happened to him. Something must be troubling him."

The cab pulled away, and Kelly stood on the sidewalk, her back to us. Fog enshrouded everything, visibility only a few feet away. A car drove up, and a couple of young guys whistled at Kelly when they slowed down.

"Looking for a little action, honey?" one of them cooed.

"The action I want to see is your foot pressing down on the accelerator, dude."

"You don't know what you're missing," the driver said, peeling rubber.

"Sorry about that, they must be from some other part of town. It's usually pretty quiet out here. Where's Mike?" Joan asked, turning her gaze around.

"He was out of the cab before it had stopped, headed that way." She jerked her head in the direction of town.

"Did he say what he was doing?"

"He didn't say a damn word all the way over here. He's acted strange ever since we decided to come visit you guys, kind of excited, like he was really looking forward to it." She turned and looked directly at Joan. "And now I know why."

"He never told you about what happened between him and Damon?"

"He just said they shared an apartment and knew each other in high school. Now I'm looking for the whole story. The whole goddamned dirty story."

Joan bristled with annoyance at Kelly's portrayal of the relationship. "I don't know many details, and I never asked for any from Damon. You should know that Damon has spent the last couple of years in reparative therapy."

"What the hell is reparative therapy?"

"In Damon's case it was to change his sexual orientation. It's a long, ongoing process, and he has made great strides."

"Let me get this straight." Kelly turned and walked a few steps, turned back, and rummaged through her shoulder bag. She pulled out a cigarette, tapped it on the package, stuck it in her mouth, snapped the lighter, and inhaled deeply. The momentary flash of light showed the anger on her face, mouth twisted, eyes snapping, shoulders hunched forward. She exhaled a cloud of smoke and drilled her eyes into Joan.

"So Mike and Damon were fucking in high school and got an apartment together afterwards."

"Look, Kelly, Damon was honest with me. I'm sorry that Mike wasn't with you. But it's in the past."

"You coulda fooled me. I thought they were gonna go at it right there on the table."

"I can't speak for Mike, but I can for Damon. We discussed his concerns about Mike and the past, and Damon felt that was all behind both of them now." Her voice shook a little, and she bit her underlip. "I'm going in now. Why don't we take your luggage and get you settled. Mike needs some time to cool off. I'm sure he'll be back."

"You don't know Mike. There's no telling what he'll do."

∞

After a sleepless night for all of us, Mike called the next morning. When I answered, he demanded in a brittle voice to speak with Kelly. I handed the phone to Kelly and only heard snatches of their conversation.

Kelly appeared a few minutes later while I was tapping away on my laptop on the patio. She had her suitcase and overnight bag stashed in the hall.

"Mike's at the airport. He wants me to meet him there. We're taking the afternoon flight back."

She spun on her heel and flounced toward the kitchen.

I jumped up and followed her in and gave her a hug.

"Are you going to be okay?"

She broke down a little, and I hugged her again. She took a tissue out of her pocket and blew her nose.

"I wish to hell I knew," she mumbled, then stiffened her back. "I've called a taxi. It should be here any minute."

"Oh, Kelly, I would have been glad to drive you." I felt guilty, for some reason, and upset, although Mike had brought it onto himself.

"I know you would, but we've caused enough trouble already."

The cab honked. Kelly took a last look around as if trying to remember everything, then we went out into the hall. I carried her luggage out, and the driver put it in the trunk. We hugged again.

"Tell Joan I wish it had all turned out differently. She's a peach."

I closed her door, and she ran the window down.

"Damon, I want you to know, you didn't do anything wrong, and I have no hard feelings."

I nodded as the cab pulled away. I stood there long after it was out of sight.

Mike, I realized again, did me a great favor two years ago.

PART 3

CHAPTER

1

July 2004

In retrospect, the next eight years flashed by. Joan was unable to have a child, and that weighed on her mind. Maybe she felt a child would bring us closer together, enhance my masculinity.

Late one spring afternoon, the sky roiled uneasily with an approaching storm. I sat at my desk in the bedroom, writing out checks, when a blast of wind-driven rain hammered against the wall. The curtains billowed from a partially open window, and rain gushed in onto the carpet. I hurried to lower the sash then stood contemplating nature's violence. A dull ache in my forehead presaged another bout of low spirits.

Joan appeared at the door; I was immediately concerned by the expression on her face. A tear rolled down her cheek. She was holding an envelope in her left hand with sadness in her eyes like I had seldom seen before. Alarmed, I reached for her. She put her hand out to push me away.

"Damon," she said, "I think we should call it a day."

Tears now flowed freely. She dabbed at her cheeks with an already-damp tissue.

I stepped back, my hand clutching the bedpost.

"I don't understand. We don't need to go out in the storm." I indicated the window. Her body language forewarned me there was much more than a meal out at stake.

"I'm talking about our marriage, or what's left of it. I can't continue like this." Her shoulders sagged, and she leaned her head against the door casing. "Dammit, Damon, this is so hard to say. I've been putting it off, there's never a good time to say it."

"Divorce, legal separation, what?" My breath caught, and the familiar tightness gathered in my chest. She held a letter in her hand. What could it say? Who could it be from?

"I haven't thought that far ahead. I just know it's no good to stay together any longer, for either of us." She hesitated then went on. "I feel so alone most of the time. I can't stand it anymore."

"Alone? You have me." I couldn't believe this was happening again, just like it did with Mike. We'd been going through a ritual these past couple of years that neither of us believed in anymore. Why hadn't we been more honest with each other?

"That's the trouble, Damon, I don't have you. I never did. It's Carlos, it always has been. I saw the look on your face when you read that he's HIV positive. God help me, I can't deal with his shadow between us anymore. He's that piece of your past you can't let go of."

We stood looking at each other. The pattern in the wallpaper behind her slowly undulated. Her face blurred. We moved toward each other. This time she didn't retreat. Almost in a slow motion trance, we hugged, my face buried in her hair, my right hand behind her neck. She slipped her arms around my chest in a tight embrace and started to shake. We were both in tears, but I knew she was right.

"I'll always love you," I managed to whisper into her ear.

"I know you will," she replied softly. "And I will you." She released her hold, and we backed out to arm's length. "You have fought your true nature longer than anyone could ask for, so neither of us should have regrets."

I slowly nodded. "But—"

"But"—her face was solemn—"now it's time for us both to move on while we're still young."

Her gaze left no doubt this was not a capricious move on her part but well thought out and final.

"I feared this coming." My voice caught. "It's hard to say, but you have saved me from it, coward that I am."

"Don't berate yourself, you have tried in every way to make it work. Don't ever think I haven't noticed and appreciated it. But an end comes." Her jaw tightened resolutely.

Neither of us spoke again for several minutes. The gale continued unabated outside. This woman with whom I had spent these past eight years was still a stranger in so many ways. We had never quarreled; no bitter words ever passed between us. She was always so conscious of my needs, my struggle; she deserved better. So much more needed to be said, yet neither of us could find the right words.

The phone rang, and Joan picked it up. She blotted her eyes with the tissue, but her voice was calm and strong. "No, Ilka, with the storm and all, this isn't a good evening to go out. Besides, we're both tired." A pause before she replied. "Oh no, we're both fine, it's just been a busy week, and we need the evening to rest." Another pause. "We'll speak to you tomorrow." She hung up the phone. "Ilka wanted to play cards this evening."

"I doubt she has a clue," I said.

"Don't underestimate her. She just doesn't want to believe it. She forced me onto you nine years ago, and we have been her pride and joy. She had turned her baby brother…"

"Straight," I finished for her. "We've all fooled ourselves long enough. Those goddamned support groups, 'I'm finding myself, it's so wonderful to be normal again.' A crock and we all knew it— every one of us." My heart had quieted, and a feeling of relief spread through me. I felt guilty, but I was glad it was Joan who was bringing things to an end.

"We could have gone on as we were, but I honestly don't think it would be good for either of us. And to tell the truth"—she paused, a feeble smile starting to lift the corners of her mouth—"I've been looking at other men, I have to confess." We looked at each other, and suddenly the tension was eased. We laughed rather guardedly.

"What kind do you prefer?" I asked, and it set us off again.

"Gay, of course." She covered her mouth, and her face sobered. "That was unfair and unkind. I never should have said it. It just slipped out."

The remark hit me between the eyes at first. I was not quite sure how to take it, so unlike Joan. But dammit, she was right. Good for her. I hoped she didn't think she was offensive. I put my arms around her, and she looked up at me, her face troubled.

"You know," I said, "why couldn't we have been honest with each other so much sooner? I feel like a wall has been ripped away from between us."

She buried her face in my shoulder, and her body shook. I let her cry and somehow found the warmth of her body against mine comforting, yet there was no sexual need or arousal. Did I feel less of a man now? Probably. But with all the counseling I had received these past nine-plus years, I was okay.

She handed me the envelope. It had a San Diego postmark with the initials CSB in the upper left corner. I held it in both hands to keep them steady. I studied it for several seconds. Then Joan and I looked at each other.

She spoke as she turned away.

"I'll start dinner so you two can be alone together."

I detected resignation rather than bitterness in her words. Perhaps a bit of relief. I went to the window, the envelope almost alive in my hand. I stared out as a bolt of lightning struck the ground a couple of hundred feet away, followed immediately by a deafening roar. Tree limbs and vegetation erupted in all directions.

Did I sense what the letter relayed? Was it something I would want to know? Why did I have such trepidations about opening it?

Was he sicker than I knew? Was he alone, needing someone? Who might be living with him now? I paced the room; the first letter I had ever received from him was in my hand, a phantom from my past. I had every one of his CDs hidden away in a drawer, the cellophane still intact.

I sat at the desk, the letter in my hand, torn between slashing it open or delaying it for later in the evening. What was stopping me? An invisible presence seemed to guide my hand to the letter opener. The phone rang, and I jumped. Should I answer? It was probably Ilka. I didn't want to talk with her. Joan picked up in the kitchen; I could faintly hear her side of the conversation. I moved to the hall door to better hear.

"A letter came from him just today," Joan said. A pause. "Under those circumstances, you had no choice." She was obviously listening to Ilka speak. "I have no idea, when I came out to the kitchen, he hadn't opened it. No, Ilka, I don't think you should come over." Another pause. "Listen to me," she continued sharply. "Don't come over."

It was refreshing to hear her speak sharply to Ilka. I'm sure she wanted to many times before. I went back to the desk, picked up the letter, and ran the opener across the top. Just touching the paper sent a shiver through me. It was a one-pager written on a yellow legal pad in a small, tidy script.

Dear Damon,

My dear friend, I have never finished a letter to you before, but I have started one a hundred times. I'm sure you have read about my problem (HIV positive), payment for the foolish life I have led. I'm an addict and an alcoholic, reformed, I'm happy to say.

You have never been far from my mind though. When the end may be in sight, it makes me want to tie up loose ends. I finally got up nerve enough to call Ilka and coerce her into giving me your address. She sounds the same as ever. I was surprised to hear you were still in Fort Worth. I threatened to come looking for you, and she panicked, I guess. She reluctantly gave your address. She told me you were happily married and was not interested in the "likes of me" anymore.

I am so happy for you, you deserve the best! Do you have any children? Maybe I can meet her and them (?) someday.

I have had more professional success and money than I deserve, but that is now in the past. Washed up at thirty-five, ha ha. My habits brought my success and popularity to a screeching halt. Remember Jerry Haines? He's in rehab somewhere, and Night Paving Now has a new lead singer. I'm not bitter, I knew what I was doing and can blame no one else.

I was so absorbed in reading the letter I was oblivious to the storm. A streak of lightning convulsed the front lawn, and the lights went out. Sparks flew from an overhead transformer across the street, and an electric wire hit the pavement. Joan rushed from the back of the house to see if there was any damage inside. I hugged her as we peered out to see a few brave souls wearing slickers gather beside the damage. A wisp of smoke curled up from behind the bed. I screamed at Joan to call 911 while I pulled the bed away from the wall. I could hear a crackling sound, and an acrid smell filled the room. I crammed Carlos's letter into my pocket.

Joan appeared at the door, alarm shown on her face.

"The telephone's dead," she gasped.

The flames in the wall sounded increasingly ominous. My body felt paralyzed, and every move was an effort. My heart pounded; the terrible nightmare was real.

"Use the cell phone if you can get through. I'll see if we can get help outside." I rummaged through garments on the hall coatrack and threw on Joan's slicker. People were on the lawn now, and the fire was erupting under the eaves. Strangers raced up onto the grass, pointing and chattering. My heart sank when smoke emanated farther along the eave line, and flames spit out the eave vent. The fire was spreading rapidly. I rushed back into the house followed by several onlookers willing to help.

We pushed a chair under the ceiling hatchway. My knees felt like jelly, and someone supported me as I lifted the hatch. Choking smoke and flames engorged the space. A pasteboard box carefully labeled Christmas Decorations caught fire as I watched helplessly.

A young man grabbed a fire extinguisher I had overlooked in my panic, and another young person boosted him up into the inferno. My entreaties not to get injured or overcome went unheeded. He foamed the area, and the flames subsided somewhat. Joan appeared with a wet cloth for him to cover his mouth.

Others out in the street asked for towels. Joan threw an armful out the front door. They laid towels and sheets on the lawn, which soon became soaked. A brigade of teenagers clambered into the attic and beat the flames with the wet cloths. One of them shouted, "The whole fucking roof is on fire." The storm raged on. My "firefighters" were soon soaked, smoke and soot covering their faces and clothes. No attempt on my part dissuaded them. They seemed to be making headway by the time the fire trucks arrived, but the firemen ordered everyone outside.

Before I left, I looked into the bedroom. The wall near where the fire started was charred. The curtains caught fire and flamed brightly then burned out, the smoky remains swinging from the rods. Our wedding picture, hanging over the bed, hung at an angle, burned beyond recognition. I could hear the firemen chopping holes in the roof. The hydrant was pumping water full force into the attic. Water poured down the walls and puddled on the floors. A mixture of rain and hydrant-fed water covered everything. The dining room ceiling sagged dangerously then collapsed onto the table and china closet in a shower of black water and charred timbers. Dishes and everything breakable lay in ruin on the floor. A cuckoo clock on the one undamaged dining room wall nonchalantly chirped seven times.

The storm finally let up, and the sky cleared. The crowd thickened outside as the weather improved. The house, just like our marriage, was in shambles. Water, covered in ugly black scum, rushed out the front door. The firemen announced the fire appeared out but a team would stay the night to watch for further outbreaks and to discourage looting. Electrical fires were particularly vicious as wires run all through the house, we were informed. Police lines pushed the crowd back, and the perimeter of the house was cordoned off with yellow tape on sticks driven into the ground. *Scene of the crime*, ran through my mind. A stubborn flame shot out the back roof vent over the kitchen. The firemen hosed it down and discovered the wall was on fire as well. Axes chopped away at the wall. The back patio was a tangle of broken clapboards, charred rafters, and destroyed furniture. The scene of many pleasant evenings was a tangle of ruins, both of property and memories.

The house would have to be gutted. Water damage had destroyed every wall and ceiling. Joan and I were numb at the loss of the home and the marriage we had shared for the past eight years. Carlos's letter, partly read, rustled in my pocket as my nervous fingers ran along the folds.

"Do you folks have a place to stay tonight?" a police officer asked as he nodded toward the house.

"We have relatives here in Fort Worth. We'll be okay, thanks," I assured him.

"Do you need to talk with a grief counselor? It takes time for something like this to settle in. Don't be afraid to ask."

He headed toward the front door and pulled it together then conversed with one of the men.

"Don't worry about your valuables, we watch for looters. The devils prey on folks like you, but we see to 'em. Don't go back in until tomorrow. It's dark now, and you might get injured.

The detached garage was untouched, and we sat in my car for an hour or so, talking very little, silently pondering the future. I kept my arm around Joan, who wept occasionally, twisting a handkerchief in her fingers. Could I ever face going into that house again? Three hours ago we were a married couple, presumably happy and living in a nice home.

CHAPTER

2

"I can't face Ilka. Not tonight. Too much has happened. She'll want to know every last detail." I was worried about Joan. Her face was ashen; she suddenly looked very fragile. She had been testier with Ilka than I had ever seen. It would not be good for them to get into a real tangle now.

"She'll be incensed, you know," Joan replied. "It's all been too much. I don't want to spend the night with her, and you shouldn't either. If I can just get to sleep. I want to forget everything and sleep for a month."

"Same here. Look at us, we look like we've fallen down a chimney."

We had streaks of black on our cheeks and chins. My left sleeve was ripped and barely hanging to my shirt. Joan had fared better because she had been getting cloths for volunteers to soak and relaying messages. My pant legs were still wet and likewise Joan's skirt. The cell phone rang in my pocket. I checked the number.

"Shit, it's Ilka. She's heard, you can be sure of that." I was tempted not to answer.

"What's happened?" she asked, her voice strained, almost breathless.

"The house was struck by lightning. There's been a fire, but we're both okay."

"I'm coming over." She clucked her tongue. "Your own sister, you weren't going to tell me tonight, were you?" she exclaimed in an anger-filled voice.

"Can it, Ilka, we were busy fighting the fire. What were you going to do, hold a hose? There's nothing you can do, we're fine, really," I said in a calmer voice. The connection was broken. I looked at Joan. "She didn't even listen to me. She's on her way over."

Hands shaking, I jabbed the garage door opener. We jumped in, and I floored the accelerator and screeched out into the street.

"We won't be her victims any longer."

I slammed the car into drive and drove like a maniac until we were out of the area Ilka would be coming from. After about five minutes, I let up on the gas. I had a death grip on the steering wheel, and my shoulders ached from tension.

It was after eleven, and neither of us had eaten since lunch. I swerved into an attractive-appearing restaurant and pulled into a spot near the entrance, hoping they weren't about to close. Another car pulled in, and two people got out and entered.

"Come on, Joan, let's eat."

She brightened a bit and smiled. "We look like pigs."

She ran her hand down a sooty sleeve.

I put my arm around her and pulled her close. I felt very emotional. Here, the most wonderful woman in the world was in my arms, but I would soon be leaving her. I prayed she would find happiness, real happiness. I dreaded the day we would part, but it was the best thing for both of us. We would be headed in new directions. The thought excited and scared the hell out me, both at the same time.

I fished around in the glove box and found some tissues, which helped remove the worst of the soot. We always left a jacket or two in the backseat. We sponged each other's faces, slid on jackets, and entered the dining room. It was nearly empty, so we would get decent service.

The waiter, a handsome young man, seated us and inquired about drinks. Joan and I looked at each other then nodded. The thought of wine sounded wonderful, but the last thing I needed was to get picked up for DUI.

"Any motels in this area?" I inquired. "It would serve us well after the evening we've been through."

"There's a Serendipity Inn out on Lenore Drive. Only about five miles out."

He stood near my left shoulder, holding a bottle of Merlot in his left palm, the neck resting in the fingers of his right hand.

"This would be a fine wine to start your dinner with," he suggested, looking intently at me.

I glanced at him, and he held my stare for a second. I felt uneasy and turned away. Is it all going to start over?

I looked to Joan, lifting an eyebrow for her opinion. She nodded assent, so we ordered a glass.

"Leave the bottle," I ordered.

He took great pains in pouring and made brief contact with my hand. We thanked him and studied the menu. He hesitated, and I looked up at him again. He smiled and then withdrew.

"He's making a play for you," Joan remarked after he was out of earshot.

"Don't be ridiculous," I snorted, glancing at her from the corner of my eye to ascertain if she was serious.

Her face betrayed nothing I could read.

Then, in a calmer voice, I asked, "You think?"

She nodded.

We decided on a pasta dish. She excused herself to go to the ladies' room. As she stood up, I whispered in her ear, "And leave me here with Casanova?"

"What the hell."

She trailed her fingers across my neck and shoulder as she kissed me on the cheek. Very unlike Joan to be demonstrative in public. Already the proposed marital breakup was changing her, in some ways for the better, I hoped. We were too much alike, easygoing and nonassertive. She needed to have more spunk. I worried about her.

The waiter returned as Joan disappeared into the foliage plants placed everywhere.

"Is the wine satisfactory, sir?" he inquired. His face somewhat flushed behind a deep tan, and his breathing appeared a bit rapid.

"Yes, fine," I replied, avoiding his gaze.

"Can I guess you and the lady were involved in a fire this evening?"

"Our house was struck by lightning late this afternoon and destroyed by fire."

Just thinking and speaking of it again made me shudder visibly, and I was feeling uncomfortable with his hovering. He expressed regret and hoped we would be able to rebuild. I thanked him, and he moved away, adjusting chairs, retrieving a napkin and several straws from nearby tables, anything to kill time, I guessed. I poured us each another glass.

"I don't wonder you need a drink, several drinks," he said, coming back to our table a few minutes later. "Tell you what"—he snapped his fingers as though the thought had just come to him— "you and the lady take your time and enjoy yourselves." A sly look came to his face as he leaned in closer. "I'm off in an hour. I live near the inn, and I can drive your car there easily. It's only a couple of blocks from my house. I can walk home, and my roommate can drive me to work in the morning."

"We would really appreciate that," Joan remarked, suddenly reappearing. The waiter was taken off guard and nearly tipped over the wine bottle. He scrambled to help her with the chair. "My husband is very tired and needs to relax." She sat down calmly and announced she was ready to order. We consulted again and agreed as he wrote feverishly on his pad and scurried off to the kitchen.

Joan had a Mona Lisa smile cross her face.

"What?" I asked, new facets of her personality surfacing before my eyes.

"I'm suddenly starting to feel free. To hell with the house and to hell with Ilka."

"And to hell with me?"

"You know that's not true." She patted my hand, her face sobering.

"I know." A shiver ran through me, and my throat tightened as I placed my other hand on hers. "Am I that obvious?" I nodded toward the kitchen where the waiter had disappeared.

"I bet he tries to put the make on every nice-looking man that comes in." A tear suddenly rolled down her cheek. "I'm going to miss you, you know." She picked up a saltshaker and ran an edge of it along a groove in the table then set it back. She started to speak, paused, then looked at me. "What is Carlos really like?" She laid her hand on mine. "Be honest."

"Nothing like the tabloids have portrayed." I squeezed her hand. "I did something bad to him ten years ago, and Ilka, damn her soul, did worse." A lump developed in my throat, and I couldn't talk for a few seconds. "I think a lot of his troubles have been caused by the way I treated him the last time I saw him." I couldn't continue; the room was a blur.

"How did you meet him?" She stroked my hand, her index finger circling my wedding band.

I somewhat regained my composure and continued, raising an eyebrow. "Ilka never told you?"

She looked away for several moments, pulled her hand back, played with the seal around the top of the wine bottle, and set it back in place. "I always doubted her story. She seemed so bitter. She was so sure that some fellow years ago back in New Hampshire had molested you and that Carlos had—well, let's not get into that."

"I met Carlos on the bus from Boston to Fort Worth," I replied. "The attraction was instant, like a spark of electricity jumped between us. Physical, you've seen pictures of him, but more than physical, a lot more. I would have gone anywhere, done anything to be with him. And the feeling was mutual." I glanced at her to get some reaction; her expression remained serious. "Ilka liked him, at first. He charmed her, but she knew she was losing me, and she couldn't stand it."

Our salads arrived, and the waiter set the plates carefully in front of us, unrolling the napkins and laying our silver out. He poured us another glass of wine at my request and assured us our entrées would be coming shortly. I avoided his eyes. We ate our salads and warm rolls ravenously. The wine relaxed me, and I needed to talk.

"You loved him," Joan said, more statement than question.

"Passionately." I touched her hand and looked her in the eyes. We were now both beyond pretense.

"A day has never gone by you haven't thought about him?"

"Not one, which never lessened my love for you." I smiled ruefully. "I thought I'd never hear from him again."

"What happened?"

"We were staying a few days with Ilka. I planned to continue to California with him. He offered to go out for a while one evening so she and I could talk. She even let him borrow her car.

"I told her about the fight with Dad before I left New Hampshire. Ilka feigned surprise, but it was just an act. Then I told her about my relationship with a man in New Castle. She accused him of making me gay. Right then I knew her tolerance was a lie. I yelled at her and ran out into the night, the early morning hours actually, like a damn fool, in a strange city, into the blackness. Carlos met me at the door and tried to stop me, but I outran him." I paused. "You didn't know, Ilka never told you?"

"She said you were beaten up, left for dead, and she felt Carlos had something to do with it."

I banged the table with my fist. "Damn her, I was beaten, raped, and my throat was sliced. I would have been murdered if a police car hadn't come by on another call. The men, four or five of them, threw me behind a bush and ran down an alley when the lights hit them. I managed to crawl to an ambulance that followed the patrol car. Carlos had nothing to do with it in any way whatsoever."

The horror of that night came back to me with a rush. The combination of our marriage ending, the letter in my pocket, and the fire suddenly overpowered me. I poured another glass of wine.

"Oh, Damon, I don't know how you ever stood it. No wonder you still have flashbacks."

"I was scared shitless of men after that. The rapist could have figured out who I was and come after me again."

"No, Damon, I never knew."

I could read the pain in her eyes. Her right hand closed over mine again.

I couldn't go on. I felt like every bit of life had been bled out of me. The wine tasted good, and I needed it. We fell silent; the only sound was traffic and city noises in the distance. I touched my pocket for the reassuring rustle of Carlos's letter. She didn't mention it, but I'm sure she must have been curious.

The waiter returned with our entrées. We had consumed the bottle of wine, and the liquor was having an effect. I needed to go to the restroom but didn't want to stumble. More bread and the meal would help, I was sure. The food was hot and rich, the perfect antidote for the staggers. The waiter lingered until I assured him everything was fine.

Relaxing somewhat, feeling I owed Joan the whole story, I related some of my experiences with Seth Porter fifteen or so years ago. It must have been like picking a sore to her, but one you can't refrain from in spite of the pain. It sounded worse to me the more I talked, and I hesitated when it came to the money he left me. Once more I had told most of the story and again wished I hadn't. I could have at least spared her these details.

I felt in control enough now to head for the restroom; besides, I needed to get up and move around. The place was empty, and I splashed cold water on my face. After relieving myself, the letter came to mind. There was not much more to read, and the need and temptation were overpowering. I went into a stall and sat on the toilet, clutching the letter as though someone might snatch it away. My hand shook as I pulled it out of my pocket.

> I have bought a two-bedroom house on the beach. It has a large deck that looks toward the ocean a couple of hundred feet out at high tide. I have become quite the beachcomber. I fancy the sun gives me energy. I'm taking a lot of meds and hope, on good days, to beat it.
>
> I am alone here now and find all my so-called friends have moved on to more exciting things. I lived with a fellow for about a year, but he turned out to be a gold digger, and he finally found someone else.
>
> I have a piano again and still compose songs when the mood strikes. I think of you often and remember our bus trip. I still regret my harsh departure from you ten years ago. I was thinking of myself instead of you and what you had been through. That is now best all in the past.
>
> I hope you are happy and well settled in your life. My best wishes to your lovely Joan. Write me sometime if the mood strikes.
>
> Affectionately,
>
> Carlos

I sobbed without restraint for several minutes over what we had had and what we had lost. I reread it, needing to decide if he knew and felt more than he was saying. Yin and yang. Two halves of a whole. Words said long ago, were they still true? "I am alone here now." His words physically aroused me for the first time in months. What an enormous hold he still held over me. I composed myself with difficulty and returned to Joan. At last I had a view of a future. Or did I?

∽

The waiter was in charge of closing down for the night. He scurried around, tidying up and shutting off lights. Joan sat in a trance, her eyes focused on some distant spot, far beyond the confines of these restaurant walls. I came around in front of her, but she seemed unaware. I touched her arm, and she jumped. She rose from her chair, and I took her arm, and we headed outside.

Hope and sadness mixed in various amounts as we climbed into the car. Joan sat in front with the waiter who drove us as promised. We tipped him fifty dollars. He feigned reluctance, but his broad smile indicated he was pleased. Joan took special pains to express our gratitude. Whatever his intentions had been, he was soon on his way home.

The Serendipity Inn was pleasant enough. A moderate-sized building, very clean but not pretentious. It would serve our needs well. The desk clerk must have thought we were out on a binge; we were disheveled and without luggage. We showered and slept in the raw. My dreams were full of Carlos; tangled pieces of our past ebbed and flowed through my subconscious. I awoke with a start several times in the night. Joan appeared to be deep in sleep. I felt very protective of her; but my allegiances were now torn.

CHAPTER

3

Dawn slithered over the landscape like mud oozing down a California hillside after a heavy rain. I awoke from a heavy sleep that had finally descended upon me in the early morning hours. A light drizzle fell, and the air felt unusually cool for the time of year. My mind was unwilling or unable to reassemble the previous day's events in any logical pattern. Perhaps there was no logical pattern.

Joan slumbered as I slid out of bed so as not to disturb her. My brain was developing twin compartments, the heavy oppression of unpleasant work and duties to be accomplished and the lightness of promised new beginnings. The door in my mind swung easily between the passage from one side to the other involuntary. The slightest decision came with great effort, and my head was betrayed by a hangover.

The motel furnished a coffeemaker. I brewed a pot and drank a cup, hot and strong; its power slowly spread through my body. My true nature was wending its way to the surface like a drowning man disentangling himself from wreckage on the ocean's floor. Would I be able to escape the confines of the cocoon of my past and not become ensnared in the sticky webs of the future? And so I sat for the better part of an hour.

Joan stirred, and our day began.

The rapid departure from the site of last night's calamity precluded any essentials being available, if indeed any were unharmed. At least we had the cell phone. Joan must call the hospital where she worked, and I needed to call Ilka. Joan's call went well; mine did not.

"I'm sorry about last night," I said, a dull ache throbbing in my neck and down into my spine.

"Where were you? I waited in my car two hours, expecting you would be returning. I was worried sick something might have happened," Ilka said, ice in her voice.

"I told you we were fine." Anger rose in my throat. "It's not every day your goddamned house burns down, so I don't need any of your shit," I snapped back at her.

"Don't be profane with me, Damon." Then her tone changed and became almost plaintive. "You're my brother, and I worry about you."

"I realize that, but give me a little slack. I'm not thirteen years old anymore."

"Where did you spend the night?" she asked, her voice hardening again. "What's family for if they can't help each other in an emergency?"

"We rode around, just to get away from the scene. Neither of us wanted to talk with anyone else. I can't explain. We needed quiet, that's all."

"My god, Damon, you didn't sleep in the car?"

"Of course not." The conversation was going downhill rapidly; I had to end it. "We'll be over later and can talk it out." I hung up before she could say anything more.

"Is she on her broomstick again?" Joan asked, a rueful smile crossing her face.

"I think it's welded to her ass."

We had breakfast at a Subway. I called our insurance agent from the car. He was to meet us at the house sometime later in the morning.

∽

A terrible feeling of loss swept over me when we turned the corner of our street. Joan had a tissue pressed to her mouth. We pulled into the driveway where the damage seemed less severe outside than I had feared. As we circled the house, however, the damage was more evident. Bedroom windows smashed out, and several holes gaped in the roof. A policeman stationed outside asked for identification prior to our entering. He escorted us through the ruins, cautioning about broken glass and weakened ceiling rafters.

I was sick at heart at the mess inside. Our bedroom was destroyed; the outside world stared back at us through open cavities that were once windows. The ceiling had collapsed, and rain from the roof spattered and dripped from the chopped-out holes. The living room and guest room were intact save for water stains on the walls. The dining room and kitchen were completely destroyed. A blue haze and an acrid odor from smoke still hovered. I grieved over this symbolic destruction of the past eight years of our marriage. Yesterday's storm neatly severed the physical remains with the finality of a guillotine.

We collected what we could salvage of our belongings and valuable papers from my desk and bureau drawers and dumped them into black plastic garbage bags. The clothes in our closets were mostly unharmed, and I loaded them into the backseat of the car.

The insurance adjuster arrived about five minutes before Ilka appeared. He was experienced in disasters like this, but his genuine sympathy and good-hearted encouragement lifted our spirits somewhat. He arranged to have a tarp put over the roof and have the windows boarded up. We mutually agreed to have a trailer pulled onto the lot for us to live in for the duration. We discussed having the shell bulldozed and building new or rebuilding. It was impossible to keep Ilka away from him during negotiations, but she clung to us like last winter's mud. The final decision was up to Joan since she would be the one living here. Ilka scented something awry like a bloodhound tracking a fugitive.

I was vice president of the bank and had close ties with the president, whom I was being groomed to replace someday. I had parlayed my bequest from Seth Porter into several million dollars in stocks and high-interest real estate notes. The one thing I was good at was making money. Joan wouldn't need to work, and we would both have high residual income streams. It was my intention for the property to be Joan's. The least I could do was leave her financially secure.

I gave the adjuster my cell number, and he promised to be in touch no later than tomorrow regarding the trailer and securing the house while we decided what to do. Ilka paced around as we spoke, absorbing every word spoken.

In the bottom drawer of my desk, I found unopened copies of all the CDs Carlos recorded during the height of his career. I hadn't been able to listen to them, afraid of the emotions they might evoke. Yet I treasured them. His handsome face smiled back at me and the world. I straightened up and shuffled through them, my mind absorbed in the past. How foolish I had been not to follow my dream. Could I have saved him from all the problems with liquor and drugs? Or would I have been an impediment to his career? Am I now anticipating something that will once more turn to ashes? I pushed him away ten years ago; will he push me away now?

Joan was busy collecting cosmetics and medicines from the master bath. I carried another armful of clothes out to the car. I slid into the driver's seat and pulled out Carlos's letter and reread it. Was there something in there I hadn't seen in the first read? Did he have a lover he was not mentioning? I needed desperately to contact him. I needed to see him. How had I deluded myself so long that I could continue living without ever seeing him again?

I tipped my head back against the headrest, staring at the headliner, the letter resting in my lap. Something Dr. Polanski said to me years ago flooded my mind. *What do you really want, Damon?* I told him I didn't know. *The day will come when you do, don't let it be too late.*

"Damon," Ilka said at the car window, "I'm going home now to make a good lunch. You aren't eating right, and you both need to change those stained clothes."

I was startled and tried to conceal Carlos's letter. I'm sure she didn't miss it but said nothing. I felt like a little boy caught playing with matches. I flushed and then felt annoyed with myself. I still had a long way to go before being able to take charge of myself.

"About an hour?" she asked.

I nodded and managed to say thanks. I couldn't turn my back on her now; she had seen me through some rocky times and meant well in her own twisted way.

We both got a leave of absence from our jobs and stayed with Ilka the next two endless nights until the trailer arrived. Daytimes were spent on salvaging or disposal.

I discussed the future with Joan. She suddenly seemed so helpless and vulnerable. Was I doing the right thing? Would someone try to take advantage of her?

I fell apart a few nights later and said I wasn't going to leave. She faced me down and said it was the only way. Both our lives would be ruined if we didn't separate. The old song "Breaking Up Is Hard to Do" ran over in my mind.

The house was beyond salvaging, so we decided to rebuild a larger house, and then Joan could either sell it or live there. The trailer had two bedrooms, and we agreed it best to each have our own room. Unfortunately, we fell into the old habit of letting Ilka run our lives. She cooked meals for us, and we played cards in the evening at the trailer or her house. We were not up to breaking that tie until about a month into the rebuilding. We decided, in fairness to Ilka, we should be truthful with her.

We concluded it would be easier to invite her out, as she couldn't make as bad a scene in a restaurant. I was so nervous I had to change my shirt before we left the house. Joan appeared calm, but her hands were shaky.

We chose a posh nightspot with gourmet dining and a dance floor since Ilka enjoyed dancing. We all dressed for the occasion. The maître d' showed us to a special table overlooking the dance floor and asked if we would like to start with a cocktail. A waiter appeared shortly to take our drink orders. Wine and rolls were served, and we nibbled on stuffed mushrooms and oysters rolled in bacon. Joan and I agreed beforehand to wait until after the entrée to confront her.

I asked Ilka to dance. I glanced at Joan, and she nodded. I learned a lot of dance steps back in my days with Mike. Ilka was quite a dancer herself.

"You seem rather on edge tonight, Damon. Is something troubling you?"

"Nothing new. Guess the strain of rebuilding is getting to me."

"Is everything okay between you and Joan?" she asked.

Jesus Christ, what do I do now?

"I understand you got a letter from Carlos a few weeks ago."

"Yes."

"What did he want after all this time?"

"For God's sake, Ilka, can't I get a letter from an old friend without the third degree?"

"You don't need to be so defensive about it."

"I'm sorry, I didn't mean to overreact. He was wondering how we're doing here in Fort Worth, and he even asked after Joan."

"So you're going to dump Joan and go rushing back to him."

"What?" I stammered. I was soaked in sweat and tried desperately not to lose it on the dance floor. I needed air. "Let's go back to the table," was all I could say. The truth of her words hit me between the eyes. She said in a few succinct words what Joan had only implied.

Ilka headed for the door. I leaned over and whispered in Joan's ear what had happened. She looked stunned. I threw four twenties on the table and escorted Joan out. Ilka paced the parking lot. She strode over toward us and said to Joan, "Are you going to let him get away with this? Just walk out on you?"

"I was the one that started this, Ilka. Damon would have gone on as we were. Give him some credit. It wasn't working, we both tried our damnedest, but it just was not to be."

"If that snake in the grass had left you alone, this wouldn't have happened."

"I presume the snake in the grass is Carlos," I barked at her.

"Yes, and he was from day one," she shouted back. "And you're going back to him the minute he beckons."

"If he'll have me," I said, curling my lip and standing in front of her, daring her to go on.

She threw up her hands. "If he'll have you, if he'll have you! The bastard, the damned bastard, he's ruining your life again." She turned. "I'm calling a taxi."

"Get in the car," I ordered.

She started walking away.

"Now," I said as firmly as I could.

"Ilka," Joan interceded, "I'm asking you to get into the car. We have got to calm ourselves and settle it once and for all. It won't go away. Leaving won't settle anything."

Shoulders sagging, she grudgingly climbed in back. Joan got in with her. Ilka was crying, and Joan put her arm around her. They were silent for the trip home. I could see Joan's face in the rearview mirror, and there was resoluteness, a firmness that encouraged me. She would be okay.

Back at Ilka's, Joan took charge like I had not seen before. Ilka's shoulders shook with weeping, but she was quiet and submissive. Joan set a pot of coffee brewing and started making sandwiches. She took over as though it was her house. We ate mechanically, in silence, our minds flooded with questions and accusations.

Later, after we had all calmed down somewhat, Joan pulled a chair up by Ilka and stated, "Damon and I have done everything we could, but it was not enough and never will be. We have come to terms with each other. You must do the same."

"I promised Dad I'd get him over this gay business if it killed me. Tonight it just about did."

The lines in her face deepened, her jaw set; she seemed to have aged years in the past few hours.

"He had no right to ask, and you had no right to promise," Joan replied. "It was up to Damon. Nobody has the right to dictate someone else's life."

I felt anguish for Ilka in spite of myself. "What do you owe Dad after what he did to you?"

Her head snapped toward me, the tic erupting on her cheek. "What do you know about that?"

She jumped up, grabbed our dishes, and clattered them into the sink.

"Enough," I replied.

Joan looked questioningly at me.

"The nasty old bastard," Ilka spit out, yanking the dishwasher door open and slamming dishes in, "coming to my room at night. Mother would never believe me. She always defended him. I never did anything to encourage him. I knew I must be bad, or it never would have happened."

Joan looked at me, appalled. "Of course it wasn't your fault, Ilka." She jumped up and put a hand on Ilka's shoulder. "You can't blame yourself for other people's actions, you must believe that."

Ilka turned, and they hugged. Ilka sighed and pulled out of the embrace.

"I've never told this to another living soul."

She ran the dishcloth over the table and straightened the chairs.

⁂

Days went by. I was frankly scared to call Carlos. After all this time, we couldn't just pick up as though nothing had happened. We were both different people now. I filled my mind with sheet rocking, taping seams, kitchen cabinets, and hardwood flooring. Overseeing all these activities helped take up my mind. But the nights, oh, the nights. I imagined all kinds of possibilities while I tossed and turned. The head of the construction crew finally got after me in a good-natured way.

"Mr. Duncan," he said, smiling, "we're going to have to charge extra for time spent working around you."

Joan was aware of my procrastination. "Call him, it's going to be okay, whatever happens."

I called information for San Diego. My hand shook as I punched in his number. It rang several times. Is he away? Is he sick? Does he have caller ID and know it's me and not want to answer? That's crazy, how would he know it's me? I was about to hang up when a husky voice, somewhat out of breath, answered.

"Carlos here."

"Hi. It's Damon."

The line was dead for several seconds. My heart pounded.

"Damon?" His voice broke. "It's really you? I was afraid you never got my letter. I wanted to put my phone number on, but I didn't want to seem too presumptuous."

"It's me." My voice was hoarse. I swallowed and cleared my throat. "How are you doing?" I managed to say.

"I'm fine," he said more firmly. "I heard the phone and ran in off the beach. I jump every time it rings, hoping it's you."

"I never thought I'd hear from you again."

"Oh, Damon, what we had. How did we ever let it slip away from us?" His voice was so faint I barely heard the last few words. Struggling for my voice to reply, he continued. "Don't listen to me. You've made a good life for yourself, and I'm happy for you."

Why was I hesitant about mentioning my separation from Joan? "And how about you?"

"It's very peaceful here. The ocean is beautiful as I look out over it every morning. I'm doing a little songwriting now that I have the time. Taking it easy."

"I want to come see you, if you have room." My palms were sweaty on the phone as I waited for him to reply.

"Damon, you're fishing, just like you did ten years ago. No, I don't have a lover, not for years. You'd be more than welcome. Like you couldn't believe. I have room for your wife as well," he said with a chuckle.

I visualized the corner of his mouth tilting up. "No, I'll be alone. Joan and I are legally separated. She's a wonderful woman and understands me better than I understand myself. I'll always love her, but"—I paused to steady my voice—"I-I've missed you."

We were both quiet, struggling with our emotions.

"Oh god, Damon, I have thought of you every day."

"And I of you," I managed, hardly able to speak around the lump in my throat.

We continued talking for the better part of two hours. I listened in amazement as he recounted the life he had finally put behind him.

"How soon can you come?" he finally asked.

"I can clear my schedule and be along in a few days."

"The fewer the better."

"I'm sorry." At last I was able to say it. It had eaten at me all these cursed years. What hidden anger had he harbored? I had to say it to deal with what had torn me apart so long.

"For what?" he asked.

I sensed his curiosity and perhaps anxiety.

"What I did to you ten years ago."

Memories of the whole terrible episode washed back over me as I waited for his answer. My mind raced, thinking of ways to finish my business here and be on the road.

"Get your ass out here and make it up to me."

CHAPTER

4

American Airways Flight 271 hovered like a giant bird of prey on its slow descent to the Manchester-New Hampshire runway. I peered at the ground rising beneath me, trying to identify any familiar landmark in an area where I spent the first twenty-three years of my life. Nothing looked the same from above.

At last there was the thump of the landing gear as it hit the tarmac, and the plane taxied to the terminal and cut its engines. I watched the baggage attendants fill the trolleys with luggage while we waited to exit the plane. A long portable tunnel rolled up to the passenger exit door, and we all shambled through and up into the main terminal. A young man waiting at the exit gate rushed up to a pretty young brunette, and they hugged and kissed hungrily. I wondered how they would feel if they had been separated for ten years. I looked around at the bustling crowd; every passenger has a story. How many would end happily?

After retrieving my bag from the carousel, I spotted a McDonald's and stepped into line. No Diet Coke and green salad for me.

"A quarter pounder, fries, and a large soda please."

I found a small table facing the incoming planes. In another few days, I would be departing once more back to Fort Worth then driving on to California. The letter from Carlos rustled reassuringly in my breast pocket. Was I throwing away everything from the past in order to chase an elusive dream? Yes! Being the good son, good brother, and good husband have purged my soul and defecated it onto the streets of New Castle and Fort Worth. No more. A whole new world was opening.

The folks knew I was due in today, but I didn't give them a flight number or time of arrival. No welcoming committee or cross burning, as the case might be, at the airport. A stop at the New Hampshire State Liquor Store was also in the plan. The scene later in New Castle would require a good deal of liquid lubrication.

"Excuse me, sir." My reverie was broken by the young man from the gate. "Could we join you? There aren't any empty tables, and I thought maybe…"

He blushed and looked apologetic, leaving the sentence hanging.

I looked up and smiled.

"All finished. Guess my mind was somewhere else." I pushed away from the table and collected the leavings and crammed them into the paper cup. "Enjoy your lunch."

The young man thanked me and pulled out the chair for the brunette. Their minds were on each other. I quickly receded from their view. She's a lucky gal. The young man—boy, really, probably less than twenty—was a handsome specimen. What a long road I had traveled to be able to accept myself as a gay man and to appreciate other men.

A little prickle of concern surfaced every so often. How have the years treated Carlos? He's HIV positive. How long does he have? His face in the tabloids looked tired and sad. I longed to have my arms around him again, to care for him as time passed. I glanced around and then slid on my sunglasses.

∽

The day was warm, and I was glad to slip into the rented Chrysler and pump up the AC. I circled the perimeter road a couple of times. The airport was so much larger now than it was ten years ago it took time for my mind to absorb it. I pulled out onto Brown Avenue, heading toward I-93. The traffic was busy, but the two lanes north were nothing like the six suicide lanes going all directions in Dallas and Fort Worth. I headed north toward Hooksett. Plenty of time to head south later.

The road slid smoothly under my wheels; the late summer hillsides were a lush green, preparing for the fall colors a few weeks away. The state liquor store / rest stop soon came into view. A brief stab of hot sun between car and cool store interior reminded me of Texas without the humidity.

I perused the aisles looking for some good scotch for Dad, his favorite, and several bottles of wine that might sooth the "savage beasts" after dinner. I turned the corner and was flabbergasted to see Kelly. She stood inspecting a bottle in the vodka aisle. I hesitated a moment, considering whether to move on as she was apparently unaware of me. A moment too long, she turned, and our eyes met.

"Kelly, fancy meeting you here," I exclaimed tritely, hurrying over to give her a hug. I stood back, holding her forearms, looking into her eyes. A tear rolled down her cheek. "What is it, Kelly, you that glad to see me?"

"You're the last person I ever expected to see. Are you just arriving?"

"Yeah, what's happening?" I ran my finger down her cheek, tracing the trail of the tear. "Is it Mike?"

She nodded and pulled a tissue out of her purse, blotted her cheek, and blew her nose. A chill ran through me, and I guessed it was not something I wanted to hear. Thoughts of Mike hadn't surfaced for some time. It was a finished chapter for me, end of book.

"Is he here with you?"

I dreaded her answer; New Castle would hold enough challenge without this.

"No, he's at home. I should be getting back. He'll be angry if I'm late."

"Things are not going well then?" A hollowness developed in the pit of my stomach. I had come to the point of forgiveness toward Mike for the way we parted ten years ago in Portsmouth. But anger remained over the horrible weekend two years later in Fort Worth. "Time for a cup of coffee?" I could see she needed to talk.

"I guess it wouldn't do any harm. It will be good to sit a minute."

We finished our purchases and carried them to our cars. Kelly's car was an older model and had numerous nicks and dings. She saw me and flushed. I put my arm around her, and we headed for the main rest station. I wished I could do or say something that would cheer her up. Maybe just talking would help.

We found a couple of chairs in a quiet corner, and I went for coffee. Kelly sipped at hers for several seconds. I doubted she even knew what it tasted like. I waited for her to speak, trying to look sympathetic. She sighed and peered at me over the Styrofoam cup.

"Mike never really got over you, Damon. When he's depressed or drunk, he kicks himself for letting you go. He realizes it was his fault."

I didn't know what to say. It was his fault, but it was the best thing that ever happened to me. I shuddered to visualize two thirty-something fags living a closeted life in a cold-water flat in Portsmouth. It was so ridiculous I smiled.

Kelly's eyes clouded, and her lips drew thin. She felt hurt, and I felt like an ass.

"Forgive me, Kelly," I continued. "I'm tired, and my mind wandered a minute. Thinking of seeing my folks again isn't exactly a piece of cake." I chuckled then grimaced. "I was fantasizing bashing a bottle of wine against the front door and proclaiming, 'I christen thee Hell House of the Century.'"

"Oh, Damon," she said, a faint smile on her face now. "Here I am singing a sad song when you're heading for the meat grinder."

Our eyes met, and a warm current passed between us.

"Seriously, I don't see how you can stand to live under those conditions. Have you thought about leaving him?"

Sadness settling on her features again and she ran a finger along the edge of the windowsill.

"I've thought about it, of course, many times. He needs me. I don't know what would happen to him if I left."

She took a last sip of coffee and squeezed the Styrofoam cup till it popped. She continued to hold it tightly in her grip.

"Do you love him?" I looked at her as kindly as I could.

She peered at me out of the corner of her eyes and then back out at the parking lot.

"To be brutally honest, Damon"—she turned back to me—"I have spent a lot of fruitless years hating you because he wanted you more than he loved me."

I nodded, a bit startled by the honesty of her statement. I followed her gaze out the window before replying.

"I can certainly understand. And you put it so well—wanted me but not loved me. I did love him those many years ago but was able to move on. The sad thing is he apparently hasn't been able to."

I was becoming edgy, an intense scene awaited me, and here I was attempting to comfort the wife of my old boyfriend.

Kelly checked her watch and rose rather abruptly.

"It has been wonderful seeing you, Damon, a bright spot in my day." She paused, looking a bit sheepish. "Here I've been carrying on about myself and haven't even asked about Joan. How is she?"

I slid our chairs around and turned back toward her. A catch came in my voice in spite of myself.

"She's fine, I hope." Kelly's eyebrows rose at the last two words. "We have separated—amicably. I will be heading to California next week."

She sucked in her breath. "Carlos?"

"Carlos."

Our eyes met, mine starting to smart again. I pulled my dark glasses out and slid them on.

"We made promises to each other back in Fort Worth ten years ago, but I let him slip away."

Kelly squeezed my hand.

"Like Mike let you slip away."

"Yes, like Mike and me. And Carlos wants me back," I finished in a whisper. I paused to catch my equilibrium.

Back at our cars, we hugged wordlessly, emotions raw in our minds. She watched me pull out and head north. Looking in the rearview mirror, her hand was still in the air as I pulled onto I-93, then my eyes went back to the road.

I reached Portsmouth shortly after 6:00 p.m.

Turning the corner from 1B onto Beach Hill Road, I pulled over on the narrow pavement. The intoxicating aroma of the ocean wafted into my open window. Automobiles lined the hill; someone must be having a party.

Why was I doing this? I could have called or e-mailed. No, I wanted Mom to hear about my plans face-to-face.

Goddamn, Ilka's car was sitting in the driveway.

CHAPTER

5

I pulled in beside Ilka's tan Neon. She must have driven night and day to get here ahead of me. I bet she couldn't wait to tell the folks about my separation—and Carlos. Slamming the gears into park, I cranked up the AC and sat there. The house seemed smaller and the grounds less well tended than I remembered. The Piscataqua River merging with the Atlantic Ocean had hardly a ripple today but, like my emotions, could capriciously turn violent under a wind-driven storm.

Welcome home, Damon. Shit.

For all I knew, Dad had a shotgun aimed at me right now.

I cut the engine, got out, hauled the carton of liquor up to the front door, set it on the step, and pressed the doorbell. Light from the dining room chandelier shone through the windows. Several people, not family members, milled around inside. Someone poked back a curtain with their finger and peered out. What diabolical scheme had Ilka cooked up?

Thank goodness Mom answered the door. She had a broad smile and welcoming arms.

"You look wonderful, Damon. You don't know how much I've missed you."

A shiver of regret ran through me as I hugged her back—regret for all the shit the family had pulled on her, regret that she had let them get away with it, regret that I hadn't expressed my love and support better.

Over Mom's shoulder I could see Ilka heading our way. I backed off and picked up the carton. She yanked the door wider so I could pass through.

"What a surprise, wish it was a happier one," I mocked, sticking my tongue out, like I did as a kid as she moved ahead and opened the kitchen door. I set the carton on the table.

Mom leaned in the door and said she would tell Dad I was here.

A few moments later, "Send him in," filtered out. His voice sounded less vigorous than I remembered. What was he like now? It was hard to believe the stroke would have taken away all his bullshit ego.

Ilka and I silently confronted each other for several moments. I slipped off my jacket, hung it on a chairback, and started jamming bottles noisily into the wine rack.

"You couldn't wait to tell them the news, could you?"

"I haven't told them anything. It's your goddamned life, throw it away if you want." A tremor in her hands indicated she expected a major scene. "The news will probably give Dad another stroke. I wanted to be here to mend as much damage as possible."

"How noble of you."

"How long are you staying?"

"That depends."

"On what, how much chaos you cause?"

"Look, Ilka, if it wasn't for Mom, I'd walk out the fucking door right now without looking back. You never cut me any slack, do you?"

She stared silently at me, arms crossed.

"Who the hell are all these people anyway?" I asked, breaking the angry silence.

"Lower your voice, they'll hear you."

Mom appeared back at the door, stepped in, and put her arm through mine. I pulled her close and kissed her on the forehead. She squeezed my hand and looked up at me. At that moment, I knew I had done the right thing. To hell with the rest of them, Mom needed to hear it from me.

"Is everything all right? I hope you two aren't arguing."

"No more than we do every time we get together."

Liz Duncan looked from one to the other of her children and clucked her tongue. By her own admission, discord always made her uneasy. She noticed the wine rack. "Looks like someone has replenished our hooch." She smiled, trying to ease the tension.

"Yeah," Ilka replied, "Damon's bringing a peace offering."

"You're right, sis," I said in a light voice. "It's gonna be needed."

She flushed and grabbed a sponge to wipe an invisible spot on the counter.

"Damon," Mom continued, "I'm sorry you didn't bring Joan. You know how fond your father is of her." The tone of her voice showed concern, but I surmised she had already guessed the truth.

I looked at Ilka and then at Mom. "No, we have mutually agreed on a separation. It was amicable. We're still friends. She's probably my best friend, come to think of it."

"But friends a marriage does not make." A rueful look spread over her face. "It's Carlos, isn't it?" She picked up a bottle of Merlot and inspected the label then set it back on the table. "It always has been." The remark was as matter-of-fact as if speaking about the weather.

My face must have turned scarlet; and burned right into my ears. "Yes."

"Bastard," Ilka spit out.

I ignored her and loosened my tie and the top button on my shirt.

"It was Joan's idea, about the separation, I mean."

Mom's eyes were swimming, and she took my hands. "No matter what your father says, I never loved you less when you told us you were gay." She straightened up and brushed at an errant tear. "I have to confess." Her face now became animated. "I've been a fan of Carlos ever since his first appearance on TV."

Her words meant everything to me. Tears spontaneously gushed down my cheeks. We put our arms around each other and wept. My relief at her support was overwhelming; to hell with what dad thought. I gave my pound of flesh nine years ago at House of Change.

"What a bunch of crap!" Ilka intoned. "I'm going in with Dad and smoke a cigar." It was intended to be irony, but I could just picture her doing it.

"Let it go, Damon." Mom dried her eyes, and we both sat down side by side at the table.

"She's good at heart."

"If she's got one."

"I don't know how she can be so kind to her father after what he put her through." She sighed and took my hand again. "I suppose you know all about that."

"As much as I need to. Still, it's time she got over it and moved on."

Mom nodded. "You must go in and see him."

"I know, into the lion's den."

She leaned over and straightened my collar and gave me a rueful look.

"By the way, who are all the people in there?"

"Some of your father's friends and investment partners. He wanted to have them meet you and to show off Joan." She tipped her head and shrugged her shoulders as if dismissing a foolish happenstance.

I jumped up and scurried to the liquor cabinet, pulled out several bottles, and inspected them for alcoholic content.

"Get the wineglasses, Mother, we're going to have a toast."

"Oh no, you wouldn't."

But I could tell she saw that I would. Just a trace of a smile flitted across her lips.

Mom led the way with glasses on a tray. I followed with the wine. I was startled to see how much weight Dad had lost. His right cheek drooped, and there appeared to be a weakness in his arm when we shook hands. I couldn't help but remember a quite different scene ten years ago in this same room. He came out from behind his desk and introduced me to the gathered group. Their faces were all a blur, but I dutifully shook hands with each one.

I uncorked a bottle of Chardonnay, and Mom carefully poured out a glass for each person. We handed them around. Everyone lifted a glass, and someone proposed "to the visiting son and his beautiful wife."

Dad looked toward the door.

"Where is Joan? Bring her in so I can brag about your good taste."

"No, Dad, she didn't come. She's still in Texas."

My voice was somber, and he immediately picked up on it.

"Nothing's wrong, is it?" he asked sotto voce.

"Well, yes and no."

He cuffed my arm but looked wary, his eyes traveling my face. "You sound like my goddamned lawyer."

The guests chuckled and nodded.

This was going to be more difficult than I thought. Some of my courage in the kitchen had evaporated. But it had to be done. This could be sweet revenge, but I tried not to look at it that way.

"Joan will not be coming." I paused, sweat sopping my underarms. "We've separated."

The room became deadly quiet, all eyes on me. My mind recalled Jim McGreevey, former governor of New Jersey, and I paraphrased his words. "The truth is, Dad, I am a gay man." I paused, needing to steady my voice, now full of emotion, then resumed. "You know how hard I tried to overcome it."

Dad's mouth twisted, but he was silent. The blood drained from his face, and his breathing became rapid. Ilka rushed to him.

"Ilka," I spoke up, "back off."

"Christ, Al, give the boy a pat on the back," one of the guests said. "He has the guts to say what my brother never did. He's lived thirty years with another man, they're millionaires, living in Europe, but the word *gay* is never spoken." He grasped my hand and shook it vigorously.

An embarrassed silence developed, everyone else avoiding eye contact. The front door opened, and someone left quietly. Dad leaned against the desk, his jaw set. Others approached me, gave weak handshakes, and mumbled a couple of trite words but did not look me in the eye. My gaze steady, I asked each one their name, repeated it, and thanked them for coming. They gave their excuses to Dad and left.

"Why did you bother to come?" Ilka broke the trance, contempt in her voice, after they had all left. "Did you have to rub it in? You could have at least kept it in the family. A telephone call would have sufficed."

"I thought the family deserved to hear it from me in person. I stupidly hoped there would be more understanding, considering the hell I went through trying to change." I addressed Ilka and Dad indirectly. "Have you ever wanted something so badly you'd die to get it?"

"And you probably will if you shack up with him. He's sick now and probably needs a nursemaid," Ilka remarked, setting her untouched glass on a trivet.

"So much for following the twisted news stories."

Ilka's face reddened "You have spoken to him?"

"Oh no. I just thought I'd drop in one day." I bottomed out my wine and held the glass by the stem.

She made a dismissive hissing sound with her mouth. "What if he gets sick of you and throws you out?"

"What if?" I challenged. "What if one of us was diagnosed with cancer? What if this house burned down in the night?" Dad looked startled but remained mute. "What if someone broke in in the night and murdered every fucking one of us in bed?" I paused. "Life is all about choices. We can't just give up because of the what ifs." I peered at the wall where the vase had smashed ten years ago. "Haven't either one of you understood a word I've said?"

"Damon," Ilka persisted, "can't you get it through your head. It's wrong. It's against God's will."

"Then I guess Carlos and I will roast in hell for all eternity. But together!"

I spent a sleepless night in my childhood bedroom. Memories filled the space like refuse in a bag waiting for the garbage truck. So many wasted hours, full of self-doubt, I spent sprawled on this bed, looking at the floor.

Dawn streaked the sky before I nodded off for a couple of hours of exhausted sleep.

Stirrings downstairs started around seven thirty. I stretched and pulled myself out of bed around eight. No rush for me. I took a leisurely shower and shaved, hoping I was holding up Ilka from her morning ablutions.

It was a warm day, and my first choice—shorts, muscle shirt, and sandals. Instead I reached for slacks, T-shirt, and loafers. No neck chains today, as Dr. Kessler said, "Dress like a man." Why hassle Dad any further?

Mom slept late, but Dad and Ilka chatted in the kitchen. Ilka scrambled eggs and made toast, and Dad sat at the table. They fell silent as I entered the room. We each moved around the space as though no one else was present. Ilka fixed plates for Dad and herself, scrambled eggs, bacon, and toast.

"Help yourself," Ilka offered.

"Thanks. Where do you store the ground glass?"

"Very funny. Texas turned you into a real comedian."

I reached for a cup and poured myself coffee, took cream from the fridge, stirred in sugar, sipped the hot liquid, and paced around. Ripples on the ocean sparkled and danced in the morning sun. I pushed the French door open and stepped out onto the stone patio. Mike and I laid those years ago while Dad bossed and complained if each stone was not perfectly aligned.

I slumped onto a teakwood settee and perched my coffee cup on a plastic Parsons table. The Isle of Shoals was visible on the cloudless horizon. I put my feet up on a tree stump, which also served as a seat.

The departed tree blew over in a violent winter storm fifteen years ago. Memories everywhere.

I scrounged around in my shirt pocket for the cell phone. A pleasant young female voice inquired how she could help me.

"When is the next flight out to Dallas-Fort Worth?"

CHAPTER

6

Joan met me at the airport. Chills ran up my spine. Am I doing the right thing, or am I throwing away a comfortable life and a wonderful wife? What lies ahead? This is my last attempt at happiness. Take it!

We were silent on the trip back to the house. I would be leaving tomorrow for San Diego—for good.

We clung to each other the following morning. I knew it would be hard, but not this hard. I slid into the car, fully laden with my possessions, and reached for Joan's hand once more.

"Friends forever?" I asked.

"And beyond," she said.

We both mouthed, "I love you."

I backed into the street. Joan turned and headed for the house, wiping her eyes and waving her handkerchief. I missed her already.

I drove through the night and much of the next day. When I hit the outskirts of San Diego, I was in a frenzy and had goose bumps all over. I memorized driving up his street and catalogued it in my mind like a flower pressed into an album. Carlos had given excellent directions, and I soon found the house. It appeared small compared to the others but gorgeous. Trimmed boxwood hedges and bougainvillea on trellises framed the side of the building. I smelled the essence of the ocean and the gorgeous cascading flowers of every kind.

And there he stood.

The most beautiful, the most wonderful man in the world.

The sun shone behind him, and the hair on his arms and legs glistened like dandelion floss. He hesitated a moment then raced out to my car. I threw the door open. His lips were on mine before my feet touched the ground. He swept me into his arms. We hugged a long time.

His shirt was open, and I could feel his heart pounding against my cheek. It was almost like ten years ago—almost. But now I could feel his ribs. Were we again two halves of the same whole? Had we passed too many years being two halves of the wrong whole? We slid back to arm's length and inspected each other. Carlos was still the handsome devil, his face thinner, hair receding just a bit, and a touch of gray peppering the black. I couldn't take my eyes off him, the handsomest man I have ever seen. Only thirty-five but the medications already taking their toll.

"I'm going to beat this HIV, you know," he said firmly.

"Of course you are. We are," I said, struggling to keep my voice steady.

"You're staying a while?"

"For good. I'm here for you, if you still want me."

His eyes clouded, and I stood buried in his arms. "Just try to get away, champ. We've got years to make up for."

A tear rolled down my cheek. All the mistakes of the past reverberated in my mind. What good to live the past? It's over. Still the gall tasted bitter in my mouth, the regrettable "what ifs," the "why didn't Is," the "if onlys," but we at least have the "nows."

He took my arm, and we walked out to the deck. The view over the Pacific was spectacular. We stood wordlessly for several minutes, taking time to control our emotions. His hand slid down into mine. A young couple strolled by, their feet bare in the sand.

After all this time apart and even so few days together ten years ago, we suddenly acted a bit reserved with each other, testing this new beginning, perhaps afraid it would evade us once more.

Somehow, the breeze and the salt air have a healing quality. Would that it could.

Carlos encircled my shoulder with his arm and gave me a squeeze then a kiss on the lips—a long kiss. It felt so right to be near him. I desperately wished some of my strength could flow into his diminished body, that my presence could bind some of the wounds left by the departure of fair-weather friends.

"What about Joan?" he asked, finally, wrinkling his brow, concern showing on his face.

"We separated several months ago." I hesitated for some reason, habit, I suppose, then added, "She always knew." Words spoken with irony. Another life altered, needlessly. "She loved me, knowing the truth, hoping it could work out somehow. One of the hardest things I have ever done was leaving her yesterday, but she'll be okay."

"Always knew?" he asked, gazing at me with a puzzled expression.

"Shortly after we married, Ilka bragged to Joan, in one of her more stupid moments, that she had cured me of being gay. Joan has wonderful instincts. She knew better."

"Ah yes, Ilka." Carlos peered out to sea. "She still thinks I was behind the attack on you that night, I suppose." His glance turned back to me.

"It was never anything personal. In actuality, she just couldn't deal with my being gay, and you stood in the way."

"I guess." His brow wrinkled in thought. "She wanted it to be me though, didn't she?" he said with a trace of resentment still in his voice.

"You're gonna laugh, but she had the hots for you when we first arrived in Fort Worth."

"You've got to be shittin' me," he snorted, one eyebrow raised, his lips starting to twist into one of his wonderful lopsided grins.

"No, honest. Remember when she picked us up at the bus terminal? She thought you were some hot guy chatting with me. There was another fellow standing beside us, and she figured he must be my new love. I read it in her diary."

"You what?" He shot me a look like I was going daft.

"After I finally came to my senses, you know, and ended her control over me, I went into her room. It lay on the bureau. I couldn't help myself. I had to find what was on her mind the night I ran out.

"'C is the man I always dreamed of,' she wrote. 'He flatters me but then won't give me the time of day. It is wrong in God's eyes for D to have him. I must break them up!'

"But no mention of the fight you two had. Curious."

Carlos shook his head; disbelief registered on his face. He studied the horizon for several minutes. A chuckle started, and then he broke into a laugh. Then we both started to laugh hysterically, tears running down our cheeks.

We finally composed ourselves. He was growing tired. I suggested we move to the deck chairs. We sat in silence for an hour or so, except when one of us would start to chuckle. Neither of us spoke; neither of us felt the need. He held my hand now and then, pointing out a gull in its gawky flight or a plane so high it made no sound, only the vapor trail frosting a slice of the sky. The warm sun infiltrated our bodies. Calmness permeated my mind. The gentle lap of the ocean against the beach helped to allay some of the regrets, at least temporarily. A shiver of disbelief ran up my spine. He was really here. I could actually touch him.

Somewhat later, we moved over to the two-person hammock filled with plump, luscious pillows, where we could snuggle. Carlos dozed, and I studied him in repose. He had done everything: singer, songwriter, dancer, musician, world tours, TV, even a bit part on Broadway, the consummate showman. What is there about life that throws two such dissimilar people together? The world may say it's wrong, yet that spark, that very special chemistry, that chain reaction strikes. Two meteors collide in a fiery explosion, meld, become inseparable, a fusion of energy in motion. Too soon that energy forges into the atmosphere, a momentary streak of light, a spectacle on earth, and then it disappears.

Forever.

Carlos stirred, rubbed his eyes, and looked at me.

"You're still here. I prayed you weren't just a dream."

Twilight was settling in; the breeze had an edge as it picked up again. We untangled ourselves from each other's bodies. Time to move inside. As the sun slowly dipped into the ocean, it reflected an orange flaming arrow straight into our beings. The sea was calm except for tiny, reflecting iridescent half-moons dipping and swaying in rhythm to the soft breeze caressing the water.

We stood shoulder to shoulder, admiring the sunset through the wall of sliding glass doors. A log spit and glowed on the grate. A motorboat ground by, the engine revving then idling, the last run for the day. The only sound remaining was the rusty squawk of the gulls and the endless lap of the sea on the shore.

Later, we sat cross-legged on a gorgeous oriental carpet in front of the blazing fire, balancing our dinners on plastic plates in our laps. We toasted with plastic glasses of Pepsi, liquor not allowed with his meds or his alcoholic recovery. The firelight danced on the bleached ceiling beams and walls. The moon rising in the east painted pale golden stripes between the row of cottages and out onto the sand.

After dinner, we lay naked before the open fire. If I were struck dead now, I could have no regrets.

Later, as we prepared for bed, I was relieved to see, in spite of being thinner, his body was not emaciated as I feared. I clung to every positive sign and scrap of hope. I was alarmed to see all the pill bottles on his nightstand. I silently prayed they could make the difference.

"You may want to sleep in the other bedroom." He pointed to the door. "I tend to be restless during the night, and I don't want to disturb you. I made it up for you."

"Right," I said. "You got rocks in your head?" Then I snickered as I broke into to the most obsequious English fan. "I have not driven the last twenty-four tedious hours, Gov'nor, to sleep in Carlos Bravara's guest room. Although even that would be, indeed, a bloody honor."

"Then get your horny little ass into the bedroom straight ahead."

"Oh heavens, sir, I hope you're not going to take advantage of me."

"Only in every way I can think of." He hugged my back as we stumbled into the bathroom.

We brushed our teeth in the huge master bath with double sinks then showered together.

He wore a shorty pajama bottom while I climbed in beside him, naked since I hadn't unpacked anything yet. He rolled over and hugged me. His breath smelled of toothpaste as his lips found mine, and we kissed. As much as I wanted sex, I could tell he needed rest. He cuddled against me and fell asleep almost immediately. I read a while then kissed him on the forehead and shut off the light. He didn't stir.

I lay awake for several hours, my mind going over the past. Seeing Kelly again reminded me once more of that terrible weekend in Fort Worth. In some strange way it may have helped me finally come to terms with myself. Mike's struggle became my struggle although I couldn't admit it at the time. Did we ever really love each other? Or were we too young to know the difference between love and lust?

The next morning was warm and sunny. Clad in shorts and straw hats, we were glad of the huge umbrella. The view of the ocean was a natural high, better than tranquilizers.

"Remember the first time we met?" I asked Carlos.

"Yeah, I remember." He nodded and glanced at me. "I still have that yellow silk shirt you liked so well."

"You're kidding. Get it and put it on."

He smiled that wonderful smile. "Just remember, we don't have a bus restroom handy."

"We can always improvise," I said, slapping his butt when he walked by.

His cell phone rang on the coffee table.

"Want me to get it?" I called to him.

"No, I'm nearer."

I caught a word or two here and there, the name Shirl then, "My god, you're kidding." Then a door closed, and I couldn't hear anything more.

Shirl—it couldn't be the one from Fort Worth. He probably knows a hundred Shirls. Ten minutes dragged by, and I finally got up and strolled out onto the beach. Uneasiness filled my mind. I couldn't shake the feeling. I turned and headed back. Carlos came through the sliders with the shirt in his hand. His eyes were downcast, and his shoulders seemed to slump.

My mouth felt dry. "Are you okay?" I grabbed him by the arm. Once more, I realized how raw my nerves were. I would have to learn to roll with the punches better than this. I forced a smile.

"Yes, fine," he answered. "That was Shirl, can't remember her last name. She's the girl I stayed with those three weeks you were in the hospital."

"Back in Fort Worth? You're kidding." Relief rushed over me. She was supposed to be the start of my 'cure.'"

Carlos raised an eyebrow but went on. "She's here in LA. She wants to see me."

"That's wonderful."

"There's more." Anguish shown on his face.

"More? I don't understand."

He took hold of my hand. "She's bringing my son with her." He searched my face for a reaction.

I opened my mouth, but no words came out. We continued looking at each other. I felt him start to shake. I squeezed his hand. His eyes welled up, and a tear ran down his cheek. He made no attempt to hide his emotions.

"Your son?"

"Yes. I haven't heard from her since I left Fort Worth. She read about my having...about my trouble and knew she had to tell me about him. She wants to stay awhile, to let my son and I get to know each other."

"You never knew before today?"

"Nothing." A suggestion of a smile returned. "He must be about ten."

I took the yellow shirt out of his hand and spread it over my knees. I smoothed it out, tracing around the buttons with my index finger. A beach ball bounced onto the deck. A young boy rushed up to retrieve it. He was about the right age. I could imagine it might be Carlos Junior.

"When are they coming?"

"A couple of hours, she said."

My heart sank. I needed to get away. But what to do? What kind of an excuse?

"I've been thinking about taking a ride up the coast. This might be a good time to do it," I blurted out, panicked.

Too much was happening too soon. It was hard to breathe. I felt like heaving. It was 1995 again with Ilka.

"I don't want you to go."

"I'll be back. You need this time together. I don't want to rob you of this opportunity. You must be free to…I don't know, you must be free."

I avoided his gaze. My gut was so twisted I was afraid I'd collapse.

"Promise you'll come back."

He took me roughly by the arm, swung me around, my body pressed against the smooth stonework wall. My arms flew up around his neck, our lips welded, reluctant to separate. I could feel his need pressing against me.

"I lost you ten years ago. I swore if you ever returned, you'd never leave me again." His lips brushed my ear as he whispered. "I wanted you last night, but I wasn't sure about you, about me." I nodded and tasted his lips again. "God, Damon, let me love you." His hands kneaded my body as he slid down, fumbled with the buttons on my shorts.

❧

I remember nothing of the beginning of the trip up the coast except his lips on mine, our bodies locked together. After half an hour or so, I had to pull off the highway. I got out, slammed the door, and pounded the hood with my fists until they bled. I smeared the blood onto my shorts. Why did she have to show up now?

I walked along the highway for several hundred feet, kicking at stones and feeling sorry for myself. I turned and headed back to the car. I slammed into drive and tramped on the accelerator. Scenery rushed, by but my mind was on San Diego. By late afternoon I swung into a small town and filled the car up with gas.

My mind raced, and I began to feel guilty. Carlos looked so upset when I ducked out. I had to do something or go nuts. Then it occurred to me. Dr. Polanski. Call Dr. Polanski.

Thank God he was available. After the usual salutations, I explained the situation and asked him what I should do.

"What do you want, Damon? What do you really want?"

"I don't know," I replied.

"Of course you do."

"I want yesterday to last forever."

"This is today, Damon, and there will be tomorrow and then the day after."

"I can't bear to share him anymore, I want him to myself."

"What about Carlos, what do you think he wants?"

"I wish I knew."

"For God's sake, Damon, the man showed his desire for you and his commitment before you ran out on him. What do you want, to have him handcuff himself to you? Stop playing the martyr. Do what you need to do. If that means driving away forever, then drive. But if it means going back, go. Stake your claim."

"Thanks, Doc, I owe you."

"You're damn right you do. Let me know where to send the bill."

We both laughed, and I thanked him again. It was okay. I stared at the cell phone in my hand for a long time. I started to laugh again, poor me, poor Damon. "A delicate child," Mom would say to Dad when he wanted me to go hunting with him. Delicate child, bullshit, Mom, a fucking queer is what I was—am.

Three messages on my cell phone, all from Carlos. I finally realized how selfish and inconsiderate I had been. I tried to make myself think it was best for Carlos to have time alone with them. Such a big day for Carlos and I still wasn't there for him. I punched in his number. I could hear the worry in his voice.

"I'm on my way back…home. Are you okay?"

"I'm fine. I love you," he said.

"I know, I love you too."

"Where are you?"

"Coupla hundred miles up the coast, I guess."

"Get your ass home."

"Yes, sir."

I somehow felt older. I glanced in the rearview mirror several times, looking for white hairs. I hoped there were some. What a dope I've been. Always the easy way out, don't take chances, hope for the best, let someone else do the dirty work. Me first. One of the few times I ever asserted myself was with Dad ten years ago.

And Ilka. What about Ilka? For all those years I allowed her to rule my life. It wasn't her fault. I let her do it. My mind continued to wander until I noticed the speedometer—ninety-five miles an hour.

The sun was setting when I finally swung into the driveway. A shiny red Cadillac crowded the space. Holy shit. I thought she was poor. I tucked in my shirt, combed my hair back with my fingers, and took a deep breath.

The only thing I could think of to say as I climbed the three steps to the deck was, "Margaret, I'm home," in my best *Father Knows Best* imitation.

Apparently no one heard me arrive as they all looked surprised when I appeared. Carlos jumped up and came to meet me. He put his arm around my waist and led me over for introductions. Neither of us mentioned the blood on my shorts.

"How are you, Damon?" Shirl asked in a supercilious voice, looking me over from head to foot, eyes resting on my bloody shorts.

I shrugged. "Just fine!" She gave me a hug and a peck on the cheek.

She didn't look like I remembered her at all. Her hair was jet-black, carefully coiffed, obviously dyed, I thought in my bitchy mind, and she was quite heavy. She still had nice legs and dressed well in a soft blue chiffon sleeveless dress and matching shoes. A diamond ring sparkled on the left third finger. She had on matching diamond earrings and a diamond pendant on a gold chain around her neck. Fags notice things like this, I said to myself. I hugged her back and pecked her on the cheek, smiling broadly.

"And who is this fine-looking young man?" I asked, spying the boy. He was stocky, rather short, with a surly manner.

"Damon," she said, pride in her voice, "this is Carlos Junior." The emphasis on *Junior*.

Carlos Junior, huh? I was suddenly in a family situation in which I had no legal sway.

He reluctantly got up and shook hands, following his mother's orders. Shirl's attention immediately returned to Carlos, and she requisitioned him to assist her in the kitchen, so I turned to Junior.

"Have you been out in the ocean this afternoon?" I asked.

"I don't like the water."

"Have you played out in the sand?" I tried again.

"That's for sissies."

"I used to love building sand castles back in New Hampshire when I was your age."

I sensed his desire to say, "I rest my case," but to his credit, he refrained.

"After dinner, maybe we can walk up the beach and look for seashells," I said hopefully.

"I don't like sand in my shoes."

I clamped my jaws together and said in a low voice, "Then take 'em off, you little shit, or I'll break your goddamned neck."

The boy looked up at me, startled, and covered his mouth. I expected a kick in the balls, but he snickered.

"I like you, Damon, we're gonna get along."

I grabbed him around the chest, lifting him off the deck, and said, "You devil. You've been yanking my chain."

"Gotcha," he snorted, struggling free and running out onto the beach.

When the two of us came back in, the table was set with crystal, china, and silver. There were even linen napkins and a tablecloth. Candles flickered on various surfaces around the room. Shirl seated Carlos at one end of the table and her at the other. The symbolism was not lost on me, but I let it go. Carlos Junior and I sat opposite each other. She must have brought an arsenal of food with her. I noticed several coolers through the kitchen door opposite me.

"What's this black stuff, Mom?" Junior asked, wrinkling his nose. He caught my eye, and I made a face. Shirl was busy looking at Carlos, so they both missed it.

She finally looked over at him. "That's caviar, dear. Try some."

"Ugh, fish eggs."

"Look, Junior, I'll try some with you. It looks delicious," I said. Shirl beamed.

"I have wine cooling. I'll get it," she bragged.

"Let me help," I jumped up and gallantly pulled her chair out. I caught a smirk on Carlos's face as I walked by. He touched my hand, looked up at me, and stuck out his tongue. Shirl got a bottle of champagne out of the fridge. She had a matching set of crystal to the water glasses on the table. The kitchen was hot, so I turned on the AC. She asked me to uncork the liquor. It was still too warm, and the bubbly mixture blew up onto the cabinets and down onto the floor. I tried to aim some of it into the glasses.

"You men," she said. "I'm going to have to get you cleaned up these next few weeks."

"How long you staying, Shirl?" I asked, trying to sound innocent.

"No plans. I suppose you'll be moving on soon," she said.

No fucking way, I said to myself, my gore rising.

One of the delicate glasses splintered in my hand. A shard pierced my palm, and the blood squirted. I swore and rushed to put it under the cold-water tap while she looked on, more concerned over the broken glass than my cut, I felt sure. She wrapped a towel tightly around my hand. She had Junior hunt around for gauze and surgeon's tape.

Her gaze dropped to my bloodstained shorts.

"Looks like you've had quite a day. You must be accident prone." She officiously strode over and switched off the AC. "We don't want our boy to get a chill in his condition."

"Heaven forbid," I said, teeth clenched. "Shall we serve the wine?"

"You go ahead back to the table. I'll handle the rest of these delicate glasses."

I resolved then and there not one of them would leave this property in one piece.

Junior reported to Carlos what the commotion was about. He came into the kitchen and put his arm around me.

"You okay, love?" he asked. "Did you get all the glass out?" He unwrapped the bandage and inspected my hand.

"Love," he never called me that before, and he said it in such a natural way. Shirl was busy cleaning up the broken glass. Carlos went over and turned the AC back on.

"Sorry about the glass, Shirl," he said. "But I can't drink anything alcoholic. How about a Coke for me and the boy?"

There was a great deal of silence through the balance of the meal. Shirl had little to say other than to have something passed. Carlos pressed his knee against mine and gave me a sly look. After dessert, we thanked her for a wonderful meal. As much as I would have liked to, we couldn't throw away the dishes as we had the paper ones last evening. I offered to load the dishwasher and commandeered Junior to help.

Carlos and Shirl retired to the living room as I had planned. I wanted them to have time alone to chat. I hoped Carlos would be setting her straight on things. Junior and I turned off the kitchen light and joined them in the living room. Carlos and Shirl were sitting on the love seat, deep in conversation.

I sat in a recliner across the room, and Junior perched on one arm. He was a smart kid, way beyond his mother. She would have her hands full. Maybe I would too. He had a deck of cards and was busy showing me tricks. I was more interested in the talk across the room but interacted with him the necessary amount.

A bit later, I checked the time and suggested to Carlos he needed to take his pills.

I went into the bedroom, and he followed me.

Is it okay if she stays here with us for a couple of weeks? After that, she needs to get Junior back to Fort Worth for the fall term."

"Of course it's okay, it's your house."

"It's our house now."

I melted.

"I want to sleep with Damon," Junior announced when we came back into the living room.

"That's fine, dear," Shirl broke in. "I can share the other room with Carlos."

I looked at Carlos, and he looked at Shirl. It was obvious she was serious.

"That's fine," I said to Shirl. Junior ran out to get his suitcase. "You sleep with Carlos, and I'll sleep with Junior. I can make love to him."

"Junior will sleep on the couch," she said firmly.

Carlos snickered. He came over and hugged me and gave me a kiss. "Just for tonight, okay?"

"Are you serious?"

"No big deal, it's just for tonight." He winked and squeezed my shoulder, his hand slid down my arm.

I returned the wink. "Think I'll get a little night air." I snickered to myself, slipping out onto the deck. Shirl deserved the trick we were playing.

I waited and paced. Okay, guys, the joke's over. This foolishness had to come to an end. I was anxious to feel Carlos's arms around me.

Half an hour later the lights extinguished. I heard Shirl giggle. Then all was quiet. The joke appeared to be on me. Should I storm in and throw the bedroom door open? What if I didn't like what I saw? Was Carlos wanting an open relationship? In retrospect, I knew so little about him. It didn't make sense fatherhood had taken precedence over our relationship.

I walked to the railing, knelt, and clutched the spindles so tightly my knuckles ached. Flashes of light went off in my head. I tried to justify what had happened. I couldn't. I willed Carlos to come out for me. He didn't. The minutes dragged into an hour. A strong wind came up. The ocean pounded and roared; the rest of the world was quiet.

Sometime in the middle of the night, I got into my car and headed out.

CHAPTER

Blackness all around me, blackness. The sky was black. The road was black. My emotions were black. I traveled this road two days ago with excitement, anticipation, and hope. Now blackness enveloped me. A terrible despair clutched at my soul. My one great hope of the last ten years, consciously or unconsciously, had been carelessly ripped from my heart. That horrible black night ten years ago bore into my mind like a laser-guided rifle site. I was shaking so badly I had to pull off the road. What had been done to my body then was being done to my mind now. Shirl's callous laugh rang again in my ears. I turned the radio on full blast, but it couldn't drown it out. I covered my ears and screamed for it to stop. I willed calmness and pulled back out onto the empty highway and drove mechanically several more hours.

The blackness abated somewhat by the sunrise in the east, peeking through breaks in the clouds. The radio station predicted rain. Why not? Everything else had gone to hell. So much had happened in the past twenty-four hours my mind was now on autopilot. It felt like a dream, as though I were a voyeur visiting another person's mind. I could neither cry nor laugh. I bit onto my finger to be sure I was not dreaming. It hurt. The wound in my right hand throbbed.

The yellow light on the dash indicated gas was low. A convenience store sign showed on the horizon, and I swerved in. Three pumps registered out of order. An elderly woman, confused by self-service, tried unsuccessfully to make gas run out of a fourth pump. I stepped out and assisted her. It took some time for her to maneuver the credit card numbers and the receipt request. She was nearly in tears as she pulled away. I gave her a hug.

My tank full again, I pulled the car forward to a parking space and went into the restaurant. I wasn't hungry, but food would keep me awake, and I wanted to drive as far as I could before resting. It was the typical rest stop. Fake marble counter, stools with worn red Naugahyde seats, dark wood floors stained from long usage, and an unused jukebox loomed in one corner. An old menu still tacked to the wall, badly discolored with cigarette smoke from the days when it was still allowed, flittered and twisted in the breeze from the paddle fans above.

All the booths were occupied. One seat was empty across from an old geezer, probably in his late sixties, working on a plate of eggs and pancakes. He needed a haircut, and his clothes were rumpled like he had slept in them. I pointed to the seat, and he nodded, so I slid in across from him. I thanked him and struck up a conversation, anything to take up my mind so I wouldn't have to think.

A middle-aged waitress appeared, pad in hand. She had long since lost the battle of the bulge. Her legs looked like sauna tubes stuck into black-laced shoes, and a flab of fat between her shoulder blades undulated as she moved. Her ample breasts stretched her arms out as she proceeded to jot down as I ordered eggs, toast, and lots of black coffee. A smile crossed her pleasant, once-pretty face.

"Say, you aren't on TV, are you, young man?"

She seemed absorbed in studying me.

I shrugged. "Hardly." I lifted an eyebrow. "Why do you ask?"

"You're a dead ringer for a fellow on a TV show years ago. Thought you might be a relative." She scratched her head with the end of her pencil and nodded her head. "Yes, it was about the FBI. I watched it every week. His last name was, let's see, Brooks. Yes. What was his first name?"

"Not that one with Zimbalist?" the old guy asked.

"Yeah, but he isn't the one." She looked embarrassed. "Here I'm running on and you must be hungry." She turned, puffing, and came back with the coffee pot and filled my cup. "Stephen!" she exclaimed.

"Beg your pardon, ma'am?"

"Brooks, Stephen Brooks was his name. A gorgeous young man, never missed a show." She paused, reflecting, then hobbled side to side back to the kitchen.

The old guy and I watched her disappear.

"Them were the good old days. The sixties, not much like the troubles today."

We both remained silent a bit, minds taken up with the present. I looked out the window at the gray sky.

"Hope the rain won't last all day. I've got a long way to drive."

"Hard tellin'. Where ya headed, stranger? Don't sound like you're from around these parts."

"New Hampshire, originally."

"I wouldn'ta guessed it."

"I spent the last ten years in Texas, Fort Worth."

"Going back there now?"

"Nah, thinking of Maine, maybe Vermont. Trying to put my life back together." The same words I had used ten years ago on the bus with Carlos.

"Sounds like things ain't turned out the way you wanted."

"I'm beginning to wonder if they ever do."

"Maybe, maybe not. Take me, been married to the same woman thirty-five years. She threw me out last night. Don't know what I'm gonna do. No place ta stay. I slept out in the barn last night. At least the horses still like me." He cackled in a high-pitched whine. "Wife throw you out or a girlfriend?" he asked, looking at my naked ring finger.

"No, she decided to sleep with another man last night. Asked me if I minded." No need for him to know the gay issue, so I fudged the genders.

"She asked you if you minded?" he repeated, emphasizing the last word as he stabbed into the scrambled egg on his plate.

"Just for one night though."

"Whatja tell her?" he asked, fork in midair with the egg falling off.

"I said it was okay, and then I left."

"Man, what kind of a goddamned fool are you anyway? She was beggin' you ta say no. You shoulda marched her into the bedroom, thrown her on the bed, and well, you know what." He leaned over his plate to take another mouthful of egg. He held the fork, stabbing it at me as he talked. "You two been having trouble for a while?" He stared me in the eye.

"No. I thought everything was fine."

"Well, why'd she do it then?"

"This person had been good to her years ago, and she thought she owed him a favor."

"Good Christ alive, man, I've done favors for women, but I never fucked 'em afterwoods."

I knew it sounded foolish to say out loud. We both fell into silence, just the rustle of the stuffing in the seats as we shifted around. I sipped on the black coffee to keep me awake.

By the expression on the aging waitress's face, I could see I had made her day as she shuffled back with my order and the bills. I smiled at her and reached for both of them.

I turned to my breakfast companion. "The meal is on me. I appreciate your listening to my sad story."

"I'll pay the tip then." He threw a five-dollar bill on the table. "My advice, young man, since you're payin' for it, is ta go back and claim your filly. Throw that other bastard out on his ear. She owed him? Shit. Buy him a necktie or some other goddamned fool thing."

We walked out together after finishing breakfast. He'd given me a lot to think about. I wished my father and I could have talked like this. Much to my surprise, he got into a recent silver-colored Cadillac. I would have guessed a rusty pickup.

He ran the window down and said, "You take my advice, young man, go back and throw that son of a bitch out on his ear. Good luck."

"And you go back and show that wife of yours who's boss."

"She already knows that." He chuckled and drove back out onto the highway.

I watched him leave; a light, steady rain blanketed the parking lot. My shoulders were soaked by the time I got back into the car, resolution now muddied. Had I done the right thing, or was I just continuing a pattern I had set up? When the going gets tough, turn and run. Words swirled in my mind.

What do you really want, Damon?

Go back and claim your filly. Stake your claim. Throw the bastard out.

This is today and then there's tomorrow.

She's bringing my son.

Oh, God, tell me what to do. I can't stand the thought of that woman sleeping with Carlos.

She was begging you to say no.

A bell rang way back somewhere in my mind. Of course, what a fucking idiot I'd been. He made a commitment to me hours before, and now he was begging me to do the same to him. I broke out in a sweat. I could hardly breathe. My hand shook when I stabbed the key into the ignition. I checked my cell phone. No calls. He hadn't called. It's time I make the calls. Had I finally turned a corner? Could I finally stand on my own and be a real partner?

The trip back home felt endlessly long and stressful. What was I going to say? How was I going to feel seeing them both again? Could I handle the next few weeks with Shirl and their son? I pulled off the highway. Still no answer on the cell phone. He knows who it is. Why doesn't he answer? Why didn't he call?

The red Caddy was missing when I finally pulled into the driveway. Thank God. Maybe she will stay away long enough for us to talk. I prepared myself for the scene ahead.

No one was in sight.

"Carlos!"

No answer. Everything inside was in order. The bed was made; the guest room looked unused. Not a soul in sight either way on the beach.

I returned to the kitchen to make a cup of tea, picturing myself on the deck calmly sipping tea when they returned, red-faced with guilt. I went to the sink to fill the kettle. Bloody cloths. Oh Jesus, there's been an accident. *Call the hospital.* My fingers shook thumbing through the telephone book There were seventeen hospitals listed. Which was the nearest?

On the eighth call I got lucky, or unlucky, as the case might be.

"Yes, a Carlos Bravara was admitted four hours ago."

Any details she could tell me about his condition? No, she wasn't allowed.

A trip over unfamiliar territory would be difficult at best, with this, a disaster. *Call a cab.* Five minutes seemed more like five hours.

I pulled the door open before the cab had come to a stop. "An emergency," I blurted.

Fifteen minutes later we pulled up in front of admissions, and I threw fifty dollars for a thirty-dollar ride onto the front seat. He thanked me heartily and tipped his hat as he pulled back onto the street. Hopefully it helped his day.

The rain had let up, but the heat and humidity lingered. I ran my hand over my face and felt thirty-six hours of stubble as the receptionist looked up. The foyer was cool from the whisper of the air-conditioning. The receptionist was likewise.

I identified myself and asked for Carlos's room number.

"Relationship," the receptionist asked.

I struggled to think of how to answer so they would let me in.

"Significant other," I finally said.

She gave me a very strange look, a bit of disgust even.

So you don't like gays, lady. Tough shit.

She directed me to a waiting room and suggested inquiring at the nurses' station for further information.

To my amazement and relief, Carlos and Shirl were seated, deep in discussion in the lounge area. Then it struck me. Oh no, it must be Junior. Carlos looked up as I approached.

"Well, where in hell have you been?" he demanded, jumping up to face me.

"What's happened?" I asked, ignoring his callous remark. "Has Junior had an accident?"

Shirl nodded, her face red from crying.

"He went out looking for you on his bike this morning. He thought he saw you across the street and swung out in front of a car," Carlos said in the same terse voice.

"How bad?" I dreaded the answer.

"Two broken ribs, a fractured arm, and a broken ankle."

"How bad are the ribs? Did they puncture anything internal?"

"We're waiting to hear."

Carlos motioned me to follow him down the hall. He stopped in a deserted corner lounge, wheeled around, and grabbed me by the shoulder. His grip was strong, but I shrugged it off.

"Where in hell did you go this time, Damon? Another one of your childish disappearing acts?" he demanded, curling his lip.

I had never seen him so angry. I saw hate in his eyes as he looked at me. I was tongue-tied, unable to speak for several seconds. We stood glaring at each other.

"Did you and Shirl enjoy the little romp in bed last night?" I finally asked in a taunting voice.

His face turned scarlet, and I could see him clenching his fists.

"Why don't you hit me?" I asked, daring him.

He turned away and started down the hall.

"Don't you turn your back on me, you bastard," I shouted.

Carlos kept walking.

"I'm going back with Shirl. You can go to hell."

I had never spoken like this to anyone else, except Dad. He continued out of sight around the corner.

Shirl was still sitting where I had first seen her. She looked a wreck, no makeup, her hair caught up in a ribbon. I pitied her in spite of myself.

"Can I get you some coffee or something to drink?"

"No, thank you, I'm okay." She paused, as if trying to decide what to say next, what to tell me. Finally she asked, "Where did you go last night, Damon?"

"Out."

"I don't understand why."

"Well then, you've got one thick skull. You're a married woman, for God's sake, or were anyway, Shirl," I said, looking at her ring. "How would you feel if your husband asked if you minded if he slept with a woman friend?"

"This is different."

"What's different about it Shirl, tell me!" I said coldly.

"Well, you're both men and you're..." Her voice trailed off.

"Both queer," I finished. "So we have no feelings except sexually."

"You said it, I didn't," she replied in a weak voice.

I glared at her in a cold fury with a strength and determination I had never experienced before. There would be no more running away. Carlos would never treat me like this again either. I clenched my hands into fists and fought the urge to wrap them around her neck.

A surgeon wearing operating-room greens approached us.

"Mrs. Bravara, your son is very lucky. The internal injuries were minor, but he'll need a transfusion. He has a rare blood type, maybe you or his father can donate. We've set the ankle and bound his ribs. He's a pretty sore young man, but he'll be fine. He's asking to see you, and he keeps mentioning Damon."

"I'm Damon. Would it be okay for me to see him?"

"Under the circumstances, I think it would be advisable. He's pretty upset, and the pain medication doesn't do it all. He'll be groggy, so don't stay too long, he needs rest."

We walked up a long tiled hallway. Several unused beds were angled along the walls. It was a scary scene as we entered Junior's room. He was lying in bed, his leg elevated, ankle in a cast, chest strapped, and a splint on his arm. The side of his face was covered with scratches, and a bandage covered his left cheek. His features looked different somehow despite the injuries. I held Shirl's arm when her legs became wobbly.

"You came back. Dad said you might not. I had to find you." A tear rolled down his cheek.

"You bet I'm back, I just went out for a little air. I'm not going away, you can count on that."

I poked Shirl with my elbow. She looked confused as she took Junior's hand to reassure him everything was okay. I sensed Carlos's presence in back of us. I winked at Junior, swung away, avoiding contact with Carlos, and left the room with no eye contact between us.

I went to the nurses' station to ask about donating blood. Junior's type was the same as mine. Carlos's blood type was O positive. I'd seen it listed on his pill bottles. He couldn't donate anyway. I had hoped to donate for him when the time came, but our types did not match. So it would be Shirl's, and she was in no shape to donate anything.

I was ushered into a sterile white-walled room. Blood pressure was taken, allergies questioned, "HIV positive or infected with AIDS" questioned. The nurse swabbed my arm and inserted the needle. I watched the blood slowly fill the bag. Finally it was full, and she removed the needle and pressed a fold of gauze on the needle exit and had me double up my arm. I started to sit up, but she gently pushed me back down.

"You need to stay lying down for five minutes."

Another nurse appeared and said the Bravaras were asking for me. A thought hit me.

"Should you check with Mrs. Bravara about donating as well? Maybe the pint won't be enough."

When my vital signs were approved, they had me drink a glass of orange juice. A few minutes later, the nurse returned and had me sit up. I felt fine. The nurse followed along as I returned to the waiting area. Shirl and Carlos came toward me; she was eyeing the bandage inside my left elbow. I passed by them, my expression set.

"I will see you later, back at the house," I said coldly. The words "Back home" stuck in my throat. I doubted at that moment it ever would be again.

Fatigue overtook me on the taxi ride to the house. I had not slept since the night before last and had driven a couple of hundred miles, plus the loss of blood. As I was stepping up onto the deck and looking out to sea, it occurred to me. I had gained half a house and alienated the only person I ever loved. A nice day's work.

I wondered where the best place to sleep would be. The guest room seemed the logical choice. Lying down eased my body, and I shielded my eyes with my left forearm. The harm I had done so unknowingly to Junior finally sank in. Tears of regret and loss ran down the side of my face onto the pillow. I finally slept.

CHAPTER

8

The sounds of Carlos and Shirl arguing awakened me. It was nearly 5:00 p.m. I lay with my eyes shut for several more minutes trying to make sense of the last forty-eight hours but not feeling ready yet to talk it out with anyone.

A shower and shave might lift my spirits or at least take up my mind for a bit. All my clothes and belongings were either in Carlos's room or the trunk of my car. I decided to do without shaving since my razor was in Carlos's bathroom but at least take a shower in the guest bath. After, feeling only somewhat refreshed, it was time to plot my next move. Going out for dinner would avoid having to endure more than passing interaction with them. I slipped back into my shorts and jersey and slid my feet into my sandals and headed for the living room.

"Sorry, Damon, we didn't mean to waken you."

Carlos studied my face, probably gauging my mood. He looked haggard and deflated.

"No, that's fine, I slept long enough. What's the current word on Junior?"

"He's doing well. We left him about an hour ago. His meds are making him sleepy." Shirl rose from her chair and turned toward the kitchen. "Would you like something to eat?"

"No, thanks, I'm going to pick up something in town." I turned back to Carlos and affirmed, "But I will be back."

"Damon, we need to talk." He rose and moved toward me.

"Yes, but not now." I gestured for him to sit down again.

The early evening air was pleasantly warm as I stepped out onto the deck, but a breeze sweeping inland from the sea had a cool edge to it. I rummaged through the suitcases and boxes in the trunk of my car and pulled out a blue cotton sweater. It smelled of the softener Joan used. With some feeling of regret, I slid it on. We two had lived such a simple, uncomplicated life. What if Carlos had never sent me that letter? Would we still be living the lie?

I should call her again, just to hear her voice. I had called when reaching San Diego to let her know I had arrived. It was a difficult call for us both.

Not tonight though. Too many emotions choked my mind. Leaving New Hampshire was a wise move, but was leaving Texas a big mistake? Existing between two worlds and belonging to neither seemed forever to be my lot.

What should I do about unpacking? No need to bring my luggage inside now, maybe tomorrow, maybe not at all. I slammed the trunk lid down. No decisions tonight.

The ride into town was pleasant enough. I listened to a Joe Henry CD, which I was particularly fond of. I hummed along with "Stop." It fitted my situation so well.

I decided on takeout at a Kentucky Fried Chicken. After a bite or two, the rest landed in the trash. A young couple sat at an outdoor table, chatting while they ate. They nodded to me and commented on the weather. Conversation with anyone tonight was repugnant, so I smiled and nodded and got back into my car.

Not ready to deal with Carlos and Shirl yet, I parked a short distance from the house and took a well-worn path out onto the beach. The roar of the ocean and the vista out to the horizon was soothing. I sat on someone's bench and tried once more to make sense of it all. The one thing I was sure of, there would be no running away again. Junior would probably be back soon; children heal fast. And then there was Shirl. Carlos had said it was only for one night. Why did I foolishly agree, and how did that make me look in his eyes? When would I sleep with him again after last night? There had to be a reckoning.

A thick fog slowly rolled in obliterating the surroundings more than a few feet away. The sky darkened, and the sound of a coast guard patrol boat passing by drowned out the sound of the tide. It was chilly and damp as I went back to the car.

⤟

Carlos and Shirl still sat in the living room when I reappeared. Carlos had a fire burning on the grate, and they both had drinks in their hands. I was concerned, knowing he should not have liquor. He pointed to an aluminum Coke can on the floor beside him then pointed at his glass. We made some shallow conversation, avoiding the big questions. We all fell silent; Carlos gazed into the fire. I went down the hall to his room and collected my few things and put them into a box. They could be stored in the guest room for the time being.

I looked around the room. It was to have been our room. Not anymore. Maybe Carlos would want me to leave. It would be his choice, not mine. Was whatever we once had gone now? His expression in the hospital sealed that. And I couldn't fault him. He was dead-on. Maybe Dad was right throwing me out; maybe Mike was too.

Was my love affair with Carlos all an illusion, something still in my head but not in his heart? A chill ran through me. What if he only invited me out of friendship? My god, have I been a fool? He could have any man he wants, why me? It would be much easier to hate him if he had hit me in the hospital this morning. The problem is I don't hate him—far from it.

My quandary was interrupted by the ringing telephone.

"I'll get it," I shouted.

It was the hospital. They were calling for Mr. or Mrs. Bravara. They wouldn't say the reason. I called Shirl.

I handed her the phone. She listened several seconds.

"Is this a serious setback?" she asked, alarm in her voice. She ran her fingers up into her hair.

Carlos and I looked at each other. *Don't let him die. Please, God, don't let him die.*

"More blood? Yes, of course." She stood holding the receiver, then she burst into tears. Carlos took her into his arms. "They need another pint of blood," she said between sobs.

Carlos, arm around Shirl, took the phone and said he was the boy's father. He listened and nodded several times. "Thanks, we'll be right along."

"I'll get the car."

I headed toward the door. If they had asked me at that moment to cut off an arm, I would have asked which one. It was good to have something active to do. Carlos wrapped a sweater around Shirl's shoulders and tried to comfort her. She seemed upset beyond reason. They sat in back with his arm around her. I frequently checked the rearview mirror the rest of the way in. He has something to live for now, his own flesh and blood. Shirl and Junior can live out here now. A boy needs a father.

At the hospital, Carlos and I escorted Shirl to the laboratory for the blood donation. We stood, silent, waiting. I, lost in my own thoughts, was glad not to be privy to his. Shirl came out again, grim faced.

I was the first to react.

"Something's wrong. What is it, Shirl?"

The lab technician appeared at the door. "Mrs. Bravara, your blood type doesn't match the boy's."

"Well, it must match," Carlos said. "It has to, my blood is O positive. The doctor said he transfused the boy with AB negative."

"I don't understand," the technician repeated.

Shirl and I looked at each other. It couldn't be, but what else could explain it? Junior and I have the same blood type. Carlos caught our interchange but made no comment. Instead, he turned and strode back to the waiting room.

Bits and pieces of the past swirled around me. That terrible night ten years ago in my apartment. I needed to feel better about myself that I could make it with a woman. Shirl was aware of my affair with Carlos, and seducing his lover would be her revenge on Carlos for abandoning her.

And now I have a son. My god, I have a son. How I managed to continue as though nothing unusual had happened, now having this knowledge, was all a matter of sheer willpower—more than I ever knew I possessed.

Shirl and I idled back to the waiting area. Carlos was seated, chin leaning on one arm. Shirl sat beside him. I offered to go for coffee. I couldn't sit still. I had to move or bust. Fortunately, neither argued. So I circled around out of their view and went back to the lab, my real reason for going for coffee in the first place. The technician came to the door. He recognized me from the previous fray.

"Can I help you, sir?"

"The mother's blood doesn't match, does it? There was no mistake."

"Just what relation are you?" he asked, ignoring my question, eyebrows raised.

"The father." My knees shook as I said it.

"The father?"

"Her blood doesn't match, does it?" I asked again.

We stared at each other.

"What do you want me to do, lie?" he asked, an edge in his voice.

"No, tell her you don't need the blood. Mr. Bravara mustn't know."

"I've heard of these little arrangements before, Mr.?" he said, a touch of scorn in his voice.

"Duncan, Damon Duncan." I stared him down.

He made no comment.

"And for your information, the lady is not Mrs. Bravara."

"This could become very sticky, but I'm inclined to agree to what you're asking. We did an extra transfusion on the boy this afternoon, and we thought—"

I was alarmed and broke in, "Has his condition worsened?"

"Absolutely not. He lost a lot of blood, so he was transfused as a precaution. Since you appear to be the father and with the concern you all have, I am giving you this information. We do have extra pints on hand, but we hoped the mother could help us out due to rarity of this type." He looked me in the eye and asked, "She is the mother?" A smile played at his lips.

"Yes, no doubt of that."

I thanked him for his understanding and discretion. I turned to leave, and he spoke again.

"Mr. Duncan, since you are the boy's father, your blood type should match."

I turned back. "I donated just a few hours ago."

"I didn't realize, thanks."

The cafeteria had closed for the night, but thermos containers had been placed out for self-service. I filled three cups and added Coffee-Mate and sugar then circled back again. It was a balancing act with three cups, but now Superman, I was able to leap tall buildings in a single bound.

Shirl relieved me of one, but her hands shook so badly she had difficulty holding it. Our eyes caught, hers with a question, mine with malice. Carlos took a cup and sat down. I sat across from them, careful not to catch his eye.

The technician came out to where we were seated.

"We won't need any blood after all, we've found another donor. I know it's been a tough day. Thank you for coming."

He glanced in my direction, and I mouthed, "Thanks."

Shirl nodded and visibly relaxed. Carlos put an arm around her. We finished our coffee, and I collected the cups and pitched them into the trash while Carlos and Shirl went over to the nurses' station.

"Can we see our son now?" she asked plaintively.

"It's late. He's resting comfortably. The doctor has recommended no company. We'll let you know if there are any further problems. Better to see him in the morning," she replied, dismissing us and returning to her charts.

Shirl thanked the nurse, and we all went out to the car. Carlos helped Shirl into the backseat and slid in beside her. A momentary stab of jealousy clutched my gut, and I knew right then, dammit, I wouldn't let Carlos slip away from me again. Yet if a final blow were necessary to our tenuous relationship, Junior's paternity could do it. He's going to throw me out and let himself die. I drove in silence, my mind more unsure of the future than it ever had been.

Shirl looked exhausted when we arrived back. Her face was swollen from crying, her hands unsteady and hair falling around her face. Other things I expected, however, were even more troubling to her. In fairness, I gave her benefit of the doubt on whether she knew for sure if Junior belonged to me. She wanted so badly to have it be Carlos's. Had she tricked even herself? Where would she finally stand in this developing tragedy?

Shirl said she had nerve pills in her bag and asked me to get them. I had the evil desire to see if she had condoms there as well but didn't. I brought her purse back with a glass of water. She scrambled through the contents and popped two pills into her mouth. I wished they were arsenic. Carlos got her calmed down, and we helped her into his bed. We sat on either side, each holding one of her hands. She finally dropped off into uneasy sleep, parts of her jerking and twitching. We eased the door shut as we left.

Now we had to face each other. Bad words, hurtful words had passed between us. My little spate of servitude and acceptance of the situation came to a screeching halt.

The fire had burned down in the grate, and Carlos stirred the coals and tossed on more wood. It smoldered a bit, and then tongues of flame encircled the logs.

"Should I make us some tea?" I asked to break the silence.

"That would be nice."

Carlos followed me into the kitchen. I filled the kettle, turned on the gas, rinsed the pot with hot water, scooped in three tablespoons of loose tea, and filled it with boiling water when it boiled. Carlos got a tray and placed the cups and saucers, honey, teaspoons, and the lemon on one side. I placed the pot on the other side and covered it with a towel. We kept busy to avoid talking. "Why don't I—let me," we said together, smiling at each other.

We sat at the small kitchen table. I waited for the tea to steep. I was so tense it was difficult to pour. I scalded my thumb and rushed for cold water. Carlos made an attempt to help then pulled his hand back when I scowled. We retreated back into silence.

"Damon." He held the cup in his hand.

I had started to sip, stopped, and looked at him over the rim of my cup.

"I said some bad things to you at the hospital this morning. I'm sorry."

"No need to apologize. You were right," I replied, my heart beating faster. "The truth in your words is what hurt. I won't lie about that." We sat in silence several more minutes. "I was rude and out of line with you. In retrospect, I wish I could take my words back."

"Were you leaving me last night?" he asked, looking directly at me.

I didn't want to answer. A lie at this late stage of our relationship didn't make much difference, yet I wanted to be honest.

"Yes," I said simply.

"Because of Shirl sleeping with me?" he asked, eyebrows raised. He set his cup down, rose, and went to the window, his back to me.

A jealous fury grabbed me at his words. "Yes, goddammit." I banged my cup down onto the saucer so hard tea slopped out.

He wheeled around, anger on his face. "Why in hell didn't you say no, that I was off-limits? I wanted you to slap me, anything to show you loved me."

I paused. The old gent at the café was right. What a fool I'd been, but I was still suffused with fury.

"So it was a test then? I told you I was here for good the morning I arrived. I've put my life on hold because you were that important to me."

"Right. Were that important, *were*."

I jumped up, planted my hands firmly on the table, and stared him down. "All right, did you sleep with her or not?"

"It's none of your business, but yes, we did share the bed." He looked away.

It hit me between the eyes. "The same bed we shared the night before?" Anguish choked my voice.

"Yes, Damon, the same bed, and I wanted it to be you. Christ, Damon, you ran out on me twice yesterday—twice."

"We both needed space. You know that. We've wasted ten fucking years apart. You're the only person I ever loved or wanted. Saturday with you was heaven. And the next day you suddenly had a son. How do you think I felt?"

"I made a commitment to you Sunday afternoon and you left me anyway. I asked you to stay. I needed your support." He swung back to the window and twisted a blind cord in his fingers. "You hate her, don't you?"

"Yes," I screamed, jumping up and grabbing his shoulder. "I hate her."

"And you hate my son too." He twisted toward me, shrugging me off.

"You know that's not true, you've seen us together."

I turned to leave the room. It was on the tip of my tongue to say, "Your son, he's my son." It took every ounce of reserve not to break down in tears, once more realizing what a wimp I still was.

I bumped into Shirl at the door, disheveled from weariness and sorrow.

"For God's sake, you two, what the hell's going on?"

CHAPTER

❧ 9 ☙

"You told him, didn't you?" Shirl accused, ice in her voice.

"No. We should do that together," I said.

"Tell me, for God's sake, tell me what?" Carlos's voice rose.

"This is not a good time. Why did you bring it up, Shirl, why now?"

There was a disturbed look in her eyes, a haunted expression, something I had not seen in her before. I was concerned with what twist it might take.

"When is it going to be a good time then?" she demanded, her voice shrill.

Carlos grabbed me by both arms. "For Christ's sake, Damon, tell me, what are you two hiding?"

"There's no easy way to tell you this," I said, looking him in the eye. "I...Shirl and I...found out today, by chance...the blood tests..." My voice trailed off.

"What about the blood tests?" Carlos gripped my arms till it hurt.

"Junior is not your son."

"Whose son is he then?" His face turned red, and a nerve twitched in his cheek. "Not yours, Damon, not yours?"

I continued looking him in the eyes. "Yes, he's probably mine."

Carlos recoiled like I had struck him. He released my arms and covered his eyes. Shirl and I stared at each other.

Carlos strode to the sink and looked out the window. "You bitch, Shirl, you fucking bitch." He spun toward her, shook his head, then spun back to the window.

Shirl rushed over to him and grabbed his shoulder. "I didn't know. It could have been yours, honest, Carlos, I thought he was yours."

"If the boy wasn't in the hospital, I'd send you both packing."

"You can't blame the boy, Carlos," I pleaded. "What the rest of us have done, it's not his fault."

It worried me to see him so upset. I was afraid of violence, not for myself but for Shirl.

His eyes looked clouded, his face contorted.

"I had hoped to spend the last of my life peacefully with you, Damon. God, how I wanted it to work." He stopped, moved back to the window, and sighed. "It's all gone bad—everything. I need to be alone, to think, to figure out what's the truth. I'll put you up at a hotel near the hospital so you can be near the boy."

"You can't walk away from Junior," I protested. "He thinks you're his father. It would break the boy's heart. There's no need for him to know. Later, when he's older."

"Then you take care of him. He thinks the sun rises and sets on you anyway."

I felt sorry for Shirl in spite of all the heartbreak she had inflicted. I was torn between two factions, both out of control. She was mother of the child I never knew I had. Carlos was the person I had obsessed about the past ten years.

Where did my duty lie?

Shirl was distraught. She had a son, my son. I couldn't turn my back on her now. I went to Carlos and put my arms around him. I rested my head on his back. He stood motionless, hands over his eyes. Suddenly, he twisted and strode into the living room. His abrupt movement threw me off balance, and I landed on the floor.

Fortunately he was already out of the room and didn't realize what had happened. Struggling to my feet, I came up under a cabinet edge, banging the devil out of my head. My knees buckled, and I fell backward, striking my head on the floor. I must have been dazed for several seconds. The next thing I knew, Shirl was on her knees beside me with an ice pack against the wound. The back of my head hurt like hell.

"Where's Carlos?" I asked.

"The last I saw of him, he was out on the beach."

I struggled to get up. Her face was twisted in anger. She straightened up, ran her hand over her face, and looked at herself in a mirror.

"You do as you wish, Damon, but I've had it here. I'm leaving."

"What about Junior? We need to go down and see him in the morning."

I was afraid of what Shirl might say to Junior and concerned about Carlos. I needed some kind of plan. I prayed to keep my head and get us through this crisis. I had an obligation to Carlos and to Junior.

Shirl stamped into the bedroom in a fury and began throwing things into her suitcase. Whatever Carlos had gone through in the past ten years, he was now a stranger to me. Still I wouldn't leave now, even if he asked me to. He was so upset. I was concerned about his state of mind.

Darkness settled in. No sign of him. I was worried sick. Should I call the coast guard? I relaxed a bit when I heard him moving a chair on the deck.

I went into the bathroom and took two double-strength aspirins. My head throbbed, but I didn't want it to cloud my thinking. Junior was all right for the night. I must keep Shirl from upsetting him. I could find a hotel for her, keep on her good side. Junior's welfare depended on it. No, she should stay here. I can keep watch of her more easily.

I went into the bedroom where she was packing.

"Shirl, please don't leave tonight. Stay here, we need to go see Junior in the morning."

"I want to get out of this fucking house as fast as I can," she said, brushing by me. "You two can stay here and laugh about Shirl and her bastard son. Neither of you will see him again, I promise that."

"Neither of us are laughing about you and my son. He's a wonderful boy, and we have to think of his welfare first."

My headache was picking up again, and I cursed myself for stumbling in the kitchen. I had no legal hold over her and could not stop her from taking the boy.

"Let her go," Carlos said from the bedroom doorway. "My life has been in turmoil ever since you two arrived. Go and let me fight this thing out on my own. I want to lie down and die. My friends are gone. My fans are gone. My career is over. I have nothing left."

"You still have me." I struggled desperately to stay calm.

"I never had you, and I don't now. You listened to Ilka rather than me ten years ago, if you remember. It wasn't ever me. It was your sister. Carlos never came first in your life."

"I had been through hell, if you remember, I wasn't thinking straight." I looked away from him. "I'm not proud of that part of my life." I headed for the bedroom.

"You sent me away. You had a restraining order. I came to see you anyway, and you sent me away, Damon."

"I never had anything to do with that fucking restraining order!" I pounded the bedpost. "It was Ilka's doing. I hounded her after you left and made her confess and cancel it."

Carlos and Shirl both stared at me. Doubt showed on his face. What other lies had he believed?

"You want to talk about sorrow and regrets, then let's talk about sorrow and regrets. It took me six goddamned months to go outside after the attack. I used to sit and shake if Ilka left me alone at night. I still have flashbacks. And those terrible ninety days at House of Change! We all lied to ourselves—we were changed, we were cured.

Bullshit, we weren't changed, and we weren't cured because we weren't sick."

My breath came in gasps. My body was wound up so tight I couldn't have stopped if I had tried. I clutched the bedpost for support. Both of them listened in stunned silence.

"Do you remember performing in Dallas five years ago?" Not waiting for an answer, I plunged on. "I lied to Joan and went to see you. Tears ran down my cheeks during the performance. You were wonderful. I tried to see you afterwards. I wrote a note and asked a stagehand to deliver it to you. I waited and waited. He finally came back and said you had gone.

"I tried a hundred times to phone you. I even spoke to Jerry Haines. I bet he never told you that. And your manager, Hudson, the bastard, he laughed at me. He said, 'You cocksuckers are all alike, you want a piece of the star.'" I paused for breath, afraid of my knees crumpling. "How many letters did you receive? I wrote you a dozen those first years. You never answered, and I gave up."

Carlos started toward me, and I held him off with my hands.

"I was living a double life as a straight married man and as a man racked with guilt over his real feelings. Some days I could make myself believe I loved Joan and everything was okay. Then I'd see your name in the paper, and the lie would come back like a kick in the guts.

"The only happy day I've had in this past ten years was when you called last month."

I stopped, unable to go on. My heart pounded. My eyes blurred. My mouth went dry. I swung around onto the bed, attempting to get my equilibrium back. The room was deadly silent. Carlos and Shirl stood like statues. At last Carlos started to speak, but I cut him off.

"And then I read you were HIV positive. My world—what there was left of it—crumbled. I took indefinite leave of absence from the bank and came here as soon as I could arrange it. Saturday could have been the best day of my life if I hadn't known what was ahead. And now Shirl."

I raised my head and looked her in the eye.

"Out of nowhere comes this woman bringing your child. And then you had to sleep with her that night." I eyed Carlos. "I still see the anger and hatred in your face when you confronted me in the hospital the next day."

Tears ran down Shirl's cheek. "When Junior is able to travel, I'll be going back to Fort Worth. I promise to keep in touch." She walked out of the room.

A deadly calm fell over me. All my emotions of the past ten years had been spilled out on the floor. I was suddenly free of them. Free at last—free from my parents, free from Ilka, and yes, free from Carlos. He sat on the bed beside me as if in a trance.

I touched his arm.

"I won't leave you. I'm going to look for a place nearby so you can have your space here. I'll be around days to care for you as time goes by."

"My nursemaid," he said bitterly.

"If that's the way you want to put it," I replied calmly. I was dead tired; my head ached, and my spirit was gone. I went into the living room and lay on the sofa on my side, hands between my knees. I was glad Carlos had not protested during my diatribe; this made my release from all people on earth.

Shirl brought a blanket and covered me. Carlos was nowhere in sight.

I awoke with a start around 6:00 a.m. My legs were stiff from my cramped position on the couch. I arose painfully and went to the bathroom, ran the cold water, and pressed a wet washcloth against the welt on the back of my skull. Back in the kitchen, I put on the kettle for tea. Shirl was rustling around in the living room.

Carlos was nowhere around. I didn't care. I hoped he could have plenty of time to himself. I felt of no further use to him other than seeing he medicated as he should.

"Shirl," I called, "do you know if Carlos took his meds?"

"I have no idea," she called back.

And she probably doesn't give a shit either.

Junior was the only one who needed us; the rest had messed up our lives so badly it could never be straightened out. I had been so sure of the situation last night. Now, it was all mixed up in my mind. Carlos had not been able to vent. I had pushed too hard with my own agenda. How did I feel about him today? Had I been wrong about him all these years?

Shirl and I prepared to go to the hospital. She was silent when we got into the car. Carlos appeared on the deck stairs. I ran the window down and asked if he wanted to go. He shook his head. I backed out. Time, space, people whirled by me. I had promised to stay no matter what.

Chapter

10

When Shirl and I arrived at the hospital, Junior had finished breakfast, and his dressings were being changed. I felt sobered from one rueful encounter I had fathered a child. It had been a pleasure to neither of us, quite the contrary, but I felt a bond to him already.

Shirl sat on the edge of the bed and hugged him. I stood rather awkwardly beside them, trying to accept the three of us as a family. I had purchased a model plane kit and a couple of comic books on the way in. He looked from one to the other and then decided to assemble the plane.

He stopped and looked up at Shirl.

"Where's Dad? Is he coming in to see me?"

I sucked my breath in as silently as I was able under the circumstances at the thought of what the boy would face in the future sorting out his parent's deeds. I had not noticed any connection between Carlos and the boy, and it troubled me. I reached for Junior, and we hugged.

"He has a headache, but he said he loves you and will be in later," Shirl announced, looking to me for reassurance.

"You bet he will," I said firmly.

A shiver ran through me. Was I up to this new challenge? Time would tell. There was no doubt in my mind he was a smart and savvy kid. He would have our number soon enough.

"Thanks for these cool things, Damon. I love Spiderman." He turned to his mother. "How soon can we go back to Dad's place?"

I could see she was close to falling apart.

"Why don't we go out and ask the doctor?" I said.

What was I going to do with these three needy people? We hadn't eaten breakfast, so I got coffee and Danish for both of us.

I checked at the nurses' station regarding Junior's condition and prospects for going home. The nurse assured me she could not give any specific information, only family members and then only from the doctor.

"I am the boy's natural father," I informed her. "But he doesn't know it yet." I regretted telling her since she might let it slip. "Please don't say anything about it to upset him."

"Of course, I can't and wouldn't. I hope you'll tell him as soon as he's better. It's a terrible thing for a child not to know," she said frostily.

"When can we speak to the doctor?" I asked coolly.

She checked the chart. "He'll be in soon. I'll tell him the family wants to speak with him."

I handed the coffee and Danish to Shirl and told her the doctor would be in soon.

I stood up and dropped the car keys into Shirl's hand. She looked at me questioningly.

"I'm taking a taxi back to the house. You stay here with Junior and talk to the doctor. Tell Junior I love him and I'll be back later. Please don't tell him about Carlos or me. We need to do that together."

∽

I found Carlos slumped on a cedar chaise, head in hands, staring at the deck floor. He needed a shave and a change of clothes.

"You look like you've just lost your last friend," I said.

He looked up at me, sadness in his eyes. "Have I?"

I bent and gave him a noisy kiss on the lips. "What do you think?"

A smile slowly radiated over his handsome face. "I need you… more than you know."

I knelt beside him and laid my head in his lap. "I know." He ran his hand through my hair. "I've grown up a lot in the past three days. I didn't run away this time. And I won't again."

He made no comment, just nodded.

I sprang up and pulled at his arm.

"I'm fixing us some breakfast. When was the last time you ate?" He followed me into the kitchen. "You're shivering." I draped a sweater over his shoulders, and he perched on a barstool while we chatted. I was in the midst of pouring eggs into a pan to scramble. "Tell me about Jerry Haines."

He looked at me quizzically. "Whatever for?"

I shrugged. "He's a piece of your past. I really know so little about that portion of your life."

"Yeah, and not a very good part in most cases." He slid off the stool, rummaged in a cupboard, and hauled out his basket of meds.

"Jerry was always the big shot. Actually though, just a lot of hot air. Promise anything, but don't come through."

He popped some pills and took a swallow of water.

"His rock group was big in Boston then, but nowhere else yet. I was barely nineteen at the time. His world seemed so glamorous. I was gaga over him. He had a regular following, both teenaged girls and boys. I was attracted to him but steered clear. I meant nothing to him. The story of my life. My looks opened doors, but the wrong ones."

"You opened my door," I said, laughing.

"You're the best thing that ever happened to me."

He slid his arms around me.

He thought a moment then continued, "I tried my hand at songwriting a couple of years later. I was good. Nobody was more surprised than I. Jerry recorded them, and one turned into a hit. The record listed him as the songwriter. No contract was signed. I trusted him, but no commission. He encouraged me to open a joint account with the pittance amount I had earned from him and playing piano at a bar on my time off. My first big mistake.

"Jerry had dreams of going to Miami and hitting the big time. He wanted me to go with him. I wanted to go on my own to LA. That's when you and I met."

I piled two plates with scrambled eggs and toast and poured two mugs of coffee. He paused, and we both ate in silence for several minutes. A comfortable calm pervaded, and we looked at each other from time to time. No words were spoken. He set his coffee cup back down, took a bite of toast, and laid the rest on the plate. He cleared his throat.

"I never told you this before, but it's a part of the whole catastrophe in Fort Worth. I had twenty-seven thousand dollars in the bank when we met. Jerry pulled it all out, so I was flat broke. I had a couple of thousand in cash and traveler's checks with me when I left Boston. What if we had started to California with me penniless?"

"Jesus, what did you do?"

We were interrupted when Shirl pulled my car into the driveway. She stormed up onto the deck and into the kitchen, her face twisted in anger. She stood speechless, glaring from one to the other of us.

"What?" Carlos said.

"You two are some fucking worried about Junior! I've waited four goddamned hours since you walked out on me, Damon."

It was on the tip of my tongue to snap back at her but thought better of it. Junior would be the loser no matter what. Her rage filled the room. I could see the angry interplay between the two of them. Enough of this shit, he needs some loving.

I piloted him into the bedroom, pushed him gently down onto the bed, and eased off his tank top and shorts.

"Where's the yellow silk shirt?"

He hesitated. "On the bureau, in the gray box. Why?"

"For old time's sake, the good times." I held it out for him to put on.

"Damon, I can't. My mind isn't working right. Don't ask me to do it."

Not to be deterred, he needed me and, for God's sake, I needed him, I grabbed the box and shook out the shirt. He had kept it all this time.

I fed one of his arms into a sleeve like dressing a child then pulled the shirt around and pushed in the other arm. He was naked before me save for the open silk shirt.

My T-shirt and shorts soon landed on a chair. Carlos was becoming aroused. I stood naked in front of him, hard.

"Stop it, Damon, stop it." Shirl gasped from the doorway.

I slid into bed beside Carlos, my body against his. We kissed deeply, passionately, our bodies rolling and kneading, flesh against flesh. His eyes were closed; tears welled and slid down his cheeks. I slowly pushed between his legs while rolling on a condom. I took saliva and moistened myself and slowly, ever so slowly, pushed forward.

All the hurt, anger, and jealousy flowed from my mind. Let the hinges of hell creak. Let the world cast its judgment. For what time he had left, we would be together as one. Ten years of frustration, turmoil, separation, longing—forgotten. Nothing mattered now; we were oblivious to everything around us. Our bodies finally bonded. His breathing accelerated; my breathing accelerated. He tightened his legs around my torso and raised his body to mine, his arms engulfing me. His lips were on mine in a long, tender, passionate kiss. He slid back down, prone. We teetered on the edge of paradise in a world of our own making. My urgency finally increased as I pushed deeper into him, the bond once more complete. The final release was mutual. I slid slowly forward into his encircled arms. He was now yin and I yang.

All the while, Shirl stood in the doorway like a statue, perhaps trying to accept what she was witnessing. I was unaware of her leaving.

We lay together for several hours. I was unwilling to break the bond we had reestablished. Carlos finally drifted off to sleep. I pulled a sheet over us and slept. I awoke later to his even breathing. I gently untangled myself from his arms and slid on a robe.

Shirl sat in a chair in the living room. I closed the bedroom door behind me.

"He hates me now," she sighed, childlike. "And you hate me too, I suppose."

"Shouldn't I?" I asked unkindly. "I can't speak for Carlos. What I can't forgive easily, Shirl, is you trying to break us up." She sat in a state of dishevelment, her face streaked with mascara, her nose red from tissues, her hair uncombed and tangled.

"That was some spectacle you staged in there," she snorted.

"You didn't have to watch."

"You didn't ask me to leave."

"Maybe I wanted you to watch," I said, rubbing my chin. "This may get it into your head where the three of us stand."

"I've spent more time with him than you have."

"Not anymore." My mind streaked back to ten years ago as a slim thread of understanding flashed through me. "I do appreciate your taking care of him those three weeks, whether you believe me or not."

She looked up at me with a sly smile on her face. "What if it had been Carlos's child? Where would you have fit in then?"

I found this game of cat and mouse repulsive. She hadn't seemed like this ten years ago. Something had hardened her. I had to watch myself; she might take it out on Junior.

"He would probably have chosen you," I said to placate her.

Her eyes gleamed.

Carlos came out into the living room wearing his robe. He put his arms around me and asked me to come back to bed with him.

"I need the sleep, but I want you with me when I wake up."

Shirl's face twisted. She grabbed one of her prize goblets off the table and smashed it against the wall. Carlos looked startled. I handed her another, and she flung it. Then Carlos handed her one.

She fired it at him, but he ducked. It hit the wall over the fireplace, exploding. Shards of glass glittered around his feet.

"Stay where you are," I said. "I'll get the broom. The last thing you need now is a cut on your foot."

Shirl's anger subsided as quickly as it flared. She must have realized the jig was up. She had lost Carlos. Not that she ever really had him. But hope dies hard. How well I knew.

She collapsed into a chair when I came back with the broom. I brushed carefully around Carlos's feet. The glass made a rattling sound as it fell into the metal dustpan.

Broken glass on the floor ten years ago in New Castle. The beginning of my odyssey.

Junior came home several days later. He and his mother spent many hours on the beach. He developed a nice tan and tossed stones into the ocean with his good arm. She frequently hugged him, and they seemed to be in deep conversation. For the rest of the visit his exuberance disappeared, and he remained polite and remote.

The school season was fast upon us, and Shirl made good her plans to return to Fort Worth. I felt it preyed upon Junior's mind that Carlos paid so little attention to him. It troubled me that we all seemed to withdraw into our own worlds. When the two of them departed for Texas, I never observed a less emotional parting.

Shirl backed out into the street, Junior raised his hand slightly, and I blew him a kiss. In spite of paternity, I was caught between Carlos and Shirl until such time as we were honest with Junior.

Carlos grew lethargic and spent a lot of time watching television in our bedroom. A wall had developed between us, and I agonized over where we were headed. He often fell asleep in the middle of the day. Whatever was bothering him was not to be shared with me.

We both needed direction, but the communication lines had faltered.

CHAPTER

⊰ 11 ⊱

A few days later, I stepped into the living room off the deck. Carlos had just hung up the phone.

"Who was that?" I asked.

It was a near-perfect California day, and I'd been catching some rays on the cedar chaise.

"Just a couple a guys that worked with me in the recording studio back in Miami." He walked nonchalantly over to the desk and flipped through the day's mail, tossing most of it into the wastebasket. "They're at a bar over in town." He hesitated then added, "They want me to come over and bullshit about old times."

"That's great. Can I come along? I'd like to meet some of your old cronies."

I reached for my shirt and slipped into my sandals.

Carlos's face clouded for a moment, and he cleared his throat.

"It will be boring for you. Stay here and soak up some more sun."

He must have caught my expression of surprise out of the corner of his eye as he turned to leave.

"They don't know about me, do they?" I yanked off my shirt and heaved it at a chair. "Is this some kind of goddamned test to see if I love you enough to stop you?"

"Fuck you, Damon. We've been penned up here together for the last coupla months, I need some air." He grabbed the keys to the Jag and headed for the door. "No, they don't know about you."

Anger flared, and a suffocating bond tightened around my chest till my fingers tingled. This had happened several times in the past couple of weeks. Sweat cascaded from under my armpits, and my head pounded. Damn, I don't want him to notice.

I gathered enough strength to retort, "And it won't ever be, will it, Mr. Macho Man? Go, have a good time with the boys, eat, drink, and be merry."

"For tomorrow I die," he replied in a hoarse voice.

It was so near the truth it clogged my breath. Our eyes met, mine smarting, Carlos's contrite. He approached, grabbed my hand, and crushed me in his arms. His breathing against me was a half-choke.

"You're soaking wet and shaking. Are you okay?"

"Yeah, I'm fine," I lied. "Just a touch of indigestion. Go, I shouldn't have said what I did. I got a little too much sun. It's okay." He had torn me apart with a casual remark, and I needed to be alone. "Go, see your friends. I'm fine."

"Not unless you go with me. To hell with them anyway, you're all that matters." He pulled me over to the love seat, his arm around me.

I smiled in spite of myself. "You know something, Carlos, my good man, what you said a few seconds ago was the first honest thing you've said since we got back together."

I shrugged out of his arms, stood up, and headed for the deck.

"I've been thinking, why don't we get married?" His face was all seriousness.

I stopped dead and chortled. "You've got to be shittin' me," I snorted, the idea the farthest thing from my mind.

He twisted his shoulder around and leaned his head on one hand, staring at me. "Are we ever going to get beyond what I said earlier?"

I could see he was serious. "You forget, I'm already married and have a son. The thing that bothers me most is all the years we were apart. Do you think we would have stayed together, or would it have ended somewhere between?"

"I saw a lot of marriages and relationships fold while I was on the road." He looked reflective and sighed. "It happened to a real good friend. She dumped him and threw herself at me." He fell silent.

"There's more to the story." I stood up, stretched, and yawned.

"She was handy. I was lonely. The guys were wondering if I was queer. So we had a little affair. She dug me, but in a possessive yet offhand way. I was high on drugs and blamed my impotence on that." He leaned forward, head in hands. "Her ex got jealous, and we had a hell of a fight. We were both too wasted to carry through." He paused, reached in his empty shirt pocket. "Shit, I could use a cigarette."

"He's one of the guys who called a while ago?"

He nodded.

"I think you should go and see them. It would be good for you and probably them too."

"It sounds like it's me going, not us." He put his arm on my shoulder and looked me in the eye.

My resolve weakened somewhat, but I returned his intense stare. "No, not this time. I was wrong before and acted like a fool. Bring 'em back here later. This is your space. You need it. Go."

I knew how important it was for him to see some of his old cronies. I should have shut my mouth before.

He flipped open his cell phone and punched in some numbers. He chatted several minutes and made a date to meet them at Riley's Bar in a half hour. He snapped the phone shut and made a high sign with his thumb and index finger. He wrinkled his brow.

"Will you be here when I get back?"

"I might take a stroll on the beach, the weather's perfect."

That was not what concerned him. I could tell by his hesitation that he was still unsure of me, maybe afraid to leave.

"You might as well know at the outset, one of them is a past lover."

His confession made me realize I had hit the nail on the head. "And you're unsure of how you feel about him now." I had to admit a touch of jealousy ran up my spine.

His hand was on the doorknob; he paused, turned back. "Why have any secrets? It will come out sooner or later." I must have blanched. "I had a hot and heavy romance with Kylle. He was going to stay with me if you hadn't decided to come out. We had become just friends several years ago. The romance had ended in a hell of a fight. I knocked one of his teeth out."

I was suddenly unable to swallow. Fortunately, Carlos was upset enough about his confession he was looking away. My knees buckled, and I managed to land in a chair. My breath was coming in spasms, and I dug my fingernails into the palms of my hands. It let up as fast as it started, but I was wet with sweat. I had to get him out before he noticed.

"Go and see the guys. Bring 'em back later if you want. I'd like to see my competition."

Carlos's head jerked sharply toward me to see if I was serious. A little breeze off the ocean had picked up. It felt good on my face as it blew in through the open slider. If I could rest a little, everything would be all right.

He blew me a kiss and was off. He seemed the most charged up he'd been in days; his footsteps bounced.

The day was hot, and the tourists and regulars in the bar drowned out the noise of the AC. Carlos looked around in the crowded space and finally spotted Kylle and Jott seated at the bar, probably on their second or third beer.

"Well, look at the two boozehounds." He stepped between them, putting an arm around each of them. Kylle put both arms around Carlos's waist and gave him a squeeze. Jott slid Carlos's hand off his shoulder and took another swig of beer.

"Man, it's great to see you again," Kylle exclaimed. He rose up and gave Carlos a quick peck on the cheek. "You look great. I didn't know what to…"

"Expect?" Carlos finished. Carlos was all too aware of Kylle and the good times they had had several years ago. He felt a stirring as Kylle ran his hand up under his shirt.

"I'm feeling great and have one humpy nurse. Wait till you see him." Carlos ordered a Coke and another round of beer for the guys. "Let's go over to a table where we can talk." He collected the drinks in both hands after tossing a bill to the bartender. They headed for a table in a secluded corner. "Tell me, what's happening in the big world of music?"

"The usual, too much time on the road. It raises hell with your personal life. It's a ballbuster, but I still love it. Not the same without you though." Kylle took a swallow of beer and set the bottle back on the table, rolling it around on its bottom, then cocked an eye at Carlos. "Any chance of you coming back?"

Carlos caught his eye, and a vibration ran between them. "Never say never, but it's day to day with me, more like month to month now, I'm happy to say." He shifted around in his chair and fiddled with his Coke bottle, avoiding Kylle's attentive scrutiny. "Think the fans will ever forgive me for the last year or so?"

"Fuck yes! Write a book, man, for Christ's sake. George Michael has, and the fans are swarming around him like a bear eatin' shit."

"Bears don't eat shit, asshole," Jott said, disgust in his voice.

"Now just how in hell would you know that? Ever lived with one?"

"Present company excepted, don't believe so," Jott replied.

"How you two lovebirds, do carry on." Carlos snickered.

Jott shot him a steely glance then broke into an embarrassed grin. Carlos nodded.

"Seriously, guys, I'm taking a shitload of meds now, but the old HIV is still down there waiting to nail me." They remained quiet a few moments, the finality of his words sinking in. Carlos broke the silence. "Say, guys, what do you hear from Jerry?"

"In bad shape, man." Kylle shook his head ruefully. "He's on the wagon again, but his liver's shot. A coupla drinks and he'd be dead meat."

"Good old Jerry, the snake. We had our differences, but I wouldn't wish that on anybody. What is he now, forty-five?"

"Shit no, he's fifty if he's a day," Kylle replied.

"Really?" Carlos rolled the cold can on his forehead.

"And what the fuck are you up to these days, Harpo?" Carlos asked good-naturedly. Harpo was a nickname Jott picked up because he talked so little.

"Sloggin' along, trying to keep this guy out of trouble." He nodded toward Kylle.

"Hey, guys, come on over to my place and meet Damon. We've got a house on the ocean, you can go skinny-dipping tonight."

Kylle reached for the empty bottles and grabbed Carlos's arm. There was no mistaking what was happening between them now. Jott headed for the door, a scowl on his face.

"Right on, man. I've gotta see this retard you're shacking up with."

"Watch it, brother. Wait till you see him, he's one hell of a guy."

"Does he like practical jokes?"

"Whatcha got in mind? I hate to think," Carlos said, a grin spreading on his face.

❧

Several hours later, I awoke with a start. Someone was kissing me. And it wasn't Carlos. I shot up to a sitting position and gave the guy a shove. He staggered backwards and sprawled on the floor. I looked to my left, and someone lay on the bed beside me. I jumped up and grabbed a book and was ready to belt him with it. My heart pounded. Had I left the slider unlocked?

Carlos stepped into the room and laughed.

"Honest, Damon, this wasn't my idea. See what I put up with these past ten years?" He sat on the edge of the bed and pulled me into an embrace. "Kylle is the one who kissed you, and Jott's on the bed with you."

I slid out of Carlos's embrace and turned to the guys.

"My god, look at you, Kylle, you handsome devil, I don't wonder you guys were an item."

He colored and boosted himself up off the floor. He was one fine-looking man, tall, slim, but muscular. His longish brown hair framed a tanned face, deep-set hazel eyes, and the most kissable lips. I had my perfect revenge for things said earlier.

I slid out of bed naked except for my undershorts, sauntered over to Kylle, put my arms around him, and pulled him into a deep, tongue-probing kiss. The only sound in the room was the ocean lapping at the sandy shore and our noisy kissing. Kylle fell in with it immediately, and we hugged and mauled each other. I broke away enough to say, "I think Kylle wants to give me a blow job."

"Fuck yes," he spouted.

Carlos was silent a moment, then he broke into a big grin.

"Okay, guys, playtime is over. House rules: no one touches Damon."

I slipped into shorts and a T-shirt. Carlos took me firmly by the arm and piloted me into the living room.

"Sorry, guys, he didn't react the way I thought he would. The joke's on us."

He gave me a playful cuff on the butt.

Jott had yet to say a word. He looked like a nice guy, short, thin, average looking. His nose had probably been broken at some time. He had an easy demeanor that appealed to me right away. He smiled a lot. I shook hands with him, and a nice vibe shot through me.

I encouraged the guys to go to the piano and do a little something for old time's sake. I hadn't heard Carlos sing since we got back together. Tears sprang to my eyes hearing the three musical pros together for a jam session. No wonder he, with their backing, had earned so many gold records.

CHAPTER

⊰ 12 ⊱

Gotta say, I felt jealous of Kylle. Carlos had been forthcoming about the affair, or had he? The more I thought about it, the more it came back to me. Kylle would have cared for him as the disease progressed were it not for me. They had been lovers. Could they still be?

Was it happenstance that Kylle showed up now? It was supposed to be just for a day as he and Jott were passing through. Three days later, Kylle remained in town and was usually here—like tonight.

It was a warm evening, and we sat on the deck, enjoying the sunset over the ocean. Jott was off somewhere, so it was the three of us. I went in to prepare snacks and iced tea.

The passageway was dark as I glanced out the window. The moon reflected on Carlos's gold neck chain as he chatted with Kylle. Suddenly their heads were so close together it obscured the shiny metal. Were they kissing? I hated myself for snooping and being suspicious.

My mind was in overdrive as I tossed snacks onto a tray, pausing at the sliders to listen. For what? I sauntered out and dropped the tray about an inch from the table. It made a satisfying racket, and the guys made a grab for the drinks. Kylle scarfed into the crackers and cheese, crumbs flying as he waved his arms, extolling Miami. They continued to chat about the great times the band members had on tours and the wild things they did. This was good therapy for Carlos. I wasn't involved, and they were oblivious to me anyway. This went on for fifteen or twenty minutes until I finally hoisted myself up and collected the empty glasses and other remains. Was I imaging it, or did they both have erections?

Some past event was brought up by one of them, and they broke out laughing hilariously as I passed through the sliders to return to the kitchen.

What a fool I had become. Probably fifty million adoring fans would give their right arms to be in my shoes. Loading the dishwasher and clearing the counters took a few minutes, and I snapped off the kitchen light to return to the deck. They had gone out by the water, and their laughter filtered up over the cliff. Should I join them? I was unusually weary, so I flopped onto a recliner and stared at the moon. Their voices trailed off, and I must have fallen into a catnap.

I felt the vibration on the deck as they came back to the house. I pretended to be asleep as they tiptoed by.

"I've got dozens of scrapbooks of the tours we made. They're in the bedroom. I'll get 'em." Carlos headed in that direction. Kylle must have followed because their conversation became muffled. After waiting for several minutes while they were still in the bedroom, I got up and slid back into the house. The light was on, and the bedroom door was open, and they seemed lost in reminiscing. No need to bother them now, so I went into the guest room, slipped off my clothes, and slid under the sheet.

My head was pounding, and a shiver ran through me. An extra blanket didn't help much. I tried to read. After rereading the same page three times, I gave up, shook out a couple of aspirin from the nightstand drawer, and swallowed them with a swig of water. I shifted around, trying to get comfortable, and finally conked out.

I roused around 2:00 a.m. The house was dark and quiet. Kylle must have left. I scratched around for the light, threw back the covers, struggled up half-asleep, and stumbled into our bedroom. Ten to one Carlos had forgotten his meds; he was doing so well I didn't want any setbacks. Maybe his warm body would dispel my chills and the doubts about the evening's activities.

I snapped on the light and sucked in my breath. What the fuck. They were in bed together, sound asleep. Filled with an uncompromising rage, I let out a yell and grabbed for a weapon, anything I could find to hammer them senseless. They awoke wild-eyed and disoriented as I landed in the middle of the bed with a shoe in my hand.

"You goddamned fucking sons a bitches," I screamed, hammering Kylle over the head. "You're sleeping in my bed with my lover. You get your ass out of here, and never come into my sight again, do ya hear?"

He scrambled out fully dressed, I noticed, and made for the door while I continued to beat on his body.

"Fucking scumbag. I'd shoot you if I had a gun."

I was so damn mad I paid no attention to what he was saying or the protests he was making. He was bleeding around the mouth. I may have broken his nose. I didn't give a shit.

Carlos rushed out after us, trying to pin my arms down and get the bloody shoe away from me. I turned on him. He was fully clothed as well. Despite my rage, verbal abuse was my only safe weapon against him.

"Listen, Damon," he shouted over my yelling.

"Fuck you, Bravara. Keep your filthy, two-timing hands off me or I'll deck ya."

My voice was giving out, breath stuck in my windpipe, and pain exploded in my chest. I fell backward onto the floor, exhausted and only semiconscious.

I awoke to oxygen flowing through a nosepiece and a needle stuck in my arm. I stared at an unfamiliar ceiling as a nurse checked my blood pressure. The pain was gone from my chest, and I felt eerily calm. I wiggled my fingers and toes. No paralysis, thank God.

Carlos materialized from a chair near my bed. He took my hand. I shook my head.

"Go home, take your meds. See me in the morning."

I squeezed my eyes shut. Tears I couldn't stop ran down my cheeks.

"Mr. Bravara, you must leave. The patient needs his rest," the nurse said in an understanding but firm voice.

"Give me a minute. I need to straighten something out."

"I don't think it's a good idea. Let him rest."

I nodded.

"Five minutes, that's all. Nothing upsetting, I'll be back."

Carlos knelt by the bed and took my hand.

"That was some performance you put on last night."

He looked gray; ten years seemed to be added to his face. I continued to stare at the ceiling.

"It was no performance," I muttered. "I am fighting with everything I've got to make this relationship work. Why does everything seem to go against it?"

"It was my idea, I mean Kylle and me last night. It was a practical joke. We had gotten into bed together to fool you. We were both dressed, if you remember. But you didn't come in. It had been a long day, and we zonked out."

"Yeah, I know. I've kind of figured that out laying here."

Our eyes caught for a moment. But there was more going on. I could feel it. He struggled to his feet as though the weight of the world lay on his shoulders. Near the door, he turned and came back and pecked me on the forehead.

"I love ya, babe. See ya later."

⬄

Carlos stopped at a soft drink machine and stuffed a bill in. A can rolled down. He glommed it out. The day was hot, and the carbonation squirted out over his hand as he pulled the tab. He jammed it up to his lips, took a swig, and then wiped his mouth with the back of his hand.

He flopped down onto a chair, his head thrown back, trying to sort out his feelings. Kylle was so full of life. What if there was still a spark between them?

The red emergency room sign caught his eye. Could Kylle still be in there? Carlos felt light-headed as he edged in that direction.

Kylle was seated in the waiting area, his nose bandaged. Carlos slid into an adjacent chair and threw an arm around Kylle's shoulders.

"Broken?" he asked without preamble.

"No, I was lucky, but I'm going to have a real lump."

"You mean that beautiful face of yours is going to be marred?"

Kylle gave him a lascivious look and elbowed him.

"Look, dude, sorry it ended this way, but let me make it up to you."

"Your place or mine?" Kylle said, his eyes wide.

⌘

I remained in the hospital for the next several days, enduring one test after another. The news finally came, and it was not as bad as I had feared—a congenital hole in my heart that was repairable. Surgery was scheduled for the following week. Plenty of rest and no stress in the meantime. Right! Maybe I should have croaked last night.

Carlos came in each day but only remained a half hour or so. There seemed to be little to talk about. I didn't bother to tell him about the surgery, and dammit, he didn't ask. His mind seemed elsewhere, as though he was only going through the motions of visiting me. At first, I thought he might be upset at having to see to himself again. That was bullshit, but any small hope as the ship starts to sink. I badgered him about taking his meds as he should. He assured me he was, for what little his words were worth.

Several days went by with no mention of Kylle. I finally asked about him, not that I gave a shit. In fact, I was hoping he and Jott had skedaddled. Carlos flushed, stood up, moved over to the window, and fingered blossom stems in a vase of flowers he had sent me. I hate yellow roses, but the thought was kind, I guess.

"He's doing okay. He's bandaged up, but no great damage was done. He sends his understanding and best wishes."

Big fucking deal, I thought. Carlos couldn't look me in the eye as he wandered around the room, straightening pictures and rearranging chairs—deck chairs on the *Titanic*?

Annoyance built in me, and I felt like telling him to leave the goddamned chairs alone. I reached for his hand, and he took mine, albeit with hesitation.

I patted a place on the bed for him to sit down. The pressure of his weight allowed my legs to slide against him. He moved farther away.

"He's staying at the house, isn't he?"

I knew the answer by his body language.

"Yeah." There was sadness in his expression. "He needed a place to stay so the doctor could check his nose." He glanced apprehensively at me to get my reaction.

"There's plenty of hotels around," I replied caustically. "How does he like the guest room?"

He squeezed my hand and dropped his head.

"I figured."

"Damon, I'm so damned sorry! I never meant this to happen."

He released my hand and stood up. He finally caught my eye as a tremor came to my lips.

"Are you in love with him, or has this just been a little fling?"

"Where did that come from?" His body seemed to slump, and sweat beaded his forehead. An angry look briefly flashed across his face as he looked down at me. "I never know when you're going to take off."

"Or what you're going to do to force me into it." I clinched my fists so hard on the sheets it probably left permanent wrinkles. I caught his eye and held it. "Dammit, Carlos, I came back both times though, didn't I?"

He looked rueful and nodded.

"Come down with me to the cafeteria, it's time for lunch."

I swung my feet to down the floor and humped my toes into my slippers.

"I'm not hungry. We need to talk."

I sat back on the edge of the bed and motioned for him to pull up a chair. He stood facing me, grasping the back of a chair. He cleared his throat as if to speak but remained silent.

"What are you planning to do about us?" I asked, breaking the silence.

He swallowed and slipped a mint into his mouth and licked the dryness on his lips. "It has meant a lot to me to have Kylle back in my life. Everything else has been wrapped up in pills and more pills. I feel like I'll bust if I can't perform one more time." He swung around, arms in the air. "Jesus, Damon, you can't understand what it's like." He clutched the back of the chair again.

"You could have shared that with me instead of 'Damon, I lost you once, and I'm not going to let that happen again,'" I said in a mocking manner.

A touch of anger registered around his mouth, his voice stronger as he replied, "You kept slipping away from me. I didn't know what to think. You need to grow some balls."

"And someone ought to cut yours off," I snapped.

He looked stunned. I was tiring and wanted him to leave. He was looking by me as if he would rather be anywhere else but here.

I was alone in this "land of paradise." With a sharp twinge, I realized, belatedly, it must have been the way he felt when I last saw him ten years ago in Ilka's living room. If I had only stopped him. My eyes burned with the realization of how much my present predicament was my own doing.

"Then Kylle comes along, a bright spot in an otherwise humdrum life." I brushed at my eyes. Words hung like an impenetrable glass wall between us. "I'm not going to make it hard for you."

He turned to me with a sharp look in his eyes. "What's that supposed to mean?"

I swung myself back around onto the bed. "I'm suddenly very tired."

His face softened into a momentary look of concern, and he knelt by the bed. He slowly put his hand out and touched mine. "Can I get you anything?"

"Yeah, a bus trip to Fort Worth ten years ago."

The wonderful smile that had so enchanted me flashed and then was gone.

His face sobered again.

"Damon, don't, I feel lousy enough already."

He looked awful, his hair rumpled, his face unshaven and drained of color. It frightened me.

"Promise me you'll take your meds no matter what else happens. I can't have you on my conscience."

He nodded and moved toward the door, turned back, wiped his eyes, and muttered, "Promise. Thanks." He was in mental agony and guilt, and so was I.

The words "I'd rather you didn't come to see me anymore" suddenly sprang from my lips, unwanted on a conscious level.

His head jerked around, and his mouth twisted. "Is that the way you want it?"

"It's not the way I want it, but I'm out of choices. Who the fuck else is going to come out of your past?" I wanted so desperately for him to hug me, to say he loved me. "I always seem to be odd man out."

"I don't know what to say." Sweat stood out on his forehead, and his shoulders sagged.

"There's no need, your eyes say it all." I turned away, hoping he'd leave before I fell apart.

∾

"Damon's figured out what's been going on between us," Carlos announced to Kylle as he pulled his shorts back on. Kylle lay naked on another chaise on the deck.

"Oh yeah. Big fucking deal," he replied, a smirk on his face. "He acts like you two are married or some other fucking thing." He stubbed out his cigarette on the deck floor and slid back into his shorts. "I've been thinkin', it's not all that wise for me to continue staying here, if you know what I mean."

Carlos looked startled and a little defensive. "You haven't liked it?"

Kylle flicked a match in the air between his thumb and middle finger after he lit another cigarette, took a drag, but made no reply.

"Does Jott know you've been staying here and we've been…"

"Hell yes. As a matter of fact, he's shacking up with some friend as we speak." Kylle gave Carlos an incredulous stare. "Don't be a fool. I've seen the look Damon gave him. This little performance he gives of some fuckin' long-suffering monogamous saint hasn't fooled me one bit. Wake up and smell the roses, buddy." He patted Carlos on the shoulder and tut-tutted.

"Leave Damon out of this, ya hear?" Carlos snarled.

Kylle wriggled into his T-shirt, zipped up his shorts, and scuffed into his sandals.

"See ya later!"

He bounded off the deck.

"Hey, where ya going? Wait a minute. I'll get some clothes on and come along," Carlos shouted to Kylle's rapidly disappearing figure.

Kylle turned and sauntered back to the deck stairs with a bored expression.

"Forget it. You're a drag anyway. Take your meds and warm tea. Don't forget the shawl."

With a wave, he jumped into his rented yellow Mustang and disappeared up the street.

"Fucking bastard," Carlos spit out, gritting his teeth.

He grabbed the handle on the slider and rammed it open full force. A crack shivered up one of the glass panels. He strode into the kitchen, snatched a glass, threw open a cupboard door, and pawed around for a bottle of brandy secreted behind canned goods. A plastic container of pills fell out onto the table. He snarled as he struck it with the back of his hand, crashing it against the wall. Pills exploded from the impact.

He hauled the bottle into the living room and dropped into a chair. The ocean shimmered in the sunset Damon and he had enjoyed so many evenings together.

"Here's to the two loves in my life," he bellowed, slopping the glass full and spilling it onto his clothes.

He glared at it, put the glass up to his lips, broke into a sweat, jumped up, and heaved glass and all into the fireplace.

The flames hissed and flashed.

CHAPTER

13

Carlos roused from a deep sleep. Someone was hammering on the slider. He checked his watch and yawned. It was going on 11:00 a.m. He pulled himself up from the chair, rubbed his eyes, and ran his hand over a stubbly chin.

"Yeah, yeah, who's there?" he called.

Kylle stepped in. He surveyed the disheveled room and snorted. They had done nothing to clean up since Damon left. Clothes were tossed around, ashtrays full, and fast-food containers littered the coffee table and the floor around it.

"Jott and I are heading out for Miami, thought you ought to know."

"Big fucking deal, don't let me stop ya."

"That's not what you were saying a few days ago."

"I had rocks in my head." He glared at Kylle.

"Here I have the best guy in the world worrying about me taking my meds and I'm screwing around with you."

"Have you called him?" Kylle looked dour. He dumped out a chair and dropped into it.

"He told me not to visit him anymore."

Kylle looked startled and studied Carlos for a moment. "Not to visit him anymore? Why the hell not? Isn't he coming back here?"

"Fuck off, man. I don't know what his plans are. Got any cigarettes, Kylle? I need one, bad."

Kylle fumbled in his shirt pocket and tossed him a half-empty pack of Marlboros. Carlos shook one out and slid it between his lips. Kylle had to steady his hand and flick his lighter. He drew deeply, held it a couple of seconds, and let it drift slowly out through his nose.

"Man, you look like shit. Get shaved and put some clothes on. I'll take us out for breakfast," Kylle said.

"Hell, I don't need any food, just someone to clean up this dump."

"Don't look at me."

"You helped make it."

"Don't you have a cleaning woman, for God's sakes, or does Damon have to do that too, you cheap bastard?"

Carlos gave him a dirty look. "I fired her. She kept asking about Damon."

"Probably looking for some dirt to sell to the *Inquirer*."

"Cunt. Yeah, probably checking the wastebaskets for condoms," Carlos said.

"Well?"

"Well what? Maybe the first night." Kylle made up a face.

"You didn't have to stay if it was so bad."

"I might as well have left, for all you're worth."

He wandered around the room, grabbing up arms full of clothes, disappearing in the bathroom, and heaving them into the hamper.

"Hey," Kylle questioned, reappearing and checking his watch, "aren't you supposed to pick up Damon?"

"I'm afraid to face him." He got up and leaned an arm against the mantel, staring into the ashes. "Jesus, Kylle"—his voice was hoarse—"what have I done. What have we done to Damon?"

Anger flashed across Kylle's face. He advanced threateningly toward Carlos.

"What the fuck is this 'we' shit? You came on to me from the first day I got here." His eyes shown steely, and he hefted a fire tong in his right hand. "You had a hard-on when we met at the bar." He slammed the poker back into the holder, curled his lip, and sneered. "Face it, loser, you don't give a shit about Damon."

The full force of Kylle's words staggered Carlos—like his first day without a drink in rehab. Was it too late to make amends? He whirled at Kylle, gritted his teeth.

"For your information, asshole, Damon is the only guy I ever really loved."

"You coulda fooled me."

"I want you out of this house, you fucking opportunist. I'm going to spend the rest of my life—what there is left of it—making it up to Damon."

Kylle turned to leave.

"Lotsa luck, buddy boy, hope things work out."

Carlos dropped back into the recliner, eyeing the brandy bottle sitting on the mantel.

⁂

I was released at 11:00 a.m. with a bag full of meds from the hospital pharmacy. I scrounged out my cell phone and called for a taxi. The cabbie was very solicitous. He ran around, took my bag, and opened the rear door for me. I settled myself then leaned forward and gave directions to Carlos's place.

I had mixed feelings as the house came into view. I paid the driver and tossed my overnight bag onto the backseat of my car, stepped up onto the deck, and stopped a moment to look out over the magnificent Pacific. A stiff wind had blown up, and the tide crashed in. A ragtag group of dedicated surfers caught the huge swells and curled ten in the waves spouting around them, ready to paddle out and catch the next big one. That seemed to be about what my relationship with Carlos had turned into. I sighed and turned to grab the slider door handle. Shit. The glass was cracked. Had there been a fight? I stepped in. The room was a wreck. A chill ran through me.

Carlos rushed to me, arms outspread, looking concerned but also alarmed.

"Jesus, Damon, I could have picked you up. Are you okay?"

I let my arms hang limp as he hugged me. "Couldn't be better."

"You look beat." He kissed me, but I didn't return it. I could feel the tension in his body.

Anxiety and emotional strain finally sapped my strength. Carlos eased me down into a huge upholstered lounge chair, and I laid my head back.

Hours later, I awoke with a start, yawned, and stretched my arms over my head. Carlos appeared, shut the sliders, and checked the windows. The room had been straightened up as well.

"Sorry about the noise. A breeze blew the bedroom door shut."

"It was time to waken anyway." I arose and moved nearer the fire; the hot embers reflected a reddish glow on Carlos's face. He leaned against the mantel.

"I've been doing a lot of thinking these past few days," I said, finding it harder to say than I had fooled myself into thinking. "Maybe it's a good thing Kylle has come back into your life."

Carlos whirled, startled, and snorted. "A good thing? You've got to be kidding. Look at what's been happening."

"My point exactly. You're excited about life again, happier than I've seen you," I lied.

"What have you been smoking? I've never been so fucking miserable."

"We're trying to live out those few wonderful days we had together so long ago." My voice had a catch in spite of my best intentions.

Carlos scratched his head and looked away. "I've given you a hard time. I'm not proud of that." He took the poker and stirred up the fire and threw on another log. The heat felt good as a heavy fog had settled in, and there was a chill in the air.

"You did what your heart told you to do."

"It wasn't my heart." He flushed when I flinched. "It was poor judgment, and I regret it, more than you will ever know."

I shook my head. "Joan told me to be honest with myself and go back to you." I stretched my hand out to him. "But was it wrong?"

He ignored my gesture with a shrug. "Maybe on your part, not mine." He ran his hand over his unshaven chin, the whiskers made a scratching noise against his watchband. His eyes were red rimmed as he asked, "What do you want to do?"

"I'm a lost soul here in California with no friends or support system. It's an alien world, fast-paced and fake. I'm thinking about going back to New Hampshire for my surgery."

"Then I'll be a lost soul in New Hampshire."

I flopped onto a blue leather recliner and didn't make any comment. The fire crackled, and wind-driven sparks raced up the flue.

The weight of my remark settled.

"But I'm not going, right?" he spit out.

"Right," I snapped. "I spent five days in that goddamned palace hospital while you and Kylle were back here fucking around in the bedroom I thought was half mine."

"Damon!" He jumped up. "How many fricking times did you run out on me since you got here? Answer me that."

"All right, you bastard, I'm fed up to here"—I held my hand above my chin—"with that lame excuse you keep throwing at me. The second day I was here, who should appear but Shirl and her bastard son, your son, at least that was the operating premise. Skipping out, in retrospect, was a bad choice on my part, but I thought it would be easier for everyone if I spent the afternoon away. I can't turn back the clock now."

"It would have been a hell of a lot better if you'd stayed, a unified front."

"Granted. So then you were pissed with me. I suppose that was cause enough to feel justified for you and Ms. Shirl to spend the night in our bed."

"Which you let happen." His voice was strained with anger.

"Right! I suppose I said, 'Why don't you two sleep together tonight?'"

"You're a big boy, you could have said no fricking way."

"And you could have called it off and come after me."

"Sure, when you were two hundred miles away."

"Hardly. I waited on the deck until 3:00 a.m." I hammered on the arm of the chair. "Remember what I said?"

Ignoring my question, he blathered on. "More like you went into a pet, jumped into your car, and drove away," he spit out, headed toward the kitchen, turned back, and asked in a softer tone, "Remember what?"

"You winked at me when you and Shirl went into the bedroom. I assumed it was all a big joke. I waited and waited for you to come out. It got to be 3:00 a.m."

He dropped into a swivel chair that squealed under his weight and the quick turn. "That's a detail I didn't know about. I guess I've been wrong about a lot of things."

He patted his shirt pocket, pulled out a crumpled pack of cigarettes, and scratched around for the lighter. I was gratified to see his hand shake when he held the flame up to the tip. He turned his head away, blowing out smoke.

"It would be easier for me to overlook what happened with Kylle if I wasn't in the hospital with an unknown disease. I needed you. I was scared." My voice turned flat and dead. "You could hardly look at me. You wanted to be anywhere else but there."

A tear rolled down his cheek, and he stubbed out the cigarette in a candy dish on the end table. I sat dry-eyed, looking at him.

"We both knew that things weren't working out as we had hoped," he said. I nodded ruefully. "All my old feelings toward Kylle came back. I couldn't be dishonest with you as much as I knew it would hurt you."

"And you thought I wouldn't figure it out."

"Let's just say I hoped you wouldn't. I'm a lousy liar. It was an act of insanity, a compulsion I couldn't ignore, an opportunity I was too weak to deny."

He broke off, and we both remained silent several long seconds. The wind was howling now, and the waves crashed noisily against the beach.

"Then you're in love with him."

He dropped down in front of me, his voice low and hoarse. "No! No, I was never in love with him. God help me. It was only physical. I hoped it never would come to this." His voice was just over a whisper. "It's over, kaput, gonzo. I had forgotten what a creep he is, vain, self-centered, selfish, a bore. I finally threw him out."

"Until he decides to come back." With a strength I never knew I had, I reached for his hand. "Or so you're telling me. I won't stand in your way."

He pressed my hand against his cheek. I wrenched it away, struggled up, and forced myself to stay calm though my mind was racing.

"That's the last thing I want to do."

He jumped up and tried to hug me.

I stepped back.

"Don't try to jerk me around."

Talk about metamorphosis, my beautiful butterfly had turned back into an ugly caterpillar.

They say love and hate are closely related. The latter emotion won. If he touched me again, would he be fantasizing about Kylle? In a self-flagellating way, I wanted out of this house as badly as I ever wanted to leave New Castle ten years ago.

"I'm sleeping in the guest room tonight. We can make other arrangements for me tomorrow."

He looked hurt and forlorn. Good. I made up my mind then and there, no more tears or moping around. I hadn't a clue what the future held. I doubted I would ever sleep through a night again. He stood dazed as I slammed the mahogany-paneled guest-room door.

I slid out of my clothes, wearing only my briefs, and struggled into bed, exhausted.

Five minutes later, he tapped and peered around the door, entered, and crouched by the bed.

"Is there anything I can do for you?'

I shook my head.

"Nothing?"

"Nothing," I replied.

He straightened up and looked down at me. Both our hearts were breaking, but so be it.

"Nothing," I repeated and turned over.

Miraculously, I did sleep, soundly, probably the belated reaction to the meds. Lights were on in the living room, but it was deadly quiet. I half-hoped he had called Kylle. Finally, around 7:00 a.m., I tossed back the covers and swung my feet to the floor. I tiptoed to the door and peeked around the casing. I could see Carlos through the sliders, scrawled on a chaise, head tipped back, eyes closed.

I grabbed my clothes and snuck into the master bedroom as quietly as I could, not wanting to alert him to my movements yet. I dressed rapidly. No shower this morning. I searched in the closet for my old duffel bag kept for sentimental reasons. What a stupid jerk. I thought better of it and took one of Carlos's suitcases with wheels. The few clothes I packed took up little space, and the rest landed in a pile on the floor. Salvation Army, Goodwill, whatever.

I turned to see Carlos standing by the suitcase, staring at my clothes.

"So you're really leaving?"

He reached for my arm, and I shook loose, just like I had in Fort Worth, that fateful night.

"Don't try to stop me. The sooner I'm out of here the better."

I continued packing and checked around for anything I had overlooked, slammed the cover shut, and zipped it up.

I finally looked at him and was alarmed. He had obviously been crying, he was unshaven, and his gorgeous face was lined and puffy.

"Have you been drinking?" I asked as sternly as I could muster.

"No, but I'm damn sure thinking about it now." His husky voice sounded more like gravel scraping on the floor.

"In God's name, why? You've got what you wanted! Rejoice. Damon is finally leaving." I forced a wry smile. "Have you been in touch with Kylle?"

He stopped pacing and glanced at me.

"As a matter of fact, I called him around four this morning. I hadn't slept all night, and I needed to set him straight."

"Well, well, couldn't wait to let the body get cold." I snorted and slid the suitcase onto the floor. "How did he take his new position and wealth?" I tugged the suitcase toward the door.

"Not too well, I'm afraid." He cleared his throat.

"The perks will set in soon enough."

"I doubt it. I told the son of bitch I'd shoot him between the eyes if I ever saw him again." He advanced toward me and clutched me by the forearms and wouldn't let me go in spite of my struggle. "We belong together, Damon. Every waking hour these past ten years have been filled with thoughts of you." He pulled me to him and kissed me.

I recoiled and slapped him.

"You dirty lying bastard. When you found out I planned to stay, you did everything you could to push me away. Shirl, Kylle, how many others I don't know about. Anybody you want…" My voice trailed off.

He finally let go and dabbed at his eyes and fumbled in his trouser pocket for a handkerchief.

"Damon, how can I ever make it up to you?"

"You can't, it's over. Don't you understand? I've been made a fool of, pushed aside, insulted, and neglected. That's love?"

"I know you love me."

I stepped back. "Did love you. If you wanted an open relationship, why didn't you discuss it with me? Love is honesty, compassion, caring. What am I missing here? How would you feel if Mike should appear from New Hampshire and I decided to spend the night with him here in our bed while you were in the hospital?"

Anger flared on his face, and he punched the wall beside him then turned to me.

"I'd go wild and kill the bastard."

"You're funny." But I wasn't smiling. "How the hell do you think I felt—feel? Do you have some special code of conduct I don't know about?"

"Fair enough." He bit his lip and continued. "When I got out of prison ten years ago, I stopped by Ilka's. I needed my arms around you, hoping you might have had second thoughts about the letter you sent me."

"Prison? Letter? I haven't a clue what you're babbling about. You were in prison overnight, sent a good-bye letter back with Ilka, and then flew blithely to California the next day."

His manner suddenly turned angry, agitated.

"Whatdaya mean a letter from me? After Ilka set me up, the police nabbed me when I left her house."

"I knew about the setup after the fact, but I forced Ilka to have the charges dropped the next day. She called the precinct that night. I heard her."

"She came down the next day, all right. With false pity in her voice, she handed me a letter from you."

"My brain was garbled with medications, but I would remember if I wrote one. What did it say?" My knees felt weak.

"The usual Dear John letter: 'It's been fun, but it's over' and something about possible involvement in your rape."

The room started to spin. I clutched desperately for something to support myself. Carlos grabbed me behind the shoulders and under the knees and hauled me in onto his huge bed. He propped my head up and went for water and a cold towel. I saw fear in his eyes as he held the glass for me.

I didn't resist his arm being around me. My breathing eased, and my stomach grumbled.

"Neither of us have eaten breakfast. Let me fix us something." He leaned down and kissed me. "I love you so much," he whispered.

But not as much as Kylle, I thought.

He rattled around in the kitchen and soon returned with a loaded tray and sat it on the bed beside me.

"I'm okay now." I reached for coffee—decaffeinated, he assured me. "Let's eat in the kitchen."

I slid off the bed, balancing the cup. My knees were weak, and I fell back onto the bed, slopping hot coffee onto my stomach.

Carlos ran to the bathroom and wet a towel to swab me up the best he could. What was happening to me?

An uncomfortable silence stretched out as we picked at our food in silence.

He finally reached for my hand, and I didn't pull back.

"Will you stay here today while we figure what to do?"

"I was so sure what to do this morning until a half hour ago."

"I know. I'll keep out of your way if you want, but stay. Please."

At this point returning to New Hampshire was out of the question. More was wrong with me than I had been told. Of that I was sure.

"This damn surgery is hanging over my head. I've acted so badly they'll probably refer me to another health facility." Feeling better, I tried to change my shirt. He reached to help me with the buttons. "Please don't touch me."

"We're back to that." He whirled around, holding his forehead, looking down. "Damon, I'm in agony. Give me some sign we can work this out." He went to the window; the cerulean ocean was calm and still, hardly any current.

"We need counseling."

He swung back to me. "Whatever you say." But he looked dubious.

I went through the things I had packed and spotted my cell phone. Dr. Polanski answered on the second ring. My voice shook a little.

"I'm delighted to hear from you, Damon. It's been such a long time since we last saw each other. Are you okay?"

"It's wonderful to hear your voice as well. I'm not doing so well, but that's a long story. How are you these days?"

"I'm fine, enjoying partial retirement. Just seeing special patients like you."

"Seems like the only time I call is when I need advice."

"Anything I can do for you. My door is always open."

"Doctor, I need you, bad. We do."

"You and Carlos?" His words were tinged with concern.

"Yes." My voice broke, and I had a hard time speaking.

"How does Carlos feel about it?"

"Would you speak to him?"

"Of course. Is he nearby?"

I motioned to him. He took the phone and put his arm around me.

"Hello, Dr. Polanski, this is Carlos." His voice was low and modulated.

Pause.

"Thank you, I know he is." He lowered his voice. "I don't want to lose him. Thank you, here he is back."

CHAPTER

14

It was a toss-up between surgery and counseling. Carlos was for surgery, and I was for the latter. Since the surgery seemed fairly simple, as the surgeon had explained it to me, and it was already scheduled for the following Monday, three days hence, I decided to go forward with it here in San Diego. I needed to report to the hospital the next day for additional tests.

We slept in separate rooms again that night. Carlos wanted me to be in the master bedroom, where he could see if I needed anything. He was exhausted from lack of sleep the night before and finally agreed to my staying in the guest room one more night. He kept the doors open between the rooms. He zonked out the minute his head hit the pillow.

I slept fitfully and dreamed most of the night, awakening with a start around three thirty, trying to catch my breath. My mouth was dry, and the bed was soaked with my sweat. I didn't want to waken Carlos, so I drifted in and out of sleep until seven.

Carlos was kneeling by the bed when my mind finally cleared. I felt like shit. There was some numbness in my left arm, which alarmed me. He propped my head up with pillows and brought me a cup of tea that I promptly threw up. He kept his left arm around me and dialed 911 with his right hand.

The procedure to repair the hole in my heart was a relatively noninvasive operation. By inserting state-of-the-art instruments up through a vein in the groin while the surgeon watches on a monitor, a tiny "umbrella" bridges the aperture, and closure is accomplished, much like a button slipped through a buttonhole.

Later, however, in the recovery room, I suddenly went into cardiac arrest. No one could explain how a faulty valve in my heart could have been missed. Carlos was distraught. After I was finally stabilized, he phoned several leading hospitals and finally persuaded one of the most prestigious heart surgeons to fly in to perform the delicate operation. I was in ICU for three days.

Recovery from open-heart surgery is a long and difficult road. Fits of depression and paranoia are the rules of the game. Carlos was never far from my side night and day. I was not a good patient. There must have been times when he could have strangled me, but he never showed it.

As the days passed, our initial bond haltingly returned. We found every book on relationships, reestablishing trust, philosophy, and healthy outlooks. Carlos was not, by nature, much of a reader, being more the person of action, but during our many hours of forced leisure, he showed a quick and perceptive mind and immersed himself unstintingly in literature. If I tired, he held my hand and read to me in his wonderful deep voice. He also spent many hours playing the piano, very soothing to me, and even dabbled at composing a couple of new songs.

During this period, we both had a chance to discover each other, much as we should have ten years ago. I wouldn't leave him now if he asked me to.

CHAPTER

⁘ 15 ⁘

The nearer the plane approached Dallas, the more subdued Carlos became. I suspected he was concerned about meeting Dr. Polanski and where the counseling might lead. I was hopeful he would finally resolve issues from the past that haunted both of us.

We landed at Dallas International at 11:10 a.m. on a fine but intensely hot late-summer day. We rented a white Chevy Impala and skirted the center of the city. Our destination was Dr. Polanski's lush home and office in Plano, featured in *Architectural Digest* several months ago. The languorous midday sun shimmered on avenues of upscale homes, many with fountains, waterfalls, and winding stone paths leading to sumptuous estates set well back from the street.

I recognized Polanski's magnificent house from the magazine article as Carlos slowed and pulled into the driveway paved with chevron-pattern bricks leading to a five-car garage. The residence walls were faced with flat fitted stone with exterior arches constructed from brick. Manicured shrubbery encased the triple-story mansion with long sloping rooflines and wide overhangs that resisted the sun and storms.

Dr. Polanski met us at the door. A broad smile lit his still-unlined face as we embraced. He was attired in a white shirt with black pinstripes and a red, white, and black regimental striped tie. The sharp creases in his black woolen slacks could slice French bread.

He was shorter than I remembered with a slight build and a full head of longish, well-groomed white hair. He seemed diminished somehow from what I remembered of him.

"Damon," he said, "can it be ten years? I have often thought of you. I hope your surgery was a great success."

"Indeed it was. I've never felt better." I turned to Carlos, who extended his hand. "And this is my partner, Carlos Bravara."

"It is so nice to meet you at last." They shook hands rather awkwardly, I thought.

"The pleasure is mine. Damon has often spoken of you."

"We have been admiring your house," I said. "I saw the spread in *Architectural Digest,* and it hardly does justice."

"Would you like a quick tour of the first floor?"

The house was as lovely as the magazine photos conveyed, perhaps more.

We ended up in the huge screened gazebo, where his maid/cook had laid out sandwiches and lemonade. She was thrilled to meet Carlos. He even offered to autograph one of his CDs for her.

Dr. Polanski initially turned out to be a mixed blessing. We began with one-on-one sessions. Carlos was at first uneasy. Maybe he felt I had an unfair advantage due to our previous relationship.

"Mr. Bravara," Dr. Polanski opened with Carlos, "tell me a little about yourself. Is there some issue or issues you want to discuss about your relationship with Damon that might be helpful as we move forward?"

"Call me Carlos. I'm thirty-five, and I've fucked up pretty bad most of my life." Carlos waited for some kind of reaction. "Damon is far too good for me. He's one classy guy. I do stupid things, hurtful things."

"It sounds like you have done something recently, something you need to explore."

Carlos flushed and arched his shoulders. "Something I wish to God I could undo, but there's no way I can."

Polanski made no comment but nodded for Carlos to continue. Carlos took a deep breath then let it out slowly. His eyes reddened.

"I cheated on Damon with a former lover. While Damon was first in the hospital."

"And now you're both trying to deal with it."

"We almost broke up over it."

❧

My interview went well, to start with, that is. Dr. Polanski asked me about my recovery, how I was feeling now. For some reason tears started, and I couldn't stop them. I felt like such a fool. It was a brief storm, and the rain soon ended. But it cleared the air.

"I really am fine now. Better every day, as a matter of fact." I took a handful of Kleenex, blew my nose, and wiped my chin. "I am so glad you were able to see us."

"My pleasure, Damon. You have always been very special."

"The feeling is mutual."

"I can see why you value Carlos. He is a very sensitive young man, unusually so, considering his profession. He puts very high stock in you, Damon, very high."

We chatted some more, but I was careful not to mention Kylle or his implications.

That afternoon, we sat rather stiffly in Polanski's office. He glanced up at us while studying notes he had taken. Carlos's leather chair protested under his weight as he shifted uneasily.

"After our interviews, I developed some questions that may help you both to better understand the events which have brought you here. Shall we begin with the interlude in Fort Worth after Damon was attacked?" Polanski smiled encouragingly at Carlos.

Carlos cleared his throat and poured ice water into a glass from a carafe on a tray between us. "One of the worst periods of my life." He took a sip and set the weighted tumbler back onto a coaster. He leaned forward, his mind obviously struggling with the past.

He detailed his stop at Ilka's that night, his search for me, and the TV report of an attack on a young man answering Damon's description, including the birthmark. "Ilka, Damon's sister, did everything in her power to stop me. I needed so desperately to see Damon." He sighed, settling back in his chair.

Polanski consulted his notes again. "Let's go back now to your visit with Damon at his sister's house after Damon was released from the hospital."

"For several nights I watched the house waiting for a chance to see Damon alone. My chance finally came."

He hesitated and expelled his breath, momentarily reliving that momentous night when both our worlds catastrophically collided.

Carlos continued, "When Damon finally answered the door, he was like a different person, nothing like the wonderful guy I met on the bus. I was horrified."

"Horrified. Tell me what you saw."

"He was pallid, emaciated, not making a lot of sense, completely under his sister's spell, almost scared. He wouldn't let me touch him or get close." He colored and took another sip of water "We had been intimate from the first day we met and even made firm commitments to each other. Now we were strangers." He became increasingly agitated, squirming in his chair, voice rasping as though unable to inhale enough oxygen as he continued recounting the excruciating events. "Then Damon offered me money. I couldn't believe it." His voice became stronger and with an edge. "He implied I might have been involved with his rape."

I was aghast and violently shook my head.

"I have since realized I was wrong. I was just so damned hurt."

"Damon"—Polanski turned to me—"what are your recollections of this encounter?"

"Ilka, my sister, must have found out somehow that Carlos had been watching the house. Figuring he would violate the restraining order, she set up a sting operation with the police. I'd bet she injected me with an extra amount of pain medication so I would be woozy and disoriented. She convinced me Carlos hadn't tried to see me at the hospital. She said if I saw him again, he would try to turn me against her."

It was hard to read Carlos's face; he had a stoic expression, like his mind had metastasized.

"She said, 'Offer him money, you'll see the last of him,' and dammit, I did."

Carlos reached for a tissue and blew his nose.

"Did you in any way believe or imply Carlos was somehow involved in your attack?"

"No, dammit, never. There was never any question in my mind. I don't know where he got that idea."

Polanski raised an enquiring eyebrow to Carlos.

"I asked him if he really thought I had something to do with it, and he said he couldn't remember anything. I jumped to the conclusion that he thought I might have."

"Understandable. Go on, what happened next?"

"The police were waiting outside the door. They grabbed me, and I struggled, which only made matters worse." He hesitated, caught between remembering and trying to forget. Anger twisted his lip; he looked at me and then away. "Dammit, I had been betrayed. I was a caged animal."

Dr. Polanski bent forward. "You were held overnight?"

Carlos loosened his tie and shirt collar and addressed me. "Overnight," he spit out, "how about six months with one month off for good behavior."

"No!" I shouted.

"Yes," he replied in a tired voice, "and someone planted steroids in my jacket pocket."

I shook my head. "I never knew about any of this." I was scarcely able to speak, my heart thumped, but no tightness in the chest. Thank God for the surgery. "And the letter?" I asked.

"A letter?" Polanski looked from one to the other of us.

"Yeah, his sister"—he nodded at me—"brought a letter, supposedly from Damon." He lowered his voice. "It said, 'It's been fun, but it's over, don't bother to call.'" He leaned forward, elbows on the chair arms, looking down, shaking his head. "I didn't." His voice grew firm again. "I was thrown into a cell with a pervert who tried to molest me. I near killed the bastard."

A roar of silence engulfed the room. When I could finally manage my voice again, I choked out, "Ilka brought back a letter from you. I thought it was real. 'I'll be in California when you read this. Good luck with your injuries. Don't call.'"

"No, never, never! It was all Ilka's doing. When I got out of jail," Carlos pressed on, "I stopped by Ilka's, hoping to see you. She said no one knew where you were." He had an "answer me that" look in his eyes.

"By that time I was enrolled in that farce at House of Change."

Dr. Polanski grimaced. We three sat in silence for several minutes broken only by distant sirens and a ludicrous motorcycle backfiring.

Dr. Polanski held a hand out to each of us. "This seems like a good point to end the day. Will you be staying in Dallas this evening?"

"In the area."

"Tomorrow. About the same time?"

I put my hand out.

"That would be fine."

We walked out to our rented vehicle. I still struggled to comprehend the terrible injustices perpetrated on Carlos ten years ago. He opened the door for me and then went around and slid behind the wheel. Until today, we had only tapped the lightest touch on this incredibly hurtful period in our lives. Our fingers entwined, and he kissed me lightly on the cheek. I turned to him; my heart was full.

"How ya doing, champ?" he said.

For the next seven days we had afternoon sessions with Dr. Polanski and went through as many boxes of tissues. It was very intense, and we got into issues from both our backgrounds neither of us knew about the other.

Carlos was abandoned, in essence, by his birth parents, the Santoses, and had no idea if they were even still alive. His adopted parents, the Bravaras, failed to even come to his debut performance and lost touch with him years ago. He was never able to bond with his adopted father, who shipped him off to an aunt in Boston when he was fifteen. From that time on, he had been on his own—sex, drugs, booze, overnight binges, plenty of money and opportunities, but few restraints.

Carlos was shocked to hear how my own father had disowned me, which precipitated my trip to Fort Worth. I was extremely emotional recounting my stint at House of Change and the horrible death of Paul Gatsas.

I recited the highlights of my marriage and how difficult its eventual dissolution became.

Near the end of what was supposed to be our final session, Carlos, under careful probing by Polanski, came out with the crux of why we were here.

"Were you really going to leave me after the unforgivable business with Kylle?"

"Yes. I couldn't get beyond the fact that you had betrayed my trust. When you found me packing, I had every intention of facing you down before I left."

Carlos looked stricken and didn't speak for several seconds. "Then I was that close…to losing you for good?"

I sighed, and our eyes locked. "Maybe temporarily, but I would've returned. We've proven nothing can ultimately keep us apart. I didn't handle myself well during that period. I have now come to the point of accepting that you and Kylle have a special friendship. I don't like the man, and I don't trust him, but you two are colleagues in the music business, and your paths will cross again."

Dr. Polanski excused himself and left the room. We turned to each other, our fingers interlaced.

"We need to get back to the hotel," he said.

"My thoughts exactly."

CHAPTER

⚔ 16 ⚔

"Are you up to it?" I asked, clutching the steering wheel. "It's a little late for that."

"No, it's not." I slammed on the brakes, and the car skidded on loose gravel on the shoulder.

"What are you doing?" Carlos grabbed my arm, his face screwed into a scowl.

"Turning around. I'm not putting you through the family thing. It was a rotten idea on my part." I wheeled the rented Chrysler 300 onto a side road. The late summer sun shone lazily on the fluttering green limp-wristed leaves. Goldenrod blossomed by the thousands along Route 16 as we moved south toward Portsmouth. Crickets chirred, and a crow cawed in the distance then landed on a branch, shook its feathers, and settled itself.

"Turn the engine off a minute. I want to hear the sounds." He ran the window down to listen. "So this is New Hampshire." After another pause, he said, "I love it."

"Wait till you see the ocean, it's a deep blue this time of year."

"Let's get going. I want to meet your mother." He was smiling again, his face anxious, like a puppy dog waiting for a stick to be thrown.

I eased back onto the highway, and we rode in silence as Carlos drank in the new sights and sounds.

We finally pulled into the family driveway beside Dad's antique Mercedes. Straight ahead the ocean shimmered in the afternoon breeze. My heart beat faster in foreboding of the scene I knew was going to happen. Carlos reached over and squeezed my hand.

"It's going to be okay, babe. I'm fine, relax."

I was almost annoyed that he could be so calm and collected when I was such a nervous wreck.

He was agog with the ocean view, so different from the Pacific. We stepped out of the car, and he headed toward the path leading down to the shoreline a couple a hundred feet beyond. He dipped his hand in and shouted for me to come down. I shook my head and motioned him back. I turned and saw Mom and Ilka through the glass door. I pumped my arm to Carlos and pushed the door open and into Mom's arms. Ilka wordlessly scurried out. We kissed each other on the cheeks, our eyes afloat. Carlos bounded up the steps and filled the door with his presence. He towered over Mom as he came forward, a bit out of breath, and gave her a big hug. She angled out her cheek for a kiss, and he gave her a real smacker.

"It's so wonderful to finally meet you Mr. Brav—Carlos." Her face was flushed, and she was clearly impressed. They stood back at arm's length. "My goodness, Mr. Ravenal, you are one handsome gentleman."

"*Show Boat*, 1951," I muttered.

It was Carlos's turn to redden. "If that be the truth, ma'am, I can take no personal credit for it."

"What movie was that from?" I asked.

"Can't remember, but I always wanted to use it."

"Where's Dad?" I mouthed to Mom, and she nodded her head in the direction of the den. She was enthralled chatting with Carlos as I slipped off to the lion's den to face my father and sister. He was little changed from a few months ago, when I had been here for what seemed likely to be my last time.

Ilka stood by his side with her hand on his shoulder. He made no effort to get up or greet me.

"Whose damn fool idea was this anyway?" His bloodshot eyes bore into me.

"Hi, Dad," I replied as lightly as I could. "Now what damned fooled idea are you referring to?"

Our eyes met in a tug of war.

"You know damned well what he means," Ilka snapped.

"And hello to you, sister dear. Why don't you get back onto your broom?"

"Bastard."

"Now, now, enough of the sweet talk," I retorted.

"Seriously, Dad, how are you feeling?" A flicker of warmth crossed his face but left just as quickly.

"As if you really care." The scowl returned.

"We've had our differences, sure, but you are my father, and I do care." He flinched as I looked him in the eye and smiled. Anger and hostility he could handle, warmth and compassion, anathema.

He picked up a paperweight and rolled it in his hand. I wasn't sure he didn't plan to throw it at me. "Have a seat, boy." He indicated a chair a short distance from his desk. "I'm doing okay if my children don't give me another heart attack."

I made no reply. It became eminently clear that my main duty on this visit was to defang the python that lay in wait, ready to pounce on its next victim. Yet a slight tremor of the hand and a trace of sweat on his brow indicated a bit of nerves on his part.

Enter Mom and Carlos, arm in arm, chatting like old friends. Carlos strode across the room and, with a flourish, presented Dad with a box of Cuban cigars. Where he had kept them was beyond me. I was amazed. Dad stood up as they clasped hands. The cigars were a genius stroke. Dad's favorite. And Cuban!

"Hi, I'm Carlos. Wonderful to meet you, sir," he exclaimed, still holding Dad's hand. "Damon has told me so much about you."

Dad gave me the most furtive, barely noticeable glance. What must have been going through his mind?

"Do sit down again, sir, so we can chat." Carlos pulled up two chairs near the desk, gestured to Mom, and they both sat down. I grabbed a chair, and we formed a semicircle around the desk.

"Oh hello, Ilka." He stood up again as if just seeing her. "You're looking well."

He extended his hand.

She barely lifted hers as they shook.

Dad hadn't uttered a word. He was completely outclassed. The old Bravara charm was in full sway. Talk about taking the bull by the horns. This was taking the bull by the balls and squeezing.

Taking the initiative and getting to the point, I said, "It must have been a blow when Damon and Joan broke up. I haven't met her but have spoken to her on the phone. She sounded like a wonderful person. She even encouraged Damon to come back to me."

Dad remained deadly still. Mom snuck a quick glance at me. Her shoulders straightened, and her hands unclasped. Dad pushed his chair back, crossed his legs, and rested one hand on the desk.

"Mr. Bravara."

"Carlos."

"Whatever. Your sweet talk and gifts won't take away from the fact that what you and my son are doing is wrong. It's against God's will. Do you want him to go to eternal damnation?"

Mom leaned forward. "Oh, Al."

"No, ma'am, that's a fair question." Carlos squeezed her hand and turned back to Dad. "That may be your interpretation of the Bible, but it's not mine." We exchanged glances, the meaning of which could not be misconstrued. "Besides, Damon is a grown man and makes his own choices."

Dad snorted and hitched around in his chair.

"I hope we can get beyond this today," Carlos said, waiting for Dad's reaction.

Dad uncrossed his legs, pulled his chair back up to the desk, and laid his hands flat on the surface. "You showfolks in Hollywood and the goddamned Democrats are screwing the country up and destroying the moral fiber of the young people." He arose and came around the desk. "I understand you've got AIDS."

"I'm HIV positive."

"Same damn thing.

"Early stages perhaps, but it's responding well to treatment now. With your son's good care, I'm feeling fine."

He glanced over at me, and I nodded.

"I suppose you want me to give my blessing to a Sodomite that will probably infect my son." He clenched his jaw and stared belligerently at Carlos, defying him to refute.

I had never seen Carlos speechless before. Never one to be afraid of confrontation, he seemed unwilling to verbally attack my father and most of all over such an obviously touchy subject.

Rage grew in me though, the kind I have fought all my life to control, the kind that leaves a bitter taste in my mouth, the kind that must be satisfied at any cost. Once again, this man of whom I had always sought approval had thrown me to the lions.

Better judgment no longer mine, I squeezed between them, my voice unsteady with emotion.

"What does the Bible say about incest?"

His eyes turned into blazing orbs, and a trickle of saliva glimmered at the corner of his mouth.

"Goddamn you to hell, boy. That's a vicious lie."

He struck me full force across the mouth with the back of his hand, his ring slicing my upper lip. Knocked off balance, I staggered backwards, landing against an antique table. One of the legs snapped with a loud percussion, and I landed sprawled on the floor amid wood splinters and broken glass from a lamp.

Ilka, with both hands pressed to her mouth, raced from the room screaming, "No, no, no!"

Carlos rushed to help me up. "Are you okay?"

"I'll live."

Dad started toward us, face distorted, breathing heavy. Carlos whirled and grabbed him by the shirt collar with both hands and pushed him backwards to a sitting position on the desk.

"I may be a guest in this house, but nobody, I repeat, nobody touches Damon. He is my life. Is that understood?" His voice icily calm but the implication clear.

Blood oozed from the impact of Dad's ring against my jaw, but not before it streaked red down onto my shirt and arm.

Carlos loosened his hold, and Dad spit at him. Carlos stepped back, holding his hand up as warning that the physical interaction had come to a halt. Turning back to me, he used his handkerchief and gently pressed it against my cheek.

With an expression full of scorn, his lip curled, Dad announced, "This sniveling wimp is no son of mine. He's probably more like his biological father."

Mom, hurrying from the room to get ice, turned at the door, red blotches spotting her face.

"Al, how could you?" She turned to me, a stricken look on her face.

"Is it true?" I whispered. "Or is this just another one of his cruel jokes?"

The truth was evident on Mom's face. She reached for me. I couldn't look at her. The room seemed to shrink around me.

"Am I adopted?" I managed.

She put both hands on my arm.

"No, we waited ten years after Ilka was born for another child. We decided on artificial insemination as Al was, well, unable to..." Her voice trailed off.

"Oh sure, it was my fault, everything bad around here is always my fault." He slid off the desk, challenging Carlos to stop him, shuffled around, and sat down.

Carlos whispered something to Mom. She nodded and left the room.

My mind flashed back to Ilka's kitchen in Fort Worth when Dad collapsed on the floor and the guilt for the momentary relief I felt when he might be dead.

And what now, relief, anger, betrayal? I struggled in my mind. How did I feel?

"Were you ever told who the sperm donor was, my real father?" I asked in a cold, flat voice.

"No," he growled, "we were never to know. The records were destroyed in those days."

"Well, Al," I said, irony thick in my voice, "you must be happy for the world to know you don't really have a son after all. This genetic freak you've endured all these years was not your doing from the beginning."

The room fell deadly quiet. A U-Haul truck rumbled into a neighbor's driveway, rattling a pane of glass in the old window. The phone rang in the kitchen. Ilka picked up, her muffled voice drifting back.

"I tried to be a father, but you shut me out. Always had your nose in a book. Why couldn't you have been more like my nephew? He was a real man's man."

Carlos closed his arm around my shoulders and gave me a little squeeze.

Mom returned with ice cubes in a cloth and handed them to Carlos. I grimaced when they touched the tender spot on my lip.

"I even sent him down to Fort Worth to talk some sense into you."

"Yeah, some big fucking deal." Dad winced again at the F word. "Well, he never showed up."

I sat down again. Carlos knelt beside me, applying pressure to what had turned into a bloody nose.

"You sent Kirk down to talk to Damon? When?" Mom asked, anger ringing in her voice.

Carlos and I looked at each other.

"Did you say, Kirk?" I asked.

"What about it? That's his name."

"Your wonderful nephew Kirk. Didn't he wash out of the police force work down in Boston?" Mom chided.

I looked at a framed photo on Dad's desk. Chills ran up my spine. I caught Carlos's eye and nodded at the picture.

Carlos continued to hold the ice pack against my nose as he turned to Dad.

"Does the name McVey mean anything to you?"

Dad's eyes narrowed and his voice became brittle.

"It was his last name. So what?"

"And he's missing his left thumb."

"Yeah, some young punk down in Boston tried to take his gun away. The bastard shot his thumb off." His head jerked up, eyebrows lifted. "How do you know so damned much about him?"

"Where is he now?" The timber of Carlos's voice slowly rose.

"What is this, twenty questions? It's none of your damned business."

"You're wrong on that," I piped up. "It's very much his business. And mine."

"If you must know, he's dead. There, does that make you feel any better?"

I let out my breath in a puff. A nightmare for ten years was finally over.

"How do you know he's dead?" Carlos asked, eyes flaming.

He guided my hand to the ice pack, jumped up, hurtled toward Dad, and punched his fists flat on the desk.

"Where is he now?" he demanded.

"Dead, I told you, ten years ago. Found his body in a swamp down in Florida. Somebody crushed his head. They figure he crawled away and died."

Carlos yanked at his tie and tore his shirt open, buttons flying. "See this scar?" He jabbed his finger at the tattoo on his shoulder. "That was your crazy son of a bitch nephew's work."

"What's a crazy tattoo got to do with anything?" His voice was suddenly wary, however.

"It's covering a bullet hole, and I've got another one on my hip. Your favorite nephew came this close"—he demonstrated with finger and thumb—"to killing me." He fingered his left ear where the razor had cut. With his face five inches from Dad, he snarled, "And what's more, he's the one who raped Damon."

Dad paused. His whole body seemed to wither. A trapped animal stare seized his eyes as he glanced from Carlos to me.

"Coincidence, pure coincidence, you're just trying to stir up family trouble."

I picked up the picture and showed it to Carlos. He blanched. Kirk McVey as a young man.

A deadly calm swept over me. The past was just that, the past. This man I never really knew had turned into a pathetic being worthy only of scorn.

"Ten years ago"—I moved to Carlos's side—"you stood at this desk and told me you no longer had a son." I leaned toward him, his eyes shifted down and then back up to mine. In a calm, deliberate voice, each word was carefully enunciated. "Now, I'm leaving, and I no longer have a father."

I turned away and spoke to no one in particular.

"Where's Ilka?" I continued in a stern voice. "We also have a score to settle."

"You going to drag the whole damn family in on this?" my "father" asked in a much more subdued manner as I turned back to him.

"Damon," Carlos said softly, taking my arm and steering me toward the door, "it's not worth it. Let's leave."

We turned and strode through to the front hall. As Carlos opened the front door, his hand on my arm for me to pass through, I caught a glimpse of Ilka. I advanced a step back toward her.

"We burned the letter you forged from Carlos."

She stood stricken.

"And the one you forged from Damon to me," Carlos cut in, his voice slicing like frozen steel.

"A pox on you and that cruel old bastard in there," I snapped.

I was alarmed when Carlos let go of my arm and started toward her. She backed off as though afraid of being struck.

"Where's Damon's mother?" he demanded.

"Upstairs, I think," she said in a weak voice.

"Tell her we're leaving and would like to say good-bye."

He turned back to me and smiled reassuringly.

Ilka disappeared upstairs and shortly returned with Mom. Her face was flushed and her eyes red rimmed. Her persona was that of an abused person.

Carlos approached her as she reached out.

"It was wonderful meeting you in spite of all that has happened. Now I know why Damon loves you so much." His voice turned husky. "I don't know if my real mother is even still alive. I'd like it if I could call you Mom."

Her body shook as we had a three-person hug. Any issues he and I ever had with each other were entirely washed away in that poignant moment. I hated to leave Mom there with Ilka and him— no longer my father—but she urged us to go.

Carlos put his arm around me as we walked to the car.

"How ya doing, champ?"

"I'm okay. Not really. Christ, I don't know."

"I don't think I could have done what you just had to do."

I had the distinct feeling we were being surreptitiously observed by the neighbors.

"Kiss me," I said on impulse, turning to Carlos.

He looked puzzled but complied.

"What was that all about?"

"I mean really kiss me."

He swooped me into a hug and a long, sound kiss on the lips then gave me a questioning look.

"I just wanted the neighbors to have no doubts about my orientation."

"I think that could have done it."

"Let's take a walk. I need to work off some of this angst."

"Sounds like a plan," Carlos said as we walked back down Beach Hill Road. "Whatcha got in mind?"

"Something to eat and something to drink. Non-alcoholic for Carlos."

"That should be no problem in Portsmouth."

"No, too many people around. I'm thinking more like Henry's Market."

Carlos looked uncertain. "Have we been there?"

"No, but you'll love it. It's kind of like a log cabin with everything wonderful to eat. We can even sit outdoors under the umbrella."

"Have they got tables inside?"

"Tables and booths."

After the uplifting stop at Henry's and their hospitality, it was time to go back and get the car. On second thought, I suggested Great Island Common. They have an open, covered pavilion with a gorgeous view of the ocean. We carried a bottle of soda, cheese, and crackers and plodded in that direction. With the bracing breeze, the essence of the ocean, and the man I loved at my side, I could have walked forever. But soon the woods opened up to the magnificent Atlantic. We sat for some time, Carlos's arm around me, quietly surveying the spectacle provided free by Mother Nature.

Tears streaked down my cheeks. I felt the loss of childhood fantasies of family, however bleak they were at times. Conversely, somehow I felt release from the constricting hold of a father I never really had.

We spent the night at the Wentworth Hotel a short distance away. Then we went back home to San Diego.

POSTSCRIPT

Pandemonium broke out as Carlos gyrated out onto the stage at the American Airlines Arena in Miami six months later. He wore the same outfit he had worn ten years ago, black leather vest, unbuttoned, gold chains to the waist, tight leather jeans, cowboy boots, and a black Stetson, the latter courtesy of yours truly. Carlos, with his guitar, the strap slung over his shoulder, swung into action. Jerry Haines and the Night Paving Now crew, with a couple of new musicians, tore up the place, and the fans loved it.

This was the culmination of my plans, unknown to Carlos until a month ago. His haunting words, "You can't know how much I've lost now that my career is over," reverberated in my mind like a plucked string.

Why not some single shows, see how it goes? I could see it in my mind's eye. Maybe do another performance at the American Airlines Arena, where this all started. My stock portfolio was sailing. I could put up two hundred thou to start the ball rolling.

Following Carlos's career over the years—my little guilty pleasure at the time—gave me the list of people I needed to contact and cajole into reincarnating the good years. A key player had to be Hudson. Although hesitant when I first called him, he was anxious to try. It was important that as many of the old gang as possible would be there. He knew all the ropes of putting a show on. I called him every day while Carlos was out of earshot, working out details in a business absolutely foreign to me.

The hardest task for Hudson was reassuring the American Airlines Arena booking department to schedule a performance. The

465

big break came when NBC agreed to tape the show and broadcast it during the Thanksgiving holiday season. We were all taking a big risk, but I felt Carlos was well enough to carry it off. As early plans developed, it was difficult to keep him in the dark until we had a workable deal set up.

Seated in the front row were Mom, Ilka, Hudson, some other close friends, and a giant of a man wearing cowboy gear with his sister. Leenora had gotten hold of Hudson to tell him her brother, Simon, was the one who saved Carlos's life in Miami ten years ago at this very theater.

Simon was holding in his lap the keys to a new Chrysler Town and Country. A fifty-thousand-dollar check was in a separate envelope plus a note to meet Carlos in his dressing room after the performance. Everyone had tears in their eyes when Carlos and Simon hugged.

After the show was long over and the theater was empty, we walked out onto the stage together. Carlos's eyes swept the space, the seats now empty.

"We did it," he crowed. "We really did it." And he swung me around.

"NBC is wild about the show," I said. They texted me halfway through.

He hugged me close and muttered in my ear, "You should have been here ten years ago."

Unable to speak around the lump in my throat, I nodded.

"Let's go home, babe," he whispered.

"Yeah, home."

ABOUT THE AUTHOR

Thomas was born in a small town in Central New Hampshire and has spent his entire life in the same house in the small town of Warner. He received his BA degree from New England College in 1959. While there, his interest in English composition and design was first nurtured.

Vitally interested in historic preservation, he is involved with the Warner Historical Society and has visited many restored historic homes from Maine to Florida. Twenty years as a real estate Broker, it was not creative enough, so he returned to his first love, writing. He has participated in several writers groups and many writing courses including membership in the NH Writer's Project. He finds fiction is his field and dialogue his forte.

Remembering Lasts So Long is his first published novel.